NAG HAMMADI STUDIES

VOLUME XXVII

NAG HAMMADI STUDIES

EDITED BY

MARTIN KRAUS-JAMES M. ROBINSON
FREDERIK WISSE

IN CONJUNCTION WITH

ALEXANDER BÖHLIG-JEAN DORESSE-SØREN GIVERSEN
HANS JONAS-RODOLPHE KASSER-PAHOR LABIB
GEORGE W. MACRAE†-JACQUES-É. MÉNARD
TORGNY SÄVE-SÖDERBERGH
WILLEM CORNELIS VAN UNNIK†-R. MCL. WILSON
JAN ZANDEE†

XXVII

GENERAL EDITOR OF THE COPTIC GNOSTIC LIBRARY
JAMES M. ROBINSON

ὅμοιος [43]   πῶς 25, 32
ὁμοίωμα [45]
οὖς 6, [35]   σωτήρ [27]

πᾶς [10]   τέλειος [27]
πατήρ 34, 37, 38, [46], [49]   τέλος [29]
πίστις [32]
πλανᾶσθαι 21   φαίνεσθαι 29, 33, [40], [44]
πλῆθος [19]   φθορά [12], 13
πολύς 4   φωνεῖν [5]
πρό [50]   φῶς (contr. of φάος) [50]
προεῖναι [48]
προπάτωρ [38], [41], [46]   ὡς [13], 18, [45]
προστιθέναι [10]   ὥστε [19]

GREEK WORDS
IN
PAPYRUS OXYRHYNCHUS 1081

ἀγέννητος [34],48
ἄδηλος [32]*
ἀκούειν [7],7, [35],35
ἀναδεικνύναι 31
ἄναρχος [41]
ἀναφαίνεσθαι [45]
ἄνθρωπος [20]
ἀντωπεῖν [47]
ἀντωπός [47]
ἀπέραντος [6]
ἀπό 11, [13], [15], 18, [28]
ἀπογίνεσθαι 12, [16]
ἀποθνήσκειν [23]
ἀπόρροια [30]
ἀρχή [38]
ἀφανής 28
ἀφθαρσία [15], [18]
ἄφθαρτος [5], [17]

γίνεσθαι 1, [11], [14], [14], 19
γινώσκειν [26]

δεσπότης 36
διαφορά [3], [22]
διέρχεσθαι 27

ἐγείρεσθαι 8
ἐγώ [9]
εἰδέναι 22

εἶναι [39], [50]
εἰπεῖν [10]
εἰς [1], [29]
εἰσορᾶν [42]
ἐμφανής 2
ἔννοια [31]
ἐπί (for ἐπεί) [47]
ἔρχεσθαι 2
ἔσοπτρον [43]
ἔτι 2, 9
εὑρίσκειν [33]
ἔχειν 6, 35

θεός 46

ἰσόχρονος [49]

καλεῖν [37]
κύριος 25

λαλεῖν 9
λέγειν [24], 26

Μαριάμ [25]
μέλλειν [39]
μένειν [17]
μετά [0]
μεταξύ [4]

ὅλος [36]

THE COPTIC GNOSTIC LIBRARY

EDITED WITH ENGLISH TRANSLATION, INTRODUCTION AND NOTES

published under the auspices of

THE INSTITUTE FOR ANTIQUITY AND CHRISTIANITY

NAG HAMMADI CODICES
III,*3-4* AND V,*1*

WITH

PAPYRUS BEROLINENSIS 8502,*3* AND
OXYRHYNCHUS PAPYRUS 1081

EUGNOSTOS AND THE SOPHIA OF JESUS CHRIST

EDITED BY

DOUGLAS M. PARROTT

E.J. BRILL
LEIDEN • NEW YORK • KØBENHAVN • KÖLN
1991

The paper in this book meets te guidelines for permanence and durability of the Committee on Production Guidelines for Book Longevity of the Council on Library Resources.

Library of Congress Cataloging-in-Publication Data

Eugnostos the Blessed. English & Coptic.
　　Nag Hammadi codices III,3-4 and V,1 with Papyrus Berolinensis 8502,3 and Oxyrhynchus papyrus 1081: Eugnostos and The Sophia of Jesus Christ / edited by Douglas M. Parrott.
　　　　p. cm.—(Nag Hammadi studies. ISSN 0169-7749; v. 27) (The Coptic gnostic library)
　　Parallel text in English and Coptic.
　　Includes bibliographical references and index.
　　ISBN 90-04-08366-9 (alk. paper)
　　1. Nag Hammadi codices. 2. Papyrus Berolinensis 8502. 3. Oxyrhynchus papyri. 4. Wisdom (Gnosticism) 5. Gnosticism. I. Parrott, Douglas M. II. Sophia of Jesus Christ. English & Coptic. 1991. III. Title. IV. Title: Nag Hammadi codices III. 3-4 and V, 1 with Papyrus Berolinensis 8502,3 and Oxyrhynchus papyrus 1081. V. Series. VI. Series: The Coptic gnostic library.
BT1392.E92A3　1991
299'.932—dc20　　　　　　　　　　　　　　　　　　　　　　　　91-19243
　　　　　　　　　　　　　　　　　　　　　　　　　　　　　　　　　CIP

ISSN　0169-7749
ISBN　90 04 08366 9

TABLE OF CONTENTS

FOREWORD

The Coptic Gnostic Library is a complete edition of the Nag Hammadi Codices, of Papyrus Berolinensis 8502, and of the Askew and Bruce Codices, comprising a critical text with English translations, introductions, notes, and indices. Its aim is to present these texts in a uniform edition that will promptly follow the appearance of *The Facsimile Edition of the Nag Hammadi Codices* and that can be a basis for more detailed technical and interpretive investigations. Further studies of this sort are expected to appear in the monograph series Nag Hammadi Studies, of which the present edition is a part.

The gnostic religion was not only a force that interacted with early Christianity and Judaism in their formative periods, but also a significant religious position in its own right. General acceptance of this modern insight had been seriously impeded by the scarcity of original source material. Now this situation has been decisively altered. It is thus under a sense of obligation imposed by the discovery of these largely unique documents that the present edition has been prepared.

This edition is a project of the Institute for Antiquity and Christianity, Claremont, California. The translation team consists of Harold W. Attridge, J. W. B. Barns†, Hans-Gebhard Bethge, Alexander Böhlig, James Brashler, G. M. Browne, Roger A. Bullard, Peter A. Dirkse, Stephen Emmel, Joseph A. Gibbons, Søren Giversen, Charles W. Hedrick, Wesley W. Isenberg, T. O. Lambdin, Bentley Layton, Violet MacDermot, George W. MacRae†, Dieter Mueller†, William R. Murdock, Douglas M. Parrott, Birger A. Pearson, Malcolm L. Peel, James M. Robinson, William C. Robinson, Jr., William R. Schoedel, J. C. Shelton, John H. Sieber, John D. Turner, Francis E. Williams, R. McL. Wilson, Orval S. Wintermute, Frederik Wisse, and Jan Zandee.

The project was initiated in 1966 with only a limited number of tractates accessible, but rapidly developed as the texts became increasingly available. In view of the fact that the bulk of the material in Codices I–VI had at that time either been published or announced for imminent publication in complete editions in other languages, the edition in the Coptic Gnostic Library was envisaged in the complementary role of providing merely English translations in a single volume, which in subsequent planning was then envisaged as two volumes. It was at this stage that preliminary announcements were made in *New Testament Studies* 16 (1969) 185–90 and *Novum Testamentum* 12 (1970) 83–85, reprinted in *Essays on the Coptic Gnostic Library* (Leiden: Brill, 1970). The publisher and editorial board of Nag Hammadi Studies at their meeting in Uppsala, Sweden, in August 1973, recommended that the Coptic Gnostic Library edition be complete for Codices I–VI and BG as well as for VII–XIII. This plan was adopted by the volume editors at their September 1973 work session in Cairo. This resulted in Codices I–VI and BG being planned for six, then nine volumes. They do not correspond precisely to the seven codices, for it is preferable to publish parallel texts together. Thus the present volume presents in parallel columns the two copies of *Eugnostos* (III,*3* and V,*1*) and the two copies of its Christianized second edition, *The Sophia of Jesus Christ* (III,*4* and BG,*3*) in order to facilitate study of the complex interrelations involved. After it was decided to include in Nag Hammadi Studies a new English edition of the other Coptic Gnostic codices known previously, the Askew and Bruce codices, the publisher included them in the Coptic Gnostic Library to make it complete.

The volumes and the editors of the Coptic Gnostic Library are as follows: *Nag Hammadi Codex I (The Jung Codex)* : Volume 1, *Introduction, Texts, and Translation*; Volume 2, *Notes*, volume editor Harold W. Attridge; NHS 22 and 23, 1985; *Nag Hammadi Codices II,1 and IV,1: The Apocryphon of John, Long Recension*, edited by Frederik Wisse, NHS 32, in preparation; *Nag Hammadi Codex II,2–7, together with XIII,2*, Brit. Lib. Or.4926(1), and P. Oxy. 1, 654, 655* : Volume 1, *Gospel According to Thomas, Gospel According to Philip, Hypostasis of the Archons, Indexes*; Volume 2, *On the Origin of the World, Expository Treatise on the Soul, Book of Thomas the Contender, Indexes*, edited by Bentley Layton, NHS 20 and 21, 1989; *Nag Hammadi Codex III,1 and Papyrus Berolinensis 8502,2: The Apocryphon of John, Short Recension*, edited by Peter Nagel, volume editor Frederik Wisse; *Nag Hammadi Codices III,2 and IV,2: The Gospel of the Egyptians (The Holy Book of the Great Invisible Spirit)*, edited by Alexander Böhlig and Frederik Wisse in cooperation with Pahor Labib, NHS 4, 1975; *Nag Hammadi Codices III,3–4 and V,1 with Papyrus Berolinensis 8502,3 and Oxyrhynchus Papyrus 1081: Eugnostos and The Sophia of Jesus Christ*, edited and translated by Douglas M. Parrott, NHS 27, 1990; *Nag Hammadi Codex III,5: The Dialogue of the Savior*, volume editor Stephen Emmel, NHS XX, 1984; *Nag Hammadi Codices V,2–5 and VI with Papyrus Berolinensis 8502,1 and 4*, volume editor Douglas M. Parrott, NHS 11, 1979; *Nag Hammadi Codex VII*, volume editor Frederik Wisse; *Nag Hammadi Codex VIII*, volume editor John H. Sieber, NHS 31, in the press; *Nag Hammadi Codices IX and X*, volume editor Birger A. Pearson, NHS 15, 1981; *Nag Hammadi Codices XI, XII and XIII*, volume editor Charles W. Hedrick, NHS 28, 1990; *Nag Hammadi Codices: Greek and Coptic Papyri from the Cartonnage of the Covers*, edited by J. W. B. Barns†, G. M. Browne and J. C. Shelton, NHS 16, 1981; *Pistis Sophia*, text edited by Carl Schmidt, translation and notes by Violet MacDermot, volume editor R. McL. Wilson, NHS 9, 1978; *The Books of Jeu and the Untitled Text in the Bruce Codex*, edited by Carl Schmidt, translation and notes by Violet MacDermot, volume editor R. McL. Wilson, NHS 13, 1978. Thus, as now envisaged, the full scope of the edition is seventeen volumes.

An English translation of all thirteen Nag Hammadi Codices and P. Berol. 8502 has also been published in 1977 in a single volume, *The Nag Hammadi Library in English,* by E. J. Brill and Harper & Row. A first paperback edition of that preprint augmented by the inclusion of Yale inv. 1784 of the Beinecke Library at NHC III 145/146 (p. 238) appeared in 1981 at Harper & Row and in 1984 at E. J. Brill. It was not possible to include there subsequent improvements in translations. A third, completely revised edition appeared in 1988 at E. J. Brill and Harper & Row.

The team research of the project has been supported primarily through the Institute for Antiquity and Christianity by the National Endowment for the Humanities, the American Philosophical Society, the John Simon Guggenheim Memorial Foundation, and Claremont Graduate School; and through the American Research Center in Egypt by the Smithsonian Institution. Members of the project have participated in the preparatory work of the Technical Sub-Committee of the International Committee for the Nag Hammadi Codices, which has been done at the Coptic Museum in Cairo under the sponsorship of the Arab Republic of Egypt and UNESCO. The extensive work in the reassembly of fragments, the reconstruction of page sequence, and the collation of the transcriptions by the originals not only served the immediate needs of the facsimile edition, but also provided a basis for a critical edition. Without such generous support and such mutual cooperation of all parties concerned this edition could not have been prepared. Therefore we wish to express our sincere gratitude to all who have been involved.

A special word of thanks is due to the Egyptian and UNESCO officials through whose assistance the work has been carried on: Gamal Mokhtar, President until 1977 of the Egyptian Antiquities Organization, our gracious and able host in Egypt; Pahor Labib, Victor Girgis, and Mounir Basta, Directors Emeriti, and Dr. Gawdat Gabra, currently Director of the Coptic Museum, who together have guided the work on the manuscript material; Samiha Abd El-Shaheed, First Curator for Manuscripts at the Coptic Museum, who is personally responsible for the codices and was constantly by our side in the rooms of the Coptic Museum; and, at UNESCO, N. Bammate, Deputy Assistant Director General for the Social Sciences, Human Sciences, and Culture until 1978, who has guided the UNESCO planning since its beginning, and Dina Zeidan, specialist in the Arab Program of the Division of Cultural Studies, who has always proved ready with gracious assistance and helpful advice.

Gary A. Bisbee (Chiron Inc.) in conjunction with the Computer Based Laboratory of Harvard University has designed the Coptic characters, keypunched the manuscript and produced the camera-ready copy for this volume with great commitment and competence.

Edmund S. Meltzer was kind enough to read the typescript and make valuable suggestions before the volume went to press.

We also wish to acknowledge our great indebtedness to the directors of E. J. Brill during the years in which this volume was in preparation, F. C. Wieder, Jr., Director Emeritus, the late T. A. Edridge, and Dr. W. Backhuys, Director Emeritus, and Drs. M. G. Elisabeth Venekamp, Vice-President, who is in charge of Nag Hammadi Studies for Brill.

James M. Robinson
General Editor

PREFACE

This project was begun in 1967, while I was a graduate student at the Graduate Theological Union. In connection with the Coptic Gnostic Library Project at the Institute for Antiquity and Christianity, James M. Robinson suggested that I try to produce the parallels of *Eug* and *SJC*, using the only source then available to us, namely, the text of Till's edition of BG and his footnotes, which contained the variants from *SJC*–BG found in *Eug*–III and *SJC*–III. His hope was that we might be able to test the then recently published arguments of Krause regarding the priority of *Eug*. The result was somewhat less than satisfactory because of the gaps in *Eug*–III in Till's edition—gaps made necessary by restricitons imposed upon him. When photos of the Nag Hammadi texts became available to the Institute for Antiquity and Christianity later in the decade, I began working on the parallels of *Eug*–III and *SJC*–BG in translation (with variant readings in footnotes), which would have been part of the then projected volume of Codices I–VI in English translation only.

When that was replaced in 1973, as a result of the decision to publish critical editions of all the texts, I put aside the parallels project in order to complete *Nag Hammadi Codices V, 2–5, and VI and Papyrus Berolinensis 8502, 1 and 4*, which was published in 1979. I have worked on various aspects of this edition since that time, using portions of the earlier work.

I want to express my thanks to a number of persons who have helped with this project. Stephen Emmel, while working as the Cairo representative of the Coptic Gnostic Library Project, recollated *Eug* III and retranscribed *SJC*–III, both with the aid of ultraviolet light, identified important fragments in *Eug*–V (after publication of the facsimile edition) and provided invaluable feedback for textual questions about *Eug*–V. Bentley Layton, while he was also in Cairo, recollated the whole of *Eug*–V with the use of ultraviolet light and made numerous important suggestions regarding the filling of lacunae. Martin Krause made available an early draft of his anticipated parallel edition. Hans-Martin Schenke provided photos of BG. And Harold Attridge lent his infrared photos of P. Oxy. 1081 for the new edition of that fragment included here.

Egyptologist Leonard Lesko (then at UC Berkeley, now at Brown University) and his assistant David Larkin gave expert and invaluable advice regarding knotty translational problems during a week in Berkeley in the spring of 1981.

Also, this edition has benefited in a variety of ways from the discussions at the fortnightly meetings of the Coptic Texts Seminar at Claremont Graduate School during the 1983–84 academic year. The regular participants in that group, besides myself, were James Goehring, Edmund S. Meltzer and James M. Robinson, all three from the CGS faculty; graduate students Jon Daniels,

Clayton Jefford, Stephen Patterson and Leif Vaage; and Richard Smith, then Instructor in Coptic at Fuller Theological Seminary.

Finally I want to thank Howard Jackson, Tulane Peterson, Jirair Tashjian and Leif Vaage, graduate students at CGS, who assisted me at various stages in the preparation of this volume. I am also grateful to Lenore Brashler for mediating expertly between me and her word processor.

The editing of this volume was made possible in part by grants from the Committee on Research of the University of California at Riverside.

Readers are requested to communicate to the general editor of the Coptic Gnostic Library any errors that may be found so that a list of corrections can be published.

Although this volume was accepted for publication in 1984, for a variety of reasons, including the special problems involved in setting it up, actual publication has been delayed for some time. During this time, of course, scholarship has continued, and I have been able to take some of it into consideration, but by no means all. I especially regret that limitations on the number of changes have not allowed me to incorporate references to Michel Tardieu's translation, with notes and comments, of *Eugnostos* and the *Sophia of Jesus Christ* in his *Ecrits gnostiques: Codex de Berlin*, Sources gnostiques et manichéennes 1 (1984). I anticipate making good use of it in a future commentary.

                                                          Douglas M. Parrott

TABLE OF TRACTATES IN THE
COPTIC GNOSTIC LIBRARY

The following table lists, for the thirteen Nag Hammadi Codices and Papyrus Berolinensis 8502, the codex and tractate numbers, the tractate titles as used in this edition (the titles found in the tractates themselves, sometimes simplified and standardized, or, when the tractate bears no surviving title, one supplied by the editors), and the abbreviations of these titles. The abbreviations in parentheses are used only in this volume, for the sake of brevity.

ABBREVIATIONS

(Abbreviations commonly found in standard English dictionaries are omitted from this list. Nag Hammadi tractates are listed at the beginning of the volume.)

A	Achmimic dialect
A$_2$	Subachmimic dialect
ADAIK	Abhandlungen des Deutschen Archäologischen Instituts Kairo
alt.	alternative
Apoc. Mos.	*Apocalypse of Moses*
Att (in notes)	*Attridge**
B	*Bohairic dialect*
BASP	*The Bulletin of the American Society of Papyrologists*
BDF	Blass, Debrunner and Funk*
BG	Berlin Gnostic codex (Papyrus Berolinensis 8502), ed. by Till (1955)* and Till–Schenke (1972)*
Corr.	Correction by scribe
D (in notes)	Doresse (1960)*
do.	ditto
Epiphan. *Pan.*	Epiphanius, *Panarion*
F	Fayyumic dialect
Gen	Book of Genesis
H (in notes)	Hunt*
JAC	*Jahrbuch für Antike und Christentum*
K (in notes)	Krause (1974)*
LSJ	Liddell, Scott and Jones*
LXX	Greek Version of the Old Testament (Septuagint)
NHC	Nag Hammadi Codex
NHLE	*Nag Hammadi Library in English*, 3rd ed., ed. by James M. Robinson*
NHS	Nag Hammadi Studies
NovT	*Novum Testamentum*
OLZ	*Orientalistische Literaturzeitung*
PO	*Patrologia orientalis*
P.	Papyrus manuscript
P. Oxy.	Papyrus Oxyrhynchus
par(r.)	parallel(s)
Pist. Soph.	*Pistis Sophia*
Plat. *Tim.*	Plato, *Timaeus*

---

* See "Works Consulted."

Pu (in notes)	Puech (1963)*
Rom	Letter to the Romans
S	Sahidic dialect
SBL	Society of Biblical Literature
sugg.	suggestion
TDNT	Kittel, G. and Friedrich, G., eds. *Theological Diction-ary of the New Testament*, 10 vols. Trans. and ed. by G. W. Bromiley. Grand Rapids: Wm. B. Eerdmans, 1964–76.
T–S (in notes)	Till–Schenke*
Tr (in notes)	Trakatellis*
TU	Texte und Untersuchungen
W (in notes)	Wesseley*
VC	*Vigiliae christianae*
ZRGG	*Zeitschrift für Religions- und Geistesgeschichte*

---

* See "Works Consulted."

WORKS CONSULTED

Attridge, Harold W.
1975

"P. Oxy. 1081 and the Sophia Jesu Christi." *Enchoria* 5: 1–8.

Barns, John W. B.
1975

"Greek and Coptic Papyri from the Covers of the Nag Hammadi Codices: A Preliminary Report." In *Essays on the Nag Hammadi Codices: In Honour of Pahor Labib.* NHS 6. Ed. by Martin Krause. Leiden: E.J. Brill.

Barns†, John W. B.; Browne, G. M.; and Shelton, J. C., eds.
1981

Nag Hammadi Codices: Greek and Coptic Papyri from the Cartonnage of the Covers. NHS 16. Leiden: E.J. Brill.

Bellet, Paulinus
1978

"The Colophon of the Gospel of the Egyptians: Concessus and Macarius of Nag Hammadi." In *Nag Hammadi and Gnosis: Papers read at the First International Congress of Coptology (Cairo, December 1976).* NHS 14. Ed. by R. McL. Wilson. Leiden: E.J. Brill.

Bickerman, E. J.
1980

Chronology of the Ancient World. Revised ed. London: Thems and Hudson.

Blass, F.; Debrunner, A.; and Funk, Robert W. (BDF)
1961

A Greek Grammar of the New Testament and Other Early Christian Literature. University of Chicago.

Böhlig, Alexander and Labib, Pahor, eds.
1963

Koptisch-gnostische Apokalypsen aus Codex V von Nag Hammadi im Koptischen Museum zu Alt-Kairo. Sonderband. Wissenschaftliche Zeitschrift der Martin-Luther-Universität. Halle-Wittenberg.

Böhlig, Alexander and Wisse, Frederik, eds.
1975

Nag Hammadi Codices III, 2 and IV, 2: The Gospel of the Egyptians (The Holy Book of the Great Invisible Spirit). NHS 4. Leiden: E.J. Brill.

Bultmann, Rudolf
1968

The History of the Synoptic Tradition. 2nd ed. Trans. from German (2nd ed., 1931) by John Marsh. Oxford: Basil Blackwell.

Colpe, Carsten
1976

"Heidnische, jüdische und christliche Uberlieferung in den Schriften aus Nag Hammadi V." *JAC* 19.

Crum, W. E.
1939

A Coptic Dictionary. Oxford: Clarendon.

De Santos Otero, Aurelio, ed.
1956

Los Evangelos Apocrifos. Madrid: Biblioteca de Autores Cristianos.

Dillon, John
1977

The Middle Platonists: 80 B.C. to A.D. 220. Ithaca, N.Y.: Cornell University.

Doresse, Jean
1948

"Trois livres gnostiques inédits." *VC* 2: 137–60.

1960

The Secret Books of the Egyptian Gnostics: An Introduction to the Gnostic Coptic manuscripts discovered at Chenoboskion. Trans. from French (1958, 1959) by Philip Mairet. New York: Viking.

Emmel, Stephen
1978

"Unique Photographic Evidence for Nag Hammadi Texts: CG II *1*, III *1–4* and IV *1–2*." *BASP* 15: 195–205.

1979

"Unique Photographic Evidence for Nag Hammadi Texts: CG V–VII." *BASP* 16: 179–91.

Facsimile Edition—V
1975

The Facsimile Edition of the Nag Hammadi Codices: Codex V. James M. Robinson, et al. Leiden: E.J. Brill.

Facsimile Edition—III
1976

The Facsimile Edition of the Nag Hammadi Codices: Codex III. James M. Robinson, et al. Leiden: E.J. Brill.

Fallon, Francis T.
1979

"The Gnostic Apocalypses." *Semeia* 14: 123–58.

Hedrick, C. W.
1981

"Christian Motifs in the Gospel of the Egyptians: Method and Motive." *NovT* 23: 242–60.

Hunt, Arthur S.
1911

The Oxyrhynchus Papyri. Part 8. London: Egypt Exploration Fund.

Kasser, Rodolphe
1964

Compléments au Dictionnaire copte de Crum. Bibliothèque d'études coptes 7. Cairo: L'institut français d'archéologie orientale.

Klostermann, Erich, ed.
1929

Apokrypha 2. 3rd ed. Kleine Texte 8. Berlin: W. de Gruyter.

Krause, Martin
1964

"Das literarische Verhältnis des Eugnostosbriefes zur Sophia Jesu Christi." *Mullus, Festschrift Theodor Klauser.* JAC Ergänzungsband 1: 215–23.

1974

"The Letter of Eugnostos." In *Gnosis: A Selection of Gnostic Texts* 2: *Coptic and Mandean Sources.* Ed. by Werner Foerster. Trans. from 1971 German ed. by R. McL. Wilson. Oxford: Clarendon.

Krause, Martin and Labib, Pahor, eds.
1971

Gnostische und hermetische Schriften aus Codex II und Codex VI. ADAIK, Koptische Reihe 2. Glückstadt: J. J. Augustin.

Liddell, Henry George; Scott, Robert; and Jones, Henry Stuart (LSJ)
1968

A Greek-English Lexicon with a Supplement. Oxford: Clarendon.

MacRae, George W.
1970

"The Jewish Background of the Gnostic Sophia Myth." *NovT* 12: 86–101.

Ménard, Jacques E.
1980

"Normative Self-definition in Gnosticism." In *Jewish and Christian Self-definition* 1: *The Shaping of Christianity in the Second and Third Centuries.* Ed. by E. P. Sanders. Philadelphia: Fortress.

Pape, W. and Bensler, G.
1911

Wörterbuch der griechischen Eigennamen. 3rd ed. Braunschweig: Friedr. Vieweg & Sohn.

Parrott, Douglas M.
1971

"The Significance of the Letter of Eugnostos and the Sophia of Jesus Christ for the Understanding of the Relation Between Gnosticism and Christianity." *SBL Seminar Papers* 2.

1975   "Evidence of Religious Syncretism in Nag
                                  Hammadi Tractates." In *Religious Syncre-
                                  tism in Antiquity: Essays in Conversation
                                  with Geo Widengren.* Series on Formative
                                  Contemporary Thinkers 1. Ed. by Birger A.
                                  Pearson. Missoula, Montana: Scholars.

1979   Ed., *Nag Hammadi Codices V, 2–5 and VI
                                  with Papyrus Berolinensis 8502, 1 and 4.*
                                  NHS 11. Leiden: E.J. Brill.

1987   "Gnosticism and Egyptian Religion." *NovT*
                                  29: 73–93.

1988   "Eugnostos and 'All The Philosophers'."
                                  Religion im Erbe Ägyptens: Beiträge zur
                                  spätantiken Religionsgeschichte zu Ehren
                                  von Alexander Böhlig. Manfred Görg, ed.
                                  Ägypten und Altes Testament 14. Wies-
                                  badn: Otto Harrassowitz: 153–167.

Perkins, Pheme   "The Soteriology of Sophia of Jesus Christ."
1971   *SBL Seminar Papers* 2.

1980   *The Gnostic Dialogue: The Early Church
                                  and the Crisis of Gnosticism.* New York:
                                  Paulist.

Przybylski, B.   "The Role of Calendrical Data in Gnostic
1980   Literature." *VC* 34: 56–70.

Puech, H.-C.   "Les nouveaux écrits gnostiques découverts
1950   en Haute-Egypte." In *Coptic Studies in
                                  honor of Walter Ewing Crum.* Boston:
                                  Byzantine Institute.

1963   "Gnostic Gospels and Related Documents."
                                  In Edgar Hennecke, *New Testament Apo-
                                  crypha* 1: *Gospels and Related Writings.*
                                  Ed. by Wilhelm Schneemelcher. Trans.
                                  from German (1959) by R. McL. Wilson.
                                  Philadelphia: Westminster.

Robinson, James M.
1979

"Codicological Analysis of Nag Hammadi Codices V and VI and Papyrus Berolinensis 8502." In *Nag Hammadi Codices V, 2–5 and VI with Papyrus Berolinensis 8502, 1 and 4*. NHS 11. Ed. by Douglas M. Parrott. Leiden: E.J. Brill.

1984

The Facsimile Edition of the Nag Hammadi Codices: Introduction. Leiden: E.J. Brill.

1988

Ed., *The Nag Hammadi Library in English*. Trans. by Members of the Coptic Gnostic Library Project of the Institute for Antiquity and Christianity. 3rd, completely revised ed. New York, et al.: Harper & Row.

Schenke, Hans-Martin
1962

"Nag-Hamadi (sic) Studien II: Das System der Sophia Jesu Christi." *ZRGG* 14: 263–77.

1966

Review of Böhlig-Labib. *OLZ* 61: Cols 23–34.

Smyth, Herbert Weir
1956

Greek Grammar. Rev. by Gordon M. Messing. Cambridge: Harvard.

Stern, Ludwig
1880

Koptische Grammatik. Leipzig: T. O. Weigel.

Till, Walter C.
1955

Ed., *Die gnostischen Schriften des koptischen Papyrus Berolinensis 8502*. TU 60. Berlin: Akademie-Verlag.

1961

Koptische Dialektgrammatik mit Lesestücken und Wörterbuch. 2nd ed. Munich: C.H. Beck.

1966

Koptische Grammatik (saïdischer Dialekt) mit Bibliographie, Lesestücken und Wörterverzeichnissen. 3rd improved ed. Leipzig: Verlag Enzyklopädie.

Till, Walter C. and Schenke, Hans-Martin, eds.
1972

Die gnostischen Schriften des koptischen Papyrus Berolinensis 8502. TU 60. 2nd ed. Berlin: Akademie-Verlag.

Trakatellis, Demetrios
1977

Ο ΥΠΕΡΒΑΤΙΚΟΣ ΘΕΟΣ ΤΟΥ ΕΥΓΝΩΣΤΟΥ (*The Transcendent God of Eugnostos*: An Exegetical Contribution to the Study of

the Gnostic Texts of Nag Hammadi).
Athens.

Treu, Kurt
1982

"P. Berl. 8508: Christliches Empfehlungs-
schreiben aus dem Einband des koptisch-
gnostischen Kodex P. 8502." *Archiv für
Papyrusforschung* 28: 53–54.

Wesseley, C.
1924

"Les plus anciens monuments du christian-
isme écrits sur papyrus, II." *PO* 18: 493–95.

Wilson, R. McL.
1968

Gnosis and the New Testament. Philadelphia: Fortress.

Wisse, Frederik
1975

"Nag Hammadi Codex III: Codicological
Introduction." In *Essays on the Nag Ham-
madi Texts: In Honour of Pahor Labib.*
NHS 6. Ed. by Martin Krause. Leiden: E.J.
Brill.

TEXTUAL SIGNS

.   A dot placed under a letter in the transcripton indicates that the letter is visually uncertain, even though the context may make the reading certain. Dots on the line outside of brackets in the transcription indicate missing letters that cannot be reconstructed but of which vestiges of ink remain.

[ ]   Square brackets in the transcription indicate a lacuna in the MS in which there is every reason to believe that writing existed at one time. When the text cannot be reconstructed, or when it can only be partially reconstructed, the number of estimated missing letters, up to five, is indicated in the transcription by dots; beyond that an Arabic number is used, followed by a plus or minus sign (±). In the translation, brackets are used not only for lacunae but also for letters or portions of letters that do not make translatable sense units. Three dots in brackets indicate an unreconstructed, and therefore an untranslated, portion of indeterminate length. Brackets are not allowed to divide words: words are placed either entirely inside brackets or wholly outside, depending on an estimate of the certainty of the words they translate.

< >   Pointed brackets indicate an editorial correction of a scribal omission or error. In the latter case a footnote records the MS reading.

{ }   Braces indicate letters or words unnecessarily added by the scribe.

\ ´   High strokes indicate that the letters so designated were written above the line by the scribe.

( )   Parentheses in the translation indicate material supplied by the translator for the sake of clarity.

† †   Two daggers indicate that the words between them are considered corrupt.

INTRODUCTION

I. DISCOVERY

The thirteen Nag Hammadi codices were discovered in December, 1945, on the right bank of the Nile, near the town of al-Qasr (ancient Chenoboskia) and close to the larger town of Nag Hammadi, which is on the opposite bank.[1] Facsimile editions of all thirteen have been published. The MSS are now preserved in the Coptic Museum in Old Cairo, Egypt.

Evidence in the cartonnage used to stiffen the leather covers suggests the library was buried sometime in the last half of the fourth century C.E. (Barns et al.: nos. 63–65). It is possible the codices had been used by monks in the nearby Pachomian monasteries and were buried during a time of heresy-hunting.[2]

P. Berolinensis 8502 (commonly designated simply BG) was purchased in or near the city of Achmim, Egypt, and acquired for the Berlin Museum in 1896. At first Carl Schmidt, who initially proposed to edit it, gave it a fifth-century date, although subsequently he thought it should be dated later. Stegemann placed it in the early fifth century (Till–Schenke: 6–7).[3]

II. PUBLICATION HISTORY

The four tractates published here are two versions of *Eugnostos* and two of *The Sophia of Jesus Christ*. They are presented in parallel form because of the large amount of common material.

Eugnostos (abbreviated, *Eug*–V) is the first tractate of Nag Hammadi Codex V (1,1–17,18) and has not been published before in a critical edition. *Eugnostos, The Blessed* (abbreviated, *Eug*–III) is the third tractate of Nag Hammadi Codex III (70,1–90,13). The portions of the text and translation of *Eug*–III that are variations of sections in *The Sophia of Jesus Christ* were published in Till (1955) and Till–Schenke. However, non-parallel parts, including all the frame material, were omitted. The text and translation (modern Greek) of *Eug*–III was published by Trakatellis as part of his Harvard dissertation. His text was based on preliminary work of my own with

---

[1] The most authoritative account of the discovery and subsequent history of the codices is to be found in Robinson's introduction to the facsimile edition (1984).

[2] See Barns: 9–18. But for cautions about Barns's conclusions, see Shelton's introduction to Barns et al.

[3] For a brief account of the unsuccessful efforts of Schmidt to publish BG during his lifetime, see Till–Schenke: 1–2.

some modifications by George MacRae, who was the dissertation director (corrrespondence with MacRae). Translations of *Eug*–III by Krause (1974: 27–34) and myself (*NHLE*[3]: 206–43) have been published. In both cases the portion of *Eug*–V covering the missing two pages of *Eug*–III (79–80) was also published.

The two versions of *The Sophia of Jesus Christ* (hereafter, *SJC*) vary from each other in relatively minor ways. One version is the third tractate of BG (77,8–127,12), which was edited (text and German translation) by Till (1955). His edition was later revised by Schenke (Till–Schenke). Translated portions were also published by Puech (77,9–79,18; 124,9–126,16; 126,17–127,10) (1963: 246–47).

The other version is the fourth tractate of NHC III (90,14–119,18). It was published by Till with the BG version, in the sense that places where it varied from the BG text were printed in the footnotes. Unfortunately, in many instances the Till edition (and its revision) did not completely reflect the variations, particularly the orthographic ones. Krause translated the portions of *SJC*–III that vary from *Eug*–III and published them in endnotes (1974: 35–39). A translation by myself of all of *SJC*–III is published in *NHLE*[3]. In both cases, the parts of *SJC*–BG covering the missing four pages of *SJC*–III (109–10; 115–16) were also published.

In addition to the two Coptic MSS of *SJC*, one leaf of a Greek copy has survived among the Oxyrhynchus papyri. It is numbered 1081 and is presented here in a new edition, following the parallels.

III. TITLES

The title of *Eug*–III in the incipit is ⲉⲩⲅⲛⲱⲥⲧⲟⲥ ⲡⲙⲁⲕⲁⲣⲓⲟⲥ , "Eugnostos, the Blessed," which agrees with the subscript title (90,12–13). But *Eug*–V has only faint traces of its subscript title and the incipit is very fragmentary. Enough of the latter is visible, however, to make clear that ⲡⲙⲁⲕⲁⲣⲓⲟⲥ , "the Blessed," was not part of the line. It is also evident that ⲡⲙⲁⲕⲁⲣⲓⲟⲥ could not have been part of the subscript title (see V 17,18n.). But what of "Eugnostos"? It appears nowhere in the tractate. The correct number of spaces is available in the incipit. And the same is true of the subscript, where, in addition, the only visible letter (omicron) is in the correct position for the reconstruction of "Eugnostos." But since other names would also be possible, the designation of "Eugnostos" as the title of the tractate depends on the recognition of the similarity of this tractate and *Eug*–III.

The titles of both copies of *SJC* appear in superscriptions and subscripts. The superscriptions are the same in both, except that the spelling of the *nomina sacra* in BG (ⲓ̅ⲥ̅ and ⲭ̅ⲥ̅) differs from that in Codex III (ⲓ̅ⲏ̅ⲥ̅ and ⲭ̅ⲣ̅ⲥ̅). In *SJC*–BG, the same title appears in the subscript, except that this time the *nomina sacra* are spelled as they are in the superscription of *SJC*–III. The subscript of *SJC*–III omits ⲭ̅ⲣ̅ⲥ̅, "Christ," perhaps through scribal error (see III.A, below). In regard to the difference between the *nomina sacra* in the superscription and subscript of BG, it is noteworthy that while the former conform to the usage elsewhere in the codex (based on the Till–Schenke index), the latter are unique, suggesting a copyist's adjustment.

Till leaves coϕιa untranslated, on the ground that the word refers to the divine hypostasis who appears prominently in the tractate (1955: 55). Doresse (1948: 146) and Puech (1963: 245), however, prefer to translate it, on the ground that it refers to the teachings of Jesus found in the tractate. The latter view seems preferable because Sophia is not the dominant figure in the tractate, as one would expect if the tractate were titled after her. However, we have adopted Till's practice because it seems to have become generally accepted.

IV. THE RELATIONSHIP OF THE TRACTATES AND ITS SIGNIFICANCE

Because most of *Eug* is found in *SJC,* where it is attributed to Jesus, and because *Eug* seems to be without any obvious Christian elements, the question of priority was raised very early. It was thought that if *Eug* were composed first and had been used in the editing of *SJC,* then we would have a clear example of the movement from non-Christian Gnosticism to Christian Gnosticism.

Doresse argued for the priority of *Eug* (1948: 137–60) and was followed by Puech (1963: 248). Till, however, took the opposite position (1955: 54), without arguing the point. Schenke joined him, after carefully examining and rejecting the arguments of Doresse (1962: 265–67). (Schenke has since changed his mind [personal conversation in November, 1982].) A more persuasive approach (than that of Doresse) in favor of the priority of *Eug* was taken by Krause (1964). He began by distinguishing between the material common to both *Eug* and *SJC* and the material each has separately, and argued that that tractate was primary in which the common material and its separate material were most compatible. Using this criterion he concluded that the material special to *Eug* fitted better with the common material than did that of *SJC,* and that *Eug* therefore preceded *SJC.*

Although individual points of Krause's argument are not convincing (Parrott, 1971: 399–404), his method has had a significant effect: since he wrote, no one has attempted to argue the priority of *SJC.* It appears that as scholars have examined the tractates for themselves, in the light of his approach, they have become convinced of the greater likelihood of the priority of *Eug* by observing the artificiality of the dialogue framework of *SJC* and the differences in vocabulary and ideas between the common material in *SJC* and its separate material (on the latter point, see Parrott, 1971: 405–06). The priority of *Eug* is now usually simply assumed (e.g., Perkins: 35).

That conclusion would diminish in importance, however, if *Eug* could be shown to be Christian in some significant way. Schenke maintained that there were signs of Christian influence, without giving any specifics (1962:

265). Wilson listed terminology that might be Christian (115), but admitted that it fell short of demonstrating Christian influence. I suggested that the so-called summary section of *Eug*–III (85,9ff) was deliberately edited in a Christian direction, but it is also possible that haplography occurred (1971: 412–13; 1975: 180–81), and in any case *Eug*–V lacks the changes. The one rather clear indication of Christian influence in *Eug*–III is found at the conclusion, where editing appears to have sharpened the reference to the one who is expected (90,7–11), so that it easily is seen to refer to Christ in the next tractate, which is *SJC*. Since that sharpening is not found in *Eug*–V, it is possible that *Eug*–III has been subject to some Christian modifications, but that does not alter the basic non-Christian character of the original form of *Eug* (similarly, Ménard: 137). One should perhaps note here that the last sentence in *Eug*–V may be a direct quote from Mark 4:25 or one of its parallels, but it could also have been drawn from the common treasury of secular proverbs assumed by Bultmann as the source for the passage in the gospels (102–04).

There is another aspect of the relationship between these two tractates that needs to be discussed, namely, what appears to be their symbiosis. This is immediately suggested by their juxtaposition in Codex III. It is further suggested by the above-mentioned ending of *Eug*, which in its clearest expression, in Codex III, looks forward to the coming of one who will not need to be taught but who will "speak all these things to you joyously and in pure knowledge" (90,7–11), clearly (in Codex III) pointing to Christ in *SJC*. What could be the reason for this juxtaposition and interconnection?

When Doresse discussed *SJC*, he assumed the tractate was an attempt to make Christians think that Christ taught Gnosticism (so also Krause, 1964: 223) and suggested that the knowledge Christians had of the existence of *Eug* would have made clear to them that that was in fact a fraud (1960: 198). One suspects that problem would have been obvious to the Gnostics, which suggests then that they had something else in mind for *SJC*, something which would have made the relating of these two tractates more than a mistake.

An alternative would be that Christian Gnostics were interested in having those who knew and revered *Eug* come to know that Christ fulfilled the prophecy of Eugnostos (probably initially known by them in its more ambiguous form found in Codex V). That would make it possible for them to accept Christ as the new revealer and recognize that he had triumphed over the sinister powers, thereby opening the way for them to do so also. In other words, the intention may have been to convert non-Christian Gnostics to Christian Gnosticism.

Supporting this is the allusive nature of the references to traditional gnostic doctrines in the material added to *Eug* to produce *SJC*. The reader learns something, but not very much, about the ignorant and bad creator god (III 107,5–11), the sin of Sophia (III 114,14–18), the fall of the divine drops of light into the prison of this cosmic order (III 106,24–107,6, par.), the evil of sexuality (III 108,10–16, par.), and the punishment of the creator god and his minions (BG 121,13–122,5). In no case is one of these doctrines presented in a fully developed way. That suggests that the intended audience was made up of those who already knew those doctrines; that is, that the intended audience were Gnostics. The one doctrine that is fully developed is the doctrine of Christ. (For a similar argument and conclusion, see Perkins, 1980: 98; see also Perkins, 1971: 177.)

Eug and *SJC* could both have a life of their own, as is demonstrated by Codex V, which has *Eug* but not *SJC*; and BG, which has *SJC* but not *Eug*. But it is the symbiotic relationship as seen in Codex III that seems to reveal the reason for the creation of *SJC*.

V. DATING

The dating of the composition of the tractates is difficult because no date-able events are referred to in them. Krause has suggested the first or second centuries C.E. for *Eug* without specifying the reasons (1974: 26). D. Trakatellis is more specific, suggesting the beginning of the second century C.E., because he thinks that *Eug* belongs early in the period in which the leading figures of Gnosticism made their appearance (32). However, those figures produced systems with clear Christian elements, whereas *Eug* has none. A date no later than the first century C.E. seems justified. An even earlier date is likely. *Eug* is directed against the views of "all the philosophers" (III 70,15). From the brief descriptions of these views, the philosophers can be identified as Stoic, Epicurean, and the theoreticians of Babylonian astrology. The latest time when these could be thought of as "all the philosophers" was probably the first century B.C.E. (Parrott, 1988).

As to the date of *SJC*, Puech has dated P. Oxy. 1081 early in the fourth century, thus providing a *terminus ad quem* (1950: 98 n. 2; 1963: 245). He also suggests that *SJC* might have been composed in the second half of the second century, or at the latest, the third century, but gives no reason (1963: 248). Till suggests a relative dating between *Ap. John* (NHC II,*1*; III,*1*; IV,*1*; BG *1*) and *Pist. Soph*. Assuming that *SJC* is an integrated whole, he argues that in it the understandable philosophical viewpoint found in *Ap. John* and its consistent development are diminished, while *SJC* seems to represent an early state in the development of a *Weltbild* that ends in *Pist. Soph*. (Till–Schenke: 56). Doresse puts *SJC* close to the first books of *Pist. Soph*. (1948: 159).

In contrast to these rather late datings, there are certain crucial elements that taken together suggest an early date. The likelihood that *SJC* was produced to persuade non-Christian Gnostics to accept Christian Gnosticism has already been mentioned. That suggests an early date, especially in view of the fact that it seems to be assumed that the intended audience knows little or nothing about Christ, although one cannot deny the possibility of a continuing body of non-Christian Gnostics to whom Christian Gnostics might have wanted to appeal.

Further, there is the absence of polemics connected with the gnostic-orthodox struggle. This is seen rather dramatically when the frame material of *SJC* is compared with that of *Ap. John*. In *Ap. John*, both the beginning and the ending contain elements that seem to refer to the conflict. John is depicted as a traditional Jewish Christian (going to the temple) at the start, who is confronted with charges against Christ by the Pharisee Arimanius. He is unable to answer them and so turns away from the temple and goes to the desert (II 1,5–19). John, then, is seen as moving from the inadequate ortho-dox way (based on Jewish tradition) to the gnostic way.

At the end of *Ap. John*, we sense the defensive posture of a group that anticipates attack in the instructions from Christ that the words of the revela-tion are to be given only to John's fellow spirits ("for this is the mystery of the immoveable race"), that John is to write down and keep secure what he has heard, and in the curse that follows against anyone who might sell what is written (probably to opponents) (II 31,28–37). There is none of that in *SJC*. In the beginning the disciples are perplexed (no reason is given) and go to the place where they have reason to think they will receive answers from the risen savior. And in the end, they are simply told to continue the savior's mission, which, according to the account, they begin to do by preaching the Gospel (i.e., what they have just heard).

Another reason for assigning an early date is the fact that *SJC* contains nothing that would clearly indicate that it had been influenced by the great systems of the middle third of the second century. There are numerous points of contact, of course, but nothing that demonstrates dependence. Finally, when one examines the attempt in *SJC* to integrate the person of Christ into the system of *Eug,* it is clear that problems remain: Christ is identified with Son of Man, but not with Savior; but a major section on the work of Christ (III 106,24–108,16, par.) is placed immediately after the sec-tion on the appearing of Savior, who is the son of Son of Man (III 106,15–24), which would lead one to think that a second identification of Christ — this time, with Savior — was being made. Perhaps in an attempt to resolve this confusion, the bridge section, which provides a summary of sorts, in *SJC* identifies Savior with Son of Man and ignores the son of Son of Man (BG 108,1–7) (although he is mentioned in the *Eug*–V parallel). All this suggests that in *SJC* we are at the beginning of the process by which Christian Gnosticism was to become rationalized or theologized.

Taken together, then, these points tend to the conclusion that *SJC* should be dated early. If *Eug* is dated in the first-century B.C.E., then *SJC* should probably be dated late in the first or early in the second century.

VI. ORIGINAL LANGUAGE

Prior to the identification by Puech of P. Oxy. 1081 as a leaf from a Greek copy of *SJC* (1950: 98, n. 2), Doresse asserted that *SJC* was composed originally in Coptic (1948: 152). But once the identification was made, a Coptic original became improbable. And given a Greek original of *SJC*, a Greek original of *Eug* is very likely. Further confirmation of this is provided by the presence in *Eug*–III of an untranslated conjugated Greek verb (75,8); evidently it was unfamiliar to the scribe-translator, so he left it as it was.

VII. PROVENANCE

Trakatellis holds that nothing can be concluded about the provenance of *Eug*. The fact that the scribe of *Gos. Eg.* has the name Eugnostos as his spiritual name, and could therefore be the same person as the writer of *Eug* (on the unlikelihood of which, see the next section), might suggest Egypt. But Trakatellis argues (following Böhlig–Wisse) that one cannot be certain that *Gos. Eg.* was in fact directed to the Egyptians (32).

There is, however, another element in *Eug* that suggests Egypt, namely, the reference to "the three hundred sixty days of the year" (III 84,4–5). In *Eug* the number of days of the year is thought of as existing because it is a reflection ("type") of the 360 supercelestial powers. Hence it is part of the necessary ordering of things. From ancient times the Egyptians had calculated the year as having 360 days, divided into twelve months of thirty days each, plus five epagomenal days (Bickerman: 42). Furthermore, when the Romans conquered Egypt they left the 360 day period intact, decreeing only that every four years another day should be added to the epagomenal days (Decree of Augustus, 26 B.C. [Bickerman: 49]), thus bringing the Egyptian year into line with the Julian year, which was standard elsewhere in the Roman Empire.

Przybylski has suggested several possible sources other than Egypt for the 360 day reference (1 Enoch, Jubilees, a purely theoretical rather than a practical calendar, ancient Babylon) (60–62), but it seems unlikely that any of them would have been the source without some word of explanation to the reader. It was only in Egypt where such a reference would have been taken for granted.[4]

A further reason for believing in an Egyptian provenance is found in the discussion of sources in Section IX.

If *Eug* had an Egyptian provenance, it is reasonable to think that *SJC* had one also.

---

[4] As noted, 360 days did not constitute the whole year for the Egyptians. But the references in *Eug*–III and *Eug*–V do not claim that, and indeed *Eug*–III seems to suggest that it is only a part of the year, with its strange word order and odd (for the context) preposition: ⲡϣⲙⲧ{ⲧ}ϣⲉⲥⲉ ⲛ̄ⲧⲛ̄ ⲧⲉⲣⲟⲙ<ⲡ>ⲉ ⲛ̄ⲍⲟⲟⲩ, lit., "The three hundred sixty *from* the year days" (84,4–5). It should be noted that the Valentinians also assumed a 360 day period (Iren., *Haer.* 2.15.1, and *Val. Exp.* [XI,2] 30,34–38).

VIII. WRITERS AND AUDIENCES

Eug

The name Eugnostos is not widely attested, but there is one reference to it (Pape and Bensler: s.v.; contra Bellet [47]). From the tractate there is no reason to think that it is anything other than a proper noun (derived from an adjective). It may be a spiritual name here (in contrast to a birth name), since Eugnostos is the spiritual name of the scribe of the colophon of *Gos. Eg.* (III 69,10–11). Or, if we can assume that the non-Christian *Eug* was earlier than the colophon of the Christianized *Gos. Eg.*, it may be that the name became spiritual within a gnostic community because it was the name of the revered writer of our tractate. Bellet's conjecture that Eugnostos is the title of an official in a gnostic circle requires for credibility an unlikely transposition, since the title should be in second position in relation to the name of the person possessing the title. Such a transposition has not been found in other sources, as Bellet himself admits (47 and 55–56).

The designation пмакариос , "the Blessed," which appears only in *Eug*–III, would probably not have been applied by the writer to himself, since it is honorific, and should therefore be considered secondary. It may have been inserted to indicate that Eugnostos was dead. Such usage was not limited to Christian communities, contrary to Bellet (55) (see *TDNT* 4:362 [Hauck] and LSJ: s.v.).

The writer of *Eug* may have been a teacher of some significance, since his writing is preserved in two quite different versions, testifying to long usage. In view of the fact that the compiler of Codex III placed *Gos. Eg.* and *Eug* side-by-side, he may have identified Eugnostos with the scribe of the colophon of *Gos. Eg.* If that was the case, it seems unlikely that he was correct (contra Doresse, 1948: 159; 1960: 196), in view of the probability that *Eug* was considerably earlier than *Gos. Eg.*

Eug is ostensively addressed to "those who are his" (III 70,1–2). "His" may refer to Eugnostos himself, in which case the audience would be his disciples. But one gains the impression from the tractate that the audience may not be familiar with some of Eugnostos' teachings (see, e.g., III 74,12–14). If that is the case, "his" could refer to a deity to whom the audience is thought to belong. "Sons of Unbegotten Father" are mentioned in III 75,22.

SJC

The author of *SJC* wants it to appear that he is a disciple (III 91,12–19, par.).[5] However in point of fact we have no knowledge of who the author is.

---

[5] In *Pist. Soph.*, Philip, Matthew and Thomas, all of whom are named in *SJC* (along with Bartholew and Mary), are designated as "those who are to write everything that Jesus says" (71,18–72,1; 72,11–20).

It seems clear, however, who the audience is. It is made up of those who, like the disciples in *SJC,* seek answers to basic questions about the meaning and purpose of the whole cosmic system, and about their place in it. As mentioned above, they are probably non-Christian Gnostics who are being encouraged by the writer to adopt Christianized Gnosticism.

IX. SOURCES OF EUGNOSTOS

It may be that *Eug* originally existed without the letter format, as a cosmogonic text, as Krause has suggested (1964: 222). The minor items that make it a letter could easily have been added, but there is no way to be certain (see XVII below).

There is evidence, however, that *Eug,* as we have received it, in both its versions, is the result of major earlier editorial activity. That can be seen in two places: in the first major portion of *Eug* (III 70,1–85,9, par.) (Part A), where two originally separate speculative patterns seem to have been combined; and in the second major part (III 85,9–90,3, par.) (Part B) where evidence is found that it may originally have been an independent unit.

A. *Two Speculative Patterns in Part A*

The two patterns emerge when a comparison is made of the first group of major deities and the second, the latter of which is described as "the type of those who preceded them" (III 82,10–11, a phrase omitted in *Eug*–V!), that is, the type of the first group. The following chart shows the comparison:

First Group (III 71,13–82,6, par.)   *Second Group* (III 82,7–83,2, par.)
(Variant terms found in only one text are indicated.)

1) He Who Is; Unbegotten; Father of the Universe; Forefather; First Existent (III) (III 71,13–75,2,3)

1) Unbegotten (III); Unbegotten <Father of> All things (V). *Consort*: All-Wise Sophia.

2) Self-Father; Self-Begetter; Confronter (III); Self-grown, Self-constructed Father (III); He who Put Forth Himself (V) (III 75,3–11; 76,14–17)

2) Self-begotten. *Consort*: All-Mother Sophia (III).

3) Man (V); Immortal Man; Immortal Androgynous Man (III); Self-perfected Begetter (V); Begetter Mind who Perfects Himself (V); Begotten; Perfect Mind (III); Father; Self-Father Man; Man of the Depth (V); First Man (III).

3) Begetter (III); Begotten (V). *Consort*: All-Begettress Sophia (III).

Consort: All-wise Begettress Sophia; Thought, She of All Wisdoms, Begettress of the Wisdoms (V); Truth (V); Great Sophia (V). (III 76,19–V 8,32)

4) First-begotten Son of God (V); First Begetter Father (III); Adam of the Light (III); son of Man. *Consort*: First-begotten Sophia, Mother of the Universe; Love. (V 8,33–III 81,21)

4) First Begetter (III); Begotten of the First (V). *Consort*: First Begettress Sophia (III).

5) Savior, Begetter of All Things; All-Begetter (84,13) Son of Son of Man (V 13,12–13). *Consort*: Sophia, All-Begettress (III); Pistis Sophia (III 81,21–82,6)

5) All-Begetter (III); All-begotten (V). *Consort*: Love Sophia.

6) Arch-Begetter (III) (V, in lacuna). *Consort*: Pistis Sophia.

The most obvious and significant thing to observe is that the second group has one more deity than the first. It is also notable that the name of the consort of the fifth deity in the second group, namely, Love, is one of the names of the consort of the fourth being in the first group. Also, the name Pistis Sophia, which belongs to the consort of the sixth deity in the second group, is one of the names of the consort of the fifth deity in the first group. Notable also is the fact that the second group lacks the terms Man, Son of Man, Son of Son of Man, and Savior.

Contrary to III 82,10–11, then, the second group is not now the type of those who preceded them in any complete sense.

If we ask which list is primary, the answer seems to be the second, since the number six is important subsequently in the tractate (see discussion below), whereas the number five is not.

If we assume that III 82,10–11 originally was correct, the first group once had six members; now it lacks Arch-Begetter.

The reason for the dropping of the antetype of Arch-Begetter seems to be that another pattern was superimposed on the first group, the pattern of Immortal Man, Son of Man, and son of Son of Man—Savior. This pattern had no figure to identify with the antetype of Arch-Begetter.[6]

---

[6] The name Arch-Begetter (by some translators, simply transliterated as Archigenetor) does not appear in *Eug* after III 82,18; however, it does appear in *SJC*, in a non-*Eug* section, where it is identified with Yaldabaoth, the ignorant and malevolent creator god (BG 119,14–16).

The original form of the first group, then, would have resembled that of the second, except raised to a higher level of perfection. Thus, Unbegotten Father in the second group has a consort, while Unbegotten in the first is simply one. Moreover, Unbegotten in the second group is merely father of the multiplicities ("all things"), while Unbegotten in the first group is Father of the Universe. Therefore the first group would originally have looked something like the following:

1) He Who Is; Unbegotten; Father of the Universe; Forefather; First Existent.

2) Self-Father; Self-Begetter; Confronter; Self-grown, Self-constructed Father.

3) Begotten; Self-perfected Begetter; Perfect Mind; Begetter Mind who Perfects Himself (V). *Consort*: All-wise Begettress Sophia; Thought, She of All Wisdoms, Begettress of the Wisdoms; Truth; Great Sophia.

4) First-begotten; First Begetter Father. *Consort*: First-begotten Sophia, Mother of the Universe.

5) Begetter of All Things; All-Begetter. *Consort*: Love Sophia.

6) Arch-Begetter. *Consort*: Pistis Sophia.

The pattern here is one that is found in Egyptian religion: An initial all-encompassing divinity (Amun, in Egyptian thought), creates a separate divinity by himself (i.e., no consort is involved). This divinity is then responsible for the creation of four other divinities, each of whom have a single female consort, thus making a total of eight (in Egyptian thought, the Eight *Urgötter* of Hermopolis). These, in turn, are responsible for the creation of various heavenly realms and other divine beings, leading ultimately to the structures of this world (in Egyptian thought, they create the gods who bring structure to the cosmos). This pattern can be traced to the Theban theology of the Ramesside period and (judging from *Eug*) became more abstract and hence more universal by the end of the Ptolemaic period. Since the pattern was not found elsewhere in the period under study, it seems reasonable to think that Egyptian religion is its source (Parrott, 1987: 82–88).

The pattern imposed on this reconstructed original pattern, namely, the pattern of three androgynous men, Immortal man, Son of Man, and Savior, appears to be the result of speculation on the first five chapters of Genesis. An important clue to that is the identification of Son of Man with Adam. He is not earthly Adam, of course, but his antetype, Adam of the Light (III 81,12), who exists in the transcendent realm. Another clue is the identification of Son of Man as also "Son of *God*" (V 9,2–3).

The idea that Adam was androgynous comes from Gen 1:27 and 5:1, where it is said that God created Adam male and female. He also created him in his own image, which can be taken to mean that God himself is man and that he too is androgynous. Hence, if antetype Adam is Son of Man, antetype God is Immortal Man, Adam's father. Son of son of Man–Savior should then in all probability be identified with the antetype of Seth, since only of Seth is it said that he was begotten in Adam's image (Gen 5:3) (and hence was androgynous).

The three man pattern appears to presuppose a myth like that found in *Apoc. Mos.,* where God is the benign ruler and Seth is the eschatological savior of Adam's progeny (13.1–3). One can speculate that the reason for combining this pattern with the Egyptian one was that those who thought of Seth as a savior felt the need to give their beliefs the support of a broader theological-philosophical context. The beginning of *Eug* makes clear that the writer, at any rate, felt that he was having to deal with a spiritual threat from various philosophical teachings — teachings that presupposed either that there was no transcendent world (Stoicism and astrology) or, if there were, that there was no connection between that world and this one (Epicureanism) (Parrott, 1988: 166–67).

The two patterns were combined by the simple expedient of adding the names of the second pattern at appropriate places. This is the same method used in *SJC,* where, in the Christianization process, Christ is identified with Son of Man. Probably the same thing has occurred in such tractates as *Ap. John* and *Gos. Eg.* (see Krause, 1964: 223; Hedrick, 1981). Since the names of the consorts are present in the second group, which was not affected by this combining, it seems likely that the three-man pattern lacked such names, and was simply identified as androgynous. As we have noted, because there was no fourth man, the antetype of Arch-Begetter (in the second group) was dropped. But instead of merely dropping his consort Pistis Sophia, the editor identified her with the consort of the preceding figure, which led, then, to the shifting of the name "Love" from that figure to the next preceding one. These names must have had some importance in the conceptuality of the editor, but what it might have been at the early date of *Eug* is not clear.

Part A then permits us to see the combining of a universalized Egyptian cosmological system and a speculative system based on Genesis. To the extent that these or similar elements are present in combined and elaborated form in later tractates, such as *Ap. John* and *Gos. Eg.,* we are probably justified in thinking of *Eug* as the source.

B. An Originally Independent Second Part:
Part B (III 85,9–90,3, par.)

The originally independent character of Part B is suggested by the fact that it is at odds in a number of important ways with the earlier part of the tractate. The following analysis will show the points of conflict.

Part B is introduced by a bridge section, whose purpose is to relate it to the foregoing. In particular, the intention is to relate the number of aeons in Part B to those in Part A and to suggest that the aeons to be described are the types of the preceding ones. It is here that the problems begin.

The earliest version of the bridge section is undoubtedly in *Eug*–V (13,8–20), as Krause observed (1964: 221), which states that three aeons preceded (the same number as in Part B), with another aeon (that of Unbegotten, presumably) embracing them. The three are the aeons of Immortal Man, Son of Man, and Son of Son of Man. Left out of account, however, are Self-Begetter (the reflection of Unbegotten) and the twelve aeons created by All-Begetter for the twelve angels (III 84,13–17, par.). To be sure, no aeon is mentioned as having been created for Self-Begetter in Part A, but neither is one mentioned for son of Son of Man. So the three aeons of the bridge section (in *Eug*–V) do not accurately reflect the preceding material. It appears that they were designed to meet the need created by the presence of three aeons in Part B, in the light of what might be called the typological dogma.

What is described subsequently is called "the Eighth that appeared in Chaos" (III 85,19–21, par.). "Eighth" is probably to be thought of as the highest sphere of the visible cosmos (Chaos), perhaps the sphere of the fixed stars (the seven planets—including the sun and moon—each having their own spheres below it; for the fixed stars, see the description of the "multitudinous lights" in III 86,6–8). However, one cannot rule out the possibility, in view of the discussion below, that "Eighth" refers to the eighth day of creation.

The creation described in Part B is said to be the work of Immortal Man, even though his work seemed to have been concluded in Part A (V 8,15–18). The whole section appears to be based on Genesis 1–5, as was the case with the three-man pattern earlier. The clue to the Genesis connection is in the discussion of the androgyne "Assembly" (εκκλησια), which begins in III 86,24, par. Its female portion is called "Life" (ζωη), and it is explained that in this way (by giving her this name) "it might be shown that from a female came the life in all the aeons" (III 87,5–8, par.). That is closely parallel to the LXX version of Gen 3:20, where the woman is given the name Ζωή rather than Eve, and where it is explained that she has that name "because she is the mother of all living things" (ὅτι αὕτη μήτηρ πάντων τῶν ζώντων).

Her mate, however, retains the name of the androgyne, as also happens in Genesis 3, but here he is called Assembly rather than Adam. The replacement of "Adam" with "Assembly" seems strange at first, since the Greek for "Assembly" is feminine. It thus breaks with the convention that the gender of names taken from common nouns should be the same as the sex of the being who is named (but see III 112,7–8, where it also occurs). However it seems clear that the writer is simply following the pattern of Genesis 3, without giving much thought to the convention. (Knowledge of the Hebrew Bible, where the word usually translated ἐκκλησία in the LXX is masculine [קהל], is unlikely in view of the general lack of such knowledge among Egyptian Jews [e.g., Philo].) In any case, there is no hint of this change of terminology in Part A, where, as has been noted, the term Adam is used (III 81,12, par.).

The change suggests that behind the account in Part B lies a body of speculative thought identifying antetype Adam (taken in a collective sense) with the type of an assembly that would subsequently appear, perhaps the assembly of the Gnostics. This seems unrelated to the statements in Part A that antetype Adam was Son of Man, "of the Light" (III 81,12, par.), and the type for time (III 83,22–23, par.).

The editor of *Eug* seems unaware of the tension here, or, indeed, that speculation on Adam lies behind Assembly. In what appears to be an editorial expansion (since it relates Part B to Part A), he identifies Assembly as the type not of Son of Man / Adam of the Light but of "the Assembly that surpasses heaven" (III 86,22–24, par.), which is described in III 81,3–10, par., and is in fact the creation of Son of Man / Adam (III 81,1–12, par.).

Assembly and his mate begin the spiritual generation that leads to the appearance of multifarious immortals (III 87,8–88,3, par.). The creation of the immortals is surprising, since the aeons of the immortals had earlier been described as above the sphere of the Eighth (III 85,17–18, par.). (This generating activity suggests typological speculation on Gen 4:25–5:32, where the sons of Adam and Eve are listed, along with their amazingly long life spans.)

The immortals in turn provide themselves with great kingdoms, through the authority of Immortal Man and his consort Sophia (III 88,3–89,3, par.), who is here given the name "Silence," which is different from her name in Part A, namely "All-wise Begettress" (III 77,3–4, par.). This realm, then, is said to provide the types for all subsequent creations (III 89,6–15, par.). That would seem to be in tension with the statement in Part A that our aeon is the type of Immortal Man (III 83,20–22, par.) (not the type of a separate realm created by him) and that temporal aspects of our aeon are the types of other beings described in Part A (III 83,22–84,11, par.).

In addition to these points of tension, it is worth noting that Part B seems to have been diminished in size as a result of being connected with Part A. The three aeons that have already been mentioned (V 14,3–7; III 86,8–13) are (1) beginning (V) or first (III), (2) the middle, and (3) the unending (V) and/or the perfect (V and III). Little is said about the first two in Part B and attention is concentrated on the third. However, the identification of the first two is important for our discussion, and that can be attempted by looking more closely at the third aeon.

The third aeon is named for Assembly (III 86,14–17, par.). If Assembly is initially antetype Adam and Eve (as androgyne), and then antetype Adam alone, then it would be reasonable to think that the third aeon is to be related (as antetype) to the account of creation that begins in Gen 2:4. The term "unending" would be appropriate, since there is no concluding formula for creation there, as there is in Gen 2:1. The term "perfect" would also be appropriate, since the third contains the ideal patterns for subsequent creations.

If that is the third aeon, then the first ("beginning") would perhaps be connected with the creation account that starts with Gen 1:1 ("In the beginning. . . ."). The second, "the middle," then might refer to the divine sabbath in Gen 2:2–3, which identification would be supported by V 14,7–9, as it is restored ("[The first] in it was called ['Above] Unity [and Rest']," implying that "Unity and Rest" was the Second aeon) (but note the *Eug*–III and *SJC* parallels).

These three, then, may well have reflected the whole of the Genesis creation account and been intended to present a complete account of cosmic origins. One can conjecture that the description of the three was truncated by the elimination of most of the discussion about the first two aeons, in order to fit the account into the scheme established in Part A.

When one takes into consideration the other differences we have noted, it is not unreasonable to think that originally Part B (minus the bridge section and the conclusion, and with the inclusion of the deleted material) stood by itself, as an account of the creation of the cosmos by the antetype of the creator God of Genesis, namely androgynous Immortal Man. The first aeon would perhaps have been the super-celestial and invisible realm, the third, the visible realm, and the second, the space that separated the two. The account may well have ended where it ends now, just at the point where our part of the visible cosmos would come into existence.

To summarize, in its present context, Part B appears to be a description of the highest level of the visible universe (the Eighth), and its three aeons are seen as types of three supercelestial and hence invisible ones. The evidence suggests, however, that Part B was originally an independent speculative account based on Genesis 1–5, which provided a total description of the universe, up to the point of the creation of the world as it is.

Looking back on the whole of this section, we have found that Part A is made up of two originally different speculative systems that have been combined; and now, in the discussion of Part B, we have found a third speculative scheme, which an editor has attempted to bring into some sort of harmony with Part A.

One must ask why it would have seemed necessary to combine these three. Why not simply start fresh in constructing a speculative system that would be inwardly consistent? First, as we have learned from the critical study of the book of Genesis, the bringing together of accounts that speak essentially of the same thing (e.g., the accounts of creation, the flood, etc.) may be a sign of the alignment of groups for whom these accounts had sacred significance before that alignment. The recognition that one of the systems contains an indirect reference to Seth, suggests the identity of one of the groups — Sethians, or more likely, proto-Sethians. It was this group that made use of the Egyptian cosmological pattern. An ideological reason has already been suggested for that — to have a broader theoretical structure for dealing with philosophical challenges. But the fact that it was Egyptian may suggest a strong Egyptian component in the group, for whom the pattern

would have had special significance. As to Part B, it is not possible to identify what group might have held it in special regard, but it is so different from
Part A that there must have been a separate group of origin. Second, there is
the conviction that truth is a self-consistent unity (V 6,9–14; 17,13–15). That
is, the various parts of truth must agree among themselves. If one believes
that different parts of truth are communicated separately, as the final editor of
Eug appears to, then one could conclude that when those parts are put
together, probably under the guidance of Thought (V 3,29–4,5, par.), one
would have a broader, but, *ex hypothesi*, still consistent, expression of Truth.
Obvious differences among the parts could be ascribed to human error in the
reception of revelation and therefore could be thought of as correctable at a
later time (III 90,4–11).

It may be that this explanation would also account for later developments
in gnostic systems, where disparate elements seem often to be involved.

It should be noted here that there is nothing in the sources of *Eug* that can
be considered classically Gnostic. The use of the theory of types means that
both parts of *Eug* assume that the structures of this world are reflections of
the supercelestial world, and not the creation of an inferior deity. There is
only one reference to distinctively gnostic ideology, and that seems clearly
editorial (III 85,8). However, *Eug* should nonetheless be considered proto-
Gnostic, since it provided a theoretical basis for later developments that led
to classic Gnosticism, as *SJC* shows.

X. RELATIONSHIP OF THE TEXTS

We have already noted that *Eug* was prior to *SJC* and that *Eug*–III was
apparently edited in the light of *SJC* by sharpening the prediction at the end.
Since that sharpening is only apparent because of the parallel in *Eug*–V, the
latter's reading is probably to be thought of as earlier here. In addition to the
prediction, there are two other places, which we noted, where *Eug*–V seems
earlier than *Eug*–III, namely, the titles in the incipit and subscript.

We must now look at other evidence that bears on the question of the relationship of the texts.

An examination of the parallels shows that the two texts of *SJC* are very
close. Differences in vocabulary and sentence structure mostly seem to
reflect different Coptic translators rather than different Greek *Vorlagen*.
Gaps in one text in comparison with the other, which are infrequent, can be
explained as the result of homoioteleuton (e.g., BG 89,16–17, which is lacking in *SJC*–III) or minor editorial activity (e.g., BG 83,17–19, which is also
lacking in *SJC*–III). If we take into consideration P. Oxy. 1081, which is
very similar to the two Coptic texts, we are probably justified in thinking that
there was only one major edition of *SJC*.

A further examination shows that the text of *Eug* used in composing *SJC*
generally was closer to *Eug*–III than to *Eug*–V. A good indication of that is
the bridge section (III 85,11–21 ‖ BG 108,1–18; V 13,8–18). *SJC*–BG has

two aeons, which are embraced by a third. *Eug*–III has the same pattern, although the first two are listed in reverse order. But *Eug*–V has three aeons, embraced by a fourth. Beyond that we can observe that the parallels between *Eug*–III and the two copies of *SJC* are very close, both in terms of the extent of text in parallel sections and in language. On the other hand, *Eug*–V differs, in regard to the extent of text alone, some eighteen times, at points where the other texts agree with each other.

It seems impossible to tell which text of *SJC* might be closer to *Eug*–III. At four points *Eug*–III agrees with *SJC*–BG in having more text than *SJC*–III (III 72,3–6 ‖ BG 84,13–17; III 74,3–4 ‖ BG 89,16–17; III 86,22–24 ‖ BG 111,3–5; III 89,5–6 ‖ BG 115,14–15). In two of these instances, however, the lack in *SJC*–III might well be the result of homoioteleuton. In the other two, scribal error of some sort would not be surprising. There are also a few places where *Eug*–III and *SJC*–III agree against *SJC*–BG (e.g., III 72,11–13 ‖ 95,5–7 ‖ BG 85,6–9; III 73,12–13 ‖ 96,7–10 ‖ BG 87,1–4; III 76,23–24 ‖ 101,7–8 ‖ BG 94,9–11; III 87,9 ‖ 111,12 ‖ BG 112,3), but these are minor and attributable to coincidence, and may have arisen in the process of translation into Coptic.

Although the text used in the composition of *SJC* more closely resembled *Eug*–III than *Eug*–V, there are two significant places where *Eug*–V is closer to *SJC*. First, after the address proper, *Eug*–V has the same verb as the *SJC* parallels (V 1,3 ‖ III 92,7 ‖ BG 80,4), ⲧⲟⲩⲱϣ, "I want" (Gr. θέλω). Neither that verb nor an equivalent is found in *Eug*–III. And second, in the last sentence of *Eug*–V, both it and the two *SJC* parallels have the word ⲛ̄ϩⲟⲩⲟ, "more." That word and the sentences it is found in have no parallel in *Eug*–III. Although the sentences are not exact parallels, there is a similar idea in both (*Eug*–V: "To everyone who has, more will be added"; *SJC*: "that you [the disciples] might shine in Light [even] more than these."), which suggests that at this point the writer of *SJC* was looking at a text of *Eug* closer to *Eug*–V.

We can conclude that the text used in the composition of *SJC* was generally like that of *Eug*–III, but that in a few places it was closer to *Eug*–V. Changes in the text that resulted in *Eug*–III, as it stands, would have occurred subsequent to the composition of *SJC*.

In comparison with *Eug*–III, *Eug*–V appears to have undergone considerable expansion. Although *Eug*–V has one significant gap (it lacks III 73,14–20), there are fourteen instances where it has more text (according to the arrangement of parallels in this text and excluding the section corresponding to the missing pp. 79–80 in *Eug*–III). It should probably be thought of as later than the text represented by *Eug*–III. However, as we have noted, it seems to have some readings that are earlier. *Eug*–V, then, appears to have developed independently and to have been subject to modification over a longer period of time.

The following time chart diagrams the conclusions about text relationships arrived at above:

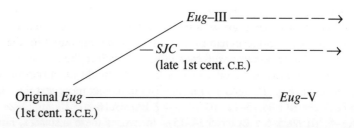

It is not clear why *Eug*–III and the *SJC* texts did not share the extensive kind of modification that is found *Eug*–V. It may have had to do with the pairing of *Eug*–III and *SJC*, which could well have acted as a brake on normal scribal tendencies to add glosses, since it would have been evident that the texts had to remain quite similar. (That assumes that *Eug*–III and *SJC* were paired for most of their textual history.) It is also possible that both texts came to be thought of in some measure as scripture among certain groups of Gnostics.

The Coptic versions of *Eug* and *SJC* were translated by different persons. That is shown by the passage left untranslated in *Eug*–III, and its parallels (75,7–8 ‖ III 99,8–9 ‖ BG 91,10–12 ‖ V 4,21–3). In no case is that passage treated the same. While *Eug*–III does not translate it, *SJC*–III attempts to do so, but does it incorrectly, and *SJC*–BG also tries and succeeds. In *Eug*–V, the passage is translated, but quite differently from *SJC*–BG. (For a reconstruction of the Greek, see the section later in the volume on P. Oxy. 1081 [lines 46–50].)

As to the Coptic translations in their totality, *Eug*–III, *SJC*–III and *SJC*–BG all seem related. The grammar, sentence structure and vocabulary are frequently the same. In contrast, *Eug*–V is often quite different. The similarities of *Eug*–III, *SJC*–III and *SJC*–BG may be accounted for by assuming that they were translated by members of the same or related scribal groups, which had developed more or less common translation traditions. (For individual differences between the translators of *Eug*–III and *SJC*–BG, see endnote 4.)

XI. THE CODICES

A codicological analysis of NHC III has been done by Frederik Wisse (1975). In the process he has also described the characteristics of the scribal hand. Codicological analyses of NHC V and BG have been done by Robinson (1979: 16–30; 36–44). His analysis of BG supersedes the one in Till–Schenke (331–32). Further developments in the analysis of these codices are to be found in Robinson (1984: chaps. 3 [The Quires]; 4 [The Rolls]; 5 [The Kollemata]; and 6 [The Covers]).

As to the dating of the codices themselves, the material in the cartonnage of the leather cover of NHC V is dated between 298 and 323 C.E. (Barns, et al.: 3), which provides a *terminus a quo* for the inscribing of the codex, but is only suggetive of the *terminus ad quem,* since the scraps used for the cartonnage could have come from a time considerably before the time of inscribing. Unfortunately the cartonnage of Codex III is no longer extant (*Facsimile Edition*: xiii). The date of BG was discussed above (see I). A recent examination of the cartonnage from the BG cover suggests that the cartonnage should be dated sometime late in the third century or early in the fourth (Treu).

XII. PHYSICAL STATE OF THE TRACTATES

Eug–V. The Codex as a whole is unevenly preserved (Parrott, 1979: 3–4), and *Eug* is the least well preserved of all the tractates. Substantial portions of the tops and bottoms of all the leaves are missing (more of the latter than the former). In addition, the first eight pages have significant gaps in the midst of the remaining text. Fading occurs throughout and is particularly marked on the first three right-hand pages. Flaking is found on p. 11.

It should be added that the quality of the papyrus is among the poorest in the library. Examples of this can be found on pp. 1 and 5, in the breaks in the vertical fibers, and the heavy, discolored horizontal fiber on p. 6, all of which forced the scribe to compensate in one way or another.

Numerous fragments were placed prior to the publishing of the facsimile edition (1975) and therefore need no comment here. However, two were placed subsequently. On August 8, 1977, Stephen Emmel, working at the Coptic Museum in Cairo, placed two fragments, nos. 1 and 40, in the inside lower margin area of pp. 5 and 6, thus providing more text at the beginning of 5,27–29 and at the end of 6,29–31 (see 9*f/10*f in Addenda et Corrigenda in Robinson, 1984).

Eug–III and SJC–III. Three leaves are missing from the tractates: 79–80, 109–10, and 115–16. Wisse has proposed that they (and three others in the codex) were removed by a dealer for showing to prospective buyers, which would sugget that they may still be extant (1975: 227).

Damage attributable to age and rough handling by the discoverers or middlemen is very limited in comparison with Codex V. Reconstruction of the text is required on pp. 70–74 (lower inner margin area), 73–88 (middle of the top area, extending down to the 5th line at one point), 87, 89, 93 (top outer corner), 95–100 (top, toward the inner margin), 105–14 (middle, inner margin area), 117–19 (middle third of page, from the inner margin to approx. 3 cm. from the outer margin). The MS is remarkably free of flaking or fading.

SJC–BG. The leaves on the whole are well preserved. Restorations are needed on pp. 96 (outer margin area), 97–106 (top margin area) and 111–18 (inner upper margin area). Fading occurs on pp. 77–79 and 118. One leaf

(85–86) was cracked or torn in antiquity subsequent to inscribing and was repaired with narrow strips of papyrus pasted over the break on both sides of the leaf. The strips on p. 86 partially cover letters of the text.

XIII. SCRIBAL CHARACTERISTICS

A. Errors and other Peculiarities

Eug–V

I have earlier listed some of the errors found here (1979: 4–5). The present list is based on a more intensive study of the tractate and is therefore more complete.

1. Errors corrected by the scribe
   a. Haplography corrected by letters written above the line or in the margin at the place of omission: 6,6.24; 7,17. In each case a stroke is placed above the letter. That occurs elsewhere in the codex only in 28,8.22. For similar corrections without a stroke, see 26,6.10.18; 27,3; 31,9.13; 56,23. This difference suggests there may have been more than one corrector of the codex.
   b. Deletion of incorrect letters by dotting: 7,26.33.
   c. Replacement of incorrect letters by letters written on top of them (i.e., covering them) without erasure: 2,18; 9,1; 10,3; 14,4.
   d. Marking out of an unnecessary letter: 14,4.
2. Errors not corrected by the scribe.
   a. Haplography: 2,16; 8,10; 9,17; 10,18.
   b. Unnecessary letters: 5,18; 15,4.
   c. Incorrect letters: 5,18; 6,29; 7,16; 7,20–22; 7,27; 8,7; 10,19.
3. Other peculiarities
   a. Omission of a circumflex with ⲍⲱ at 17,7.
   b. Use of a dot ("stop") to set off an attributive from the noun it depends on (5,4; 7,10; 17,14), perhaps as a way of rendering a Greek attributive adjective in the second position (note that the parallels for 5,4 and 17,14 have relative clauses in place of the attributives).
   c. Use of low dots as word separators in 8,7.16; 12,10 (see also 34,10).
   d. In 7,25 a dot may replace a sentence pronoun.
   e. Numeral written at end of 11,20 (a gloss, similar to those later in the codex [Parrott, 1979: 5]), with a stroke above.
   f. Instead of using a second present with a noun and an adverbial expression, the scribe in one instance uses a sentence pronoun and puts the adverbial expression in first position (11,14). Also sentence pronouns are used as shorthand for ⲱⲱⲡⲉ ⲉ- in 7,24–29 and for ⲱⲁⲩⲙⲟⲩⲧⲉ ⲉⲣⲟⲟⲩ ⲭⲉ in 11,18–20 (cf. III 106,22).
   g. ⲭ is mistakenly written for ⲭ in 6,29; 7,20–22.

Eug–III and SJC–III

The scribe of Codex III is much more error prone than his counterpart in Codex V.

1. Errors corrected by the scribe.
   a. Haplography, corrected by letters written above the line at the place of omission: 72,14; 91,11; 95,2; 105,8; 113,11.
   b. Replacement of erased or partially erased letters by letters written on top of them: 70,2; 71,21; 72,8.21; 73,12.19.22; 77,16; 84,3; 85,9.16; 87,10; 89,10.12; 91,2; 94,15.20; 96,15 (correction of dittography); 97,11; 100,21; 102,7; 106,13; 107,1.6; 113,11; 118,2.5.6; 119,7.
   c. Erasure of unnecessary letters, etc.: 81,11 (erased point); 85,8; 87,22; 92,24 (erased dot); 95,24; 96,14 (erased stroke).
   d. Replacement of marked out letters by letters written above them: 72,12; 95,6 (marking out omitted); 97,18; 113,8. In all of these a change of meaning occurs.
   e. Marking out of unnecessary letters: 72,12; 89,10; 95,6; 106,19 (dialectal change); 113,8.
   f. Re-forming of a letter to make another without erasure: 73,4.

   It is possible that a second scribe made some of these corrections. The letters written by the corrector under "d" seem somewhat different from letters in the rest of the tractate, but the differences are not sufficient to make a determination of a second scribe certain (see Böhlig–Wisse for a similar judgment regarding III,2 [4]; Wisse expresses more assurance about there being only one scribe in his later essay [1975: 236]).

2. Errors not corrected by the scribe.
   a. Haplography: 71,5; 73,10.14; 76,14; 83,5; 86,3.4.10.14.17; 89,10; 94,13(?); 95,22; 96,2.23; 97,7.17; 98,24.25; 99,8; 102,9; 103,6.10.23; 104,1; 107,7.8.21; 111,18.20; 113,7.
   b. Unnecessary letters: 74,10; 76,5 (dittography); 77,7; 84,5 (dittography).16; 85,4; 86,17; 95,6; 97,3 (dittography).18; 99,11; 113,8; 118,1 (dittography).
   c. Incorrect letters: 78,22–23 (reversal of letters); 82,2; 83,13.14; 84,13; 86,7; 87,23; 89,2; 91,15; 93,22; 101,20; 105,22; 106,14; 107,11; 113,1.
   d. Corruptions: 86,17; 99,8–9.19–22; 112,7–11.

3. Other Peculiarities.
   a. In 99,8–9 a Greek phrase is partially, and incorrectly, translated. It is left untranslated or rendered correctly in the parallels.
   b. The status pronominalis of cⲱⲧⲙ is always spelled ⲥⲟⲧⲙⲉ⸗.
   c. The lack of care of the scribe is further attested by random drops of ink that appear here and there; e.g., at 92,1.10.14; 94,12–13; 100,8.
   d. A sentence pronoun is used as shorthand for ϣⲁⲩⲙⲟⲩⲧⲉ ⲉⲣⲟⲥ ϫⲉ in 106,22 (cf. V 11,18–20).

SJC–BG

1. Errors corrected by the scribe.
   a. Haplography, corrected by letters written above the line at the place of omission: 84,1; 89,14; 92,2; 102,15; 112,16; 127,8.
   b. Replacement of erased letters by letters written on top of them: 92,18; 116,18.
   c. Erasure of unnecessary letters: 93,13; 108,15; 109,12; 116,17.
   d. Marking out of unnecessary letters: 78,10.
2. Errors not corrected by the scribe
   a. Haplogrpahy: 84,3.12; 86,11; 89,17; 91,16; 93,10; 95,10; 98,6; 101,12.18; 102,9; 110,4.5.11; 111,3.7; 112,7.10.12.16; 113,16; 114,7; 116,5; 118,15; 119,2; 123,9; 125,8 (misplacement).
   b. Unnecessary letters: 91,1; 95,10; 102,18; 105,7; 108,16; 110,12; 112,12; 115,16; 120,16; 124,15.
   c. Incorrect letters: 84,12; 87,5; 90,16; 92,11–12; 95,1.6; 99,4; 102,11; 103,15–16; 104,11; 105,8; 107,13; 109,15; 110,10; 112,14.16; 113,1.4.7 (mistranslation of Greek); 115,17; 119,11; 120,15; 121,4; 125,9–10 (misplacement). Of the above, the following may be errors of hearing: 84,12; 87,5; 105,8.
   d. Corruptions: 87,5; 103,15–16; 105,8; 116,8–9.
3. Other peculiarities
   a. Strokes are used instead of diereses over the diphthong ⲁⲓ in 104,11; 115,11; 123,16 (for the use of the dieresis, see 97,9).
   b. ⲇⲉ appears three times in the phrase ⲉⲃⲟⲗ ⲇⲉ ⳩ⲛ, when ⲉⲃⲟⲗ is not in first position in the sentence, in 111,3–4; 112,10; 126,2. It may be that ⲇⲉ simply provides a mild emphasis in these instances.
   c. Plene writing occurs in 83,7–8 (ⲉⲙⲡⲉⲁⲣⲭⲏ and ⲉⲙⲡⲉⲉϩⲟ ⲩⲥⲓⲁ) and 122,15 (ϣⲟⲣⲉⲡ).
   d. ⳣ is used for ⲝ in 112,15.17.
   e. Asterisks and diples in the body of the text highlight certain questions and answers (see detailed description below under Transcriptions).

B. Dialectal Influences

Eug–V

Although the dialect is basically S, there are numerous signs of other dialects, as is the case in the rest of the codex (Böhlig–Labib: 11–14):

1. The regular use of the demonstrative ⲡⲏ, ⲧⲏ, ⲛⲏ with the relative, as in B and F.
2. The regular use of ⲉⲧⲁⳅ for the first perfect relative and the second perfect, as in BAF[A₂] (for second perfect: 12,6; 14, 18).
3. The frequent irregular (from the point of view of S) use of ⲛⲧⲉ in the genitive construction.

4. The occasional appearance of the pronominal form ⲛ̄ⲧⲉⳉ, as in A₂ (e.g. 3,8.15).
5. The consistent use of ⲉ as the qualitative of ⲉⲓⲣⲉ , as in A and F.
6. The use of ⲙⲁⲍ-, as in A, A₂, and B, for the prefix for ordinal numbers (13,9.12), although ⲙⲉⲍ- (S) occurs also (10,19).
7. The single appearance of ⲉⲗⲉ-, as in F, instead of ⲉⲣⲉ- (7,18).
8. The single appearance of the F form of the sign of the future (ⲛⲉⳉ) (17,16).
9. The BAF form of the second perfect used as a temporal, a practice frequent in B and F (6,21; 10,13; 11,22; 14,18).
10. The AA₂ form of the negative third future (16,4).
11. The AA₂ form of the negative consuetudinis (2,17), although the S form also occurs.
12. ⲣ̄ regularly precedes Greek verbs as in A and A₂ (but this occurs in early S MSS also—Crum: 84a).
13. The following non-standard (for S) orthography:
    a. ⲙ̄ⲙⲉ as in A and A₂ (4,25);
    b. ⲛⲁϭ as in A, A₂ and F (6,22.25; 9,10);
    c. ϭⲁⲙ as in A, A₂ and F (6,10; 7,29; 12,27);
    d. ⲭⲁⲉⲓⲥ as in A, A₂ and F (6,30).

I have not mentioned ⲡⲓ-, ϯ-, ⲛⲓ- in the above. This form of the article is identified by Till as most characteristic of B and F (1961: sec. 64), but Krause subsequently noted that at least the plural is quite characteristic of early upper-Egyptian dialects as well (Krause–Labib: 29). In Codex V these forms are found intermingled with ⲡ-, ⲧ-, ⲛ-, without discernible difference in emphasis to a modern reader. Nor is it possible to see that one form of the article is preferred to the other with certain words.

As mentioned, these characteristics are essentially the same as in the rest of Codex V. Böhlig–Labib accounts for them by positing a Middle Egyptian (presumably, F) translator who intended to render the original into S but occasionally reverted to his native dialect (12). Schenke disagrees, seeing a pre-classical S dialect with A₂ features and only occasional signs of F (1966: col. 24). For *Eug*–V, Schenke is correct regarding the small number of items that occur only in Middle Egyptian (7. and 8. above). But his characterization of the dialect as pre-classical S makes it hard to understand the variations that go beyond spelling differences, since even the pre-classical stages of a language would need to have the internal consistency necessary for satisfactory communication. It is perhaps better to think of those differences as having appeared in the course of transmission as scribes from different regions adjusted the text in an *ad hoc* fashion (see Böhlig–Wisse, for a similar explanation as applied to Codex III [11–12]).

Eug–III and SJC–III

The dialect employed is S with no significant indications of other influences. Occasionally one finds orthography more familiar in other dialects according to Crum (e.g. ⲁⲛⲏⲍⲉ [A A₂] for ⲉⲛⲉⲍ; ⲉⲙⲁⲍⲧⲉ [A₂] for ⲁⲙⲁⲍⲧⲉ and ⲙⲉⲟⲩⲉ [A] for ⲙⲉⲉⲩⲉ, all of which are found along with standard S spelling). But these are also found in S texts that have become available since Crum (see Kasser) and therefore are best accounted for as reflecting an earlier non-standardized state of S spelling rather than A or A₂ influences, as proposed by Till–Schenke (21) (Böhlig-Wisse has made an observation similar to the one adopted here on the orthography of III,2 [6–7]).

SJC–BG

The dialect is basically S with some features that are similar to other dialects, especially A₂. Those features are not sufficient to make one think that we are dealing with a mixed dialect. Till–Schenke agrees with this and thinks that the translator intended to translate into pure S, that some forms were in doubt, and that in those cases he would sometimes revert to his native (non-S) dialect (21). Although all the orthographic forms referred to by Till–Schenke (18–20) are also found in S texts, the other features are not (the irregular use of the preposition ⲛⲧⲉ-, and the doubling of the ⲛ before an initial vowel), and therefore support Till–Schenke's view. The fact of the widespread nature of these peculiarities in the tractate makes Till–Schenke's explanation preferable here to the one proposed above for *Eug*–V.

It should be noted here that the use of ⲡⲓ-, ϯ-, ⲛⲓ- is frequent in BG. This form of the article is preferred with words beginning with ⲁ. Mostly its use adds nothing discernible to the emphasis of the word to which it is attached beyond an ordinary article. When demonstrative force is desired, ⲉⲧⲙⲙⲁⲩ is normally added (105,7; 111,4; 119,12–13; 120,11–12; 121,5.8). In at least one instance, however, this form of the article (without ⲉⲧⲙⲙⲁⲩ) does have demonstrative force: 96,6.

C. Scribal Style

1. Script

In Codex V, the script is small and ligature occurs frequently where the line of one letter can naturally be extended to meet another, often without regard to word separation. The letters ⲙ, ⲩ and ⲱ regularly lean to the left, giving many lines the appearance of a bias in that direction. The scribe often ends a long vertical stroke (as with a ⲣ, ⲧ, ϥ and ϯ) with a slight curve to the left, showing a certain flair. The scribe also varies the width of his strokes (e.g., the middle horizontal stroke of the ⲉ is thinner than the rest of the letter). He enlarges the ⲝ when it comes at the beginning of a line. Often ⲩ, when it appears at the end of a line (and sometimes elsewhere too), will have a non-cursive form (like a printed "y").

Codex III has a larger script than Codex V. Ligature often occurs where lines can be naturally extended, but there is less here than in Codex V. The scribe's strokes are uniformly thin in width with little interest shown in decorative accents. Letter size tends to be uniform throughout. No letters regularly lean, which gives a sense of verticality to the whole. Altogether, the impression is of ascetic spareness.

In BG, the script is bold and square in character, with strokes that tend to be heavier than in Codex III, but that vary in width, as in Codex V. Ligature occurs often within words. Letter size tends to be uniform, although some-times letters become smaller toward the end of a line, as a result (apparently) of an attempt to stay within a margin (unmarked). It should be noted that an unusually large ψ begins 120,1, for no apparent reason. Final letters (in a line) are occasionally enlarged, perhaps in an effort to make the right margin straighter (see the discussion of diples below). The letters ч and γ (the non-cursive form is used throughout) often resemble each other, resulting in occasional difficulties in transcription (see note to 107,13). Sometimes the vertical stroke of ч, φ, and the like is extended into the line below.

2. *Superlinear Strokes*

The five uses of the superlinear stroke common to these tractates, and indeed throughout the library, are these: (1) It signals that two consonants are part of a single syllable and are united by a sub-vocalic sound; (2) It signals that an initial consonant is a sonant; (3) It is used to tie three consonants together in a sense unit (i.e., мнт); (4) It marks abbreviated Greek nouns (particularly *nomina sacra*); (5) It signals the omission of an н at the end of a line.

The scribe of Codex V is quite careful. In regard to the first use, he places the stroke over both consonants; for the second, he places it over only one; for the third and fourth he puts the stroke above all the letters, although typi-cally he begins at the end of the first letter. As noted earlier, the scribe also places a stroke over letters that have been omitted in the course of copying and that are placed either above the place of omission or in the margin. In addition, at 11,20 a stroke is placed over a numeral written in the margin as a gloss for a number in the text (similar to other such numerals later in the codex).

Wisse has discussed the use of superlinear strokes in Codex III (1975: 235). I would only add to his careful analysis that they are regularly omitted with final п, т and z in two-consonant combinations.

In BG, the scribe is inconsistent in his use of superlinear strokes. He gen-erally omits them over the initial н of the perfect relative/second perfect prefix (but see 97,9; 105,17; 113,11; 117,15; 126,1), as he does frequently with other initial н's or м's. Also they are omitted normally over the third person masculine singular pronoun when it is suffixed to a consonant (but see 100,10), and over the final two consonants of such words as ϣⲟⲣⲡ and ⲟⲩⲱⲛⲍ (but see 125,15). The strokes are made with a certain casualness. Often the stroke over an initial sonant begins late and is continued over a portion of the following letter. Also when one expects two strokes side by side, the scribe makes only one (e.g., 101,19). For the editorial policy on strokes, see below under Transcriptions.

3. *Articulation Marks*

In Codex V, the scribe places curved vertical hooks on ⲅ, ⲣ and ⲧ when they are in the final position in a sense unit; i.e., always when they come at the end of a word, but also with ⲉⲧ, ⲙⲛⲧ, ⲁⲧ, etc., apparently to make clear syllabic closure. Sometimes ⲕ has a hook on it also, but there is no consistency about its use and we have therefore ignored such hooks in this edition.

In Codex III the scribe uses dots or short curved lines unattached to the letters in place of vertical hooks. These have been considered by Wisse (1975: 234).

BG has no such marks, except for the one in 88,11.

4. *Page Numerals*

Becasue of the method of presentation of the texts here, it has not been possible to show visually how the page numerals are related to the body of the text. A description is therefore provided here.

In Codex V, the few numerals that remain are found above the text just within the outer text margin. The numerals are placed between two horizontal strokes.

In Codex III, the page numerals appear in the center of the upper margin. No strokes accompany the numerals.

In BG, the page numerals are also written in the center of the upper margin. The numeral on p. 94 has, in place of the normal delta (after the fai), a figure resembling an alpha, although it is different in form from alphas found elsewhere in the text. The numerals have one horizontal stroke above them.

5. *Asterisks, External and Internal Diples and Paragraph Markers*

Asterisks are found only in BG. They occur in the left margin on the following pages: 86, between lines 6 and 7; 86,9; 87, between lines 8 and 9; 87,12; 106,11.14; 107,17. These serve to identify questions asked by Philip and Thomas (see textual note for 107,13) as well as the responses. On 86 and 87, the initial asterisks are accompanied by very large diples placed in the body of the text where the introduction to the question begins. In each case the scribe has lengthened the lower line of the diple so it ends on the next line between the end of the introduction (ⲭⲉ) and the first word of the question proper.

A similar diple is found in the body of the text at 82,19, this time introducing a question by Matthew. The marginal indicator in that case, however, is not an asterisk but a *paragraphus cum corone*. Another diple marks the introduction to the response to Matthew (83,4).

Asterisks are also used at the beginning and end of each of the lines at 127,11–12, in order to highlight the title.

No paragraph markers occur in the extant text of *Eug*–V. In *Eug*–III, a *paragraphus cum corone* appears in the left margin on p. 76, between lines 12 and 13, and two are found at the conclusion of the tractate, setting off the subscript title. In *SJC*–III, a *paragraphus cum corone* is found in the left margin between 96,14 and 15. In the first instance a major shift is indicated ("another knowledge principle"). In the second, a question by Thomas is signaled. In BG a *paragraphus* in the right margin is used to mark the introduction to the first general statement of the disciples' concerns by Philip at 79,18. A *paragraphus cum corone* occurs also in the left margin on p. 126 between lines 16 and 17, marking the beginning of the conclusion of the tractate.

External diples, used as line fillers in Codex III and BG (but not Codex V, except as concluding decorations), have been removed from the texts involved but have not been listed in footnotes. It is appropriate to list here the lines where they are found in the MSS.

In the two tractates in Codex III diples occur at the end of the following lines: 72,7; 73,4; 81,14.18; 82,6.22; 83,23; 85,14.23; 86,21(2); 87,15; 88,16; 91,11.23; 93,6.19; 94,8; 97,6; 98,21; 100,5; 102,16; 104,1; 106,1; 114,24; 117,10; 118,25. In *SJC*–BG diples are found at both the beginnings and ends of lines. They are at the beginning in the following lines: 80,5.6; 87,13; 108,6–10.16.17; 117,7.8; 123,14–17; 124,17; 127,3–7. They are at the ends of the following lines: 83,1–4; 89,1; 106,5.17.19; 107,1.2; 108,5.6.13(2); 109,8; 110,3.7(2); 111,11; 112,7(2).12; 115,15–17; 116,6(2).15.16; 117,9.15; 119,6.13; 120,10.13; 121,1–6; 122,5; 123,12; 124,11; 125,14; 126,8.12.15; 127,10.

In BG 108,13, the tip of the second diple is extended and curved back (as with the final ⲉ in 127,3), giving Till–Schenke the impression of a third diple, which would be anomalous. Diples are also placed in the body of the BG text at a number of points, all of which are noted in the footnotes. In 116,8, one precedes the final two letters, perhaps as an indicator of an anacoluthon.

XIV. TRANSCRIPTIONS

The transcriptions of the three Nag Hammadi tractates presented here were made on the basis of careful examination of original MSS at the Coptic Museum in Cairo and a number of sets of photographs of those MSS in the possession of the Institute for Antiquity and Christianity, by the editor and other members of the Claremont team (see the preface). They have been compared with a preliminary draft of parallels prepared some years ago by Martin Krause. *Eug*–III was also compared with the version published by Trakatellis (see II above). The *SJC*–BG transcription was made on the basis of the editio princeps (Till–Schenke) with the aid of photographs of the original MS.

Because of the similarities of the texts and the Coptic, as well as the relatively intact character of the MSS, occasional restorations and corrections of *Eug*–III, *SJC*–III and *SJC*–BG were done mostly without great difficulty. The same was not true, however, with *Eug*–V, where extensive lacunae made numerous restorations desirable. As noted above, the text is considerably expanded in comparison with the parallel texts, and the Coptic translator was from a different translation tradition. These factors made the use of the parallels problematic in the restorations. I want to acknowledge again the aid I received, particularly in regard to *Eug*–V, from Bentley Layton and Stephen Emmel.

As to the citations in the footnotes, since Krause's parallel version is only in draft form, it is not cited. However, Krause's translation of *Eug*–III, *SJC*–III and various portions of *Eug*–V and *SJC*–BG (1974) has often made it possible to extrapolate the Coptic text that lies behind it and refer to it in relation to the transcriptions.

The following, then, are the citation policies in this edition regarding restorations and emendations in each of the tractates.

Eug–V. Only Emmel is cited. Those citations occur where he lists photographic evidence for particular readings.

Eug–III. Divergences from Krause and Trakatellis are noted. They are also cited in support of this edition in case of disagreements. Till–Schenke is always cited where it takes a clear position. Silence in regard to Till–Schenke should be taken to mean lack of evidence, since only parts of *Eug*–III are published in that edition.

SJC–III. Divergences from Krause are noted (where they can be determined). Support for this edition is also cited, except for pp. 117–19, where there are numerous restorations and Krause has a continuous text; then, only divergences are noted. Till–Schenke is cited when it is clear; the text of *Eug*–III was dealt with in Till–Schenke only as it related to the editing of *SJC*–BG and therefore there are places where *Eug*–III is not printed. Silence in this edition regarding Till–Schenke means no evidence.

SJC–BG. Till–Schenke emendations are followed except where noted, and in those cases the Till–Schenke emendations are specified. Minor divergences, such as the dotting of a letter or the position of brackets, are not noted.

In regard to superlinear strokes, the following policies have been adopted for purposes of standardization. When a stroke spans two consonants in the MS, it is here only shown over the second, with two exceptions: where an initial м or н is a sonant and has a stroke that continues over an immediately following consonant (common in BG), the stroke is placed over the first letter only. The same policy is followed in regard to the conjunctive conjugation.

When a stroke spans three consonants in the MS, it is here placed over the middle letter only. Exceptions are made in the case of proper nouns and where the stroke is the sign of an abbreviation.

XV. TRANSLATION POLICIES

Since this is a parallel edition of four tractates, it has been necessary for the translations to be fairly literal to make comparison between the texts as easy as possible.

The following translation policies have been adopted here:

1) Abstract and predicate nouns that were (presumably) anarthrous in Greek (see BDF: sec. 252, 258) seem often to have been translated with an indefinite article in Coptic (Stern: sec. 232). In rendering these Coptic words in English, I have routinely omitted the article in the case of abstract nouns (but note III 77,11) and supplied a definite article in the case of the predicate nouns. Examples: V 4,11 (cf. parr.); 7,4; 7,6–9, parr.; III 101,18, par.

2) I have translated demonstrative plurals as singulars if they appear to reflect Greek demonstrative neuter plurals, which are routinely understood as singular.

3) There is some difficulty in distinguishing among names, titles, roles and attributes for the various divine beings. I have tended where possible to take terms as names, since knowledge of them seems to have been important among the Gnostics (see V 4,14–16).

4) Ethical datives have by and large not been translated since they are generally archaic in English. Examples: V 6,22; 6,26; III 88,12 (but see 88,21!).

5) Occasionally the adverb ⲛ̄ϣⲟⲣⲡ, which is usually translated "at first," or the like, is here translated "very soon," because "at first" does not seem appropriate in the context and something akin to the lexical rendering "early" does. Examples: V 6,16; 12,25; III 111,14.

6) The translation of ⲁⲣⲭⲏ has been difficult at times because of the problem of knowing whether it means "beginning" or "principle." I have sometimes opted for giving both possibilities in the text.

7) In regard to the notes, I have attempted to give the significant alternative renderings. In some cases I have noted incorrect readings that may have attained some currency. For ease of comparison, I have translated quotations from the German and modern Greek versions into English.

8) The Greek of Greek loan words is omitted in this edition. These can be readily identified in the Coptic text by anyone with facility in Greek. Highlighting them in the translation is not only esthetically jarring but potentially misleading, since it suggests that the words have not been integrated into Coptic, which might be true in some cases, but certainly not in all. A Greek Loan Word index is provided at the end of the volume.

XVI. FOOTNOTES AND ENDNOTES

The footnotes and endnotes have been kept as brief as possible. Attention has been focused on issues connected with editing and translating. Matters of interpretation have been dealt with only in passing, in view of an anticipated commentary. Special abbreviations for earlier editions have been adopted for the notes and are identified in the list of abbreviations. A separate set of notes is provided for each text, with transcription and translation notes combined. The endnotes deal with matters involving two or more texts, and the need to refer to them is signaled by a footnote in each instance.

XVII. LITERARY FORMS

Although *Eug* is in letter form, it quickly becomes apparent that it is basically a religio-philosophical controversy discourse, which has a form of its own. This form begins with a description of the position that is opposed. There is then a refuation of that position (often very brief). Finally the alternative proposed by the writer is presented, which is often the bulk of the piece. It can be found elsewhere as a separate form (e.g., *Orig. World* [II,5]), and in combination with the letter form (e.g., *The Letter of Ptolemy to Flora* [Epiphan., *Pan.* 33.3,1–7,10], first noted by Doresse [1948: 154–55]).

SJC is the account of a revelation discourse of a heavenly being (Christ) who appears in a special place, in response to the perplexities of his followers. There are twelve disciples, of whom only Philip, Thomas, Matthew and Bartholomew are named, and seven women, of whom only Mary (presumably Magdalene) is named. The discourse is punctuated by the questions of the followers. *SJC* concludes with a commission to the followers by Christ, who then disappears. The disciples then set forth to carry out the commission. The form of *SJC*, while unique among the Nag Hammadi writings, has close resemblances to *Ap. John.* (For further discussion of the form of Gnostic revelatory tractates, see Fallon, and Perkins, 1980: 25–58.)

GUIDE TO THE PARALLELS
of *Eug* and *SJC*
(Minor similarities and differences are not reflected)

Eug–III alone is referred to for "*Eug* Only" and "Common Material," except for those places found only in *Eug*–V. *SJC*–III is referred to for "*SJC* Only," except for those places found only in *SJC*–BG.

Sections opposite each other in the outside columns are so placed not because they are parallel in language (although they may be) but because they occupy the same relative space in the tractates.

Names of deities and other "realities" are italicized only at their first appearance.

Eug Only	*Common Material*	*SJC* Only
1. Address of letter (III 70,1–3).		1. Male disciples and women go to mountain in perplexity and meet resurrected savior; *Philip* states the general query. (III 90,14–92,7).
	2. Disputed views of philosophers about God and the cosmos (III 70,3–22).	
		3. Self-disclosure by savior (III 93,8–12).
	4. Refutation of philosophers (III 70,22–71,5).	
5. Invitation to another approach (III 71,5–13)		5. True knowledge to be given to elite (III 93,16–24).
		Matthew's request: "Teach us the truth" (III 93,24–94,4).
	6. Description of *Him Who Is, The Unbegotten One*, primarily in negative terms (III 71,13–73,3).	
		7. *Philip* asks how he (Unbegotten) appeared to the perfect ones (III 95,19–22).
	8. He embraces all and is characterized by certain mental qualities (III 73,3–13).	
	Their whole race is with Unbegotten (omitted by *Eug*–V) (III 73,14–16).	

9. *Thomas* asks why these came to be (III 96,14–21).

Response: "Because of his mercy and love" (III 96,21–97,16).

10. They have not yet become visible (omitted by *Eug*–V). The difference between what comes from perishableness and imperishableness. Ignorance of this brings death (III 73,16–74,7).

11. Transition to new topic (III 74,7–14)

11. *Mary* asks how "we" will know that (III 98,9–12).

12. The way to true knowledge: go from visible to invisible with the aid of Thought (III 74,14–19).

13. This is a knowledge principle (III 74,19–20)

14. Distinction between Forefather and Father. *Self-begotten Father* appears (III 74,20–75,12).

Revealing of the *Generation over Whom There is No Kingdom*. Rejoicing over Unbegotten Father (III 75,12–76,10).

15. Transition to another knowledge principle (III 76,10–14).

15. *Matthew* asks how Man was revealed (III 100,16–21)

16. Revealing of *Immortal Man* (III 76,14–77,2).

17. About the female part of Immortal Man (III 77,2–77,9).

17. Role of Immortal Man in salvation; his consort (III 101,9–19).

18. First appearance of names; creation of aeon for Immortal Man and the granting of authority (III 77,9–78,5).

Immortal Man's mental qualities (III 78,5–9).

The hierarchical differences among these qualities (III 78,9–17).

19. Elaboration of differences. The relationship of numbers shows the relationship among these qualities (III 78,17–V 8,6).

20. The coming to appearance of other things from these qualities (V 8,6–18).

21. Rejoicing in Immortal Man's kingdom (V 8,18–30).

21. *Bartholomew* asks whether the Son is related to Man or Son of Man (III 103,22–104,6).

22. Revealing of *First-begotten (Begetter) Son of Man* and his *Sophia* (V 8,31–III 81,3).

Identified as *Christ*

23. The multitude of angels are lights (III 81,3–10).

23. *Disciples* request more details about Man (III 105,3–11).

24. Son is called *Adam.* Rejoicing in the kingdom of Son of Man (III 81,10–21).

Additional material

25. The savior is the revealer (III 106,5–9).

Disciples ask how those who truly exist came to the world (III 106,9–15).

26. Revealing of *Savior, Begetter of All Things,* and his *Sophia* (III 81,21–82,6).

27. Revealing of the six spiritual powers by Savior (who then are identified as twelve by counting the consorts), and those that came from them. Antetypes of our aeon are provided by these and earlier revelations (III 82,7–84,11).

27. Saving work of the savior (III 106,24–108,16).

Thomas asks how many are the aeons that surpass the heavens (III 108,16–23).

28. Creation by All ("Self"—BG) Begetter of twelve aeons for the twelve angels (III 84,12–17).

29. Creation of heavens and firmaments in these aeons (III 84,17–85,6).

30. Summary statement; defect of femaleness appears (III 85,6–9).

31. *Thomas* asks how many are the aeons of the immortals (BG 107,13–108,1).

32. Description of aeons: (*Eug*–V has four aeons; *Eug*–III and *SJC* have three. The order differs between *Eug* and *SJC* [III 85,9–21]).

Description of the revealing
of the *Eighth* ("*Seventh*"
SJC) by Immortal Man, with
aeons, powers and kingdoms;
the naming of aeons (III
85,21–86,16).

Designation of the third aeon
as "*Assembly*" (III
86,16–87,9).

Assembly and his consort
begin the engendering that
leads to the revealing of all
the immortals (III 87,9–88,3)

Authority of immortals
comes from Immortal Man
and Sophia. Immortals use it
to provide themselves with
domains and retinue (III
88,3–89,6).

33. (Inserted at III 88,21)
The Apostles ask about those
in the aeons (III
112,19–113,2).

From this area come the types
of subsequent aeons and
worlds (III 89,6–15).

General rejoicing by all
natures (III 89,15–90,3).

34. Conclusion: Words of
Eugnostos are to be accepted
(preserved) until one who
need not be taught comes (III
90,4–11).

34. Reason for the revelation
(III 114,5–8).

35. *Mary* asks where the disciples came from, where they
are going and what they
should do in the world (III
114,8–12).

The coming into the lower
regions of the drop from the
Light (III 114,12–BG
119,16).

Development of psychic man
(BG 119,17—121,13).

Coming of the savior and his
work (BG 121,13–III 118,3).

Commissioning of disciples
(III 118,3–119,8).

Disappearance of the savior
and beginning of disciples'
mission (III 119,8–17).

THE PARALLEL TEXTS

Please note: A new page of Coptic text always begins at the left margin of a line marked by a Coptic page number. It is not otherwise indicated.

NHC III 90,14–91,9   BG 77,8–78,10

NHC III 90,14–91,9	BG 77,8–78,10
[ϥ] ⲧⲥⲟⲫⲓⲁ ⲛ̅ⲓ̅ⲏ̅ⲥ̅ ⲡⲉⲭ̅ⲣ̅ⲥ̅ ⲙⲛ̅ ¹⁵ⲥⲁ	ⲧⲥⲟⲫⲓⲁ ⲛ̅ⲓ̅ⲥ̅ ⲡⲉⲭ̅ⲥ̅ | ⲙⲛ̅ⲛ̅ⲥⲁ ⲟ̅ⲍ̅
ⲧⲣⲉϥⲧⲱⲟⲩⲛ ⲉⲃⲟⲗ ⲍ̅ⲛ̅	ⲛ̅ⲧⲣⲉϥⲧⲱⲟⲩ̅ ¹⁰ ⲉⲃⲟⲗ ⲍ̅ⲛ̅
ⲛⲉ|ⲧⲙⲟⲟⲩⲧ̇	ⲛⲉⲧⲙⲟⲟⲩⲧ | ⲛ̅ⲧⲉⲣⲟⲩⲉⲓ ⲛ̅ϭⲓ
ⲛⲉⲣⲉⲡⲉϥⲙⲛ̅ⲧ̅ⲥ̅ⲛⲟ|ⲟⲩⲥ	ⲡⲉϥ|ⲙ̅ⲛ̅ⲧⲥⲛⲟⲟⲩⲥ
ⲙ̅ⲙⲁⲑⲏⲧⲏⲥ ⲙⲛ̅ ⲥⲁϣϥⲉ | ⲛ̅ⲥ̅ⲍⲓⲙⲉ	ⲙ̅ⲙⲁⲑⲏ|ⲧⲏⲥ ⲙⲛ̅ ⲥⲁϣϥⲉ ⲛ̅ⲥ̅ⲍ̅|ⲙⲉ
ⲙⲁⲑⲏⲧⲉⲩⲉ ⲛⲁϥ ⲉ|ⲁⲩⲉⲓ	ⲉⲧⲉ ⲛⲉⲩⲙⲁⲑⲏ¹⁵ⲧⲉⲩⲉ ⲛⲁϥ ⲉⲍ̅ⲣⲁ̈ⲓ
ⲉⲧⲅⲁⲗⲓⲗⲁⲓⲁ ⲉⲝⲙ̅ ⲡⲧⲟⲟⲩ	ⲉⲧⲅⲁ|ⲗⲓⲗⲁⲓⲁ ⲍ̅ⲙ ⲡⲧⲟⲟⲩ ⲉⲧⲉ
ϥⲁ ⲉϣⲁⲩⲙⲟⲩⲧⲉ ⲉⲣⲟϥ ϫⲉ ⲙⲁⲛⲧⲏ |	ϣⲁⲩⲙⲟⲩⲧⲉ ⲉⲣⲟϥ ϫⲉ ⲙⲁ̅|ⲧⲏ ⲍⲓ ⲟ̅ⲏ̅
ⲍⲓ ⲣⲁϣⲉ ⲛ̅ⲧⲉⲣⲟⲩⲥⲱⲟⲩⲍ	ⲣⲁϣⲉ ⲉⲩⲁⲡⲟⲣⲓ ⲟ̅ⲩ̅ | ⲉⲧⲃⲉ
ⲍⲓⲟⲩ|ⲥⲟⲡ̅ ⲉⲩⲁⲡⲟⲣⲓ ⲉⲧⲃⲉ	ⲑⲩⲡⲟⲥⲧⲁⲥⲓⲥ ⲙ̅|ⲡⲧⲏⲣϥ ⲙⲛ̅
ⲧⲍⲩⲡⲟⲥⲧⲁ|ⲥⲓⲥ ⲙ̅ⲡⲧⲏⲣϥ· ⲙⲛ̅	ⲧⲟⲓⲕⲟⲛⲟⲙⲓ ⁵ⲁ ⲙⲛ̅ ⲧⲉⲡⲣⲟⲛⲟⲓⲁ
ⲧⲟⲓⲕⲟⲛⲟⲙⲓⲁ ⁵ ⲙⲛ̅ ⲧⲉⲡⲣⲟⲛⲟⲓⲁ	ⲉⲧⲟⲩ|ⲁⲁⲃ ⲙⲛ̅ ⲧⲁⲣⲉⲧⲏ
ⲉⲧⲟⲩⲁⲁⲃ· ⲙⲛ̅ | ⲧⲁⲣⲉⲧⲏ	ⲛ̅ⲛⲉ|ⲍⲟⲩⲥⲓⲁ ⲉⲧⲃⲉ ⲍⲱⲃ ⲛⲓⲙ |
ⲛ̅ⲛⲉⲍⲟⲩⲥⲓⲁ ⲁⲩⲱ ⲉⲧⲃⲉ | ⲍⲱⲃ ⲛⲓⲙ	ⲉⲧⲉⲣⲉⲡⲥⲱⲧⲏⲣ ⲉⲓⲣⲉ ⲙ̅|ⲙⲁⲩ
ⲉⲧⲉⲣⲉⲡⲥⲱⲧⲏⲣ ⲉⲓⲣⲉ | ⲙ̅ⲙⲟⲟⲩ	ⲛ̅ⲙⲙⲁⲩ ⲙ̅ⲙⲩⲥⲧⲏⲣⲓ ¹⁰ⲟⲛ
ⲛ̅ⲙⲙⲁⲩ ⲍ̅ⲙ ⲡⲙⲩⲥⲧⲏ|ⲣⲓⲟⲛ	

[90] The Sophia of Jesus Christ. After ¹⁵ he rose from the | dead, his twelve | disciples and seven | women continued to be his followers and | went to Galilee onto the mountain 91 called "Divination | and Joy." When they gathered together | and were perplexed about the underlying reality | of the universe and the plan and ⁵ the holy providence and | the power of the authorities and about | everything that the Savior is doing | with them in the secret | of the holy	The Sophia of Jesus Christ. | After 77 he rose ¹⁰ from the dead, | when his | twelve disciples | and seven women | who continued to be his followers ¹⁵ went up to Galilee | onto the mountain called "Divination | and Joy" and 78 were accordingly perplexed | about the underlying reality | of the universe and the plan ⁵ and the holy providence | and the power of the authorities, | about everything | that the Savior is doing with them, the secrets ¹⁰ of

---

SJC-III:

91,1 Preceding this line, MS has a short line of decoration with a *paragraphus cum corone* just below in the left margin.

91,1–2 See endnote 1.

91,2 Corr.: second ⲉ for erased ⲟ.

SJC-BG:

78,1–2 See endnote 1.

78,10 Corr.: ⲙ is marked out after ⲟⲛ.

NHC V

NHC III

NHC III 91,9–24

ⲚⲦⲞⲒⲔⲞⲚⲞⲘⲒⲀ ⲈⲦⲞⲨⲀⲀⲂ· ¹⁰
ⲀⲩⲞⲨⲰⲚⲌ Ⲛ̄ⲦⲒ ⲠⲤⲰⲦⲎⲢ Ⲍ̄Ⲛ̄
ⲦⲈⲩ|ϢⲞⲢⲠ̄ `ⲈⲚ´ Ⲙ̄ⲘⲞⲢⲪⲎ ⲀⲖⲖⲀ
Ⲍ̄Ⲙ̄ ⲠⲈ|ⲠⲚⲀ̄ Ⲛ̄ⲀⲌⲞⲢⲀⲦⲞⲚ·
ⲠⲈⲩⲈⲒⲚⲈ ⲆⲈ | Ⲛ̄ⲐⲈ Ⲛ̄ⲞⲨⲚⲞϬ
Ⲛ̄ⲀⲅⲅⲈⲖⲞⲤ Ⲛ̄ⲦⲈ ⲠⲞⲨ|ⲞⲈⲒⲚ
ⲠⲈⲩⲤⲘⲞⲦ̄ ⲆⲈ Ⲛ̄ⲚⲀϢ ϢⲀ ¹⁵ⲬⲈ
ⲈⲢⲞⲩ Ⲛ̄ⲚⲈϢ ⲤⲀⲢⲜ ⲚⲒⲘ
ⲈϢⲀ<Ⲥ>|ⲘⲞⲨ ϢⲞⲠ̄ⲩ ⲈⲢⲞⲤ ⲀⲖⲖⲀ
ⲞⲨⲤⲀⲢⲜ | Ⲛ̄ⲔⲀⲐⲀⲢⲞⲚ Ⲛ̄ⲦⲈⲖⲈⲒⲞⲚ
Ⲛ̄ⲐⲈ | Ⲛ̄ⲦⲀⲩⲦⲤⲀⲂⲞⲚ ⲈⲢⲞⲩ ⲌⲒⲬⲘ̄
ⲠⲦⲞ|ⲞⲨ ⲈϢⲀⲩⲘⲞⲨⲦⲈ ⲈⲢⲞⲩ ⲬⲈ ²⁰
ⲠⲀ Ⲛ̄ⲬⲞⲈⲒⲦ̄ Ⲍ̄Ⲛ̄ ⲦⲄⲀⲖⲒⲖⲀⲒⲀ· ⲀⲨⲰ
| ⲠⲈⲬⲀⲩ ⲬⲈ ⳨ⲢⲎⲚⲎ ⲚⲎⲦⲚ̄ ⳨|ⲢⲎⲚⲎ
ⲈⲦⲈ ⲦⲰⲈⲒ ⲦⲈ ⳨⳨ Ⲙ̄ⲘⲞⲤ | ⲚⲎⲦⲚ̄
ⲀⲨⲢ̄ ϢⲠⲎⲢⲈ ⲦⲎⲢⲞⲨ· | ⲀⲨⲰ ⲀⲨⲢ̄
ⲌⲞⲦⲈ· ⲠⲤⲰⲦⲎⲢ Ⲁⲩ

BG 78,10–79,14

ⲚⲦⲞⲒⲔⲞⲚⲞⲘⲒⲀ Ⲉ|ⲦⲞⲨⲀⲀⲂ ⲀⲨⲰ
ⲀⲩⲞⲨⲰⲚⲌ | ⲈⲢⲞⲞⲨ Ⲛ̄ⲦⲒ ⲠⲤⲰⲦⲎⲢ
Ⲍ̄Ⲛ̄ | ⲦⲈⲩϢⲞⲢⲠ Ⲙ̄ⲘⲞⲢⲪⲎ Ⲁ̄ | ⲀⲖⲖⲀ
ⲌⲢⲀⲒ̈ Ⲍ̄Ⲙ̄ ⲠⲒⲀⲌⲞⲢⲀⲦⲞ̄ ¹⁵ Ⲙ̄ⲠⲚⲀ̄
ⲠⲈⲩⲈⲒⲚⲈ ⲆⲈ ⲚⲈ|ⲠⲈⲒⲚⲈ ⲠⲈ
Ⲛ̄ⲚⲞⲨⲚⲞϬ Ⲛ̄|ⲀⲄⲄⲈⲖⲞⲤ ⲚⲦⲈ
ⲠⲞⲨⲞⲈⲒⲚ
ⲠⲈⲩⲤⲘⲞⲦ ⲆⲈ ⲚⲀϢ | ϢⲀⲬⲈ ⲈⲢⲞⲩ   ⲟ̄ⲑ̄
ⲘⲚ̄ ⲞⲨⲤⲀⲢⲜ | ⲈϢⲀⲤⲘⲞⲨ ⲚⲀϢ
ⲦⲰⲞⲨⲚ | ⲌⲀⲢⲞⲩ ⲀⲖⲖⲀ ⲞⲨⲤⲀⲢⲜ
Ⲛ̄ⲔⲀ⁵ⲐⲀⲢⲞⲚ Ⲛ̄ⲦⲈⲖⲒⲞⲤ Ⲛ̄ⲦⲈⲩ|ⲌⲈ
ⲚⲦⲀⲩⲦⲤⲀⲂⲞⲚ ⲈⲢⲞⲩ | ⲌⲒ̈ ⲠⲦⲞⲞⲨ
ⲈⲦⲈϢⲀⲨⲘⲞⲨ|ⲦⲈ ⲈⲢⲞⲩ ⲬⲈ ⲠⲀ
Ⲛ{Ⲧ}ⲬⲞⲈⲒⲦ | ⲠⲈ Ⲍ̄Ⲛ̄ ⲦⲄⲀⲖⲒⲖⲀⲒⲀ
ⲠⲈⲬⲀⲩ ¹⁰ ⲬⲈ ⳨ⲢⲎⲚⲎ ⲚⲎⲦⲚ̄ ⳨ⲢⲎ|ⲚⲎ
ⲈⲦⲈ ⲦⲰⲒ̈ ⲦⲈ ⳨⳨ Ⲙ̄ⲘⲞ`Ⲥ´ | ⲚⲎⲦⲚ̄
ⲀⲨⲰ ⲀⲨⲢ̄ ϢⲠⲎⲢⲈ | ⲦⲎⲢⲞⲨ ⲀⲨⲢ̄
ⲌⲞⲦⲈ ⲀⲠⲤⲰ|ⲦⲎⲢ

79

plan, ¹⁰ the Savior appeared, not in his | previous form, but in the | invisible spirit. And his likeness | resembles a great angel of light. | But his resemblance I must not | describe. ¹⁵ No mortal flesh | could endure it, but only | pure (and) perfect flesh like | that which he taught us about on the mountain | called ²⁰ "Of Olives" in Galilee. And | he said: "Peace be to you (pl.)! My peace | I give | to you!" And they all marveled | and were afraid. The Savior

the holy plan, | then the Savior appeared | to them, not in | his previous form | but in the invisible ¹⁵ spirit. And his likeness was | the likeness of a great | angel of light. But his resemblance I must not | describe. No mortal flesh | could endure | it, but only pure ⁵ (and) perfect flesh like his, | which he taught us about | on the mountain called | "Of Olives" | in Galilee. He said: ¹⁰ "Peace be to you (pl.)! My peace | I give | to you!" And they all marveled | and were afraid. The Savior |

SJC-III:

91,15 MS has ⲩ (incorrect gender—noted by T–S).

NHC V 1,1–3   NHC III 70,1–3

[ⲁ̄]   [ⲉⲩⲅⲛⲱⲥⲧⲟⲥ ⲛ̄]ⲛⲓⲱ[ⲏⲣⲉ . . .]ⲁ | ⲉⲩⲅⲛⲱⲥⲧⲟⲥ ⲡⲙⲁⲕⲁⲣⲓⲟⲥ   ⲟ
      [8±] ⲙⲛ̄ ⲛ̄ⲱ[. .] ⲛ̄ⲧⲉ | [7±] . [˙]   ⲛ̄ⲛⲉ|ⲧⲉ ⲛⲟⲩϥ ⲛⲉ ⲭⲉ ⲣⲁⲱⲉ ⲍⲛ̄
      ⲭⲁⲓⲣⲉ [˙]   ⲛⲉ|ⲉⲓ˙

[1]   [Eugnostos, to] the [sons . . .] | Eugnostos, the Blessed, to those | **70**
      [. . .] and the [. . .] | [. . .]   who are his. Rejoice in this, |
      Greetings!

---

*Eug-*V:

1,1 Stroke over ⲛ is partially visible in MS.
    "Sons": Here and elsewhere ⲱⲏⲣⲉ could also be translated "children" ("child,"
    when ⲱⲏⲣⲉ is in the sing.).

1,1–2 If the word ⲁⲅⲉⲛⲛⲏⲧⲟⲥ appeared elsewhere in the tractate or indeed the
    codex, it would be tempting to restore ⲛⲓⲱ[ⲏⲣⲉ ⲙ̄ⲡⲓ]ⲁ|[ⲅⲉⲛⲛⲏⲧⲟⲥ], "the sons
    [of]|[Unbegotten]," on the basis of 5,7–8.

*Eug-*III:

70,2 Corr.: second ⲛⲉ for partly erased ⲛⲟⲩϥ (dittography?).
    "This": lit. "these," the Coptic of which is probably a too literal rendering of a
    Greek neuter pl. demonstrative, which is often used to refer to a singular thing
    (Smyth: sec. 1003) (so rendered by K & Tr); see also BG 120,14.

70,2–3 Bellet proposes that ⲍⲛ̄ ⲛⲉⲉⲓ (incorrectly transcribed as ⲍⲛⲛⲁⲓ by him)
    equals ⲍⲛⲁⲓ and should be translated, "*It is pleasing to me* that you know. . . ."
    ⲣⲁⲱⲉ might then be taken as rendering the Greek χαίρε, "Greetings." Thus the
    initial statement would be essentially the same as the parr. (without χαίρε in *SJC*)
    (57). Attractive as that is, it is probably an impossible reading of the text as it
    stands, since ⲍⲛⲁ⸗ does not appear to be found elsewhere with the ⲛ geminated, or
    with a stroke over the ⲛ. Also the scribe has placed a stop betwen ⲍⲛ̄ ⲛⲉⲉⲓ and

NHC III 92,1–7 BG 79,14–80,4

ϥ⳿ⲃ̣ ⲥⲱⲃⲉ ⲡⲉⲭⲁϥ ⲛⲁⲩ ⲭⲉ ⲉⲧⲃⲉ ⲟⲩ |
ⲧⲉⲧⲛ̄ⲙⲉⲟⲩⲉ ⲧⲉⲧⲛ̄ⲁⲡⲟⲣⲉⲓ ⸳ |
ⲉⲧⲉⲧⲛ̄ϣⲓⲛⲉ ⲛ̄ⲥⲁ ⲟⲩ ⲡⲉⲭⲉ |
ⲫⲓⲗⲓⲡ̇ⲡⲟⲥ ⲭⲉ ⲉⲧⲃⲉ
ⲉⲩⲡⲟ⁵ⲥⲧⲁⲥⲓⲥ ⲙ̄ⲡⲧⲏⲣϥ̄⳿ ⲙⲛ̄
ⲧⲟⲓⲕⲟ|ⲛⲟⲙⲓⲁ ⸳ ⲡⲥⲱⲧⲏⲣ ⲡⲉⲭⲁϥ
ⲛⲁⲩ | ⲭⲉ

ⲥⲱⲃⲉ ⲡⲉⲭⲁϥ ⲛⲁⲩ ¹⁵ ⲭⲉ ⲉⲧⲃⲉ ⲟⲩ
ⲧⲉⲧⲙ̄ⲙⲉ|ⲉⲩⲉ ⲛ̄ ⲉⲧⲃⲉ ⲟⲩ
ⲧⲉⲧⲛ̄|ⲁⲡⲟⲣⲓ ⲛ̄ ⲉⲧⲉⲧⲛ̄ϣⲓⲛⲉ |
ⲛ̄ⲥⲁ ⲟⲩ ⲡⲉⲭⲁϥ ⲛ̄ϭⲓ ⲫⲓⲗⲓⲡ|ⲡⲟⲥ
ⲉⲧⲃⲉ ⲉⲩⲡⲟⲥⲧⲁⲥⲓⲥ | ⲙ̄ⲡⲧⲏⲣϥ ⲙⲛ̄   ⲡ̄
ⲧⲟⲓⲕⲟ|ⲛⲟⲙⲓⲁ ⲙⲡⲥⲱⲧⲏⲣ | ⲡⲉⲭⲁϥ
ⲭⲉ

92 laughed and said to them: "What |
are you thinking about? (Why) are
you perplexed? | What are you
searching for?" | Philip said: "For
the underlying reality ⁵ of the
universe and the plan." | The Savior
said to them:

laughed and said to them: ¹⁵ "What
are you thinking about? | What are
you | perplexed about? What are
you searching | for?" Philip said:
"For the underlying reality | of the   **80**
universe and the plan | of the
Savior." | He said:

SJC-III:

92,1 There is a drop of ink above π in a position that suggests it was not intentionally
placed there. Other random drops are found in the MS, e.g., 92,10 and 14;
94,12–13 (rt. margin).

SJC-BG:

79,19 MS has a *paragraphus* in the right margin next to ⲡⲟⲥ.

(*Eug*-III continued)

ⲉⲧⲣⲉⲧⲛ̄ⲉⲓⲙⲉ , indicating that he probably understood the passage as it is rendered
in my translation. Contrary to Bellet's assertion, the Coptic as it stands makes
sense grammatically. The infinitive here (ⲉⲧⲣⲉⲧⲛ̄ⲉⲓⲙⲉ) is not causative and
dependent, but rather purely nominal, in apposition to ⲛⲉⲉⲓ. It is possible, to be
sure, that errors were made in the course of transmission and that the original text
was closer to the parr.

NHC V 1,3–17   NHC III 70,3–17

ⲧⲟⲩⲱϣ | [ⲉⲧⲉⲧ]ⲛ̅ⲙ̅[ⲙⲉ] ⲭⲉ
ⲛ̅ⲣⲱⲙ[ⲉ] ⲧⲏⲣⲟⲩ ⲛ̅⁵[ⲭⲡⲟ]
ⲙ̅ⲡⲕ[ⲁ]ⲍ ⲭⲓⲛ ⲛ̅ⲧⲕⲁ[ⲧ]ⲁⲃⲟⲗⲏ
ⲛ̅|[ⲧⲉ ⲡⲓ]ⲕⲟⲥⲙⲟⲥ ϣⲁ ⲍⲟⲩⲛ
ⲉ̣ⲧⲛⲟⲩ ⲥⲉ|ϣ[ⲓⲛ]ⲉ ⲛ̅ⲥⲁ ⲡⲛⲟⲩⲧⲉ
ⲭⲉ ⲛⲓⲙ ⲡⲉ· | ⲏ̅ [ⲟⲩ]ⲁ̣ϣ ⲙ̅ⲙⲓⲛⲉ
ⲡⲉ· ⲁⲩⲱ ⲙ̅ⲡⲟⲩ|ϭⲛ̅ⲧ̣ϥ̅· ⲛⲉⲧⲙⲉⲩⲉ
ⲇⲉ ⲉⲃ̣ⲟ̣ⲗ ⲛ̅ⲍⲏ¹⁰ⲧⲟⲩ ⲭⲉ ⲍⲉⲛⲥⲁⲃⲉ
ⲛⲉ ⲉⲃⲟⲗ ⲍⲙ̅ ⲡⲓ|ⲣⲟ[ⲟ]ⲩϣ ⲛ̅ⲧⲉ
ⲡⲓⲕⲟ̣[ⲥ]ⲙ̣[ⲟ]ⲥ· ⲛⲏ ⲉⲧⲉ | ⲧⲙⲉ
ϣⲟⲟⲡ̅ ⲛ̅ⲍⲏⲧⲟⲩ ⲁⲛ· ⲡⲓⲧⲉⲍⲟ | ⲅⲁⲣ
ⲉⲣⲁⲧ̅ϥ̅ ⲛ̅ⲧⲉ ⲡ̣[ⲓ̄]ⲁ̣ⲓⲱⲛ ϣⲁⲩⲭⲟⲟ̄ϥ |
ⲛ̅ϣⲟⲙⲛ̅ⲧ̅ ⲛ̅ⲥⲙⲟ̄ⲧ̅ ⲉⲃ[ⲟⲗ]
ⲍⲓ̂ ⲧⲟ̣ⲟ̣ⲧⲟⲩ ¹⁵ ⲉⲧⲃⲉ ⲡⲁⲓ̈ ⲛ̅ⲥⲉ̣ⲧ̣
ⲙ̣ⲉ̣ⲧ̣ⲉ̣ [ⲙⲛ̅] ⲛⲉ[ⲩ]|ⲉⲣⲏⲟⲩ ⲁⲛ·
ⲁ̣ⲩ̣ⲟ̣[8±]ⲧⲟ̣ | . [..] ⁻̈ [9±]·̇

ⲉⲧⲣⲉⲧⲛ̅ⲉⲓⲙⲉ ⲭⲉ ⲣⲱⲙⲉ ⲛⲓⲙ |
ⲛ̅ⲧⲁⲩⲭⲡⲟⲟⲩ ⲭⲛ̅ ⲛ̅ⲧⲕⲁⲧⲁⲃⲟⲗⲏ ⁵
ⲙ̅ⲡⲕⲟⲥⲙⲟⲥ ϣⲁ ⲧⲉⲛⲟⲩ ⲥⲉⲟ |
ⲛ̅ϣⲍⲓⲥ ⲉⲩϣⲓⲛⲉ ⲛ̅ⲥⲁ ⲡⲛⲟⲩ|ⲧⲉ
ⲭⲉ ⲛⲓⲙ ⲡⲉ ⲏ ⲟⲩⲉϣ ⲛ̅ⲍⲉ ⲡⲉ |
ⲙ̅ⲡⲟⲩⲍⲉ ⲉⲣⲟϥ ⲛ̅ⲥⲁⲃⲉⲉⲩⲉ
ⲉⲧⲛ̅|ⲍⲏⲧⲟⲩ ⲛ̅ⲍⲟⲩⲟ ⲉⲃⲟⲗ ⲍⲛ̅
ⲧⲁⲓⲟⲓⲕⲏ ¹⁰ⲥⲓⲥ ⲙ̅ⲡⲕⲟⲥⲙⲟⲥ ⲁⲩⲧ
ⲧⲁⲛⲧⲛ̅ | ⲉⲧⲙⲏⲉ ⲁⲩⲱ
ⲙ̅ⲡⲉⲡⲧⲁⲛⲧⲛ̅ ⲧⲁ|ⲍⲉ ⲧⲙⲏⲉ
ⲧⲁⲓⲟⲓⲕⲏⲥⲓⲥ ⲛⲅⲁⲣ | ϣⲁⲩϣⲁⲭⲉ
ⲉⲣⲟⲥ ⲛ̅ϣⲟⲙⲧⲉ ⲛ̅|ϭⲓⲛϣⲁⲭ ⲉ
ⲉⲃⲟⲗ ⲍⲓⲧⲟⲟ ⲧⲟⲩ
ⲛ̅ ¹⁵ⲛⲉⲫⲓⲗ ⲟⲥⲟⲫⲟⲥ ⲧⲏⲣⲟⲩ ⲉⲧⲃⲉ |
ⲡⲁⲓ̈ ⲛ̅ⲥⲉⲥⲩⲙⲫⲱⲛⲉⲓ ⲁⲛ ⲍⲟⲉⲓ|ⲛⲉ

I want | [you to know] that all men,
who are ⁵ [born] of the [earth], from
the foundation of | [the] world until
now | [inquire] about God, who he is
| and what he is like, and they have
not | found him. And those of them
who think ¹⁰ they are wise,
(speculating) from the | care (taken)
of the world, | have no truth in them!
For | the ordering of the aeon is
spoken of | in three ways by them, ¹⁵
(and) hence they do not agree [with]
each other. | [...] | [...]. For |

that you know that all men | born
from the foundation ⁵ of the world
until now are | dust. While they
have inquired about God, | who he is
and what he is like, | they have not
found him. The wisest | among
them have speculated about the truth
from the ordering ¹⁰ of the world. |
And the speculation has not reached
| the truth. For the ordering | is
spoken of in three (different)
opinions | by ¹⁵ all the philosophers,
(and) hence | they do not agree. For
some | of

Eug-V:

1,4 First and second superlinear strokes are in lacuna.

1,5 First superlinear stroke is in lacuna.

1,9 First superlinear stroke is in lacuna.

1,10 Between the last two letters MS has space with ink marks. The scribe apparently
attempted to use the space but found he could not because of imperfections in the
sheet.

NHC III 92,7–22

ⲧⲟⲩⲱϣ ⲉⲧⲣⲉⲧⲛ̄ⲉⲓⲙⲉ | ϫⲉ
ⲛ̄ⲣⲱⲙⲉ ⲧⲏⲣⲟⲩ ⲛ̄ⲧⲁⲩϫⲡⲟ|ⲟⲩ
ⲉⲡⲕⲁϩ· ϫⲓⲛ ⲧⲕⲁⲧⲁⲃⲟⲗⲏ
ⲙ̄ ¹⁰ⲡⲕⲟⲥⲙⲟⲥ ϣⲁ ⲧⲉⲛⲟⲩ ⲉⲩⲟ |
ⲛ̄ϣϩⲓⲥ ⲉⲩϣⲓⲛⲉ ⲛ̄ⲥⲁ ⲡⲛⲟⲩ|ⲧⲉ
ϫⲉ ⲛⲓⲙ ⲡⲉ ⲁⲩⲱ ⲟⲩⲁϣ ⲙ̄|ⲙⲓⲛⲉ
ⲡⲉ ⲙ̄ⲡⲟⲩϩⲉ ⲉⲣⲟϥ ⲛ̄|ⲥⲁⲃⲉⲉⲩⲉ ⲇⲉ
ⲛ̄ϩⲟⲩⲟ ⲉⲧⲛ̄ϩⲏ ¹⁵ⲧⲟⲩ ⲉⲃⲟⲗ ϩⲛ̄
ⲧⲁⲓⲟⲓⲕⲏⲥⲓⲥ ⲙ̄|ⲡⲕⲟⲥⲙⲟⲥ ⲙⲛ̄
ⲡⲕⲓⲙ ⲁⲩⲧ | ⲧⲁⲛⲧⲛ̄
ⲙ̄ⲡⲉⲡⲉⲩⲧⲁⲛⲧⲛ̄ ⲇⲉ ⲧⲁ|ϩⲉ ⲧⲙⲏⲉ·
ⲧⲁⲓⲟⲓⲕⲏⲥⲓⲥ ⲅⲁⲣ ϣⲁⲩ|ϣⲁϫⲉ
ⲉⲣⲟⲥ ⲛ̄ϣⲟⲙⲛ̄ⲧ ⲛ̄ϩⲉ ²⁰ ⲉⲩⲁⲅⲉ
ⲙ̄ⲙⲟⲥ ϩⲓⲧⲛ̄ ⲛⲉⲫⲓⲗⲟ|ⲥⲟⲫⲟⲥ
ⲧⲏⲣⲟⲩ· ⲉⲧⲃⲉ ⲡⲁⲓ̈
ⲛ̄ⲥⲉ|ⲥⲩⲙⲫⲱⲛⲉⲓ ⲁⲛ· ϩⲟⲉⲓⲛ ⲅⲁⲣ

BG 80,4–81,5

ⲧⲟⲩⲱϣ ⁵ ⲉⲧⲣⲉⲧⲛ̄ⲉⲓⲙⲉ ⲧⲏⲣⲧⲛ̄ |
ⲉⲛⲉⲛⲧⲁⲩϫⲡⲟⲟⲩ ⲉⲡ|ⲕⲁϩ ϫⲓⲛ
ⲧⲕⲁⲧⲁⲃⲟⲗⲏ | ⲙ̄ⲡⲕⲟⲥⲙⲟⲥ ϣⲁ
ⲧⲉ|ⲛⲟⲩ ⲉⲩⲙⲉⲉⲩⲉ ⲉⲩϣⲓ ¹⁰ⲛⲉ
ⲛⲥⲁ ⲡⲛⲟⲩⲧⲉ ϫⲉ ⲛⲓⲙ | ⲡⲉ ⲏ
ⲟⲩⲁϣ ⲛ̄ϩⲉ ⲡⲉ | ⲙ̄ⲡⲟⲩϩⲉ ⲉⲣⲟϥ
ⲛⲥⲁⲃⲉ | ⲇⲉ ⲉⲧⲛ̄ϩⲏⲧⲟⲩ {ϫⲉ}
ⲉⲃⲟⲗ | ϩⲛ̄ ⲧⲁⲓⲟⲓⲕⲏⲥⲓⲥ
ⲙ̄ⲡⲕⲟ ¹⁵ⲥⲙⲟⲥ ⲙⲛ̄ ⲡⲕⲓⲙ ⲁⲩⲧ |
ⲧⲟⲛⲧⲛ̄ ⲡⲉⲩⲧⲟⲛⲧⲛ̄ | ⲇⲉ
ⲙ̄ⲡⲉϥⲧⲁϩⲉ ⲧⲙⲉ | ⲧⲁⲓⲟⲓⲕⲏⲥⲓⲥ
ⲅⲁⲣ ϣⲁⲩ
ϫⲟⲟⲥ ⲉⲣⲟⲥ ϫⲉ ⲥⲟⲩⲁⲅⲉ | ⲙ̄ⲙⲟⲥ   π̄ⲁ
ⲛ̄ϣⲟⲙⲛ̄ⲧⲉ ⲛ̄ϩⲉ | ϩⲓ̈ⲧⲛ̄
ⲛⲓⲫⲓⲗⲟⲥⲟⲫⲟⲥ ⲧⲏ|ⲣⲟⲩ ⲉⲧⲃⲉ ⲡⲁⲓ̈
ⲛ̄ⲥⲉⲥⲩⲙ ⁵ⲫⲱⲛⲓ ⲁⲛ ϩⲟⲓ̈ⲛ ⲅⲁⲣ

| "I want you to know | that all men born | on earth from the foundation of [10] the world until now, being | dust, while they have inquired about God, | who he is and what he | is like, have not found him. Now the | wisest among [15] them have speculated from the ordering of | the world and (its) movement. | But their speculation has not reached | the truth. For it | is said that the ordering is directed in three ways [20] by all the philosophers, | (and) hence they do not | agree. For some of |

"I want [5] you all to know | that those who have been born | on earth from the foundation | of the world until now, | while they have thought to inquire [10] about God, who | he is and what he is like, | have not found him. Now the wisest | among them have speculated from | the ordering of the world [15] and (its) movement. | But their speculation | has not reached the truth. | For it is said that the ordering is directed | in three **81** ways | by all the philosophers, | (and) hence they do not agree. [5] For

NHC V 1,17–24

ϩⲟ̣ⲓ̈ⲛⲉ | ⲅⲁⲣ ⲉⲃ[ⲟⲗ ⲛ̄ϩⲏⲧⲟⲩ
ⲥⲉϫⲱ ⲙ̄ⲙ]ⲟ̣ⲥ | ϫ[ⲉ ⲟ]ⲩⲡ̄[ⲛ̄ⲁ̄ ⲡⲉ
ϩ̂ⲓ ⲧⲟⲟⲧϥ] ⲟⲩⲁ[ⲁ]ϥ· ²⁰
ϩ[ⲛⲕ]ⲟ̣[ⲟⲩⲉ ϫⲉ ⲉⲧⲁ]ϥϣⲱⲡⲉ
[ϩ]ⲁ̣|[ⲧⲛ̄ ⲟⲩⲡⲣⲟⲛⲟⲓⲁ ·] ϩ̣ⲛⲕⲟⲟⲩⲉ
ϫ̣[ⲉ] | [ⲉⲧⲁϥϣⲱⲡⲉ ϩⲁⲧⲛ̄
ⲟⲩ]ϩ̂ⲓ ⲙⲁⲣⲙⲉ̣|[ⲛⲏ· ⲁⲩⲱ ⲗⲁⲁⲩ
ⲛ̄ⲛ]ⲁ̈ⲓ̈ ⲙ̄ⲡⲉϥϫ[ⲓ] | [ⲉⲧⲙⲉ·

NHC III 70,17–71,1

ⲛ̄ⲅⲁⲣ ⲛ̄ϩⲏⲧⲟⲩ ⲥⲉϫⲱ ⲙ̄ⲙⲟⲥ |
ⲉⲡⲕⲟⲥⲙⲟⲥ ϫⲉ ⲛ̄ⲧⲁⲩⲁⲅⲉ ⲙ̄ⲙⲟϥ |
ϩⲓⲧⲟⲟ ⲧⲩ̄ ⲙ̄ⲙⲓⲛ ⲙ̄ⲙⲟϥ·
ϩⲉⲛ²⁰ⲕⲟⲟⲩⲉ ϫⲉ ⲟⲩⲡⲣⲟⲛⲟⲓⲁ ⲧⲉ·
ϩⲉⲛ|ⲕⲟⲟⲩⲉ ϫⲉ ⲟⲩⲡⲉⲧⲏⲡ̄ ⲉϣⲱⲡⲉ
| ⲡⲉ ⲁⲩⲱ ⲟⲩⲟⲛ ⲛ̄ⲛⲁ̈ⲓ ⲁⲛ ⲛⲉ |
ⲧϣⲟⲙⲧⲉ ϭⲉ ⲛ̄ⲥⲙⲏ ⲛ̄ⲧⲁⲉⲓⲣ̄ | ϣⲣ̄ⲡ̄
ⲛ̄ϫⲟⲟⲩ ⲙⲛ̄ ⲟⲩⲉ̂ⲓ ⲙ̄ⲙⲟⲟⲩ
ⲛ̄ⲡ̄ ⲉⲧⲙⲏⲉ·   ⲟⲁ

some [of them say] | that [it is spirit
by] itself. ²⁰ [Others, that] it was
[subject to] | [providence]. Others,
[that] | [it was subject to] fate. |
[But] none [of] these has attained |
[the truth.

them say | about the world that it
was directed | by itself. Others ²⁰
that it is providence (that directs it). |
Others, that it is fate. | But it is none
of these. | Again, of the three voices
I have just | mentioned, none
is true.   **71**

Eug-V:

1,19 ϫ: see Emmel, 1979: 182. First superlinear stroke is in lacuna. See note to
SJC-BG par.

Eug-III:

70,21 "fate": see endnote 2.

NHC III 92,22–93,8   BG 81,5–17

ⲛ̄|ⲍⲏⲧⲟⲩ ⲥⲉⲭⲱ ⲙ̄ⲙⲟⲥ   ⲛⲍⲏ|ⲧⲟⲩ ⲥⲉⲭⲱ ⲙ̄ⲙⲟⲥ ⲭⲉ
ⲉⲡⲕⲟ|ⲥⲙⲟⲥ ⲭⲉ ⲉⲩⲁⲅⲉ ⲙ̄ⲙⲟϥ   ⲟⲩ|ⲡ̄ⲛ̄ⲁ ⲉϥⲟⲩⲁⲁⲃ ⲡⲉ ⲍⲓ̈ⲧⲟ|ⲟⲧϥ
ⲍⲓⲧⲟ   ⲙⲙⲓⲛ ⲙ̄ⲙⲟϥ ⲍⲛⲕⲟ|ⲟⲩⲉ ⲇⲉ ⲭⲉ

ⲟⲧϥ̄ ⲙ̄ⲙⲓⲛ ⲙ̄ⲙⲟϥ ⲍⲉⲛⲕⲟⲟⲩ[ⲉ] | ⲟⲩⲡⲣⲟⲛⲟⲓⲁ ¹⁰ ⲧⲉ ⲍⲛⲕⲟⲟⲩⲉ ⲇⲉ
ⲇⲉ ⲭⲉ ⲟⲩⲡⲣⲟⲛⲟⲓⲁ ⲧⲉ·   ⲭⲉ ⲟⲩ|ⲧⲉⲑⲟⲛⲧ ⲧⲉ ⲁⲩⲱ ⲟⲩⲁ
ⲍⲉⲛⲕⲟ|ⲟⲩⲉ ⲇⲉ ⲭⲉ ⲟⲩⲡⲉⲧⲏϥ̄   ⲛ̄|ⲛⲁⲓ̈ ⲁⲛ ⲡⲉ ⲧⲉⲉⲓϣⲟⲙⲧⲉ | ϭⲉ
ⲉϣⲱⲡⲉ | ⲡⲉ ⲁⲩⲱ ⲛ̄ⲟⲩⲟⲛ ⲛ̄ⲛⲁⲓ̈   ⲛⲥⲙⲏ ⲛⲧⲁⲩⲭⲟⲟⲩ ⲛ̄|ϣⲟⲣⲡ ⲉⲃⲟⲗ
ⲁⲛ ⲛⲉ ⁵ ⲧϣⲟⲙⲧⲉ ϭⲉ ⲛ̄ⲥⲙⲏ   ⲍⲓ̈ⲧⲛ ⲛⲣⲱⲙⲉ ¹⁵ ⲛⲧⲁⲩⲭⲡⲟⲟⲩ
ⲛ̄ⲧⲁⲉⲓⲣ̄ | ϣ̄ⲡ̄ⲛ̄ ⲛ̄ⲭⲟⲟⲩ ⲙ̄ⲙⲛ̄ ⲟⲩⲉⲓ   ⲉⲡⲕⲁⲍ ⲙ̄ⲛ | ⲟⲩⲟⲛ ⲙⲙⲟⲟⲩ ⲉⲃⲟⲗ
ⲙ̄|ⲙⲟⲟⲩ ⲍⲏⲛ ⲉⲧⲙⲏⲉ ⲏ̂ ⲉⲃⲟⲗ   ⲍⲛ ⲧ|ⲙⲏⲉ
ⲍⲓ|ⲧⲛ̄ ⲣⲱⲙⲉ·

93

them say about the world | that it is   some of | them say that | it is pure
directed by itself.   spirit by itself. | Others, | that it is
Others, | that it is providence (that   providence (that directs it). ¹⁰
directs it). Others, | that it is fate. | Others, that it is | fate. But it is none
But it is none of these. ⁵ Again, of   of | these. Again, these three |
the three voices I have | just   voices that have just been mentioned
mentioned, none | is close to the | are from men ¹⁵ who have been
truth, and (they are) from | man.   born on the earth; | none of them is
                                              of the | truth.

SJC-III:

92,24–25 See note to *SJC*-BG par.

92,24 Corr.: an erased superlinear stroke above ⲧⲟ.

93,3 "fate": see endnote 2.

93,8 Alt.: <ⲛ>ⲣⲱⲙⲉ, "from <*the*> men" (T–S); K has "through men."

SJC-BG:

81,7 "pure": "holy" (T–S). The Coptic can mean either. The T–S choice is based on
the assumption that "the translator of BG took a form of ἄγειν for ἅγιον
πν(εῦμ)α." That seems unlikely in view of the probable reconstruction of V 1,19.
That the world is, in some sense, (pure) spirit and is directed by it was Stoic doctrine (see *TDNT* [6], 1968: 354–56 [Kleinknecht]). The parallels in *Eug*-III and
SJC-III appear to reflect the Epicurean view that there is no directing power. Since
the text earlier says that these three opinions are different, and "pure spirit," here,
is, in essence, the same as providence, which is the next view, the readings in
Eug-III and *SJC*-III are probably to be preferred.

81,10–11 "fate": see endnote 2.

NHC V 1,24–2,4   NHC III 71,1–8

9±]ϣ[.]ⲡⲉ. ²⁵ [13±]. ⲛ̄[. .]   ⲡⲉⲧⲉⲃⲟⲗ ⲅⲁⲣ ⲍⲓⲧⲟ|ⲟ ⲧϥ̄ ⲙ̄ⲙⲓⲛ
(7± lines lacking)   ⲙ̄ⲙⲟϥ ⲟⲩⲃⲓⲟⲥ ⲉϥ|ϣⲟⲩⲉⲓⲧ˙ ⲡⲉ
                                        ϣⲁϥⲁⲁϥ ⲧⲉⲡⲣⲟ|ⲛⲟⲓⲁ
                                        ⲟⲩⲙⲛ̄ⲧⲥⲟϭ ⲧⲉ ⲧⲉⲧⲍⲁⲛⲧ˙ ⁵
[ⲃ̄]   ⲙ[7±]ⲉ ⲙ̄[12±] | ⲡⲓ ̣[ⲟⲩ<ⲉ̂ⲓ ⲉ> ⲙⲉⲥⲉⲥⲑⲁⲛⲉ ⲧⲉ˙
     ⲡⲉ]ⲧⲉ ⲟⲩⲛ [ϣϭⲟⲙ ϭⲉ ⲙ̄ⲙⲟϥ   ⲡⲉⲧⲉ ⲟⲩⲛ ϣ|ϭⲟⲙ ϭⲉ ⲙ̄ⲙⲟϥ ⲉⲉⲓ
     ⲉⲉⲓ] | ⲉ ̣ⲡ̣[ⲛ]ⲟ̣ⲩⲧⲉ ⲛ̄ⲧⲉ [ⲧⲙⲉ   ⲉⲍⲟⲩⲛ ⲙ̄ⲡ|ⲃⲟⲗ ⲛ̄ⲧⲉⲉⲓϣⲟⲙⲧⲉ
     ⲉⲃⲟⲗ ⲍ̂ⲓⲧⲛ̄] | ⲕⲉⲥⲙⲏ̣ [ⲛ̄]ⲥⲁⲃⲟⲗ   ⲛ̄ⲥⲙⲏ ⲛ̄ⲧⲁ|ⲉⲓϣⲣ̄ⲡ ⲛ̄ϫⲟⲟⲩ ⲛ̄ϥⲉⲓ

. . .] ²⁵ [. . .] | (7± lines lacking).   For whatever is from itself | is an
                                        empty | life; it is self-made.
                                        Providence | is foolish. (And) fate ⁵
                                        is an undiscerning thing.
[2] [. . .] | [. . .] Whoever, then, [is   Whoever, then, is able | to get free
     able to come] | to the God of [truth   of | these three voices | I have just
     by means of] | another voice,   mentioned and

Eug-III:

71,3 ϣⲁϥⲁⲁϥ "it is self-made": translation omitted by K & Tr (text is not emended
  by Tr).

71,4 "fate": see endnote 2.

71,5 T–S emends ⲟⲩ<ⲉⲓⲉ ⲉ>, but elsewhere in *Eug*–III and *SJC*–III only ⲟⲩⲉ̂ⲓ is
  found. "is . . . thing": "is something that is not known" (K [by an emendation?],
  followed by Tr, who does not emend the line).

71,6 "to get free of" (similarly, Tr): less likely, "penetrate to the solutions (sic) of"
  (K).

NHC III 93,8–16

ⲀⲚⲞⲔ ⲆⲈ ⲚⲦⲀⲈⲒⲈⲒ̂ Ⲉ|ⲂⲞⲖ ⲌⲘ̄
ⲠⲞⲨⲞⲈⲒⲚ Ⲛ̄ⲀⲠⲈⲢⲀⲚⲦⲞⲚ ¹⁰ †
Ⲙ̄ⲠⲈⲈⲒⲘⲀ · ⲀⲚⲞⲔ ⲄⲀⲢ †ⲤⲞⲞⲨⲚ |
Ⲙ̄ⲘⲞϥ ⲬⲈ ⲈⲈⲒⲬⲰ Ⲛ̄ⲎⲦⲚ̄
Ⲛ̄ⲦⲀ|ⲔⲢⲒⲂⲒⲀ Ⲛ̄ⲦⲘⲎⲈ·
ⲠⲈⲦⲈ ⲞⲨⲈⲂⲞⲖ | ⲌⲒⲦⲞⲞⲦϥ̄ Ⲙ̄ⲘⲒⲚ
Ⲙ̄ⲘⲞϥ ⲞⲨⲂⲒⲞⲤ | ⲈϥⲤⲞⲞϥ
ⲠⲈⲦⲈϢⲀϥⲀⲀϥ · ⲦⲈⲠⲢⲞ ¹⁵ⲚⲞⲒⲀ ⲘⲚ̄
ⲘⲚ̄ⲦⲤⲀⲂⲎ Ⲛ̄ⲌⲎⲦⲤ̄ ⲦⲈ|ⲦⲌⲀⲚ† ⲆⲈ
ⲘⲈⲤⲈⲤⲐⲀⲚⲈ ·

BG 81,17–82,9

ⲀⲚⲞⲔ ⲆⲈ ⲚⲦⲀⲒ̈ⲈⲒ Ⲉ|ⲂⲞⲖ ⲌⲘ
ⲠⲒⲞ ⲨⲞⲒ̈Ⲛ ⲚⲀⲦⲀ|ⲢⲎⲬϥ ⲀⲚⲞⲔ
ⲈⲦⲤⲞⲞⲨⲚ
Ⲙ̄ⲘⲞϥ ⲬⲈ ⲈⲈⲒⲦⲀⲘⲈ | ⲐⲎⲨⲦⲚ̄   ⲠⲂ̄
ⲈⲦⲀⲔⲢⲒⲂⲈⲒⲀ Ⲛ̄Ⲧ|ⲘⲎⲈ
ⲠⲈⲦⲈ ⲞⲨⲈⲂⲞⲖ ⲄⲀⲢ | ⲌⲒ̈ⲦⲞⲞⲦϥ
ⲘⲘⲒⲚ ⲘⲘⲞϥ ⁵ ⲠⲈ ⲞⲨⲂⲒⲞⲤ
ⲈϥⲌⲞⲞⲨ ⲠⲈⲦⲈ | Ϣ<Ⲁϥ>ⲀⲀϥ
ⲦⲈ{Ⲧ}ⲠⲢⲞⲚⲞⲒⲀ ⲞⲨ|ⲀⲤⲞⲪⲞⲚ ⲆⲈ
ⲦⲈ ⲦⲈⲐⲞⲚⲦ | ⲆⲈ ⲞⲨⲈⲒⲈ
ⲈⲘⲀⲤⲀⲒⲤⲐⲀⲚⲈ | ⲦⲈ

But I, who came | from Infinite
Light, ¹⁰ I am here—for I know him
(Light)— | that I might speak to you
about the precise nature | of the
truth.
For whatever is from | itself is a
polluted life; | it is self-made.
Providence ¹⁵ has no wisdom in it.
And | fate does not discern.

But I came | from Infinite Light— | I
know him (Light)—
that I might instruct | you about the   **82**
precise nature of the | truth.

For whatever | is from itself ⁵ is a
wicked life; it is self-made. | And
providence | lacks wisdom. And
fate | is an undiscerning thing.

SJC-III:

93,16 "fate": see endnote 2.

SJC-BG:

82,7 "fate": see endnote 2.

NHC V 2,4–8

ⲛ̄ⲧ[ⲉⲓ̈ϣ]ⲟⲙ[ⲧⲉ ⲛ̄ⲥⲙⲏ] 5
ⲉⲧⲁⲩϫⲟ[ⲟ]ⲩ· ϥⲛⲁⲣ̄ⲥⲩⲙⲫⲱ[ⲛⲓ
ⲛ̄ⲟ]ⲩ|ⲟⲛ ⲛⲓⲙ
ⲉⲧⲃⲏⲏⲧϥ̄·

NHC III 71,8–13

ⲉ|ⲍⲟⲩⲛ ⲍⲓ|ⲧⲛ̄ ⲕⲉⲥⲙⲏ ⲛ̄ϥⲟⲩⲱⲛⲍ
ⲉⲃⲟⲗ ⲙⲡ 10ⲛⲟⲩⲧⲉ ⲛ̄ⲧⲁⲗⲏⲑⲉⲓⲁ
ⲛ̄ϥⲥⲩⲙⲫⲱ|ⲛⲓ ⲛ̄ⲟⲩⲟⲛ ⲛⲓⲙ
ⲉⲧⲃⲏⲧϥ̄

ⲁⲩⲱ ϥⲉ ⲛ̄[ⲛⲁⲧⲙⲟⲩ·] | ⲉⲩⲁⲧⲙⲟⲩ
ⲇⲉ ⲡⲉ ⲉϥϣⲟⲟⲡ̄ [ⲍⲛ̄ ⲧⲙ]ⲏ̣ⲧ̣[ⲉ
ⲛ̄]|ⲍⲉⲛⲣⲱⲙⲉ ⲉⲩⲙⲟⲟⲩⲧ̄·

ⲡⲁⲓ̈ ⲟⲩ|ⲁⲑⲁⲛⲁⲧⲟⲥ ⲡⲉ ⲉϥϣⲟⲟⲡ̄
ⲍⲛ̄ ⲧⲙⲏ|ⲧⲉ ⲛ̄ⲛ̄ⲣⲱⲙⲉ ⲉϣⲁⲩⲙⲟⲩ

different from these [three voices] 5
that have been mentioned, he will
agree [in] | everything concerning
him,

come by means | of another voice to
confess the 10 God of truth and agree
| in everything concerning him,

and he is [immortal.] | But, although
he is immortal, he dwells [in the
midst of] | mortal men.

he is | immortal, dwelling in the
midst | of mortal men.

Eug-III:
71,9 "to confess": "and reveal" (K & Tr).

NHC III 93,16–94,1   BG 82,9–83,1

ⲚⲦⲰ|ⲦⲚ ϭⲈ ⲚⲈⲦⲤ̄ⲦⲞ ⲚⲎⲦⲚ
ⲈⲤⲞⲞⲨⲚ | ⲀⲨⲰ ⲚⲈⲦⲘ̄ⲠϢⲀ
Ⲙ̄ⲠⲤⲞⲞⲨⲚ | ⲤⲈⲚⲀϯ ⲚⲀⲨ Ⲛ̄ⲚⲎ ⲈⲦⲈ
Ⲙ̄ⲠⲞⲨ ²⁰ⲬⲠⲞⲞⲨ ⲈⲂⲞⲖ Ⲍ̄Ⲛ
ⲦⲈⲤⲠⲞⲢⲀ Ⲛ̄ⲦⲈ|ⲦⲢⲒⲂⲎ ⲈⲦⲬⲀⲌⲘ̄·
ⲀⲖⲖⲀ Ⲍ̄Ⲙ ⲠⲈⲌⲞⲨ|ⲈⲒϮ
Ⲉ<Ⲧ>ⲀⲨⲦⲚ̄ⲚⲞⲞⲨϥ· ⲬⲈ
ⲠⲀⲒ̈ ⲄⲀⲢ | ⲞⲨⲀⲐⲀⲚⲀⲦⲞⲤ ⲠⲈ Ⲍ̄Ⲛ
ⲦⲘⲎⲦⲈ Ⲛ̄Ⲣ̄ⲢⲰⲘⲈ ⲈⲦⲈϢⲀⲨⲘⲞⲨ·
ⲠⲈⲬⲀϥ·
[ϥ]Ⲁ̣ ⲚⲀϥ Ⲛ̄ϬⲒ ⲘⲀⲐⲐⲀⲒⲞⲤ ⲬⲈ ⲠⲬⲞⲈⲒⲤ

ⲚⲦⲰⲦⲚ̄ ⲀⲈ ⲠⲈⲦⲤⲦⲞ ⲚⲎ ¹⁰ⲦⲚ̄
ⲈⲤⲞⲞⲨⲚ Ⲙ̄Ⲛ ⲚⲈⲦⲘ̄|ⲠϢⲀ ⲚⲤⲞⲞⲨⲚ
ⲤⲈⲚⲀⲦⲀ|ⲀⲤ ⲚⲀⲨ ⲚⲀⲒ̈ ⲈⲦⲈ
Ⲙ̄ⲠⲞⲨ|ⲬⲠⲞⲞⲨ ⲈⲂⲞⲖ Ⲍ̄Ⲛ
ⲦⲈⲤⲠⲞ|ⲢⲀ ⲚⲦⲈⲦⲢⲒⲂⲎ ⲈⲦⲬⲀⲌⲘ̄Ⲉ ¹⁵
ⲀⲖⲖⲀ ⲈⲂⲞⲖ Ⲍ̄Ⲙ ⲠⲈⲌⲞⲨⲒ̈Ⲧ |
ⲚⲦⲀⲨⲦⲚ̄ⲚⲞⲞⲨϥ ⲬⲈ
ⲠⲀⲒ̈ | ⲄⲀⲢ ⲞⲨⲀⲦⲘⲞⲨ ⲠⲈ Ⲍ̄Ⲛ
ⲦⲘⲎ|ⲦⲈ Ⲛ̄ⲚⲈⲦⲈ ϢⲀⲨⲘⲞⲨ Ⲛ̄Ⲣⲱ|ⲘⲈ
ⲠⲈⲬⲀϥ ⲚⲀϥ Ⲛ̄ϬⲒ ⲘⲀ
ⲐⲀⲒⲞⲤ ⲬⲈ ⲠⲈⲬⲤ̄   Ⲡ̄Ⲅ̄

But to you | it is given to know; | and whoever is worthy of knowledge | will receive (it), whoever has not been ²⁰ begotten by the sowing of | unclean rubbing but by First | Who Was Sent,

for | he is an immortal in the midst of | mortal men."

Matthew said

[9]4 to him: "Lord,

| But to you it is given ¹⁰ to know; | and whoever is | worthy of knowing will receive | it, whoever has not been | begotten by the sowing | of unclean rubbing ¹⁵ but by First | Who Was Sent, for | he is an immortal in the midst | of mortal men."

| Matthew said to him: "Christ,   **83**

SJC-III:

93,16–19 "But ... receive (it)": "To you is given to know, and to those who are worthy of knowledge. It will be given" (K).

93,22 MS has ⲑ (error noted by T–S).

SJC-BG:

82,9–12 "But ... it": "But to you it is given to know, and to those who are worthy to know. It will be given to" (T–S).

82,9 MS has the last two letters in ligature.

82,19 MS has a *paragraphus cum corone* in the left margin and a large diple after Ⲙⲉ. The diple seems intended to show the place of the major division.

NHC V 2,8–13   NHC III 71,13–18

ⲡⲏ [ⲟⲩ]ⲛ ⲉⲧ|ϣⲟⲟⲡ ⲛ̄ⲟⲩⲟⲉⲓϣ	ⲡⲉⲧ|ϣⲟⲟⲡ ⲟⲩⲁⲧϣⲁϫⲉ ⲉⲣⲟϥ ⲡⲉ·
ⲛⲓⲙ· ⲉⲩⲁ[ϯ]ϣⲁϫⲉ ¹⁰ ⲙ̄ⲙⲟϥ ⲡⲉ	ⲙ̄ ¹⁵ⲡⲉⲁⲣⲭⲏ ⲥⲟⲩⲱⲛϥ
ⲙ̄ⲡⲟⲩⲥⲟⲩⲱⲛϥ̄ ⲛ̄ϭⲓ ⲍⲉⲛⲁⲣⲭⲏ | ⲙⲛ̄	ⲙ̄ⲡⲉⲉϫⲟⲩ|ⲥⲓⲁ ⲙ̄ⲡⲉⲍⲩⲡⲟⲧⲁⲅⲏ
ⲍⲉⲛⲉϫⲟⲩⲥⲓⲁ· ⲟⲩⲧⲉ ⲛⲏ ⲉⲧⲧⲱ[ϣ·]	ⲙ̄ⲡⲉⲫⲩⲥⲓⲥ | ⲛⲓⲙ ϫⲛ̄
| ⲟⲩⲧⲉ [ⲫ]ⲩⲥⲓⲥ ⲛⲓⲙ· ⲉⲓⲙⲏ [ⲧⲓ	ⲛ̄ⲧⲕⲁⲧⲁⲃⲟⲗⲏ ⲙ̄ⲡⲕⲟⲥⲙⲟⲥ |
ⲉϥⲉ]ⲓ̣ ⲙ̣[ⲉ] | ⲛⲁϥ ⲟⲩⲁⲁϥ·	ⲉⲓⲙⲏⲧⲓ ⲛ̄ⲧⲟϥ ⲟⲩⲁⲁϥ·

[Now He] Who Always Is, | being ineffable, ¹⁰ no principles or authorities | knew him—neither those who [ordain] | nor any creature—except [he (alone) knew] | himself.	He Who | Is is ineffable. ¹⁵ No principle knew him, no authority, | no subjection, nor any creature | from the foundation of the world, | except he alone.

Eug-III:

71,15 "principle": "power" (K).

NHC III 94,2–13   BG 83,1–17

| ⲘⲘⲚ ⲖⲀⲀⲨ ⲚⲀϢ ϬⲚ ⲦⲘⲎⲈ·
ⲈⲒ|ⲘⲎⲦⲒ ⲈⲂⲞⲖ ϨⲒⲦⲞⲞⲦⲔ'
ⲘⲀⲦⲀⲘⲞⲚ | ϬⲈ ⲈⲦⲘⲎⲈ· ⲠⲤⲰⲦⲎⲢ
ⲠⲈⲬⲀϤ ⲬⲈ
5 ⲠⲈⲦϢⲞⲞⲠ ⲞⲨⲀⲦϢⲀⲬⲈ ⲈⲢⲞϤ ⲠⲈ
| ⲘⲠⲈⲀⲢⲬⲎ ⲤⲞⲨⲰⲚϤ
ⲘⲠⲈⲈⲌⲞⲨ|ⲤⲒⲀ ⲘⲠⲈϨⲨⲠⲞⲦⲀⲄⲎ
ⲘⲠⲈⲪⲨ|ⲤⲒⲤ ⲚⲒⲘ ⲬⲒⲚ
ⲚⲦⲔⲀⲦⲀⲂⲞⲖⲎ Ⲙ|ⲠⲔⲞⲤⲘⲞⲤ ϢⲀ
ⲦⲈⲚⲞⲨ ⲈⲒⲘⲎⲦⲒ 10 ⲚⲦⲞϤ ⲞⲨⲀⲀⲦϤ·
ⲘⲚ ⲠⲈⲦⲈϨⲚⲀϤ | ⲈϢⲰⲠ ⲚⲀϤ
ⲈⲂⲞⲖ ϨⲒⲦⲞⲞ Ⲧϥ· | ⲠⲀ Ⲓ ⲈⲦⲈ
ⲞⲨⲈⲂⲞⲖ ⲌⲘ ⲠⲈϨⲞⲨ|ⲈⲒϮ
ⲚⲞⲨⲞⲈⲒⲚ· ⲬⲒⲚ ⲚⲦⲈⲚⲞⲨ |

ⲘⲚ ⲖⲀ|ⲀⲨ ⲚⲀϢ ⲌⲈ ⲈⲦⲘⲈ ⲈⲒⲘⲎⲦⲒ
| ⲈⲂⲞⲖ ϨⲒ̈ⲦⲞⲞⲦⲔ ⲘⲀⲦⲀⲘⲞ̄ | ϬⲈ
ⲈⲦⲘⲎⲈ ⲠⲈⲬⲀϤ Ⲛ5ϬⲒ ⲠⲤⲰⲦⲎⲢ
<ⲬⲈ>
ⲠⲈⲦϢⲞⲞⲠ | ⲠⲒⲀⲦϢⲀⲬⲈ ⲈⲢⲞϤ
ⲈⲦϢⲞ|ⲞⲠ ⲈⲘⲠⲈⲀⲢⲬⲎ ⲤⲞⲨⲰⲚϤ |
ⲈⲘⲠⲈⲈⲌⲞ ⲨⲤⲒⲀ ⲞⲨⲦⲈ
Ⲙ|ⲠⲈϨⲨⲠⲞⲦⲀⲄⲎ ⲞⲨⲦⲈ ⲘⲠⲈ 10ϬⲞⲘ
ⲞⲨⲦⲈ ⲘⲠⲈⲪⲨⲤⲒⲤ | ⲬⲒⲚ
ⲦⲔⲀⲦⲀⲂⲞⲖⲎ ⲘⲠⲔⲞ|ⲤⲘⲞⲤ
ⲤⲞⲨⲰⲚϤ ϢⲀ ⲦⲈ|ⲚⲞⲨ ⲈⲒⲘⲎⲦⲒ
ⲚⲦⲞϤ ⲞⲨⲀ|ⲀϤ
ⲀⲨⲰ ⲘⲚ ⲠⲈⲦⲈϨⲚⲀϤ Ⲉ15ⲂⲞⲖ
ϨⲒ̈ⲦⲞⲞⲦ ⲠⲈⲚⲦⲀϤⲈⲒ | ⲈⲂⲞⲖ ⲌⲘ
ⲠⲈϨⲞⲨⲈⲒⲦ ⲚⲞⲨ|ⲞⲒ̈Ⲛ ⲬⲒⲚ ⲦⲈⲚⲞⲨ |

| no one can find the truth except |
through you. Therefore teach us |
the truth." The Savior said:
5 "He Who Is is ineffable. | No
principle knew him, no authority, |
no subjection, nor any creature |
from the foundation of | the world
until now, except 10 himself alone
and anyone to whom he wants | to
make revelation through him | who
is from First | Light. From now on

no one | can find the truth except |
through you. Therefore teach us |
the truth." The Savior said:
5 "He Who Is, | the ineffable one
who exists, | no principle knew him,
| no authority, nor did | subjection 10
or power or creature | from the
foundation of the world know him |
until now, | except himself alone
| and anyone whom he wants (to
know him) 15 through me, who came
| from First Light. | From now on

SJC-III:

94,11 Alt.: ϨⲒⲦⲞⲞⲦ , "through me" (T–S [see BG par.], followed by K).

94,13 The sentence that follows this line in BG (83,17–19) may have been acciden-
tally omitted here. However, the text makes sense without it.

SJC-BG:

83,4 MS has a large diple after the second word.

83,14 ⲠⲈⲦⲈϨⲚⲀϤ : + <ⲈϢⲰⲠ ⲚⲀϤ>, "and whomever he wants <to make revelation
to> through me" (T–S).

NHC V 2,13–17   NHC III 71,18–72,3

ⲡⲏ ⲅⲁⲣ ⲉⲧⲙⲙⲁⲩ ⲉⲙⲛ̄ |
ⲙⲛ̄ⲧⲛⲟⲩⲧⲉ̣ [ⲉ]ⲭⲱϥ· ⲟⲩϣⲁ ⲉⲛⲉⲍ
ⲡ[ⲉ·] ¹⁵ ⲉⲩϣⲁ ⲉⲛⲉⲍ ⲡ̣ⲉ[·]
ⲙⲉϥϣⲱⲡ̀ ⲉⲣⲟϥ ⲛ̄ⲟ̣[ⲩ]| ⲭⲡⲟ·
ⲉ̣[ⲩ]ⲁ̣ⲧⲙⲓⲥⲓ ⲇⲉ ⲡⲉ <ϥⲉ> ⲛ̄ⲛⲁⲧⲧ
[ⲉⲓⲛⲉ] | ⲉⲣⲟ[ϥ·

ⲡⲉⲧⲙ̄ⲙⲁⲩ | ⲅⲁⲣ ⲟⲩⲁⲑⲁⲛⲁⲧⲟⲥ
ⲡⲉ ⲟⲩϣⲁ ⲁⲛⲏ²⁰ⲍⲉ ⲡⲉ ⲉⲙⲛ̄ⲧⲉϥ
ⲭⲡⲟ ⲟⲩⲟⲛ ⲅⲁⲣ | ⲛ̣ⲓⲙ ⲉⲧⲉ
ⲟⲩⲛⲧⲁϥ ⲭⲡⲟ ϥⲛⲁⲧⲁⲕⲟ |
ⲟ̣ⲩⲁⲅⲉⲛⲛⲏⲧⲟⲥ ⲡⲉ ⲉⲙⲛ̄ⲧϥ̄ ⲁⲣⲭⲏ |
ⲟⲩⲁⲛ ⲅⲁⲣ ⲛⲓⲙ ⲉⲧⲉ ⲟⲩⲛ̄ⲧⲁϥ
ⲁⲣⲭⲏ | ⲟⲩⲛ̄ⲧⲁϥ ⳪ⲁⲏ· ⲙ̄ⲙⲛ̄ ⲗⲁⲁⲩ
ⲁⲣⲭⲓ ⲉ
ⲭⲱϥ ⲙ̄ⲙⲛ̄ⲧⲁϥ ⲣⲁⲛ ⲡⲉⲧⲉ ⲟⲩⲛ̄|ⲧϥ̄   ⲟⲃ
ⲣⲁⲛ ⲅⲁⲣ ⲡⲥⲱⲛⲧ̀ ⲛ̄ⲕⲉⲟⲩⲁ | ⲡⲉ

For since no divinity is over him, |
he is eternal. ¹⁵ Being eternal, he
does not experience | birth. And
being unbegotten, <he is> without
[likeness.]

For he | is immortal and eternal, ²⁰
having no birth; for everyone | who
has birth will perish. | He is
unbegotten, having no beginning; |
for everyone who has a beginning |
has an end. No one rules
over him. He has no name; for   **72**
whoever has | a name is the creation
of another. | He

Eug-III:

71,21 Corr.: first ϥ for an erasure.

NHC III 94,14–24

| ⲀⲚⲞⲔ ⲠⲚⲞϬ ⲚⲤⲰⲦⲎⲢ·
ⲠⲈⲦⲘ ¹⁵ⲘⲀⲨ ⲄⲀⲢ ⲞⲨⲀⲦⲘⲞⲨ ⲠⲈ
ⲞⲨⲰⲀ | ⲈⲚⲈⲌ ⲠⲈ· ⲞⲨⲰⲀ ⲈⲚⲈⲌ ⲆⲈ
ⲠⲈ | ⲈⲘⲚ̄ⲦⲀϥ ⲬⲠⲞ ⲞⲨⲞⲚ ⲄⲀⲢ ⲚⲒⲘ
Ⲉ|ⲦⲈ ⲞⲨⲚⲦⲀϥ ⲬⲠⲞ ϥⲚⲀⲦⲀⲔⲞ·
ⲞⲨ|ⲀⲄⲈⲚⲚⲎⲦⲞⲤ ⲠⲈ ⲈⲘⲚ̄Ⲧϥ̄ ⲀⲢⲬⲎ
²⁰ ⲞⲨⲞⲚ ⲄⲀⲢ ⲚⲒⲘ ⲈⲦⲈ ⲞⲨⲚⲦⲀϥ
ⲀⲢ|ⲬⲎ ⲞⲨⲚ̄ⲦⲀϥ ⲌⲀⲎ· ⲈⲘⲚ̄ ⲗⲀⲀⲨ
ⲀⲢ|ⲬⲒ Ⲉⲭⲱϥ ⲈⲘⲚ̄ⲦⲀϥ ⲢⲀⲚ ⲠⲈⲦⲈ |
ⲞⲨⲚⲦⲀϥ ⲢⲀⲚ ⲄⲀⲢ ⲠⲤⲰⲚⲦ̄
Ⲛ̄|ⲔⲈⲞⲨⲀ ⲠⲈ·

BG 83,17–84,13

| ϥⲚⲀ|ϬⲰⲗⲠ ⲈⲢⲰⲦⲚ̄ ⲈⲂⲞⲗ ⲌⲒⲦⲞ |ⲞⲦ
ⲀⲚⲞⲔ ⲠⲈ ⲠⲚⲞϬ Ⲛ̄Ⲥ̄Ⲱ̄Ⲣ̄
ⲠⲈⲦⲘ̄ⲘⲀⲨ ⲄⲀⲢ ⲞⲨⲀⲦⲘˋⲞ´Ⲩ | ⲠⲈ   ‾Ⲡ̄Ⲇ̄
ⲞⲨⲰⲀ ⲈⲚⲈⲌ ⲠⲈ ⲞⲨ|ϢⲀ ⲈⲚⲈⲌ ⲆⲈ
<ⲠⲈ> ⲈⲘⲚ̄ⲦⲀϥ | ⲬⲠⲞ Ⲙ̄ⲘⲀⲨ
ⲞⲨⲞⲚ ⲄⲀⲢ ⁵ ⲚⲒⲘ ⲈⲦⲈ ⲞⲨⲚⲦⲀϥ
ⲬⲠⲞ | ϥⲚⲀⲦⲀⲔⲞ ⲠⲀⲦⲬⲠⲞ ⲆⲈ |
ⲘⲚ̄ⲦⲈϥ ⲀⲢⲬⲎ ⲞⲨⲞⲚ ⲄⲀⲢ | ⲚⲒⲘ
ⲈⲦⲈ ⲞⲨⲚⲦⲀϥ ⲀⲢⲬⲎ | ⲞⲨⲚⲦⲀϥ
ⲌⲀⲎ ⲀⲨⲰ ⲘⲚ̄ ¹⁰ ⲗⲀⲀⲨ ⲀⲢⲬⲈⲒ
Ⲉⲭⲱϥ ⲘⲚ̄|ⲦⲈϥ ⲢⲀⲚ ⲠⲈⲦⲈ
ⲞⲨⲚⲦⲀϥ | ⲢⲀⲚ ⲄⲀⲢ ⲠⲤⲰ<Ⲛ>Ⲧ
ⲚⲔⲈⲞⲨ|Ⲁ ⲠⲈ

| I am the Great Savior.
For he ¹⁵ is immortal and eternal. |
Now he is eternal, | having no birth;
for everyone | who has birth will
perish. He is unbegotten, | having
no beginning; ²⁰ for everyone who
has a beginning | has an end. Since
no one rules | over him, he has no
name; for whoever | has a name is
the creation of | another.

he will | make revelation to you
through | me.
I am the Great Savior.
For he is immortal | and eternal.   **84**
Now <he is> | eternal, having no |
birth; for everyone ⁵ who has birth |
will perish. And Unbegotten | has
no beginning; for everyone | who
has a beginning | has an end. And
no ¹⁰ one rules over him. He has no
| name; for whoever has | a name is
the <creation> of another. | He

SJC-III:

94,15 Corr.: ⲱ for ⲟ.

94,20 Corr.: second ⲣ for erased ⲭ.

SJC-BG:

84,3 Not emended by T–S.

84,12 MS has ⲡⲥⲱⲧⲉ, "the ransom."

NHC V 2,17–27   NHC III 72,3–14

εγα]ⲧⲧ ⲉⲓⲛⲉ ⲇⲉ ⲉⲣⲟϥ ⲡⲉ·	ⲟⲩⲁⲧⲧ ⲣⲁⲛ ⲉⲣⲟϥ ⲡⲉ ⲙⲛ̄ⲧⲁϥ |
ⲙⲁϥ|ϣⲱⲡ ⲉ̣[ⲣⲟϥ ⲛ̄ⲟⲩⲙⲟ]ⲣϥⲏ·	ⲙⲟⲣϕⲏ ⲛ̄ⲣⲱⲙⲉ ⲡⲉⲧⲉ ⲟⲩⲛⲧⲩ̄ ⁵
[ⲡ]ⲏ ⲅⲁⲣ | ⲉⲧ̣[ϣⲱⲡ ⲉⲣⲟϥ	ⲙⲟⲣϕⲏ ⲅⲁⲣ ⲛ̄ⲣⲱⲙⲉ ⲡⲥⲱⲛⲧ̇ |
ⲛ̄ⲟⲩⲙⲟⲣϕ]ⲏ ⲟⲩ[ⲥⲱⲛⲧ̇] ²⁰ ⲛ̄ⲧⲉ	ⲛ̄ⲕⲉⲟⲩⲁ ⲡⲉ
ⲕⲉ̣[ⲟⲩⲁ ⲡⲉ·	ⲟⲩⲛⲧⲁϥ· ⲛ̄ⲛⲟⲩⲍⲓ|ⲇⲉⲁ ⲙ̄ⲙⲓⲛ
. . . . .]ϭ̣ⲙ[.] ⲉⲩ. | [. .]·	ⲙ̄ⲙⲟϥ ⲛ̄ⲑⲉ ⲁⲛ ⲛ̄|ⲧⲍⲓⲇⲉⲁ
ⲉⲛ.[14±]ⲩⲉ | [ⲛ̄]ⲧⲟϥ ⲟⲩⲁⲁϥ	ⲛ̄ⲧⲁⲛⲭⲓⲧⲥ̄ ⲏ̄ ⲛ̄ⲧⲁⲛⲛⲁⲩ | ⲉⲣⲟⲥ
[ⲟⲩⲛ̄ⲧⲁϥ ⲛ̄ⲟⲩⲥⲙⲟ]ⲧ | [ⲉ]ϥⲉ	ⲁⲗⲗⲁ ⲟⲩⲍⲓⲇⲉⲁ ⲛ̄ϣⲙ̄ⲙⲱ ¹⁰ ⲧⲉ
ⲛ̄ⲛⲟϭ ⲉⲟ̣[ⲩⲟⲛ ⲛⲓⲙ ⲁⲩⲱ	ⲉⲥⲟⲩⲁⲧⲃ̄ ⲛ̄ⲍ ̣ⲟⲩⲟ ⲉⲛⲕⲁ ⲛⲓⲙ |
ⲉϥⲥⲁ]|[ⲧ]ⲡ̄ ⲉⲟⲩⲟⲛ ⲛ[ⲓⲙ 12±] ²⁵	ⲉⲥⲥⲁⲧⲡ̄ ⲉⲛⲓⲡⲧⲏⲣϥ̄· ⲉⲥⲛⲁⲩ | ⲍⲓ
[. .]ⲏ· ⲁⲩⲱ [16±] | [.]ⲧⲥ̄	ⲥ`ⲁ´ ⲛⲓⲙ ⲉⲥⲉⲓ̈ⲱⲣⲍ ⲙ̄ⲙⲟⲥ |
ⲟ̣ⲩⲁ̣ⲧ̣[17± ⲁⲧ̇]ⲧ ⲉⲓⲛ [ⲉ ⲉⲣⲟϥ	ⲟⲩⲁⲁⲥ· ⲍⲓⲧⲟⲟ ⲧⲥ̄ ⲙⲙⲓⲛ ⲙ̄ⲙⲟⲥ |
19±]	ⲟⲩⲁⲧⲁⲣ`ⲏ´ⲭϥ̄ ⲡⲉ

| And [being without] likeness, he does not | take on [form]. For [whoever] | [takes on form is] the [creation] ²⁰ of [another . . .] | [. . .] | only he [has a resemblance] | [that] is greater than [everything and better] | than everything [. . .] ²⁵ [. . .]. And [. . .] | [. . . no] | likeness [. . .]

is unnameable. He has no | human form; for whoever has ⁵ human form is the creation | of another. He has his own semblance— | not like | the semblance we have received and seen, | but a strange semblance ¹⁰ that surpasses all things | and is better than the totalities. It looks | to every side and sees itself | from itself. | He is infinite;

Eug-V:

2,18 Corr.: first ⲡ incorporates initial ϥ (cf. 9,1n.).

2,20 ⲉ could be ⲁ. Only a large dot remains immediately before the lacuna. For ⲉ with such a dot, see 3,13 (first ⲉ) *Facsimile Edition–V*. If the letter were ⲁ, one would expect the dot to be a bit lower.

Eug-III:

72,8 Corr.: second ⲁⲛ for an incomplete ⲩ.

72,12 Corr.: ⲍⲓⲥ`ⲁ´ for ⲉⲍⲓⲥⲉ, "It looks *at* every *labor*" (both ⲉ's are marked out; ⲁ seems to be in a second hand). See note to III 95,6.

NHC III 94,24–95,7   BG 84,13–85,11

ⲟⲩⲁⲧϯ ⲣⲁⲛ ⲛⲁϥ | ⲡⲉ ⲙⲛ̄ⲧⲉϥ
ⲙⲟⲣⲫⲏ ⲛ̄ ¹⁵ⲣⲱⲙⲉ ⲡⲉⲧⲉ ⲟⲩⲛⲧⲁϥ |
ⲙⲟⲣⲫⲏ ⲅⲁⲣ ⲛ̄ⲣⲱⲙⲉ | ⲡⲥⲱⲛⲧ
ⲛⲕⲉⲟⲩⲁ ⲡⲉ

ⲟⲩ|ⲛ̄ⲧϥ̄ ⲟⲩⲉⲓⲛⲉ ⲉⲡⲱϥ ⲙ̄   ⲡⲉ
ⲙⲓⲛ ⲙ̄ⲙⲟϥ ⲡⲉ ⲛ̄ⲑⲉ ⲁⲛ |

ⲟⲩⲛⲧⲁϥ ⲇⲉ ⲛ̄ⲟⲩⲍⲓ
ϥ[ⲉ] ⲇⲉⲁ ⲉⲧ[ⲱ]ϥ ⲙ̄ⲙⲓⲛ ⲙ̄ⲙⲟϥ ⲧⲉ ⲛ̄|ⲑⲉ   ⲛ̄ⲧⲁⲧⲉⲧⲛ̄ⲛⲁⲩ ⲏ̄ ⲛ̄ⲑⲉ
ⲛ̄[ⲧⲁⲧ]ⲉⲧⲛ̄ⲛⲁⲩ ⲉⲣⲟⲥ `ⲁⲛ´ ⲏ̄   ⲛ̄|ⲧⲁⲧⲉⲧⲛ̄ⲭⲓ ⲁⲗⲗⲁ ⲟⲩⲉⲓ|ⲛⲉ
ⲛ̄ⲑⲉ | ⲛ̄ⲧⲁⲧⲉⲧⲛ̄ⲭⲓⲧⲥ̄ · ⲁⲗⲗⲁ   ⲛ̄ϣⲙ̄ⲙⲟ ⲉϥⲟⲩⲟⲧⲃ ⁵ ⲡⲉ ⲉⲛⲕⲁ ⲛⲓⲙ
ⲟⲩⲍⲓⲁ ⲉⲁ | ⲛ̄ϣⲙ̄ⲙⲱ ⲧⲉ ⲉⲥⲟⲩⲁⲧⲃ̄   ⲁⲩⲱ ⲉϥ|ⲥⲟⲧⲡ ⲉⲛⲓⲡⲧⲏⲣϥ
ⲉⲛⲕⲁ ⁵ ⲛⲓⲙ ⲁⲩⲱ ⲉⲥⲥⲟⲧⲡ̄   ⲉϥⲉⲓ|ⲱⲣⲍ ⲛ̄ⲥⲁ ⲥⲁ ⲛⲓⲙ ⲉϥⲛⲁⲩ |
ⲉⲡⲧⲏⲣϥ · ⲉ|ⲥⲛⲁⲩ ⲍⲓ ⲥ{ⲉ}`ⲁ´ ⲛⲓⲙ ·        ⲉⲣⲟϥ ⲉⲃⲟⲗ ⲍⲓ̈ⲧⲟⲟⲧϥ | ⲙⲁ`ⲩ´ⲁϥ
ⲉⲥⲉⲓⲱⲣⲍ ⲙ̄ⲙⲟⲥ | ⲍⲓⲧⲟⲟⲧⲥ̄   ⲟⲩⲁⲡⲉⲣⲁⲛⲧⲟⲥ ¹⁰ ⲇⲉ ⲡⲉ
ⲟⲩⲁⲁⲧⲥ̄ ⲉⲙⲛ̄ ⲁⲣⲏⲭⲥ̄ | ⲟⲩⲁⲧⲧⲁⲕⲟ ⲇⲉ | ⲡⲉ

                                        is unnameable. | He has no human
                                        form; ¹⁵ for whoever has | human
                                        form | is the creation of another.
                                        He has | a likeness of his own—
And he has a semblance   not like | what you have seen and | 85
9[5] of his own—not like | what you have received, but a | strange likeness that
seen and | received, but a strange   surpasses ⁵ all things and is | better
semblance | that surpasses all things   than the totalities. It sees | on every
⁵ and is better than the universe. | It   side and looks at | itself from | itself.
looks to every side and sees itself | And he is infinite ¹⁰ and
from itself. Since it is infinite,   imperishable. | He

SJC-III:

95,1–2 Lacunae so restored by T–S.

95,6 Corr.: ⲍⲓⲥ`ⲁ´ for ⲉⲍⲓⲥⲉ , "It looks *at* every *labor*"; the initial ⲉ is marked out,
     ⲁ is written above the next ⲉ in what may be a second hand, and that ⲉ *is not*
     marked out. The same correction was made in the same way, and by the same
     hand, in 72,12, except that there the second ⲉ *is* marked out. The ⲁ is written over
     an erased letter, possibly itself an ⲁ.

SJC-BG:

85,top MS has a strip of papyrus pasted above the page number. This strip and two on
     the other side of the leaf seem designed either to restore a broken leaf or to prevent
     a weakened one from breaking further.

NHC V 3,1–4

(5± lines lacking)

[Г̄] [. . . oymakapi]o̦c [πε·
ε̣γατνο]ει м̄моч | [πε· 9±]
εβολ м̄[. . . .] εγατμιcε | [πε·
εγατϣ]αχε ερο[ч πε·]
ϣαγμογτε | [ερоч χε πι]ωτ̇
м̄πτ[ηρ]ч̣·

NHC III 72,14–73,3

oyaттazoч πε [15] oya εчμηн
εβολ πε ν̄αφθαρ|τοc· oya
εм̄νταч πεчεινε πε |
oyaγαθοc πε ν̄α̇τ̇ϣιβε
oyaṫ|ϣωωṫ πε oya εчμηн
εβολ | πε oymakaριоc πε
oyaτνο [20] ει м̄моч πε
εϣaчνοει м̄|моч м̄μιν м̄моч·
oyaτϣι|τч̄ πε· oyȧτχι ϭεχм̄
ν̄cωч πε | oyτελειоc πε
εμν̄τεч ϣω
ωṫ oymak[a]ριоc πε   ог
ν̄αφθαρ|τоc ϣaγχооc ερоч
χε πιωṫ | м̄πτηρч·

| (5± lines lacking)

[3] [he is blessed. Since he is unknowable] | [. . . being] unbegotten (and) | [ineffable,] he is called | ["Father] of the Universe."

he is incomprehensible. [15] He is ever imperishable | (and) has no likeness (to anything). He is | unchanging good. He is | faultless. He is everlasting. | He is blessed. He is unknowable, [20] while he (nonetheless) knows | himself. He is immeasurable. | He is untraceable. He is | perfect, having no defect. He is imperishably blessed. | He is **73** called "Father | of the Universe."

Eug-V:

3,2 Superlinear stroke is in lacuna.

Eug-III:

72,21 Corr.: aτϣ for partly erased aτχι.

NHC III 95,8–22   BG 85,11–86,9

оүаттаzоч пе ечмнн евол· |	оүаттаzоч пе аү|ω оүа
оүафѳартос пе емнтач	ечмнн евол пе | аүω мн петне
пеҁеі ¹⁰не оүагаѳос пе	ммоч | оүагаѳос пе аүω
емечϣіве | оүатϣωωт пе	меҁ¹⁵ϣіве оүатωта пе оү|ϣа
оүϣа аннzе | пе оүмакаріос	енеz пе оүмак`а́рі|ос пе
пе емеүно|еіе ммоч	оүатноеі ммоч | пе ϣаҁноï
ϣаҁноеіе ммоч | оүаатн̄	ммоч маү|ааҁ оүатϣітч пе
оүатϣітн̄ пе оүат¹⁵хі ѕехме	оү
н̄сωҁ пе· оүтеліос | пе	атхі таѕсе н̄сωч пе п̄с̣
емнтаҁ ϣωωт оүмака|ріос	оү|теліос пе емнтаҁ ϣ|та
пе н̄афѳартос ϣаүмоү|те	ммаү оүмакаріос пе |
ероҁ хе пеіωт м̄птнрч̄·	натхωzм̄ еϣаүмоүте ⁵ ероҁ
	хе пеіωт мптнрҁ | пе
| філіппос пехаҁ хе пхоеіс	філіппос пехаҁ | хе пех̄с̄
²⁰ пωс ѕе аҁоүωнz ентеліос |	пωс ѕе аҁоүω|неz ентеліос
пехаҁ наҁ н̄ѕі птеліос	пехаҁ н̄|ѕі птеліос нсωтнр
н̄сω|тнр хе	хе

| he is ever incomprehensible. | He is imperishable and has no likeness (to anything). ¹⁰ He is unchanging good. | He is faultless. He is eternal. | He is blessed. While he is not known, | he ever knows | himself. He is immeasurable. He is ¹⁵ untraceable. He is perfect, | having no defect. He is imperishably blessed. | He is called | 'Father of the Universe.'" | Philip said: "Lord, ²⁰ how, then, did he appear to the perfect ones?" | The perfect Savior said to him:	is incomprehensible and | everlasting, | and there is nothing like him. | He is good and he does not ¹⁵ change. He is faultless. He is | eternal. He is blessed. | He is unknowable; | he ever knows himself. | He is immeasurable. He is untraceable. He is | perfect, having no | defect. He is blessed | (and) without blemish, (he) who is called ⁵ 'Father of the Universe.'" | Philip said: | "Christ, how, then, did he appear | to the perfect ones?" The perfect | Savior said:

86

SJC-BG:

86,top MS has a strip of papyrus pasted in such a way that it covers most of the page number.

86,4–5 Between these lines a narrow strip of papyrus is pasted in the MS, extending from the fifth letter almost to the end of the lines.

86,6 MS has a large diple between пе and after філіппос and a large asterisk in the left margin slightly below the level of the line.

86,9 MS has a large asterisk in the left margin.

NHC V 3,4–15   NHC III 73,3–14

ⲍⲁⲑⲏ ⲇⲉ ⁵ [ⲙ̄ⲡⲁⲧⲉⲗ]ⲁ̣ⲁⲩ ⲟⲩⲱⲛⲍ̄
ⲉⲃⲟⲗ ⲛ̄ⲧⲉ | [ⲛⲏ ⲉⲧⲟⲩ]ⲟⲛⲍ̄·
ⲍⲉⲛⲙⲛ̄ⲧⲛⲟⲟ ⲙⲛ̄ ⲍⲉⲛ|[ⲉⲍⲟ]ⲩⲥⲓⲁ·
ⲡⲏ ⲇⲉ ⲉⲧⲱⲟⲟⲡ̄ ⲛ̄ⲍⲏⲧⲩ̄ | ⲉ̣[ⲩ̄ⲥ]ⲱ̣
ⲉ̣ⲩⲁⲙⲁⲍⲧⲉ ⲙ̄ⲡⲧⲏⲣϥ̄ ⲛ̄ⲧⲉⲩ |
[ⲧ]ⲏ̣ⲣ̣ⲟ̣ⲩ· ⲉⲛⲥⲉⲁⲙⲁⲍⲧⲉ ⲇⲉ ⲛ̄ⲧⲟϥ
ⲙ̄ⲙⲟϥ ¹⁰ ⲁⲛ ⲉⲃⲟⲗ ⲍ̂ⲓ ⲧⲛ̄ ⲗⲁⲁⲩ·
ⲡⲁⲓ̈ ⲟⲩⲛⲟⲩⲥ | ⲡ[ⲉ ⲙ]ⲛ̄
ⲟⲩⲉⲛⲛⲟⲓⲁ ['] ⲟ̣ⲩ̣[ⲙ]ⲉⲉⲩⲉ ⲇⲉ |
ⲙ[ⲛ̄ ⲟ]ⲩ̣ⲥⲃⲱ ⲙⲛ̄ ⲟⲩϣⲟⲭⲛⲉ· ⲙⲛ̄
ⲡⲏ | ⲉⲧⲍ̂ⲓ ⲭⲛ̄ ⲟⲩϣⲟⲭⲛⲉ ⲙⲛ̄
ⲟⲩⲟⲟⲙ ⲡⲁ | ⲛⲓⲟⲟⲙ ⲧⲏⲣⲟⲩ ⲍⲱⲥ
ⲉ̣ϥ[ϣ]ⲟ̣ⲟⲡ̄ ⲛ̄ⲛⲟⲩ ¹⁵ⲡⲏⲅⲏ ⲛ̄ⲧⲉⲩ
ⲧⲏⲣⲟⲩ·

ⲍⲁⲑⲏ ⲉⲙⲡⲁⲧⲉⲗⲁⲁⲩ | ⲟⲩⲱⲛⲍ ⲍⲛ̄
ⲛⲉⲧⲟⲩⲁⲛⲍ ⲉⲃⲟⲗ· ⁵ ⲧ̇ⲙⲛ̄ⲧⲛⲟⲟ ⲙⲛ̄
ⲛⲓⲉⲍⲟⲩⲥⲓⲁ ⲉ|ⲧϣⲟⲟⲡ̄ ⲛ̄ⲍⲏⲧϥ̄
ⲉϥⲁⲙⲁⲍⲧⲉ ⲛ̄ⲛⲓ|ⲡⲧⲏⲣϥ̄· ⲛ̄ⲧⲉ
ⲛⲓⲡⲧⲏⲣϥ̄· ⲁⲩⲱ ⲙ̄|ⲙⲛ̄ ⲗⲁⲁⲩ
ⲁⲙⲁⲍⲧⲉ ⲙ̄ⲙⲟϥ· ⲡⲉⲧⲙ̄|ⲙⲁⲩ ⲅⲁⲣ·
ⲟⲩⲛⲟⲩⲥ ⲧⲏⲣϥ̄· ⲟⲩⲉⲛⲛⲟⲓⲁ ¹⁰ ⲙⲛ̄
ⲟⲩⲉⲛⲑⲩⲙⲏⲥⲓⲥ ⲟ<ⲩ>ⲫⲣⲟⲛⲏⲥⲓⲥ |
ⲟⲩⲗⲟⲅⲓⲥⲙⲟⲥ ⲙⲛ̄ ⲟⲩⲇⲩⲛⲁⲙⲓⲥ |
ⲛ̄ⲧⲟⲟⲩ ⲧⲏⲣⲟⲩ
ⲍⲉⲛⲍⲓⲥⲟⲇⲩⲛⲁ|ⲙⲓⲥ ⲛⲉ ⲙ̄ⲡⲏⲅⲏ
ⲛ̄ⲛⲓⲡⲧⲏⲣϥ̄ ⲛⲉ
| ⲁⲩⲱ ⲡⲉⲩⲅⲉⲛⲟⲥ ⲧⲏⲣϥ̄ <ⲭⲓⲛ

Even before ⁵ anything is visible of |
[those that are visible], majesties and
| authorities, He Who Is in Himself |
[continuously] embraces the totality
of them all | but is not embraced ¹⁰
by anything. He is mind | and
thought; also thinking and | teaching
and counsel; and he is | above
counsel and power—all powers | are
his, since [he] is the ¹⁵ source of
them all.

Before anything is | visible among
those that are visible, ⁵ the majesty
and the authorities that | are in him,
he embraces the | totalities of the
totalities, and nothing | embraces
him. For he | is all mind, thought ¹⁰
and reflecting, considering, |
rationality and power. | They all are
equal powers. | They are the sources
of the totalities. | And their whole
race <from

Eug-V:

3,9 Fourth letter: see Emmel, 1979: 183.

3,11 Superlinear stroke: see Emmel, 1979: 183.

Eug-III:

73,4 Corr.: ⲛⲉⲧⲟⲩⲁⲛⲍ for ⲡⲉⲧⲟⲩⲁⲛⲍ "(in) that which is visible."

73,5 "that": omitted by K & Tr (text is not emended by Tr).

73,6 "he embraces": less likely, "He rules" (K). For the concept, see *Gos. Truth* (I,*3*)
    22,21–33.

73,8 "embraces": less likely, "rules" (K); see 73,6n.

73,10 So emended by T–S.

73,12 Corr.: ⲣ in ⲧⲏⲣⲟⲩ for erased ⲍ.

73,14 Not emended by T–S, K or Tr; ⲅⲉⲛⲟⲥ, "race": see endnote 3.

NHC III 95,22–96,10

ⲌⲀⲐⲎ ⲚⲤⲈⲞⲨ<Ⲱ>ⲚⲌ̄ ⲗⲀⲀⲨ | ⲈⲂⲞⲗ
ⲚⲦⲈ ⲚⲈⲦⲞⲨⲀⲚⲌ ⲈⲂⲞⲗ ⲦⲘⲚ̄|ⲦⲚⲞϬ
ⲘⲚ̄ ⲦⲈⲜⲞⲨⲤⲒⲀ ⲈⲨϢⲞⲞⲡ̄

ⳅ[ⳅ]   ⲚⲌⲎⲦϤ̄ ⲈϤⲈⲘⲀⲌⲦⲈ [Ⲙ̄ⲡⲞ]ⲗⲰⲚ |
Ⲛ̄<Ⲛ>ⲒⲠⲦⲎⲢϤ ⲈⲘⲚ̄ ⲗⲀⲀⲨ
ⲈⲘ[Ⲁ]ⲌⲦⲈ | Ⲙ̄ⲘⲞϤ· ⲠⲈⲦⲘ̄ⲘⲀⲨ ⲅⲀⲢ
ⲞⲨ|ⲚⲞⲨⲤ ⲦⲎⲢϤ ⲠⲈ ⲀⲨⲰ
ⲞⲨⲈⲚ⁵ⲚⲞⲒⲀ ⲠⲈ ⲘⲚ̄ ⲞⲨⲪⲢⲞⲚⲎⲤⲒⲤ
| ⲘⲚ̄ ⲞⲨⲈⲚⲐⲨⲘⲎⲤⲒⲤ ⲘⲚ̄
ⲞⲨ|ⲗⲞⲅⲒⲤⲘⲞⲤ ⲘⲚ̄ ⲞⲨϬⲞⲘ·
Ⲛ̄ⲦⲞ|ⲞⲨ ⲦⲎⲢⲞⲨ ⲌⲈⲚⲌⲒⲤⲞⲚ
Ⲛ̄ⲀⲨ|ⲚⲀⲘⲒⲤ ⲚⲈ· Ⲙ̄ⲠⲎⲄⲎ Ⲛ̄ⲚⲒⲠⲦⲎⲢϤ
¹⁰ ⲚⲈ·
ⲀⲨⲰ ⲠⲈⲨⲄⲈⲚⲞⲤ ⲦⲎⲢϤ ⲜⲒⲚ |

BG 86,10–87,5

¹⁰ ⲌⲀⲦⲈⲌⲎ Ⲛ̄ⲤⲈⲞⲨⲰⲚⲌ ⲗⲀⲀⲨ |
ⲈⲂⲞⲗ <Ⲛ̄ⲦⲈ> ⲚⲈⲦⲞⲨⲞⲚⲌ
ⲦⲘⲚ̄Ⲧ|ⲚⲞϬ ⲘⲚ̄ Ⲛ̄ⲈⲌⲞⲨⲤⲒⲀ
ⲈⲨϢⲞ|Ⲟⲡ Ⲛ̄ⲌⲎⲦϤ ⲈϤⲈⲘⲀⲌⲦⲈ |
Ⲛ̄ⲚⲒⲠⲦⲎⲢϤ ⲚⲦⲈ ⲠⲦⲎⲢϤ ¹⁵ ⲈⲘⲚ̄
ⲗⲀⲀⲨ ⲀⲘⲀⲌⲦⲈ Ⲙ̄|ⲘⲞϤ ⲠⲈⲦⲘ̄ⲘⲀⲨ
ⲅⲀⲢ ⲞⲨ|ⲚⲞⲨⲤ ⲦⲎⲢϤ
ⲞⲨⲈⲚⲐⲨⲘⲎ|ⲤⲒⲤ ⲠⲈ ⲞⲨⲈⲚⲚⲞⲒⲀ
ⲠⲈ ⲘⲚ̄ | ⲞⲨⲘⲚ̄ⲦⲤⲀⲂⲈ ⲞⲨⲘⲈⲈⲨⲈ
ⲘⲚ ⲞⲨϬⲞⲘ ⲠⲈ ⲚⲦⲞⲞⲨ ⲦⲎ|ⲢⲞⲨ   Ⲡ̄Ⲍ̄
ⲤⲈϢⲎϢ ⲘⲚ̄ ⲚⲈⲨⲈⲢⲎⲨ | ⲌⲚ ⲦϬⲞⲘ
Ⲛ̄ⲦⲠⲎⲄⲎ Ⲛ̄ⲚⲒⲠ |ⲦⲎⲢϤ

ⲀⲨⲰ ⲠⲈⲚⲦⲀϤϢⲰⲠⲈ ⁵ ⲦⲎⲢϤ ⲜⲒⲚ

| "Before anything is visible | of
those that are visible, the | majesty
and the authority are

9[6] in him, since he embraces the whole
of the totalities, | while nothing
embraces | him. For he is | all mind.
And he is thought ⁵ and considering
| and reflecting and | rationality and
power. They | all are equal powers.
| They are the sources of the
totalities. ¹⁰ And their whole race
from

¹⁰ "Before anything is visible | <of>
those that are visible, the | majesty
and the authorities | are in him, since
he embraces | the totalities of the
universe, ¹⁵ while nothing embraces
| him. For he is | all mind; he is
reflecting; | he is thought and |
wisdom; he is thinking
and power. They all | are equal to   **87**
each other | in the power of the
source of the | totalities. And all that
came to be ⁵ from

SJC-III:

95,24 Corr.: erased Ⲍ at the end of the line.

96,1 Stroke over Ⲙ in lacuna is visible.

   Lacuna is not restored by T–S.

96,10 ⲅⲈⲚⲞⲤ, "race": see endnote 3.

SJC-BG:

86,13 "since he embraces": less likely, "He rules" (T–S); see III 73,6n.

86,15 "embraces": "rules" (T–S); see III 73,6n.

87,4–5 ⲠⲈⲚⲦⲀϤϢⲰⲠⲈ, "that came to be": See endnote 3.

NHC V   NHC III 73,14–16

ⲛ̄ϣⲟⲣⲡ> ϣⲁ ⲁⲣⲏ¹⁵ⲭⲛⲟⲩ
ⲉⲩϣⲟⲟⲡ̄ ⲍ̄ⲙ̄ ⲡⲉⲍⲟⲩⲉⲓⲧ̄ |
ⲛ̄ⲥⲟⲟⲩⲛ ⲙ̄ⲡⲁⲅⲉⲛⲛⲏⲧⲟⲥ ·

first> to last ¹⁵ is in the
foreknowledge | of Unbegotten,

NHC III 96,11–20 | BG 87,5–15

ⲚϢⲞⲢⲠ̄ ϢⲀ ⲀⲢⲎⲬⲚⲞⲨ ⲚⲈⲨ|ⲌⲚ̄
ⲠⲈϤϢⲢ̄Π̄ Ⲛ̄ⲤⲞⲞⲨⲚ
ⲠⲒⲀ|ⲠⲈⲢⲀⲚⲦⲞⲤ Ⲛ̄ⲀⲄⲈⲚⲚⲎⲦⲞⲤ |
Ⲛ̄ⲈⲒⲰⲦ̄:
ⲐⲰⲘⲀⲤ ⲠⲈⲬⲀϤ ¹⁵ ⲚⲀϤ ⲬⲈ
ⲠⲬⲞⲈⲒⲤ ⲠⲤⲰⲦⲎⲢ | ⲈⲦⲂⲈ ⲞⲨ
ⲀⲚⲀⲒ̈ ϢⲰⲠⲈ· Ⲏ̄ ⲈⲦⲂⲈ | ⲞⲨ ⲀⲚⲀⲒ̈
ⲞⲨⲰⲚⲌ ⲈⲂⲞⲖ· ⲠⲈⲬⲀϤ | Ⲛ̄ϬⲒ
ⲠⲦⲈⲖⲒⲞⲤ Ⲛ̄ⲤⲰⲦⲎⲢ· ⲬⲈ ⲀⲚⲞⲔ |
ⲀⲈⲒⲈⲒ̂ ⲈⲂⲞⲖ ⲌⲘ̄ ⲠⲀⲠⲈⲢⲀⲚⲦⲞⲤ ²⁰
ⲬⲈ ⲈⲈⲒⲚⲀⲬⲰ ⲚⲎⲦⲚ̄ Ⲛ̄ⲌⲰⲂ·

ⲦⲀⲢⲬⲎ ϢⲀ <ⲀⲢⲎⲬⲚⲞⲨ> | ⲚⲀⲨⲌⲘ̄
ⲠⲈϤϢⲞⲢⲠ ⲚⲤⲞ|ⲞⲨⲚ ⲠⲒⲀ ⲦⲀⲢⲎⲬϤ
ⲚⲀⲦⲬⲠⲞϤ | ⲚⲈⲒⲰⲦ
ⲠⲈⲬⲀϤ Ⲛ̄ϬⲒ ⲐⲰ|ⲘⲀⲤ ⲬⲈ ⲠⲈⲬⲤ̄
ⲠⲤⲰⲦⲎⲢ Ⲉ¹⁰ⲦⲂⲈ ⲞⲨ ⲀⲚⲀⲒ̈ ϢⲰⲠⲈ
ⲀⲨⲰ | ⲈⲦⲂⲈ ⲞⲨ ⲀⲨⲞⲨⲰⲚⲌ ⲈⲂⲞⲖ |
ⲠⲈⲬⲀϤ Ⲛ̄ϬⲒ ⲠⲦⲈⲖⲒⲞⲤ Ⲛ̄ⲤⲰⲢ̄ | ⲬⲈ
ⲀⲚⲞⲔ ⲀⲒ̈ⲈⲒ ⲈⲂⲞⲖ ⲌⲘ̄
ⲠⲒ|ⲀⲠⲈⲢⲀⲚⲦⲞⲚ ⲬⲈ ⲈⲈⲒⲈⲦⲤⲈ ¹⁵ⲂⲈ
ⲐⲨⲦⲚ̄ ⲈⲚ̄ⲔⲀ

| first to last was | in his foreknowledge, (that of) the infinite | Unbegotten | Father." Thomas said to him: ¹⁵ "Lord, Savior, | why did these come to be, and why | were these revealed?" | The perfect Savior said: | "I came from the Infinite ²⁰ that I might tell you all

beginning to <end> | were in his foreknowledge, | (that of) the infinite Unbegotten | Father." Thomas said: | "Christ, Savior, why ¹⁰ did these come to be, and | why were they revealed?" | The perfect Savior | said: "I came from the | Infinite that I might teach ¹⁵ you all

---

SJC-III:

96,12 Alt.: <Ⲙ>ⲠⲒⲀⲠⲈⲢⲀⲚⲦⲞⲤ , "foreknowledge *of* the infinite" (T–S).

96,14 Corr.: a diagnoal stroke after the double stop is erased.

Between this line and the next, MS has a *paragraphus cum corone* in the left margin.

96,15 Corr.: ⲚⲀϤ ⲬⲈ Π Ⲭ for erased ⲐⲰⲘⲀⲤ Π Ⲉ.

SJC-BG:

87,5 Alt.: ϢⲀ <Ⲟ>Ⲩ or ϢⲀ <ⲠⲈ>ⲨⲬⲰ<Ⲕ>, "to (their) end" (T–S). This proposal is not satisfactory because ⲬⲰⲔ does not occur in this phrase (ⲬⲒⲚ ⲦⲀⲢⲬⲎ . . .) elsewhere in *SJC*–BG, while ⲀⲢⲎⲬⲚⲞⲨ does. The emendation adopted here is found in the parallels. It may be that ⲚⲀⲨ (line 6) should be included in the portion of the text to be emended (see *Eug*–III par.). Or perhaps it caused part of the initial problem through similarity of appearance.

87,7 Alt.: <Ⲙ>ⲠⲒⲀⲦⲀⲢⲎⲬϤ , "foreknowledge *of* the infinite" (T–S).

87,8 MS has a large diple after the first word and a large asterisk in the left margin slightly below the level of the line.

87,12 MS has a large asterisk in the left margin.

NHC V

NHC III

NHC III 96,21–97,12 BG 87,15–88,12

| NIM· ΠΕΠΝⲀ ΕΤϢΟΟΠ̅
ΝΕⲨ|ΡΕϤΧΠΟ ΠΕ· ΕⲨⲚ̅ΤⲀϤ Μ̅ΜⲀⲨ
| Ⲛ̅ΟⲨϬΟΜ <Ⲛ̅>ΟⲨΟⲨⲤⲒⲀ
Ⲛ̅ΡΕϤΧΠΟ

[ϥⲌ] Ⲛ̅Ρ[ΕϤϯ] ΜΟΡΦΗ ΧΕΚⲀⲀⲤ
ΕⲤΝⲀ|ΟⲨⲰ[ⲚⲌ] ΕΒΟⲖ Ⲛ̅ϬⲒ ΤⲚΟϬ
Μ̅ΜⲚ̅Τ̅|{Ⲧ}Ρ̅Μ̅ΜⲀΟ· ΕΤⲌΗΠ Ⲛ̅ⲌΗΤϤ̅
ΕΤΒΕ | ΤΕϤΜⲚ̅ΤΧΡΗⲤΤΟⲤ ΜⲚ̅
ΤΕϤⲀⲄⲀΠΗ 5 ⲀϤⲢ̅ⲌⲚⲀϤ ⲌⲒΤΟΟ Τϥ̅
Μ̅ΜⲒΝ Μ̅|ΜΟϤ ΕΧΠΕ ⲌΕΝΚⲀΡΠΟⲤ
ΧΕ Ⲛ̅|ΝΕϤⲀΠΟⲖ<Ⲁ>ⲨΕ ΟⲨⲀⲀΤϥ̅
Ⲍ̅Ⲛ ΤΕϤΜⲚ̅|ΤⲀⲄⲀⲐΟⲤ· ⲀⲖⲖⲀ
ⲌΕΝΚΕΠⲚⲀ Ⲛ̅|ΤΕ ΤⲄΕΝΕⲀ
Ⲛ̅ⲀΤΚⲒΜ· ΕⲨΕΧΠΕ 10 ⲤⲰΜⲀ ⲌⲒ
ΚⲀΡΠΟⲤ· ΟⲨΕΟΟⲨ ΜⲚ̅ | ΟⲨΤⲒΜΗ
Ⲍ̅Ⲛ ΟⲨⲀΦⲐⲀΡⲤⲒⲀ ΜⲚ̅ | ΠΕϤⲌΜΟⲦ |

NIM ΠΕ|ⲠⲚⲀ ΕΤϢΟΟΠ
ΝΕⲨΡΕϤ|ΧΠΟ ΠΕ ΕⲨⲚΤⲀϤ ΜΜⲀⲨ
Ⲛ|ΝΟⲨϬΟΜ Ⲛ̅ΡΕϤΧΠΕ ΟⲨⲤⲒⲀ |
Ⲛ̅ΡΕϤϯ ΜΟΡΦΗ ΧΕΚⲀⲀⲤ 20
ΕⲤΕΟⲨⲰⲚⲌ ΕΒΟⲖ Ⲛ̅ϬⲒ ΤⲚΟϬ
Μ̅ΜⲚ̅ΤΡⲘ̅ΜⲀΟ ΕΤⲚ̅ⲌΗΤϤ̅ | ΕΤΒΕ
ΤΕϤΜⲚ̅Τ‾Χ‾Ⲥ‾ ΜⲚ̅ ΤΕϤ|ⲀⲄⲀΠΗ
ⲀϤΟⲨⲰϢ ΕΒΟⲖ ⲌⲒ|ΤΟΟΤϤ̅ Μ̅ΜⲒⲚ
Μ̅ΜΟϤ ΕⲎ 5ΠΟ Ⲛ̅Ⲍ̅Ⲛ̅ΚⲀΡΠΟⲤ ΧΕ
Ⲛ̅ΝΕϤ|Ρ̅ⲀΠΟⲖⲀⲨΕ ΜⲀⲨⲀⲀϤ
Ⲛ̅Τϥ̅|ΜⲚ̅ΤⲀⲄⲀⲐΟⲤ ⲀⲖⲖⲀ
Ⲍ̅ΝΚΕ|ⲠⲚⲀ ΝΤΕ ΤⲄΕΝΕⲀ ΕΤΕ |
ΜⲀⲤΚⲒΜ Ⲛ̅ⲤΕΧΠΕ ⲤⲰΜⲀ 10 Ⲍ̅Ⲓ̈
ΚⲀΡΠΟⲤ ΟⲨΕΟΟⲨ ΜⲚ̅ |
ΟⲨΜⲚ̅ΤⲀⲦⲀΚΟ ΜⲚ̅ ΤΕϤ|ΧⲀΡⲒⲤ

‾Π‾Η

‾Π‾Η (88)

| things. Spirit Who Is was the begetter, | who had | the power <of> a begetter

[97] and form-[giver's] nature, that | the great | wealth that was hidden in him might be revealed. Because of | his mercy and his love [5] he wished | to bring forth fruit by himself, that | he might not <enjoy> his | goodness alone but (that) other spirits | of the Unwavering Generation might bring forth [10] body and fruit, glory and | honor in imperishableness and | his infinite

things. | Spirit Who Is was the begetter, | who had | the power of one who begets substance | and gives form, that [20] the great wealth that was in him might be revealed. | Because of his mercy and his | love he wished | to bring forth [5] fruit by himself, that he might not | enjoy his | goodness alone but (that) other | spirits of the Generation That | Does Not Waver might bring forth body [10] and fruit, glory and | imperishableness and his | infinite

88

SJC-III:

96,23 Not emended by T–S or K ("power, a begetting, form-[giving] nature").

97,7 Not emended by T–S or K, both of whom translate *"isolate* himself in." "Isolate" is somewhat removed from the lexical meaning of ἀπολύειν.

97,11 Corr.: Ⲍ for erased Ⲙ.

NHC V

ⲛⲉ|ⲙ̄ⲡⲁⲧⲟⲩⲉⲓ ⲅⲁⲣ ⲉⲡⲉⲧⲟⲩⲁⲛⲍ |
ⲛ̣ⲉⲟⲩⲛ ⲟⲩⲇⲓⲁⲫⲟⲣⲁ ⲇⲉ ϣⲟⲟⲡ· |
[ⲟ]ⲩⲧⲉ ⲛⲓⲁⲫⲑⲁⲣⲧⲟⲥ ⲛ̄ⲁⲓⲱⲛ

| for they had not yet come to
visibility. | Now a difference existed
| among the imperishable aeons.

Eug-III:

73,19 Corr.: ⲉ ⲛⲓ for erased ⲟⲩⲛ.

   Lacuna so restored by T–S.

NHC III 97,12–23

ετε ΜΝΤ϶ αρηχ϶˙ | χε
ερεπε϶αγαθον ογωνζ εβολ |
ζιτϯ παγτογενΗс ϯνογτε ¹⁵
ϯειωϯ ϯαφθαρсια νιΜˑ Μϯ |
νενταγϣωπε Μϯϯса ναϊ |
νε<Μ>πατογει δε επετογανζ
| πεˑ ογϯ ογˋϣˊ{ε}ιβε δε
εναϣω<϶> | ογτε νιαφθαρτονˑ
νε϶ωϣ ²⁰ εβολ ε϶χω Μμος χε
πετε | ογν μααχε Μμο϶
εсωτΜ ε|νιαπεραντον
μαρε϶сωτΜ | αγω νετρΗс

grace, | that his treasure might be
revealed | by Self-begotten God, ¹⁵
the father of every imperishableness
and | those that came to be
afterward.
| But they had not yet come to
visibility. | Now a great difference |
exists among the imperishables."
He called ²⁰ out saying: "Whoever |
has ears to hear about | the infinities,
let him hear"; | and "I have
addressed those

BG 88,12–89,7

ετε Μϯ αρηχϲ χε | κααс
ε϶εογωνζ εβολ | ϯϭι
πε϶αγαθον εβολ ¹⁵ ζϊτοοτ϶
Μπιατχπο϶ | ϯνογτε πειωτ
Μμϯτ|αττακο νιΜ μϯ
νεν|ταγϣωπε Μϯϯса ναει
| νεμπατογει δε επετογ
ονζ εβολ ογδιαφορα | δε
εναϣωс сϣοοπ ογ|τϣογ
ϯνιαττακο
νε϶|ωϣ δε εβολ χε πετε
ογ⁵ϯτε϶ μααχε μμαγ εсω|τΜ
μαρε϶сωτΜ ενιατ|τακο ανοκ

π̄θ

grace, | that his treasure | might be
revealed ¹⁵ by Unbegotten | God, the
father of | every imperishableness
and those that | came to be
afterward.
| But they had not yet come to
visibility.
Now a great difference | exists
among | the imperishables."
And he | called out: "Whoever has ⁵
ears to hear, | let him hear about the
imperishables! | I will

89

SJC-III:

97,13 "that . . . revealed": "for his goodness was revealed" (K).

97,17 MS has ν.

97,18 Corr.: ϣ for marked out ζα; the corrector neglected to mark out the following ε
(see similar problem in 113,8 and to a lesser degree in 95,6); originally ζαειβε ,
"shadow."

MS has с at end of line (gender agreement with ζαειβε).

SJC-BG:

88,19–89,2 "But . . . among" (so also Schenke in T–S: 340): or possibly, "But before
they have come to what is revealed, a significant difference exists, however,
between" (T–S).

NHC V 3,15–24   NHC III 73,20–74,7

²⁰ ⲙⲁⲣⲉⲛⲛⲟⲉⲓ ϭⲉ ⲛ̄ⲧⲉⲉⲓϩⲉ ϫⲉ |

ⲡ[ⲏ] ⲅ̣ⲁ̣ⲣ ⲧⲏⲣⲩ̣	ⲉⲧⲉ ϣⲁϥϣⲱⲡⲉ	ⲛ̄ⲕⲁ ⲛⲓⲙ ⲛ̄ⲧⲁⲩϣⲱⲡⲉ ⲉⲃⲟⲗ ϩⲙ̄	
ⲉⲃ[ⲟⲗ ϩⲙ̄ ⲡ]ⲧⲁⲕⲟ·	ϥⲛⲁⲣ̄	ⲡⲧⲁⲕⲟ ⲥⲉⲛⲁⲧⲁⲕⲟ
ⲁⲧϣⲱⲡⲉ·	ϩⲱⲥ ⲉⲁⲩϣⲱ|ⲡⲉ ⲉⲃⲟⲗ ϩⲙ̄ ⲡⲧⲁⲕⲟ·
[ⲡⲏ ⲉⲧⲉⲃⲟⲗ] ϩⲛ̄ ϯ|[ⲁⲫ]ⲑⲁⲣ[ⲥⲓⲁ·	ⲡⲉⲛⲧⲁϥϣⲱ
ϥⲛⲁ]ⲣ̄ ⲁ[ⲧϣⲱⲡⲉ ⲁⲛ·] ⲁ̣ⲗⲗⲁ		ⲡⲉ ⲉⲃⲟⲗ ϩⲛ̄ ⲧⲁⲫⲑⲉ̣ⲁ̣ⲣⲥⲓⲁ ⲟⲇ
ϥⲛⲁⲣ̄ ϩⲟⲩ[ⲉ ⲁⲫⲑⲁⲣⲧⲟⲛ·	ⲛϥⲛⲁ|ⲧⲁⲕⲟ ⲁⲛ ⲁⲗⲗⲁ
ϩⲱⲥ ⲟ]ⲩⲉⲃⲟⲗ ²⁰ ϩⲛ̄ ϯⲁⲫⲑⲉ̣ⲁ̣[ⲣⲥⲓⲁ	ⲉϥⲛⲁϣⲱⲡⲉ ⲛ̄|ⲁⲫⲑⲁⲣⲧⲟⲥ
6±] ⲡⲉ·	ϥ[12±]ⲱⲛ	ϩⲱⲥ ⲉⲁϥϣⲱⲡⲉ ⲉ	ⲃⲟⲗ ϩⲛ̄
[ⲟⲩⲙⲏ]ⲏ̣ϣⲉ	[ⲅⲁⲣ ⲛ̄ⲧⲉ ⲛ]ⲓ̣ⲣⲱⲙⲉ	ⲧⲁⲫⲑⲁⲣⲥⲓⲁ·
ⲁⲩⲥⲱ[ⲣⲙ̄· ⲉⲛⲥ]ⲉ|[ⲥⲟⲟⲩⲛ] ⲁ̣ⲛ	ϩⲱⲥⲧⲉ ⲟⲩ⁵ⲙⲏⲏϣⲉ ⲛ̄ⲣⲱⲙⲉ
ⲛ̄ϯⲇⲓⲁⲫⲟⲣⲁ [ⲉⲧⲉ ⲧⲁ̈ⲓ ⲧ]ⲉ·		ⲁⲩⲡⲗⲁⲛⲁ	ⲙ̄ⲡⲟⲩⲥⲟⲩⲛ̄
[ⲛ̄ⲑⲉ ⲛ̄ⲛⲏ ⲉ]ⲧϩⲉⲧ[ⲃ̄]ⲣⲱ[ⲙⲉ·	ⲧⲉⲉⲓⲇⲓⲁⲫⲟⲣⲁ ⲉⲧⲉ	ⲧⲁ̈ⲓ ⲧⲉ
ⲁⲩⲙⲟⲩ·]	ⲁⲩⲙⲟⲩ·

For all | that comes [from the] perishable | will come to naught. [Whatever is] from | imperishableness [will not come to naught] but | will be more [imperishable, since] it is from ²⁰ [. . .] imperishableness. | [. . . For] many | men went [astray because they did] | not [know] the difference; [that is,] | [as with] murderers, [they died.]

²⁰ Let us, then, consider (it) this way. | Everything that came from | the perishable will perish, since it came | from the perishable. Whatever came from imperishableness will not | **74** perish but will become | imperishable, since it came from | imperishableness. So, ⁵ many men went astray | because they had not known this difference; that | is, they died.

Eug-V:

3,16 Final letter: see Emmel, 1979: 183.

3,19 Letter immediately after lacuna and last 3 letters: see Emmel, 1979: 183.

Eug-III:

73,22 Corr.: second ⲥ for erased ⲃ (initially ϩⲱⲃ).

74,1 T–S and Tr restore [ⲑⲁ].

74,4 "so": "so that" (T–S, K & Tr).

NHC III 97,23–98,9   BG 89,7–20

ⲁⲛⲟⲕ ⲁⲉⲓϣⲁϫⲉ | ⲛ̄ⲙⲙⲁⲩ· ⲉⲧⲓ	ϯⲛⲁϣⲁϫⲉ | ⲙⲛ̄ ⲛⲉⲧⲣⲟⲉⲓⲥ ⲉⲧⲓ
ⲁϥⲟⲩⲱϩ ⲉⲧⲟⲟⲧϥ̄·	ⲁϥⲟⲩ|ⲱϩ ⲉⲧⲟⲟⲧϥ ⲡⲉϫⲁϥ ϫⲉ
[ϥ̄ⲏ] ⲡⲉϫⲁϥ ϫⲉ	
ⲛ̄ⲕⲁ ⲛⲓⲙ ⲛ̄ⲧ̄[ⲁⲩ ϣ]ⲱ|ⲡⲉ ⲉⲃⲟⲗ ϩⲙ̄	ⲛ̄ ¹⁰ⲕⲁ ⲛⲓⲙ ⲛ̄ⲧⲁϥϣⲱⲡⲉ ⲉⲃⲟⲗ | ϩⲙ̄
ⲡⲧⲁⲕⲟ ⲥⲉⲛ[ⲁⲧ]ⲁ|ⲕⲟ	ⲡⲧⲁⲕⲟ ϥⲛⲁⲧⲁⲕⲟ
ϫⲉ ⲛ̄ⲧⲁⲩϣⲱⲡⲉ ⲉⲃⲟⲗ ϩⲙ̄ |	ϩⲱⲥ | ⲉⲩϣⲱⲡⲉ ⲉⲃⲟⲗ
ⲡⲧⲁⲕⲟ·	ϩⲙ ⲡⲧⲁ|ⲕⲟ
ⲡⲉⲛⲧⲁϥϣⲱⲡⲉ ⲇⲉ ⁵ ⲉⲃⲟⲗ ϩⲛ̄	ⲡⲉⲛⲧⲁϥϣⲱⲡⲉ ⲉⲃⲟⲗ | ϩⲛ̄
ⲧⲙⲛ̄ⲧⲁⲧⲧⲁⲕⲟ ⲙⲉϥⲧⲁ|ⲕⲟ ⲁⲗⲗⲁ	ⲧⲙⲛ̄ⲧⲁⲧ`ⲧⲁ´ⲕⲟ ⲙⲁ`ϥ´ⲧⲁⲕⲟ ¹⁵
ϣⲁϥϣⲱⲡⲉ ⲛ̄ⲁⲧⲧⲁ|ⲕⲟ·	ⲁⲗⲗⲁ ϥϣⲟⲟⲡ ⲛⲁⲧⲧⲁⲕⲟ |
	ϩⲱⲥ ⲉⲩϣⲟⲟⲡ ⲉⲃⲟⲗ ϩⲛ̄ |
	ⲧⲙⲛ̄ⲧⲁⲧⲧⲁⲕⲟ
ϩⲱⲥ ⲟⲩⲙⲏⲏϣⲉ ⲛ̄ⲣⲱⲙⲉ | ⲁⲩⲥⲱⲣⲙ̄	ⲛ̄ⲑⲉ ‹ⲛ̄›ⲧⲁⲩ|ⲙⲏⲏϣⲉ ⲛ̄ⲣⲱⲙⲉ
ⲉⲙⲡⲟⲩⲥⲟⲩⲛ̄ ⲧⲉⲉⲓ | ⲇⲓⲁⲫⲟⲣⲁ·	ⲥⲱⲣⲙ | ⲉⲛⲥⲉⲥⲟⲟⲩⲛ ⲁⲛ
ⲁⲩⲙⲟⲩ·	ⲛⲧⲉⲉⲓ ²⁰ⲇⲓⲁⲫⲟⲣⲁ ⲁⲩⲙⲟⲩ

who are awake." | Still he continued	address | those who are awake!"
[98] and said:	Still he continued | and said:
"Everything that came | from the	"Everything ¹⁰ that came from | the
perishable will perish, | since it	perishable will perish, since | it
came from | the perishable. But	comes from the perishable. |
whatever came ⁵ from	Whatever came | from
imperishableness does not perish |	imperishableness does not perish ¹⁵
but becomes imperishable.	but is imperishable, | since it is from
	| imperishableness. Just as | many
| So, many men | went astray	men went astray | because they did
because they had not known this |	not know this ²⁰ difference, (so) they
difference and they died."	died."

SJC-III:

98,1 So restored by T–S.

98,7 The section found in the parr. immediately before ϩⲱⲥ, "so," may be missing
    here through homoioteleuton (so also T–S).

NHC V 3,25–4,2

²⁵ [ⲁⲩⲱ ⲍⲱ] ϣⲁ ⲡⲉ[ⲓ̈ⲙ]ⲁ· ⲉ[ⲧⲃⲉ
ⲡⲓ]|[ⲁⲫⲑⲁⲣⲧⲟⲥ] ⲛ̄ⲛⲟⲩⲧⲉ ⲍⲛ̄
[7±] | [. . . . .] . ⲟ[.] ⲛ̄ⲧⲉ
ⲧ̣[10±] | [. . . . .]ⲟ̣ⲥ ⲛ.[.]
ⲧ̇ⲙ[11±] | [7±] ⲉ⳽[ⲟ]ⲩⲱϣ
[ⲉ]ⲛ[ⲁⲍⲧⲉ ⲉⲛⲓ]³⁰[ϣⲁⲭⲉ ⲉⲧⲕⲏ]
ⲉⲍⲣⲁⲓ̈ ⲛ̄[8±] | [8±]ⲉ

NHC III 74,7–17

ⲁⲩⲱ ⲍⲱ̄ ϣⲁ | ⲡⲉⲉⲓⲙⲁ· ⲉⲡⲓ ⲙⲛ̄
ϣϭⲟⲙ ⲛ̄ⲗⲁⲁⲩ | ⲉϯ ⲟⲩⲃⲉ
ⲧⲉⲫⲩⲥⲓⲥ ⲛ̄ⲛ̄ϣⲁⲭⲉ ¹⁰ ⲛ̄ⲧⲁⲉⲓⲣ̄
ϣⲣ̄ⲡ̄ ⲛ̄ⲭⲟⲟⲩ{ⲉ} ⲙ̄ⲡⲙⲁ|ⲕⲁⲣⲓⲟⲥ
ⲛ̄ⲁⲫⲑⲁⲣⲧⲟⲥ ⲛ̄ⲛⲟⲩⲧⲉ | ⲙ̄ⲙⲏⲉ·
ⲉϣⲱⲡⲉ ϭⲉ ⲉⲩⲛ̄ ⲟⲩⲁ | ⲉ⳽ⲟⲩⲉϣ
ⲡⲓⲥⲧⲉⲩ ⲉ ⲉⲛϣⲁⲭⲉ | ⲉⲧⲕⲏ ⲉⲍⲣⲁⲓ̈

ⲁ̅ ⲙⲁ[ⲣⲉ⳽ⲃⲱⲕ ⲉⲃⲟⲗ]
ⲍ̣[ⲓ ⲧⲛ̄ ⲛⲓⲁ ⲧ]ⲭ̣ⲓ ⲏ[ⲡⲉ ⲉⲣⲟⲟⲩ
ⲉⲧⲍⲏⲡ̄] | ⲉⲧ̣[ⲙ̄ⲙⲁⲩ·
ⲙ]ⲁ̣ⲣⲉ⳽[ⲙⲟⲩϣⲧ̄ ⲇⲉ ϣⲁ ⲡⲓⲭⲱⲕ] |

ⲙⲁⲣⲉ⳽ⲙⲟ ⲩϣⲧ̇ ¹⁵ ⲭⲛ̄ ⲙ̄ⲡⲉⲑⲏⲡ̄ ϣⲁ
ⲡⲭⲱⲕ ⲙ̄ⲡⲉ|ⲧⲟⲩⲁⲛⲍ ⲉⲃⲟⲗ ⲁⲩⲱ
ⲧⲉⲉⲓⲉⲛⲛⲟⲓ|ⲁ· ⲛⲁⲧⲥⲁⲃⲟ⳽

²⁵ [But this much is enough about
the] | [imperishable] God in [. . .] |
[. . .] of the [. . .] | [. . .] | [. . .]
who wants [to believe the] ³⁰ [words
set] down (here) [. . .] | [. . .],

But this much is | enough, since it is
impossible for anyone | to dispute
the nature of the words ¹⁰ I have just
spoken about the blessed, |
imperishable, true God. | Now, if
anyone | wants to believe the words
| set down (here),

4 let [him leave]
[the numberless things that are
hidden,] | [and] let him [go to the
end]

let him go ¹⁵ from what is hidden to
the end of what is visible, | and this
Thought | will instruct him

Eug-V:

3,25 Omission of circumflex with ⲍⲱ: see 17,7.

3,26 First superlinear stroke is in lacuna.

3,30 Superlinear stroke is in lacuna, but a circumflex is visible above what would have
    been the second letter in the second lacuna.

Eug-III:

74,10 Not emended by Tr.

74,11 "true God": less likely, "God of truth" (K & Tr).

NHC III 98,9–16

ⲡⲉϫⲁⲥ ⲛⲁϥ ⲛ̄ϭⲓ ⲙⲁⲣⲓϩⲁⲙⲙⲏ ϫⲉ ⲡϫⲟⲉⲓⲥ | ⲛ̄ⲁϣ ⲛ̄ϩⲉ ϭⲉ ⲉⲛⲛⲁⲥⲟⲩⲛ̄ ⲛⲁï | ⲡⲉϫⲉ ⲡⲧⲉⲗⲓⲟⲥ ⲛ̄ⲥⲱⲧⲏⲣ ϫⲉ | ⲁⲙⲏⲉⲓⲧⲛ̄ ϫⲓⲛ ⲛⲓⲁⲧⲟⲩⲱⲛϩ | ⲉⲃⲟⲗ ϣⲁ ⲡϫⲱⲕ ⲛ̄ⲛⲉⲧⲟⲩⲁⲛϩ· ⲁⲩⲱ ⲛ̄ⲧⲟⲥ ⲧⲁⲡⲟϩⲣⲟⲓⲁ ·ⲛ̄ⲧⲉ | ⲧⲉⲛⲛⲟⲓⲁ ⲛⲁⲟⲩⲱⲛϩ ⲛⲏⲧⲛ̄

Mary said to him: "Lord, | then how will we know that?" | The perfect Savior said: | "Come (pl.) from invisible | things to the end of those that are visible, and the very emanation of | Thought will reveal to you

BG 89,20–90,9

ⲡⲉϫⲁⲥ
ⲛⲁϥ ⲛ̄ϭⲓ ⲙⲁⲣⲓϩⲁⲙ ϫⲉ ⲡⲉ|ⲭ̅ⲥ̅ ϥ̄
ⲡⲱⲥ ⲥⲉⲛⲁⲥⲟⲩⲱⲛ | ⲛⲁï ⲡⲉϫⲁϥ ⲛ̄ϭⲓ ⲡⲧⲉⲗⲓⲟⲥ | ⲛ̄ⲥⲱⲧⲏⲣ ϫⲉ ⲁⲙⲏⲉⲓⲧⲛ̄ ϫⲓⲛ ⲛⲓⲁⲧⲟⲩⲱⲛϩ ⲉⲃⲟⲗ ϣⲁ | ⲡϫⲱⲕ ⲛ̄ⲛⲉⲧⲟⲩⲟⲛϩ ⲉ|ⲃⲟⲗ ⲁⲩⲱ ⲛ̄ⲧⲟⲥ ⲧⲁⲡⲟⲣⲣⲟⲓ| ⲁ ⲛ̄ⲧⲉⲛⲛⲟⲓⲁ ⲥⲛⲁⲟⲩⲱⲛϩ | ⲛⲏⲧⲛ̄

Mary said to him: | "Christ, how will 90
that be known?" | The perfect | Savior said: "Come (pl.) from invisible things to | the end of those that are visible, | and the very emanation | of Thought will reveal | to you

---

SJC-BG:

90,2 T–S suggests the third person pl. prefix of the verb may be the result of dittography (ⲡⲱⲥ); note that P.Oxy. 1081,26 supports the reading in *SJC*–III.

NHC V 4,3–12   NHC III 74,17–75,2

ⲚⲚⲎ ⲉ[ⲦⲞⲨ]ⲞⲚⲌ̄ ⲁⲨⲱ [ϤⲚⲁϬⲒⲚⲉ   Ϫⲉ ⲠⲰⲤ ⲦⲠⲒⲤⲦⲒⲤ | Ⲛ̄ⲚⲈⲦⲉ
Ⲛ̄ⲚⲒⲀ Ⲧ]|ⲞⲨⲱⲚ̣Ⲍ̄ [ⲌⲢ]Ⲁ̣Ⲓ̈ Ⲍ̄Ⲛ̄   Ⲛ̄ⲤⲈⲞⲨⲞⲚⲌ ⲈⲂⲞⲖ ⲀⲚ· ⲀⲨ|ϬⲚⲦ̄Ⲥ̄
ⲚⲈⲦ̣Ⲟ[ⲨⲞⲚⲌ̄· ⲦⲈⲚ]⁵ⲚⲞⲒⲀ ⲄⲀⲢ   Ⲍ̄Ⲙ̄ ⲠⲈⲦⲞⲨⲀⲚⲌ ⲈⲂⲞⲖ·
ⲉ̣[ⲤⲚⲀ]ⲦⲀⲘⲞⲞⲨ[· Ⲧ̄ⲠⲒⲤⲦⲒⲤ] | ⲄⲀⲢ
Ⲛ̄ⲦⲈⲚⲠⲈ ⲦⲈ ⲚⲎ ⲈⲦⲉ̣ Ⲛ̄Ⲥⲉ̣[ⲞⲨⲞⲚⲌ̄]
| ⲀⲚ ⲚⲈ ⲚⲎ ⲈⲦⲞⲨⲞⲚⲌ̄·
ⲦⲀⲒ̈ ⲆⲈ [ⲦⲈ ⲞⲨⲀⲢⲬⲎ] |
Ⲛ̄ⲦⲄⲚⲰⲤⲒⲤ ·   ⲞⲨ²⁰ⲀⲢⲬⲎ Ⲛ̄ⲤⲞⲞⲨⲚ ⲦⲈ ⲦⲀⲒ̈·

ⲠⲬⲞⲈⲒⲤ Ⲛ̄ⲦⲈ Ⲡ̄[ⲦⲎⲢ]ϥ̣ | Ⲛ̄ⲚⲈϢⲀⲨⲦ   ⲠⲬⲞⲈⲒ̄Ⲥ | Ⲙ̄ⲠⲦⲎⲢϤ ⲔⲀⲦⲀ
ⲢⲀⲚ ⲈⲢⲞϤ ⲀⲚ ⲔⲀ[ⲦⲀ Ⲧ]ⲘⲚ̄¹⁰ⲦⲘⲈ   ⲦⲀⲖⲎⲐⲈⲒⲀ Ⲙ[ⲈⲨ]|ϪⲞⲞⲤ ⲈⲢⲞϤ
ϪⲈ ⲠⲒⲰⲦ· ⲀⲖⲖⲀ ⲠⲒϢⲞⲢⲠ̄ Ⲛ̄ⲈⲒⲰⲦ | ϪⲈ ⲈⲒⲰⲦ· ⲀⲖⲖⲀ ⲠⲢ[Ⲟ]|ⲠⲀⲦⲰⲢ
ⲠⲒⲰⲦ ⲄⲀⲢ ⲞⲨⲀⲢⲬⲎ ⲠⲈ Ⲛ̄ⲦⲈ ⲚⲎ   ⲠⲈⲒⲰⲦ ⲄⲀⲢ ⲦⲀⲢⲬⲎ Ⲙ̄
ⲈⲦⲚⲎⲞⲨ | ⲈⲂⲞⲖ· ⲈⲂⲞ[Ⲗ]   ⲠⲈⲦⲞⲨⲀⲚⲌ [ⲈⲂⲞⲖ] ⲠⲈ ⲠⲈⲦⲘ̄|ⲘⲀⲨ   Ⲟ̣[ⲉ

| of those [that are visible], and [he will find the invisible things] | in those that [are visible.] For Thought ⁵ [will] teach them. For [the] higher [faith] | is (that) those things that are not [visible] | are those that are visible. And this [is a principle] | of knowledge.
The Lord of the [Universe] | was not rightly called ¹⁰ "Father" but "Forefather." | For the Father is the beginning (*or* principle) of those that are to come | through him, but the

how faith | in those things that are not visible was | found in what is visible.

This is a ²⁰ knowledge principle.

The Lord | of the Universe is not rightly | called "Father" but "Forefather." | For the Father is the beginning (*or* principle) of what is visible. For he (the Lord)   **7[5]**

Eug-V:

4,8 Third superlinear stroke is in lacuna.

4,10 First and second superlinear strokes are in lacuna.

Eug-III:

74,21 So restored by T–S.

75,1 T–S and Tr restore [Ⲍ ⲈⲂⲞⲖ Ⲡ].

NHC III 98,16–25 | BG 90,9–91,2

ⲉ|ⲃⲟⲗ· ϫⲉ ⲡⲱⲥ ⲧⲡⲓⲥⲧⲓⲥ ⲛ̄ⲛⲉ|ⲧⲉ
ⲛ̄ⲥⲉⲟⲩⲟⲛⲍ ⲉⲃⲟⲗ ⲁⲛ· ⲁⲩϭⲛⲧⲥ̄ |
ⲍⲛ̄ ⲛⲉⲧⲟⲩⲟⲛⲍ ⲉⲃⲟⲗ

ⲉⲃⲟⲗ ϫⲉ ⲡⲱⲥ ⲧⲡⲓⲥ ¹⁰ⲧⲓⲥ
ⲛ̄ⲛⲓⲁ ⲧⲟⲩⲱⲛⲍ ⲉⲃⲟⲗ ⲁⲩ|ϫⲉ ⲉⲣⲟⲥ
ⲍⲛ̄ ⲛⲉⲧⲟⲩⲟⲛⲍ ⲉ|ⲃⲟⲗ

ⲛⲉⲧⲏⲡ̄ ⲉ²⁰ⲡⲓⲁⲅⲉⲛⲛⲏⲧⲟⲥ ⲛ̄ⲉⲓⲱⲧ̄
ⲡⲉ | ⲧⲉ ⲟⲩⲛ̄ⲧⲩ̄ ⲙⲁⲁⲭⲉ ⲉⲥⲱⲧⲙ̄· |
ⲙⲁⲣⲉⲩⲥⲱⲧⲙ̄·
ⲡϫⲟⲉⲓⲥ ⲙ̄ⲧⲏⲣⲩ | ⲉϣⲁⲩϫⲟⲟⲥ
ⲉⲣⲟⲩ ⲁⲛ ϫⲉ ⲉⲓⲱⲧ̄ | ⲁⲗⲗⲁ
ⲡⲣⲟⲡⲁⲧⲱⲣ <· ⲡⲉⲓⲱⲧ̄ ⲅⲁⲣ> ⲧⲁⲣⲭⲏ
ⲛ̄ⲧⲉ ²⁵ ⲛⲉⲧⲛⲁⲟⲩⲱⲛⲍ ⲉⲃⲟⲗ <ⲡⲉ>·
ⲡⲉⲧⲙ̄

ⲛ̄ⲧⲉ ⲡⲓⲁⲅⲉⲛⲏⲧⲟⲥ ⲛⲉⲓ|ⲱⲧ ⲡⲉⲧⲉ
ⲟⲩⲛ ⲙⲁⲁⲭⲉ ⲙ̄|ⲙⲟⲩ ⲉⲥⲱⲧⲙ̄
ⲙⲁⲣⲉⲩⲥⲱ ¹⁵ⲧⲙ̄
ⲡⲉⲭⲥ̄ ⲙ̄ⲡⲧⲏⲣⲩ ⲉϣⲁⲩ|ϫⲟⲟ<ⲥ> ⲉⲛ
ⲉⲣⲟⲩ ϫⲉ ⲉⲓⲱⲧ | ⲁⲗⲗⲁ
ⲡⲣⲟⲡⲁⲧⲱⲣ ⲡⲉⲓⲱⲧ
ⲅⲁⲣ {ⲛ̄}ⲧⲁⲣⲭⲏ ⲛ̄ⲛⲉⲧⲛⲁⲟⲩ|ⲱⲛⲍ   ϥⲁ̄
ⲉⲃⲟⲗ ⲡⲉ ⲡⲉⲧⲙ̄ⲙⲁⲩ

| how faith in those | things that are
not visible was found | in those that
are visible,
those that belong to ²⁰ Unbegotten
Father. | Whoever has ears to hear, |
let him hear.

how faith ¹⁰ in invisible things was |
found in those that are visible

| of Unbegotten Father. | Whoever
has ears | to hear, let him hear.

The Lord of the Universe | is not
called 'Father' | but 'Forefather.'
<For the Father is> the beginning (*or*
principle) of ²⁵ those that will
appear, but he (the Lord)

¹⁵ The Lord of the Universe is | not
called 'Father' | but 'Forefather.'
For the Father is the beginning (*or*   **91**
principle) of those that will appear, |
but he (the Lord)

SJC-BG:

90,16 ⲉⲛ:<ⲁ>ⲛ (T–S). Emendation is not necessary (see Kasser: 2).

NHC V 4,12–22

ⲍⲓ ⲧⲟⲟⲧⲩ̄· ⲡⲓ ⲁ ⲧ ⲁ ⲣ ⲭ [ⲏ] ⲁ ⲉ |
ⲛ̄ⲛ ⲁ ⲧ ⲣ̄ ⲍ ⲁ [ⲉ] ⲉ ⳓ ⲱ ⲟ ⲟ ⲛ̄
ⲛ̄ⲛ ⲟ ⲩ ⲱ [ⲟ ⲣ] ⲡ̄ ⲛ̄ ⲉ ⲓ | ⲱ ⲧ·
ⲍ̄ⲓⲛ ⲁ ⲭ ⲉ ⲉ ⲛ ⲉ ⲟ ⲩ ⲱ ⲱ ⲉ ⲣ̄ ⲍ ⲙ ⲟ ⲧ̄ ¹⁵
ⲛ ⲁ ⳓ ⲛ̄ⲛ ⲟ ⲩ ⲣ ⲁ ⲛ· ⲟ ⲩ ⲅ ⲁ ⲣ
ⲛ ⲧ ⲛ̄ⲥ ⲟ ⲟ ⲩ ⲛ ⲁ ⲛ | ⲭ ⲉ ⲟ ⲩ ⲡ [ⲉ]·
ⲛ̄ⲟ ⲩ ⲟ ⲉ ⲓ ⲱ ⲁ ⲉ ⲛ ⲓ ⲙ ⲉ ⳓ ⲉ ⲓ ⲙ ⲉ | ⲉ ⲣ ⲟ ⳓ
ⲛ̄ⲍ ⲏ ⲧ ⳓ̄ ⲛ̄ⲑ ⲉ ⲛ̄ⲍ ⲣ ⲁ ⲓ̈ ⲍ ⲛ̄ ⲟ ⲩ ⲉ ⲓ ⲁ ⲉ ⲁ |
ⲉ ⲥ ⲟ ⲩ [ⲱ ⲛ] ⲍ̄ ⲉ ⲃ ⲟ ⲗ ⲉ ⲥ ⲉ ⲓ ⲛ ⲉ ⲙ̄ⲙ ⲟ ⳓ·
ⲛ̄ⲧ ⲟ ⳓ | ⲁ ⲉ ⲡ ⲉ [ⲡ ⲓ ⲥ ⲙ ⲟ] ⲧ̄ ⲛ̄ⲧ [ⲉ] ⳓ
[ⲉ ⲧ] ⲁ ⲩ ⲧ̄ [ⲣ] ⲁ̣ [ⲛ] ²⁰ ⲉ ⲣ ⲟ ⳓ ⲭ [ⲉ
ⲡ ⲓ ⲱ ⲧ̄ ⲛ̄ⲣ ⲉ̣ [ⳓ ⲭ ⲡ ⲟ] ⳓ ⲟ ⲩ ⲁ ⲁ ⳓ |
ⲡ ⲓ ⲣ [ⲉ ⳓ ⲙ̄ⲧ ⲟ ⲙ̄ⲡ ⲉ ⳓ ⲍ ⲟ·] ⲉ ⲡ ⲓ ⲁ ⲏ ⲍ ⲙ̄ |
ⲡ ⲓ ⲥ̣ [ⲙ ⲟ ⲧ] ⲛ̄ [ⲧ ⲉ ⳓ ⲉ ⲁ ⳓ ⲟ ⲩ ⲱ ⲛ] ⲍ̄

NHC III 75,2–9

ⲅ ⲁ ⲣ ⲡ ⲁ̣ ⲛ̣ [ⲁ] ⲣ̣ ⲭ ⲟ ⲥ ⲙ̄ⲡ ⲣ ⲟ | ⲡ ⲁ ⲧ ⲱ ⲣ

ⲉ ⳓ ⲛ ⲁ ⲩ ⲉ ⲣ ⲟ ⳓ ⲙ̄ⲙ ⲓ ⲛ | ⲙ̄ⲙ ⲟ ⳓ ⲛ̄ⲍ ⲣ ⲁ ⲓ̈
ⲛ̄ⲍ ⲏ ⲧ ⳓ̄· ⲛ̄ⲑ ⲉ ⲛ̄ⲟ ⲩ ⁵ ⲉ ⲓ ⲁ ⲗ·
ⲉ ⲁ ⳓ ⲟ ⲩ ⲱ ⲛ ⲍ ⲉ ⲃ ⲟ ⲗ ⲍ ⲙ̄ ⲡ ⲉ ⳓ | ⲉ ⲓ ⲛ ⲉ
ⲛ̄ⲁ ⲩ ⲧ ⲟ ⲡ ⲁ ⲧ ⲱ ⲣ ⲉ ⲧ ⲉ ⲡ ⲁ ⲓ̈ | ⲡ ⲉ
ⲡ ⲁ ⲩ ⲧ ⲟ ⲅ ⲉ ⲛ ⲉ ⲧ ⲱ ⲣ· ⲁ ⲩ ⲱ
ⲛ ⲁ ⲛ | ⲧ ⲟ ⲡ ⲟ ⲥ ⲉ ⲡ ⲓ ⲁ ⲛ ⲧ ⲟ ⲡ ⲓ ⲧ ⲱ
ⲙ̄ⲡ ⲣ ⲟ | ⲟ ⲛ ⲧ ⲟ ⲥ ⲛ̄ⲁ ⲅ ⲉ ⲛ ⲛ ⲏ ⲧ ⲟ ⲥ·

Unending Non-Principle (*or*
beginning) | is Forefather
| —in order that we might be ready
to greet ¹⁵ him by name. For we do
not know | who he is.
Now he always understands |
himself within himself as in a
semblance | that appears and
resembles himself. And it | is [his
resemblance that] was [called] ²⁰
"Self-[begotten Father,] | He [Who
Is before His Presence,"] since in |
[his resemblance he appeared

is | the beginningless | Forefather.

He sees himself | within himself,
like a ⁵ mirror, having appeared in
his | likeness as Self-Father, that is, |
Self-Begetter, and as Confronter, |
since he confronted | Unbegotten
First Existent.

Eug-V:

4,13 Third superlinear stroke is in lacuna.

Eug-III:

75,1–3 "he ... sees": less likely, "he, the Forefather without beginning, sees" (K &
Tr). The lack of a sentence pronoun may result from the scribe's sensing that it
would be stylistically unacceptable to put it in its expected place, either immediately before or after ⲅⲁⲣ, "for." Or perhaps ⲡⲉⲧⲙ̄ⲙⲁⲩ is thought of as a sentence
pronoun in this context by the scribe (but see 71,18–19).

75,8 "since he confronted": "in the presence of" (K) (?).

NHC III 99,1–10   BG 91,2–13

[ϥθ] ΜΑΥΔ[Ε ΠΙ]ΑΝΑΡΧΟC | ΔΕ ΠΙΑΝΑΡΧΟC ΠΕ Ν̄ϢR̄Π |
Ν̄ΠΡΟΠΑ|ΤΩΡ[·   Ν̄ΕΙΩΤ

ΕϤ]ΝΑΥ ΕΡΟϤ Μ̄ΜΙΝ Μ̄ΜΟϤ | ΕϤΝΑΥ ΕΡΟϤ Μ̄ΜΙΝ ⁵ Μ̄ΜΟϤ Ζ̄ΡΑΪ
Ν̄ΖΡΑ[Ϊ] Ν̄ΖΗΤϤ̄ ΖΝ̄ ΟΥΕΙΑΛ ·   Ν̄ΖΗΤϤ ΖΝ ΟΥ|ΕΙΑΛ ϢΑϤΟΥΩΝΖ
ΑϤΟΥ|ΩΝΖ ΕΒΟΛ ΕϤΕΙΝΕ Μ̄ΜΟϤ   ΕΒΟΛ ΕϤ|ΕΙΝΕ Μ̄ΜΟϤ Μ̄ΜΙΝ Μ̄ΜΟϤ
Μ̄ΜΙΝ ⁵ Μ̄ΜΟϤ Ν̄ΤΟϤ ΔΕ ΠΕϤΕΙΝΕ | Ν̄ΤΟϤ ΔΕ ΠΕϤΕΙΝΕ ΑϤΟΥ|ΟΝΖϤ
ΑϤ|ΟΥΩΝΖ ΕΒΟΛ· Ν̄ΟΥΝΟΥΤΕ   ΕΒΟΛ Ν̄ϢR̄Π ΝΕΙΩΤ ¹⁰ Ν̄ΝΟΥΤΕ
Ν̄ΕΙ|ΩΤ ΖΙΤΟΟΤϤ̄ Μ̄ΜΙΝ Μ̄ΜΟϤ | Ν̄ΕΙΩΤ ΑΥΩ Ν̄|ΑΝΤΟΠΟC ΕΠΙ
ΑΥΩ <Ν̄>ΑΝΤΟΠΟC † ΖΙΧΝ̄   ϤΜ̄ΤΟ ΕΒΟΛ | Μ̄ΦΟ Μ̄ΠΕΤϢΟΟΠ
ΝΑΝΤΟ|ΠΙΤΟΝ † ΠΕΠΡΟΟΝΤΟC   ΧΙΝΝ̄ | ϢΟΡΠ ΠΙΑΓΕΝΗΤΟC
Ν̄ΑΓΕΝ ¹⁰ΝΗΤΟC

99   is [the] beginningless Forefather. | is the beginningless | Forefather.

| Seeing himself | within himself in a   Seeing himself ⁵ within himself in a
mirror, he appeared | resembling | mirror, he appears | resembling
himself, ⁵ but his likeness appeared | himself, | but his likeness appeared |
as Divine | Self-Father | and <as>   as Forefather, ¹⁰ as Divine Father,
Confronter † over the confronted   and as | Confronter, since he is | in
ones, † | First Existent Unbegotten   the presence of Him Who Is from |
                                          the First, Unbegotten

---

SJC-III:

99,1–2 Lacunae not restored by T–S.

99,8–9 ΖΙΧΝ̄ ΝΑΝΤΟΠΙΤΟΝ : The parr. make clear that the translator mistook the
    Greek subordinate conjunction, ἐπεί, for the preposition, ἐπί, and attempted to
    transform the subsequent word into a noun.

SJC-BG:

91,8–9 ΑϤΟΥΟΝΖϤ, "his likeness *appeared*": Translation assumes that the Coptic
    translator was rendering a Greek aorist middle (see P.Oxy. 1081,45). Alt. "But he
    showed his likeness as . . ." (T–S).

NHC V 4,22–32　　　　　NHC III 75,9–15

ⲉ[ⲃⲟⲗ] ⲛ̄|ϣⲟ[ⲣⲡ̄ ⲙ̄]ⲡⲓⲁ[ϯ]ϫⲡⲟϥ·　　ⲟⲩⲍⲓ ¹⁰ⲥⲟⲭⲣⲟⲛⲟⲥ ⲙⲉⲛ ⲡⲉ
[ⲛⲉⲙⲛ̄ⲧⲉϥ ⲟⲩϣⲱϣ] | ⲛ̄[ⲭⲣⲟ]ⲛ̣ⲟⲥ　　ⲙ̄ⲡⲉⲧⲍⲁ|ⲧⲉϥⲍⲏ·
ⲙⲛ̄ ⲡⲏ ⲉⲧⲣ̄ ϣ[ⲟⲣⲡ̄ ⲉⲣⲟϥ
ⲛ̄]²⁵ⲟ[ⲩⲟⲉⲓⲛ ·]
ⲉϥⲙ̄ⲙⲉ ⲉⲣⲟϥ ⲁⲛ [ⲛ̄ϣⲟⲣⲡ̄· ⲁⲗⲗⲁ]
| [ⲛⲉⲙⲛ̄ ⲟⲩⲟ]ⲉⲓϣ ⲉϥⲉ
ⲛ̄ⲛⲁ[ϯϣⲱⲡⲉ· ⲉϥⲱ]|[ⲛ̄ⲍⲏⲧϥ
ⲛ̄ⲟ]ⲩⲟⲉⲓϣ ⲛⲓⲙ· [ⲁⲩⲱ
ϣⲁⲣⲉⲍⲟⲓ̈]|[ⲛⲉ ⲙⲉⲉ]ⲩⲉ ϫⲉ
ⲉϥϣⲏ[ϣ ⲟ]ⲩ̣[ⲃⲏϥ ⲁⲛ ⲍⲛ̄] | [ⲧϭⲟⲙ·　　ⲁⲗⲗⲁ ⲛ̄ϥϣⲏϣ ⲟⲩⲃⲏϥ | ⲁⲛ ⲍⲛ̄
ⲙⲛ̄ⲛⲥ]ⲱϥ ⲁϥⲟⲩⲱⲛ[ⲍ̄ ⲉⲃⲟⲗ] ³⁰　　ⲧϭⲟⲙ· ⲙⲛ̄ⲛ̄ⲥⲱϥ ⲁϥⲟⲩ|ⲱⲛⲍ ⲉⲃⲟⲗ
[7±]· ⲛⲏ ⲉ[ϯ]ⲛ̄ⲛⲁ ̣[5±] | [. . .　　ⲛ̄ⲟⲩⲙⲏⲏϣⲉ ⲛ̄ⲁⲛ|ⲧⲟⲡⲟⲥ
ⲙⲛ̄]ⲛ̣ⲥⲁ ⲇⲉ ⲍⲛ̄ ⲟ̣[8±] | [. . . . .　　ⲛ̄ⲁⲩⲧⲟⲅⲉⲛⲏⲥ ⲛ̄ⲍⲓⲥⲟ ¹⁵ⲭⲣⲟⲛⲟⲥ
ⲛ̄ⲁ]ⲩ̣ⲧⲟⲅⲉⲛⲏ[ⲥ 10±]

before] | Unbegotten. He was not　　¹⁰ He is indeed of equal age with the
equal] | [in age] with the one [before　　one who is before | him,
him, who is] ²⁵ [light,] since he did
not know him [at first. But] | [there
was no] time when he was [non-
existent, since he was] | always [in
him. And some] | [think] that he is　　but he is not equal to him | in power.
[not] equal [to him in] | [power.　　Afterward he revealed | many
Afterward] he revealed ³⁰ [. . .],　　confronting, | self-begotten ones,
who [. . .] | [. . .] And then in　　equal in age ¹⁵ (and)
[. . .] | [. . .] self-begotten [. . .]

Eug-V:

4,22–23 ⲛ̄ϣⲟ̣ⲟ[ⲣⲡ̄ ⲙ̄-], "[before]": The context requires that the Coptic be understood
relationally, although normally it would be construed temporally.

4,24–25 "him . . . [light]": See P.Oxy. 1081,49–50 for a reconstruction of the Greek.
ⲣ̄ ϣ[ⲟⲣⲡ̄ ⲉⲣⲟϥ], "[before]": See note to 4,22–23.

4,25–27 The reconstruction of these lines is somewhat conjectural, since only the cen-
tral portion remains in the MS and there are no parr. The reconstruction of the
second lacuna in line 25 may be two letters too long.

4,30 Superlinear stroke is in lacuna.

NHC III 99,10–16 BG 91,13–92,2

Ñ€ΙωΤ ΟΥ2ΙCΟΧΡΟ |ΝΟC ΜΕΝ ΠΕ   ΝΕΙωΤ | ΟΥ2ΪΟCΟΧΡΟΝΟC ΜΕΝ
{2}ΜΠΟΥΟΕΙΝ ΕΤ2Α|ΤΕΨΕ2Η   ΠΕ ¹⁵ ΜΠΕΤ2ΑΤΕΨΕ2Η ÑΝΟΥ|ΟΪΝ

ΑΛΛΑ ÑΨωΗω ÑΜΜΑΨ | ΑΝ 2Ñ   ΑΛΛ<Α> ΨωΗω ΟΥΒΗΨ ΑΝ | 2Ñ
Τ6ΟΜ· ΜÑÑCωΨ ΔΕ ΑΥΟΥ|ωΝ2   Τ6ΟΜ ΜÑÑCωΨ ΔΕ | ΑΨΟΥωΝ2
ΕΒΟΛ Ñ6Ι ΟΥΜΗΗωΕ   ΕΒΟΛ Ñ6Ι ΟΥΑ
ÑΑΝ¹⁵ΤΟΠΟC ÑΑΥΤΟΓΕΝΗC   ΤΟ ΝΑΝΤΟΠΟC ΝΑΥΤΟΓΕ|ΝΗC   Ψ̄Β̄
ΤΗΡΟΥ Ñ|2ΙCΟΧΡΟΝΟC   ΤΗΡΟΥ Ν2ΪCΟΧΡΟΝΟˋCˊ |

¹⁰ Father. He is indeed of equal age   Father. | He is indeed of equal age ¹⁵
| <with> the Light that is before | with the one before him, who is
him,   light,

but he is not equal to him | in power. | but he is not equal to him | in
And afterward was revealed | a   power. And afterward | was
whole multitude of confronting, ¹⁵   revealed a
self-begotten ones, | equal in age   whole multitude of confronting,   **92**
    self-begotten ones, | equal in age

SJC-III:

99,11 Not emended by T–S ("*in* the light").

SJC-BG:

91,15 "with ... light": "with that from the lights, which is before him" (T–S).
ÑΝΟΥΟΪΝ is most likely an attributive. The doubling of Ν before ΟΥ is a frequent
practice in BG (T–S: 21). See P.Oxy. 1081,49–50 for a reconstruction of the
Greek.

NHC V 5,1–9   NHC III 75,15–23

ē [8±]ɣⲱ[9±]ⲛ̄ | [7± ⲍⲛ̄]ⲛ ⲉⲟ[ⲟⲩ   ⲛ̄ⲍⲓⲥⲟⲇⲩⲛⲁⲙⲓⲥ ⲉⲩ|ⲍⲁ ⲉⲟⲟⲩ
ⲛ̄ⲛ]ⲁ†† ⲏⲡⲉ | [ⲉⲣⲟⲟⲩ· ⲛⲏ] ⲉⲧⲉ   ⲉⲙⲛ̄ⲧⲟⲩ ⲏⲡⲉ· ⲉϣⲁⲩ|ⲙⲟⲩⲧⲉ
ϣⲁⲩ[† ⲣⲁⲛ] ⲉⲣⲟⲟⲩ· | [ⲭⲉ   ⲉⲣⲟⲟⲩ ⲭⲉ ⲧⲅⲉⲛⲉⲁ ⲉ|ⲧⲉ ⲙⲛ̄
†ⲅⲉⲛⲉ]ⲁ· ⲛ̄ⲛⲁⲧⲣ̄ ⲣ̄[ⲣⲟ] ⲉⲍⲣⲁⲓ̈   ⲙⲛ̄ⲧⲣ̄ⲣⲟ ⲍⲓ ⲭ ⲱⲥ ⲛ̄ⲍⲣⲁⲓ̈ | ⲍⲛ̄
ⲉ ⲭ ⲱⲥ ⁵ [ⲛ̄ⲍⲣⲁⲓ̈ ⲍⲛ̄   ⲙ̄ⲙⲛ̄ⲧⲣ̄ⲣⲁⲓ̈ ⲉⲧⲕⲏ ⲉⲍⲣⲁⲓ̈
ⲛⲓⲙ]ⲛ̄ⲧⲣ̄ⲣⲱ[ⲟⲩ] ⲉⲧⲕⲏ ⲉⲍⲣⲁⲓ̈

| [ⲡⲓⲁ ⲧⲟ] ⲇ[ⲉ ⲧ]ⲏⲣ ⲩ̄ ⲛ̄ⲧⲉ ⲛⲓⲁⲧⲣ̄   ⲡⲙⲏ²⁰ⲏϣⲉ ⲇⲉ ⲧⲏⲣ ⲩ̄ ⲙ̄ⲡⲙⲁ ⲉⲧⲉ
ⲣ̄ⲣⲟ ⲉⲍⲣⲁⲓ̈ | [ⲉ ⲭ ⲱ]ⲟⲩ· ϣⲁⲩ† ⲣⲁⲛ   ⲙⲛ̄ | ⲙⲛ̄ⲧⲣ̄ⲣⲟ ⲍⲓ ⲭ ⲱ ϥ ϣⲁⲩ ⲭ ⲟⲟⲥ
ⲉⲣⲟⲟⲩ ⲭⲉ ⲛ̄|[ϣⲏⲣ]ⲉ ⲛ̄ⲧⲉ   ⲉ|ⲣⲟⲟⲩ ⲭⲉ ⲛ̄ϣⲏⲣⲉ
ⲡⲓⲁⲧⲙⲓⲥⲉ ⲙⲛ̄ ⲡⲓⲡⲣ̄ ⲣⲉ | [ⲉⲃ]ⲟⲗ   ⲛ̄ⲡⲁⲅⲉⲛⲛⲏ|ⲧⲟⲥ ⲛ̄ⲉⲓⲱⲧ·
ⲙ̄ⲙⲟϥ ⲟⲩⲁⲁ ϥ·

5 [. . .] | [. . . in] glory (and)   power, being | in glory and without
numberless, | [are those] who are   number, who are called | "The
[called] | ["The Generation] That Is   Generation over Whom | There Is
Kingless ⁵ [Among the] Kingdoms   No Kingdom among | the Kingdoms
That Exist."   That Exist."

| [And the] whole [multitude] of   And the whole multitude ²⁰ of the
kingless | ones are called | "[Sons]   place over which there is no |
of Unbegotten and Him Who | Put   kingdom is called | "Sons of
Forth Himself."   Unbegotten | Father."

Eug-V:

5,3 Translation assumes the second half of a cleft sentence begins here.

5,4 The punctuation is not a stop but seems to be a way of dealing with a Greek attributive adjective in the second position. Note that the parr. use a relative. See also 17,14–15 and 7,10 (related).

NHC III 99,16–100,4   BG 92,3–16

ⲍⲓ ⲍⲓⲥⲟⲇⲩⲛⲁⲙⲓⲥ | ⲉⲩⲍⲁ	ⲛⲍⲓⲥⲟⲇⲩⲛⲁⲙⲟⲥ ⲉⲩⲍⲁ ⲉ|ⲟⲟⲩ
ⲉⲟⲟⲩ ⲉⲙⲛ̄ⲧⲟⲩ ⲏⲡⲉ·	ⲉⲙⲛ̄ⲧⲉⲩ ⲏⲡⲉ ⲡⲁⲓ ⲉ⁵ⲧⲉ
ⲉϣⲁⲩ|ⲙⲟⲩⲧⲉ ⲉⲡⲉⲩⲅⲉⲛⲟⲥ	ϣⲁⲩⲙⲟⲩⲧⲉ ⲉⲡⲉⲩⲅⲉ|ⲛⲟⲥ ϫⲉ
ϫⲉ ⲧⲅⲉⲛⲉ|ⲁ· ⲉⲧⲉ ⲙⲛ̄ ⲙⲛ̄ⲧⲣ̄ⲣⲟ	ⲧⲅⲉⲛⲉⲁ ⲉⲧⲉ ⲙⲛ̄ | ⲙⲛ̄ⲧⲣ̄ⲣⲟ
ⲍⲓⲭⲱⲥ	ⲍⲓ̈ⲭⲱⲥ
†ⲉ²⁰ⲃⲟⲗ ⲍⲙ̄ ⲡⲉⲛⲧⲁⲧⲉⲧⲛ̄ⲟⲩⲱⲛⲍ	ⲡⲁⲓ̈ ⲛ̄ⲧⲁ|ⲧⲉⲧⲛ̄ⲟⲩⲱⲛⲍ ⲉⲃⲟⲗ
ⲛ̄|ⲍⲏⲧϥ̄ ⲍⲱ†ⲧⲏⲟⲩⲧⲛ̄ ⲉⲃⲟⲗ ⲍⲛ̄	ⲛ̄ⲍⲏ|ⲧϥ ⲉⲃⲟⲗ ⲇⲉ ⲍⲛ̄ ⲛⲓⲣⲱⲙⲉ ¹⁰
ⲛⲓ|ⲣⲱⲙⲉ ⲉⲧⲙ̄ⲙⲁⲩ·†	ⲉⲧⲙ̄ⲙⲁⲩ
ⲡⲙⲏⲛϣⲉ | ⲇⲉ ⲧⲏⲣϥ̄ ⲉⲧⲙ̄ⲙⲁⲩ ⲉⲧⲉ	ⲛ̄ⲧⲉ ⲡⲙⲁ ⲉⲧⲉ | ⲙⲛ̄ ⲙⲛ̄ⲧⲣ̄ⲣⲟ
ⲙⲛ̄ ⲙⲛ̄ⲧ|ⲣ̄ⲣⲟ ⲍⲓⲭ ⲱⲟⲩ ϣⲁⲩⲙⲟⲩⲧⲉ	ⲍⲓ̈ⲭⲱϥ ϣⲁ<ⲩ>|ⲙⲟⲩⲧⲉ ⲉⲣⲟ<ϥ>
ⲉⲣⲟ	ϫⲉ ⲡⲁⲅⲉⲛⲏ|ⲧⲟⲥ
ⲟⲩ ϫⲉ ⲛ̄ϣⲏⲣⲉ ⲙ̄ⲡⲁⲅ[ⲉⲛⲛ]ⲏⲧⲟⲥ |	
ⲛ̄ⲉⲓⲱ†	
ⲡⲛⲟⲩⲧⲉ ⲡⲥ[ⲱⲧ]ⲏⲣ | ⲡϣⲏⲣⲉ	ⲡⲛⲟⲩⲧⲉ ⲡⲥⲱⲧⲏⲣ | ⲛ̄ⲛ̄ϣⲏⲣⲉ ⲛⲧⲉ
<ⲙ̄>ⲡⲛⲟⲩⲧⲉ ⲡⲁⲓ̈ ⲉⲧⲉ | ⲡⲉϥⲉⲓⲛⲉ	ⲡⲛⲟⲩⲧⲉ ¹⁵ ⲡⲁⲓ̈ ⲉⲧⲉ ⲙⲛⲧⲁϥ ⲉⲓⲛⲉ
ⲛ̄ⲙ̄ⲙⲏⲧⲛ̄	ⲛⲙ̄|ⲙⲏⲧⲛ̄

P (margin marker beside line ⲟⲩ ϫⲉ)

and power, | being in glory (and)	| and power, being in | glory without
without number, whose race is called	number. ⁵ His race is called | 'The
| 'The Generation | over Whom	Generation | over Whom There Is
There Is No Kingdom'	No | Kingdom.'
† from the one ²⁰ in whom you	It is in this (race) that | you
yourselves have appeared | from	appeared. And by these men
these | men. †	
And that whole multitude | over	¹⁰ of the place over which | there is
which there is no | kingdom is called	no kingdom, <he> is called |
100 'Sons of Unbegotten | Father,	'Unbegotten,
God, [Savior], | Son of God,' |	| God, Savior | of the Sons of God,
whose likeness is with you.	¹⁵ He Who Has No Likeness |
	among You.'

SJC-III:

100,3 MS has ⲛ̄ (not emended by T–S).

SJC-BG:

92,11–12 MS has ϣⲁϥⲙⲟⲩⲧⲉ ⲉⲣⲟⲟⲩ (active instead of passive).

NHC V 5,9–21

ⲡⲓⲁⲧⲥⲟⲩⲱⲛϥ ¹⁰ ⲇⲉ ⲉϥⲙⲉϩ ⲉⲃⲟⲗ
ϩⲛ ⲉⲟⲟⲩ ⲛⲓⲙ ⲛ̄ⲁⲧ|ⲧⲁⲕⲟ ⲙⲛ̄
ⲟⲩⲣⲉϣⲉ ⲛ̄ⲛⲁⲧϣⲁϫⲉ | ⲉ̣[ⲣⲟ]ϥ·
ⲉ[ⲧ]ⲃⲉ ⲡⲁⲓ ⲛⲉϥⲕⲉϣⲏⲣⲉ | ⲧⲏⲣⲟⲩ
ⲟⲩⲛ̄ⲧⲁⲩ ⲙ̄ⲡⲓⲙ̄ⲧⲟⲛ ϩⲣⲁⲓ | ⲛ̄ϩⲏⲧϥ̄·
ⲉⲩⲣⲁϣⲉ ⲉⲩⲙⲏⲛ ϩⲙ̄ ¹⁵ ⲡⲉⲩⲉⲟⲟⲩ·
ⲛ̄ⲛⲁⲧϣⲓⲃⲉ ⲙⲛ̄ ⲡⲓⲧⲉ|ⲗⲏⲗ ⲛ̄ⲛⲁⲧϯ
ϣⲓ ⲉⲣⲟϥ· ⲡⲏ ⲉⲧⲉ ⲙ̄|ⲡⲟⲩⲥⲱⲧⲉⲙ
ⲉⲣⲟϥ ⲉⲛⲉϩ· ⲟⲩⲧⲉ
ⲙ̄|[ⲡⲟ]ⲩⲥⲟⲩⲱⲛϥ ϩⲣⲁⲓ ϩ<ⲛ̄>
{ⲡ}ⲕⲟⲥⲙⲟⲥ | ⲛⲓⲙ ⲛ̄ⲧⲁⲩ ⲙⲛ̄
ⲛⲉⲩⲁⲓⲱⲛ [·

ⲉ]ⲃⲟⲗ ²⁰ ⲇⲉ ϩⲙ̄ ⲡⲉⲓ̈ⲡⲓⲣⲉ ⲉⲃⲟ[ⲗ]
ⲙ̣̄ⲙⲟϥ ⲟⲩⲁⲁϥ | ⲁ[ⲥⲡ]ⲣ̄ⲣⲉ ⲉⲃⲟⲗ

Now the Unknowable ¹⁰ is full of
every imperishable glory | and
ineffable joy. | Therefore all his sons
also | have rest | in him, ever
rejoicing in ¹⁵ their unchanging
glory and the | measureless
jubilation that was | never heard of
or | known among all their | worlds
and aeons.

²⁰ Now from Him Who Put Forth
Himself | came forth

NHC III 75,23–76,12

ⲛ̄ⲧⲟϥ ⲇⲉ ⲡⲓⲁⲧⲛⲟⲉⲓ   ⲟ[ⲋ]
ⲙ̄ⲙⲟϥ ⲉϥ[ⲙⲏϩ ⲉ]ⲃⲟⲗ ⲛ̄ⲛⲁⲩ ⲛⲓⲙ |
ⲛ̄ⲁⲫⲑⲁⲣⲥⲓ̣ⲁ̣ [ⲙⲛ̄ ⲟ]ⲩⲣⲁϣⲉ
ⲛ̄ⲁⲧϣⲁ|ϫⲉ ⲉⲣⲟϥ ⲛ̄ⲧⲟⲟⲩ ⲧⲏⲣⲟⲩ
ⲉⲩⲙ̄ⲧⲟⲛ | ⲙ̄ⲙⲟⲟⲩ ⲛ̄ϩⲏⲧϥ̄· ⲉⲩⲙ̣ⲏ̣ⲛ
ⲉⲃⲟⲗ ⁵ ⲉⲩⲣⲁϣⲉ ϩⲛ̄ ⲟⲩⲣⲁϣⲉ
ⲛ̄ⲁⲧ{ⲧ}ϣⲁⲭⲉ | ⲉⲣⲟϥ ⲉϩⲣⲁⲓ̈ ⲉⲭⲙ̄
ⲡⲉⲟⲟⲩ ⲉⲧⲉ ⲙⲉϥ|ϣⲓⲃⲉ ⲙⲛ̄
ⲡⲧⲉⲗⲏⲗ ⲉⲧⲉ ⲙⲉⲩϣⲓⲧϥ̄· | ⲡⲁⲓ̈
ⲉⲧⲉ ⲙ̄ⲡⲟⲩⲥⲟⲧⲙⲉϥ ⲉⲛⲉϩ ⲟⲩ|ⲇⲉ
ⲙ̄ⲡⲟⲩⲛⲟⲉⲓ ⲙ̄ⲙⲟϥ ϩⲛ̄ ⲛⲁⲓⲱⲛ ¹⁰
ⲧⲏⲣⲟⲩ ⲙⲛ̄ ⲛⲉⲩⲕⲟⲥⲙⲟⲥ·
ⲁⲩⲱ | ϩⲱ̂ ϣⲁ ⲡⲉⲉⲓⲙⲁ ϫⲉⲕⲁⲁⲥ
ⲛ̄ⲛⲉⲛ|ⲃⲱⲕ ⲉⲃⲟⲗ ϩⲙ̄ ⲡⲓⲁⲡⲓⲣⲟⲛ·

Now the Unknowable
[is] ever [full] | of imperishableness
[and] ineffable joy. | They all are at   **7[6]**
rest | in him, ⁵ ever rejoicing in
ineffable joy | over the unchanging
glory | and the measureless
jubilation | that was never heard or |
known among all the aeons ¹⁰ and
their worlds.
But | this much is enough, lest we |
go on endlessly.

Eug-V:

5,13 Third and fourth letters: see Emmel, 1979: 183.

5,14 First two letters: see Emmel, 1979: 183.

5,18 First superlinear stroke is in lacuna. MS has ⲙ̄.

Eug-III:

76,1 K translates "[remains] always incorruptible," apparently restoring [ⲙⲏⲛ ⲉ]ⲃⲟⲗ.
Tr translates "And the unknowable [is] in every imperishableness and in ineffable
joy." For ⲛⲁⲩ ⲛⲓⲙ as "ever," see Crum: 235a.

76,2 T–S restores [ⲓⲁ] and [ⲟ] only. Tr restores [ⲓⲁ ⲁⲩⲱ ⲟ]. K has "in" (ϩⲛ̄) for
ⲙⲛ̄.

NHC III 100,4–16

ⲚⲦⲞϤ ⁵ Ⲇⲉ ⲡⲉ ⲡⲀⲦⲢⲚⲞⲈⲒ ⲘⲘⲞϤ· |
ⲉϤⲘⲉⲌ ⲚⲈⲞⲞⲨ ⲚⲒⲘ Ⲛ̄ⲀⲪⲐⲀⲢ|ⲦⲞⲚ
ⲌⲒ ⲢⲀϢⲉ Ⲛ̄ⲀⲦϢⲀϪⲈ ⲈⲢⲞϤ |
ⲚⲦⲞⲞⲨ ⲦⲎⲢⲞⲨ ⲤⲈⲘ̄ⲦⲞⲚ Ⲙ̄|ⲘⲞⲞⲨ
Ⲛ̄ⲌⲎⲦϤ̄· ⲈⲨⲘⲎⲚ ⲈⲂⲞⲖ ¹⁰ ⲈⲨⲢⲀϢⲉ
ⲌⲚ̄ ⲞⲨⲢⲀϢⲉ Ⲛ̄ⲀⲦϢⲀ|ϪⲈ ⲈⲢⲞϤ ⲌⲘ̄
ⲡⲉϤⲈⲞⲞⲨ ⲈⲦⲈ ⲘⲈϤ|ϢⲒⲂⲈ ⲘⲚ̄
ⲡⲦⲈⲖⲎⲖ ⲈⲦⲈ ⲘⲈⲨ|ϢⲒⲦϤ̄· ⲡⲀⲒ̈
Ⲙ̄ⲡⲞⲨⲤⲞⲦⲘⲈϤ Ⲉ|ⲚⲈⲌ ⲞⲨⲆⲈ
Ⲙ̄ⲡⲞⲨⲚⲞⲈⲒ ⲘⲘⲞϤ ¹⁵ ⲌⲚ̄ ⲀⲒⲰⲚ
ⲚⲒⲘ· ⲘⲚ̄ ⲚⲉⲨⲔⲞⲤ|ⲘⲞⲤ ϢⲀ
ⲦⲉⲚⲞⲨ·

Now he ⁵ is the Unknowable, | who
is full of every imperishable glory |
and ineffable joy. | They all are at
rest | in him, ¹⁰ ever rejoicing in
ineffable joy | in his unchanging
glory | and measureless jubilation; |
this was never heard | or known ¹⁵
among all the aeons and their worlds
| until now."

BG 92,16–93,12

ⲚⲦⲞϤ ⲆⲈ ⲡⲒⲀⲦⲚⲞⲒ̈ | ⲘⲘⲞϤ ⲈϤⲘⲎⲌ
Ⲛ̄ⲚⲈⲞⲞⲨ | ⲚⲒⲘ ⲌⲒ̈ ⲘⲚ̄ⲦⲀⲦⲦⲀⲔⲞ ⲌⲒ̈   ϙⲅ
ⲢⲀϢⲉ ⲚⲀⲦϢⲀϪⲈ ⲈⲢⲞϤ | Ⲛ̄ⲦⲞⲞⲨ
ⲆⲈ ⲦⲎⲢⲞⲨ ⲤⲈⲘ̄|ⲦⲞⲚ ⲘⲘⲞⲞⲨ
Ⲛ̄ⲌⲎⲦϤ ⲈⲨ|ⲘⲎⲚ ⲈⲨⲢⲀϢⲈ ⲌⲚ
ⲞⲨⲢⲀ⁵Ϣⲉ ⲚⲚⲀⲦϢⲀϪⲈ ⲈⲢⲞϤ ⲌⲘ̄ |
ⲡⲉϤⲈⲞⲞⲨ ⲈⲦⲈ ⲘⲈϤϢⲒ|ⲂⲈ ⲘⲚ̄
ⲡⲦⲈⲖⲎⲖ ⲈⲦⲈ ⲘⲀⲨ|ϢⲒⲦϤ ⲡⲀⲒ̈ ⲈⲦⲈ
Ⲙ̄ⲡⲞⲨ|ⲤⲞⲦⲘⲈϤ ⲈⲚⲈⲌ ⲞⲨⲆⲈ Ō ¹⁰
Ⲙ̄ⲡⲞⲨⲚⲞⲒ̈ ⲘⲘⲞϤ ⲌⲚ <Ⲛ̄>ⲀⲒ|ⲰⲚ
ⲦⲎⲢⲞⲨ ⲘⲚ̄ ⲚⲉⲨⲔⲞⲤ|ⲘⲞⲤ ϢⲀ
ⲦⲉⲚⲞⲨ

Now the Unknowable | is full of
every glory | and imperishableness
and

ineffable joy. | And they all are at   **93**
rest | in him, | ever rejoicing in
ineffable joy ⁵ in | his unchanging
glory | and the measureless
jubilation | that was | never heard or
even ¹⁰ known among all the aeons |
and their worlds | until now."

SJC-III:

100,8 A probably random drop of ink is above the second Ⲛ.

SJC-BG:

92,18 Corr.: first Ⲓ for partly erased Ⲧ.

NHC V 5,21–27   NHC III 76,13–17

ⲚϬⲒ ⲔⲈⲀⲢⲬⲎ ⲈⲂⲞⲖ | [ⲘⲠⲈϤⲬ]ⲡⲟ | ⲔⲈⲀⲢⲬⲎ ⲚⲤⲞⲞⲨⲚ ⲦⲈ ⲦⲀⲒ· ⲈⲂⲞⲖ
ⲞⲨⲀⲀϤ ⲘⲘⲞⲚⲞⲄⲈⲚⲎⲤ | [Ⲛ ϢⲀ Ⲭ Ⲉ]   ⲌⲒ|ⲦⲞⲞⲦϤ ⲘⲠ<ⲀⲨⲦⲞ> ⲄⲈⲚⲚⲎⲦⲞⲤ
ⲠⲀⲚⲦ Ⲱ Ⲥ·

ⲠⲎ ⲄⲀ[Ⲣ ⲈⲦⲀϤ]|ⲟ[ⲨⲰⲚⲌ] ⲈⲂⲞⲖ   ⲠⲈⲌⲞⲨⲈⲒⲦ ¹⁵ ⲚⲦⲀϤⲞⲨⲰⲚⲌ ⲌⲀⲐⲎ
ⲌⲀⲐⲎ ⲘⲠⲦⲎⲢϤ ²⁵ ⲌⲘ [ⲠⲒⲈⲰⲚ   ⲘⲠⲦⲎⲢϤ· | ⲌⲘ ⲠⲀⲠⲈⲢⲀⲚⲦⲞⲚ
ⲚⲚ]ⲀⲦⲚⲀⲢⲎⲬϤ ⲠⲒⲰⲦ [ⲈⲦ]|Ⲧ[ⲞⲨⲰ   ⲞⲨⲀⲨⲦⲞⲪⲨ|ⲎⲤ ⲠⲈ
ⲈⲂⲞⲖ] ⲘⲘⲞϤ ⲞⲨⲀⲀϤ· ⲈⲦ[Ⲉ] | ⲚⲀⲨⲦⲞⲔⲦⲒⲤⲦⲞⲤ ⲚⲈⲒⲰⲦ·
[Ⲛ]ⲀⲢⲬⲎ[·]

another principle | [from his] Only- | This is another knowledge
begotten, Wholly Unique | [Word;]   principle from | <Self->begotten.

for it is [in] him [who] | [appeared]   The First ¹⁵ who appeared before the
before the universe ²⁵ [in the] infinite   universe | in infinity is Self-grown, |
[aeon], the Father | [Who Put Forth]   Self-constructed Father,
Himself, who [is] | [the] principle
(*or* beginning),

Eug-V:

5,22 First three letters after the lacuna: see Emmel, 1979: 183.

5,22–33 See 17,11.

5,23 [Ⲛ ϢⲀ Ⲭ Ⲉ], "[Word]": or [Ⲛ ϢⲎ Ⲣ Ⲉ], "[Son]"; see III,2 (*Gos. Eg.*) 68,25–26 (ⲠⲈϤ-
ⲘⲞⲚⲞⲄⲈⲚⲚⲎⲤ Ⲛ ϢⲎ Ⲣ Ⲉ). The next sentence makes the reconstruction in the text
more likely.

ⲠⲀⲚ: see Emmel, 1979: 183.

5,24 ⲞⲖ: see Emmel, 1979: 183.

Eug-III:

76,13 "knowledge principle from": "beginning of knowledge. Through" (K & Tr).

76,14 "<self->begotten": "unbegotten" (K); Tr does not emend but translates
"unbegotten." Support for my emendation: 82,13–14 and V 5,20.

76,14–16 Both K & Tr have a comma after "-begotten" and a grammatical break after
"infinity."

NHC III 100,16–101,1   BG 93,12–94,2

пехач | нач ѓбі маѳѳаіос хе
пхо|еіс псштнр· пшс апршме
| оүшнг евол· пехе птеλі ²⁰ос
ѓсштнр· хе †оүшш |
етретѓеіме хе
пентач | оүшнг гаѳн ѓптнрч·
гѓ | папєранⲧон піаүтофүнс
ра   ѓаүтоктістос ѓеіш†

пехач | нач ѓбі маѳаіос хе |
пшс ачоүшнг евол ѓ ¹⁵бі
пршме пехач ѓбі | птеλіос
ѓсштнр хе †|оүшш
етретѓеіме | хе
пентачоүшнг гате|гн ѓптнрч
гм паперан ²⁰тон
паүтофүнс наүтоктіс|тос   ⲭⲁ
неіш†

Matthew said | to him: "Lord, |
Savior, how was Man revealed?" |
The perfect ²⁰ Savior said: "I want |
you to know that
he who | appeared before the
universe in | infinity, Self-grown,
101 Self-constructed Father,

Matthew said | to him: | "How was
Man revealed?" ¹⁵ The perfect |
Savior said: "I | want you to know |
that
he who appeared before | the
universe in ²⁰ infinity,
Self-grown, Self-constructed |
94
Father,

SJC-III:

100,21 Corr.: first ɴ for a ү (?); п for erased ɴ.

SJC-BG:

93,13 Corr.: an ı is erased immediately after ⲑ.

NHC V 5,27–6,5   NHC III 76,18–77,1

π[ʜ] ετε πϣα[x]ε ϣο[οπ] |
[ν̄ʒʜτ]q̄·
εqμεʒ εβολ ν̄ογοε[ιν] | [εqр̄
ογ]οειν ν̄[ν]ατ[ϣα]x[ε εροq·]
| 30 [ν̄ταρχʜ] ∆ε εqμεε[γε
ετρε]|[πεqειν]ε ϣωπ[ε
ν̄ογνοσ ν̄σομ ν̄]
ο[γοειν εq̄р̄] ογ[οειν 9±] |
ν̄τογ[νογ πιр]ωμ[ε ετε
ογαρχʜ πε] | ν̄τε [πογο]ειν
ετ̄μ̄μα[γ αqογων̄ʒ̄ μ̄]|πιεων
ν̄[ʒο]ογ†cʒî̄μ[ε ν̄νατμογ·
†]5μ̄ν̄†ʒοο[γ†] μεν ϣ[αγ† ραν
εроc]

|ζ

| εqxʜκ εβολ ʒ̄μ πογοειν
ετρογ|οειν ν̄ατϣαxε εροq
παϊ αqνο 20ει ν̄ταρχʜ
ετρεπεqεινε ϣω|πε ν̄ογνοσ
ν̄σομ· ν̄τεγνογ | αταρχʜ
μ̄πογοειν ετ̄μ̄μαγ | ογων̄ʒ
εβολ ν̄ογρωμε ν̄αθα|νατοc
ν̄ʒοογ†cʒιμε ·
πεqραν
μ̄μν̄†ʒ[οογ† ϣαγxο]οc εροq   [οʒ

that the Word | dwells,
full of shining, | [ineffable] light. 30
And [in the beginning,] when he
took thought | [to have] | [his
likeness] become [a great power of]
[6] [shining light . . . ,] | [immediately
Man, who is the principle (*or*
beginning)] | of that [light, appeared
as] | the androgynous [immortal]
aeon.
[The] 5 maleness [is called]

| and is full of shining, ineffable
light. | In the beginning, he decided
20 to have his likeness become | a
great power. Immediately, | the
principle (*or* beginning) of that light
| appeared as Immortal |
Androgynous Man. His male name
is   [77

Eug-V:

5,27–29 The left side of the text reflects fragment placements made by Stephen
Emmel on August 8, 1977, at the Coptic Museum, Cairo, which are not included in
the facsimile edition. The fragments are those numbered 1 and 40 in the facsimile
edition.

6,3 Second superlinear stroke is in lacuna.

Eug-III:

76,19–20 "In . . . become": "This one comprehended ("perceived"—K) the ἀρχή, so
that his appearance became" (T–S, K [similar] & Tr).

76,23 "appeared as" (so also T–S, alt. & Tr): "revealed" (T–S, alt. & K).

NHC III 101,1–8   BG 94,2–11

ⲉϥ|ϫⲏⲕ ⲉⲃⲟⲗ ⲙ̄ⲡⲟⲩⲟⲉⲓⲛ
ⲉⲧⲣ̄ⲟⲩ|ⲟⲉⲓⲛ ⲉⲩⲁⲧϣⲁϫⲉ ⲉⲣⲟϥ
ⲡⲉ | ⲉⲁϥⲛⲟⲉⲓ ⲛ̄ⲧⲁⲣⲭⲏ
ⲉⲧⲣⲉⲡⲉϥ⁵ⲉⲓⲛⲉ ϣⲱⲡⲉ ⲛ̄ⲟⲩⲛⲟϭ
ⲛ̄ϭⲟⲙ· | ⲛ̄ⲧⲉⲩⲛⲟⲩ ⲁⲧⲁⲣⲭⲏ
ⲙ̄ⲡⲟⲩⲟⲉⲓⲛ | ⲉⲧⲙ̄ⲙⲁⲩ ⲟⲩⲱⲛⲍ
ⲛ̄ⲟⲩⲣⲱⲙⲉ | ⲛ̄ⲁⲑⲁⲛⲁⲧⲟⲥ
ⲛ̄ⲍⲟⲟⲩⲧⲥⲍⲓⲙⲉ

ⲉϥϫⲏⲕ ⲉⲃⲟⲗ | ⲙ̄ⲡⲟⲩⲟⲉⲓⲛ ⲉⲧⲣ̄
ⲟⲩⲟⲉⲓⲛ | ⲉⲟⲩⲁⲧϣⲁϫⲉ ⲉⲣⲟϥ ⲡⲉ
ⲉϥ⁵ⲛⲟⲓ̈ ⲛ̄ⲧⲁⲣⲭⲏ ⲉⲧⲣⲉⲡⲉϥⲉⲓ |ⲛⲉ
ϣⲱⲡⲉ ⲍⲛ ⲟⲩⲛⲟϭ ⲛϭⲟⲙ |
ⲛ̄ⲧⲉⲩⲛⲟⲩ ⲉⲧⲙ̄ⲙⲁⲩ ⲁⲡⲟⲩⲟ|ⲉⲓⲛ
ⲛ̄ⲧⲁⲣⲭⲏ ⲉⲧⲙ̄ⲙⲁⲩ ⲟⲩ|ⲱⲛⲍ ⲉⲃⲟⲗ
ⲍⲛ ⲟⲩⲍⲟⲩⲉⲓⲧ ⲛ̄¹⁰ⲣⲱⲙⲉ
ⲛ̄ⲛ̄ⲁⲑⲁⲛⲁⲧⲟⲥ ⲛ̄|ⲍⲟⲩⲧⲥⲍⲓ̈ⲙⲉ

being full | of shining light and
ineffable, | in the beginning, when
he decided to have his ⁵ likeness
become a great power, | immediately
the principle (*or* beginning) | of that
light appeared as Immortal |
Androgynous Man,

being full | of shining light | and
ineffable, ⁵ in the beginning, when
he decided to have his likeness |
come to be in a great power, |
immediately the light | of that
principle (*or* beginning) | appeared
in a first ¹⁰ immortal | androgynous
man,

SJC-III:

101,4–5 "in . . . become": "when he comprehended the ἀρχή, so that his appearance
became" (T–S).

101,7 "appeared as" (so also T–S, alt.): "revealed" (T–S, alt.).

SJC-BG:

94,5–6 "in . . . power": "(he) comprehends the ἀρχή, so that his appearance comes in
great power" (T–S).

NHC V 6,6–11   NHC III 77,2–6

| ⲭⲉ ˋⲡ̄ˊⲛⲟⲩⲥ ⲛ̄ⲣⲉϥⲭⲡⲟ
[ⲉ]ⲧⲭⲱ[ⲕ ⲉⲃⲟⲗ] | ⲙ̄ⲙⲟϥ ⲟⲩⲁⲁϥˑ
ⲧⲉϥⲙⲛ̄ⲧⲥⲍ̂ⲓ [ⲙⲉ ⲇⲉ ⲭⲉ] |
ⲧⲉⲛⲛⲟⲓⲁ ⲧⲁ ⲛⲓⲥⲟⲫⲓⲁ̣ ⲧ̣ⲏⲣⲟⲩ
[ⲧⲣⲉϥ]|ⲭⲡⲟ ⲛ̄ⲧⲉ ⲛⲓⲥⲟⲫⲓⲁˑ

ϣⲁⲩⲧ ⲣ̣ⲁ[ⲛ ⲉ]ⲣ̣[ⲟⲥ] 10 ⲭⲉ ⲧⲙⲉˑ
ⲉⲡⲓⲇⲏ ⲥⲉϣⲏϣ ⲍ̄ⲛ ⲧϭⲁⲙ | ⲙⲛ̄
ⲛⲉⲩϣⲟⲣⲡ̄ ⲛ̄ⲉⲓⲟ ⲧⲉ

| ⲭⲉ ⲡⲉⲭ[ⲡⲟ ⲡⲛⲟⲩⲥ ⲉⲧ]ⲭ̣ⲏⲕ
ⲉⲃⲟⲗˑ | ⲡⲉϥⲣⲁ̣ⲛ [ⲇⲉ
ⲙ̄ⲙⲛ̄]ⲧⲥ̄ⲍⲓⲙⲉ ⲡⲁⲛⲥⲟ|ⲫⲟⲥ
ⲥⲟⲫⲓ ⲁ ⲛ̄ⲅ̣ⲉⲛⲉⲧⲉⲓⲣⲁˑ
ⲥⲉⲭⲱ 5 ⲙ̄ⲙⲟⲥ ⲉⲣⲟⲥ ⲟⲛ ⲭⲉ
ⲉⲥⲉⲓⲛⲉ ⲙ̄ⲡⲉⲥ|ⲥⲟⲛ ⲁⲩⲱ
ⲡⲉⲥⲥⲩⲛⲍⲩⲅⲟⲥˑ |

| "Begetter Mind Who Perfects |
Himself." [And] his femaleness (is
called) | "Thought, She of All
Wisdoms, Begettress | of the
Wisdoms."

| "[Begotten,] Perfect [Mind]."
| And his female name (is) "All-wise
| Begettress Sophia."

It is also said 5 that she resembles
her | brother and her consort.

[She] is called 10 "Truth,"—since
they are equal in power | with their
forebears

Eug-V:

6,6 The unusual stroke over ⲡ indicates that the letter, written above the line, should
be inserted (see 6,24; 7,17 [insertion from the margin]; 28,8.22). Although the
stroke seems to continue to the left of the letter in the MS, the line is almost certainly the result of the bleeding of the ink along a papyrus fiber.

Second superlinear stroke is in lacuna.

Eug-III:

77,2 ⲡⲉⲭ[ⲡⲟ: "Begotten": "the ... [nous]" (ⲡⲉⲛ[ⲟⲩⲥ) (K). The form of the Coptic
article suggests a noun with two initial consonants, and the trace of the first letter
suggests ⲭ rather than ⲛ. Tr restores ⲡⲉⲭ[ⲟⲉⲓⲥ, "the [Lord." Support for my
reconstruction: 82,14–15; V 10,20–21.

77,6–8 "consort ... truth": "consort, a truth against which there is no contention; for
as to the lower truth, the error that is with it" (K & Tr). Line 7 is not emended by
Tr.

NHC III   BG

NHC V 6,11–14	NHC III 77,6–9
ετε ⲛ̄ⲧⲟⲥ ⲧⲉ | ϯⲙⲛ̄ⲧⲙⲉ ⲛ̄ⲛⲁⲧⲣ̄ ⲙⲁ̣ⲁ̣[ⲍ] ⲉⲥ̣[ⲥⲟⲟⲩ]ⲛ̣ ⲙ̄|ⲙⲟⲥ ⲛ̄ⲍⲏⲧⲥ̄ ⲍⲙ̄ ⲡⲉⲧⲍⲏⲡ̇ ⲉ̣ⲩ̣ⲛ̄ⲧⲁⲥ | ⲛ̄ϯⲡⲗⲁⲛⲏ ⲉⲥϯ ⲉⲍⲣⲁⲓ̈ ⲉ ⲭⲱⲥ·	ⲟⲩ|ⲙⲏⲉ ⲉ{ⲩ}ⲙⲉⲩϯ ⲛ̄ⲙⲙⲁⲥ ⲧⲉ· ⲧⲙⲏ|ⲉ ⲅⲁⲣ ⲙ̄ⲡⲉⲥⲏⲧ̇ ϣⲁⲥϯ ⲛ̄ⲙⲙⲁⲥ | ⲛ̄ϭⲓ ⲧⲉⲡⲗⲁⲛⲏ ⲉⲧⲛ̄ⲙⲙⲁⲥ
—who is | indisputable truthfulness, [knowing] | herself within herself in secret, and having | error fighting against her.	| She is uncontested truth; | for here below error, which exists with truth, | contests it.

Eug-V:

6,12 ⲉⲥ̣[ⲥⲟⲟⲩ]ⲛ̣: The space in the lacuna seems sufficient for only three letters. One must assume therefore that the scribe either wrote very small or omitted something. Although the facsimile edition makes it appear that the final letter could be an ⲉ, ultraviolet examination suggests that ⲛ is more likely.

NHC III 101,9–19   BG 94,11–95,4

| ϫⲉⲕⲁⲁⲥ ⲉⲃⲟⲗ ϩⲓⲧⲛ̄ ⲡⲓⲣⲱⲙⲉ ¹⁰
ⲉⲧⲙ̄ⲙⲁⲩ ⲛ̄ⲁⲑⲁⲛⲁⲧⲟⲥ ⲉⲩⲉϯ |
ⲙⲁⲧⲉ ⲙ̄ⲡⲉⲩϫⲁⲓ̈ ⲛ̄ⲥⲉⲛⲏⲫⲉ |
ⲉⲃⲟⲗ ϩⲛ̄ ⲧⲃ̄ϣⲉ ϩⲓⲧⲛ̄
ⲫⲉⲣⲙⲏ|ⲛⲉⲩⲧⲏⲥ ⲛ̄ⲧⲁⲩⲧⲛ̄ⲛⲟⲟⲩϥ·
ⲡⲁⲓ̈ | ⲉⲧⲛⲙ̄ⲙⲏⲧⲛ̄ ϣⲁ ⲡϫⲱⲕ ⲉⲃⲟⲗ
¹⁵ ⲛ̄ⲧⲙⲛ̄ⲧϩⲏⲕⲉ ⲛ̄ⲛ̄ⲥⲟⲟⲛⲉ·
ⲧⲉϥ|ⲥⲩⲛⲍⲩⲅⲟⲥ ⲇⲉ ⲧⲉ ⲧⲛⲟϭ
ⲛ̄ⲥⲟ|ⲫⲓⲁ· ⲛ̄ⲧⲁⲩⲧⲟϣⲥ̄ ϫⲓⲛ
ⲛ̄ϣⲟⲣⲡ̄ | ⲛ̄ϩⲣⲁⲓ̈ ⲛ̄ϩⲏⲧϥ̄ ⲉⲩⲛⲟⲩϩⲃ̄
ϩⲓⲧⲛ̄ | ⲡⲁⲩⲧⲟⲅⲉⲛⲏⲥ ⲛ̄ⲉⲓⲱⲧ

ϫⲉⲕⲁⲁⲥ ⲉ|ⲃⲟⲗ ϩⲓ̈ⲧⲙ̄ ⲡⲓⲁⲧⲙⲟⲩ
ⲉ|ⲧⲙ̄ⲙⲁⲩ ⲛⲣⲱⲙⲉ ⲉⲩⲉϯ ⲙⲉ|ⲧⲉ
ⲙ̄ⲡⲟⲩϫⲁⲓ̈ ⲛ̄ⲥⲉⲛⲏⲫⲉ ¹⁵ ⲉⲃⲟⲗ ϩⲛ̄
ⲧⲃ̄ϣⲉ ⲉⲃⲟⲗ ϩⲓ̈|ⲧⲙ ⲡⲣⲉϥⲃⲱⲗ
ⲛ̄ⲧⲁⲩⲧⲁⲟⲩ|ⲟϥ ⲡⲁⲓ̈ ⲉⲧⲛⲙ̄ⲙⲏⲧⲛ̄
ϣⲁ | ϩⲁⲉ ⲛ̄ⲧⲙⲛ̄ⲧϩⲏⲕⲉ ⲛ̄ⲛ̄ⲥⲟ|ⲟⲛⲉ
ⲉⲧⲉϥϣⲃⲉⲉⲣⲉ ⲧⲉ ⲧ
ⲥⲟⲫⲓⲁ ⲧⲛⲟϭ ⲛ̄ⲧⲁ<ⲩ>ⲧⲟϣⲥ̄ | q̄ⲉ
ϫⲓⲛⲛ̄ ϣⲟⲣⲡ ⲛ̄ϩⲣⲁⲓ̈ ⲛ̄ϩⲏⲧ[ϥ] |
ⲉⲩⲥⲩⲛⲍⲩⲅⲓⲁ ϩⲓ̈ⲧⲙ
ⲡⲓⲁⲩ|ⲧⲟⲅⲉⲛⲏⲥ ⲛⲉⲓⲱⲧ

| that through that Immortal ¹⁰ Man
they might attain | their salvation
and awake | from forgetfulness
through the interpreter | who was
sent, who | is with you until the end
¹⁵ of the poverty of the robbers. And
his | consort is the Great Sophia, |
who from the first was destined in
him | for union by | Self-begotten
Father,

that through | that Immortal | Man
they might attain | salvation and
awake ¹⁵ from forgetfulness through
| the interpreter who was sent, | who
is with you until <the> | end of the
poverty of the robbers, | since his
companion is
Sophia, the great one, | who from the   **95**
first was destined in [him] | for
union by Self-begotten | Father.

SJC-III:

101,14 MS unaccountably has stroke over ⲱ.

SJC-BG:

94,11–13 "through . . . attain": "through this immortal one men might attain" (T–S).

95,1 MS has ϥ (active instead of passive).

NHC V 6,14–24 | NHC III 77,9–17

ⲉⲃⲟⲗ ⲇⲉ̣ ¹⁵ ⲍⲙ̄ ⲡⲓⲣⲱⲙⲉ
ⲛ̄ⲁⲧⲙⲟⲩ ⲁ ϥ ⲟⲩⲱⲛ ϩ̄ | ⲉⲃⲟⲗ
ⲛ̄ϣⲟ ⲣ ⲡ̄ ⲛ̄ ϭ ⲓ ⲡ ⲣ ⲁ ⲛ
ⲛ̄ϯⲙⲛ̄ⲧⲛⲟ[ⲩ]|ⲧⲉ ⲙⲛ̄ ϯⲙ ⲛ̄ ϯ ⲭⲟⲉⲓ ⲥ
ⲙⲛ̄ ⲟⲩⲙⲛ̄ⲧⲣ̄ⲣ[ⲟ] | ⲙⲛ̄ ⲛ ⲏ
ⲉ ϯⲙⲛ̄ⲛ̄ⲥⲱⲟⲩ ⲉⲃⲟⲗ ⲍ ⲛ̄ ⲛ ⲁ ⲓ̈ · | ⲡ ⲏ
ⲇⲉ ⲉ ⲧ ⲉ ⲩ ϯ ⲣ ⲁ[ⲛ] ⲉ ⲣ ⲟ̣[ϥ] ⲭⲉ
ⲡⲓ ϣ [ϯ] ²⁰ ⲡ ⲓⲣ ⲱ ⲙⲉ ⲛ̄ⲧⲉ ⲡ ϣⲱ ⲕ
ⲟⲩⲉⲓⲱ ϯ ⲉ ⲃ ⲟ̣[ⲗ] | ⲙ̄ⲙ[ⲟ]ϥ
ⲉ ⲧ ⲁ ϥ ⲟ ⲩ ⲱ ⲛ ϩ̄ ⲙ̄ⲡ ⲁ ⲓ̈ ⲉ ⲃ ⲟ ⲗ ⲁ ϥ |ⲭ ⲡ ⲟ
ⲛ ⲁ ϥ ⲛ̄ ⲟ ⲩ ⲛ ⲁ ϭ ⲛ̄ⲛ ⲉ ⲱ ⲛ ·

[ⲡⲣⲟ]ⲥ ⲧ[ⲉ]|ⲧⲉ ⲧⲱ ϥ ⲙ̄ⲙⲛ̄ⲧⲛⲁ ϭ ·
ⲟ ⲩ ⲛ ⲟ̣[ⲩ ϣ ⲃ ⲏ ⲣ] | ⲉ ϥ ϣ ⲟ ⲟ ⲡ̄ ϩ ⲛ̄
ⲟ ⲩ ϩ ⲱ `ⲧ̄´ ⲡ̇ ·

ⲉⲃⲟⲗ ¹⁰ ϩⲓⲧⲟⲟ ⲧ ϥ̄ ⲙ̄ⲡ ⲁ ⲑ ⲁ ⲛ ⲁ ⲧ ⲟ ⲥ
ⲛ̄ⲣⲱⲙⲉ | ⲁ ⲥ ⲟ ⲩ ⲱ ⲛ ϩ ⲉ ⲃ ⲟ ⲗ ⲛ̄ϭ ⲓ
ⲟⲩⲟⲛⲟⲙⲁ |ⲥ ⲓ ⲁ ⲛ̄ϣ ⲟ ⲣ ⲡ̄ ⲭ ⲉ
ⲙⲛ̄ⲧⲛⲟⲩ ⲧ ⲉ | ϩ ⲓ ⲙⲛ̄ⲧ ⲣ̄ⲣ ⲟ · ⲡ ⲓ ⲱ ⲧ̇
ⲅ ⲁ ⲣ ⲉ ϣ ⲁ ⲩ |ⲭ ⲟ ⲟ ⲥ ⲉ ⲣ ⲟ ϥ ⲭ ⲉ
ⲡ ⲣ ⲱ ⲙⲉ ⲛ̄ⲁ ⲩ ⲧ ⲟ ¹⁵ⲡ ⲁ ⲧ ⲱ ⲣ
ⲁ ϥ ⲟ ⲩ ⲱ ⲛ ϩ ⲙ̄ⲡⲉ ⲉ ⲓ ⲉ ⲃ ⲟ ⲗ |
ⲁ ϥ ⲧ ⲁ ⲙⲓ ⲟ ⲛ ⲁ ϥ ⲛ̄ⲟ ⲩ ⲛ ⲟ ϭ ⲛ̄ⲁ ⲓ ⲱ ⲛ

| ⲡ ⲣ ⲟ ⲥ ⲧ ⲉ ϥ ⲙⲛ̄ⲧ ⲛ ⲟ ϭ

Now ¹⁵ from Immortal Man very
soon appeared | the name of divinity
| and lordship and kingdom | and
those that came afterward from
them. | And he who is called
"Father, ²⁰ Man of the Depth, Self-
Father," | when he revealed this,
created | a great aeon
[for] | his own majesty.
There is [a companion] | in
conjunction

Through ¹⁰ Immortal Man |
appeared the first designation, |
namely, divinity | and kingdom, for
the Father, who is | called "Self-
Father Man," ¹⁵ revealed this. | He
created a great aeon

| for his own majesty.

Eug-V:

6,15–17 See endnote 4.

6,24 The stroke over ⲧ: see 6,6n.

Eug-III:

77,11 "appeared . . . designation": "first appeared a designation" (T–S, K [similar] &
Tr).

77,16 Corr.: ⲧⲁⲙⲓⲟ ⲛ for partly erased ⲧⲁⲛⲟ ⲛⲁ ϥ.

NHC III 101,19–102,5   BG 95,4–14

NHC III 101,19–102,5	BG 95,4–14
ЄΒΟΛ ZM ²⁰ ΠΑΘΑΝΑΤΟС ΝΡШΜΕ	ЄΒΟΛ ZÏ ⁵ΤΜ ΠΙΑ ΤΜΟΥ ΝΡШΜΕ
† ΝΤΑЧΟΥ|ШΝZ ЄΒΟΛ ΝϢΟΡΠ ZΙ	ΑΡΑ | † ΑΝΟΥШΝZ ЄΒΟΛ ΝϢΟΡΠ |
ΜΝΤΝΟΥ|ΤΕ ZΙ ΜΝΤΡΡΟ † ΠЄΙШΤ	{Ν}ZΜ ΜΝΤΝΟΥΤΕ ZÏ ΜΝΤΡ|ΡΟ †
ΓΑΡ ЄϢΑΥ	ΠЄΙШΤ ΓΑΡ ЄϢΑΥΧΟС | ЄΡΟЧ ΧΕ
ΜΟΥΤΕ ЄΡΟЧ ΧΕ ΠΡШΜΕ·	ΠΡШΜΕ ΠΑΥΤΟ¹⁰ΠΑΤШΡ {ΠΑΪ}
ΠΑΥ|ΤΟΠΑΤШΡ ΑЧΟΥШΝZ ΜΠΑΪ	ΑЧΟΥШΝZ <ΜΠΑΪ> Є|ΒΟΛ
Є|ΒΟΛ ΑЧΤΑΜΙΟ ΝΑЧ ΝΟΥΝΟϬ	ΑЧΤΑΜΙΟ ΝΑЧ ΝΟΥ|ΝΟϬ ΝΑΙШΝ
Ν|ΑΙШΝ	

(PB)

ЄΠЄЧΡΑΝ ΠΕ ZΟΓΔΟΑС	ЄΠЄЧΡΑΝ ΠΕ | ZΟΓΔΟΑС
⁵ ΠΡΟС ΤЄЧΜΝΤΝΟϬ	ΠΡΟС ΤЄЧΜΝΤ|ΝΟϬ

from ²⁰ Immortal Man † who appeared | as First and divinity and kingdom, † | **102** called 'Man, Self-Father,' | revealed this. | And he created a great aeon, |	Through ⁵ Immortal Man, then, | † we first appeared | in divinity and kingdom, † | for the Father, who is called | 'Man, Self- ¹⁰ Father,' revealed <this>. | And he created a | great aeon,
whose name is Ogdoad, ⁵ for his own majesty.	whose name is | Ogdoad, for his own majesty.

SJC-III:

101,21 ZΙ: <ZΝ> (T–S sugg.), resulting in the following rendering: "From Immortal Man he appeared first <in> (?) divinity. . . ." See endnote 4.

SJC-BG:

95,7 Alt. {ΝZ} ΜΜΝΤΝΟΥΤΕ, etc. (T–S), which results in the following rendering for lines 6 and 7: "we first revealed divinity and kingdom." See endnote 4.

95,10 Not emended by T–S ("*he* appeared"). It may be that the Coptic translator mistook αὐτόν for αὐτός (see III 102,2).

NHC V 6,24–31

ⲉⲁϥ[ϯ ⲛⲁϥ ⲛ̄ⲟⲩ]²⁵ⲛⲁϭ
ⲛ̄ⲛⲉϫⲟⲩⲥⲓⲁ · ⲁϥⲣ̄ⲣ̄ⲣ[ⲟ ⲉϩⲣⲁⲓ̈] |
[ⲉ̣ⲭⲱⲟ]ⲩ̣· ⲉⲁϥⲥⲱⲛⲧ̄ ⲛ̣ⲁ̣[ϥ
ⲛ̄ϩⲉⲛ]ⲛ̣ⲟⲩⲓ[ⲧⲉ] ⲙ̄ⲛ̄
ϩⲉⲛⲁⲣⲭⲁⲅⲅⲉⲗ[ⲟⲥ ϩⲉ]ⲛⲧⲃ[ⲁ̣
ⲙ̄]|[ⲙ̄ⲛ̄]ⲧⲁϯϯ ⲏⲡⲉ ⲉⲣⲟⲟⲩ [ⲉϩⲣⲁⲓ̈
ⲉⲩ]ⲯ̣ⲙ̄ⲯ̣[ⲉ·]

| ⲉⲃⲟⲗ ⲇⲉ ϩⲙ̄ ⲡⲁⲓ̈ ⲁ̣ⲥ̣ⲣ[ⲁⲣ]<ⲭ>ⲓ
ⲛ̄ϭⲓ̣ [ϯⲙ̄]ⲛ̄[ⲧ]³⁰[ⲛ]ⲟⲩⲧⲉ̣ ⲙ̄ⲛ̄
ϯⲙ̄ⲛ̄[ⲧ]ⲭⲁⲉⲓ̣ⲥ̣ [ⲙ̄ⲛ̄ ϯⲙ̄ⲛ̄ⲧ]|[ⲣ̄]ⲣⲟ̣·

to whom he [gave] ²⁵ great authority.
He ruled | [over them], having
created [gods] | and archangels,
unnumbered | myriads [for] retinue.

| Now from him [originated] divinity
³⁰ and lordship [and kingdom] | and

NHC III 77,17–24

ⲁϥϯ ⲛⲁϥ ⲛ̄|ⲟⲩⲛⲟϭ ⲛ̄ⲉϫⲟⲩⲥⲓⲁ ·
ⲁϥⲣ̄ ⲣ̄ⲣⲟ ⲉϩⲣⲁⲓ̈ | ⲉϫⲛ̄ ⲛ̄ⲥⲱⲛⲧ̄
ⲧⲏⲣⲟⲩ ⲁϥⲥⲱⲛⲧ̄ ²⁰ ⲛⲁϥ
ⲛ̄ϩⲉⲛⲛⲟⲩⲧⲉ ⲙ̄ⲛ̄
ϩⲉⲛⲁⲣⲭⲁⲅ |ⲅⲉⲗⲟⲥ ⲙ̄ⲛ̄
ϩⲉⲛⲁⲅⲅⲉⲗⲟⲥ ϩⲉⲛⲧⲃⲁ | ⲉⲙⲛ̄ⲧⲟⲩ
ⲏⲡⲉ· ⲉϩⲟⲩⲛ ⲉⲩϩⲩⲡⲏ|ⲣⲉⲥⲓⲁ

ⲉⲃⲟⲗ ϭⲉ ϩⲓⲧⲟⲟ ⲧϥ̄ ⲙ̄ⲡⲣⲱⲙⲉ |
ⲉⲧⲙ̄ⲙⲁⲩ ⲁⲥⲁⲣⲭⲉⲥⲑⲁⲓ ⲛ̄ϭⲓ
ⲧⲙ̄ⲛ̄ⲧ|

He gave him | great authority, and
he ruled | over all creations. He
created ²⁰ gods and archangels | and
angels, myriads | without number,
for retinue.

| Now through that Man | originated
divinity

Eug-V:

6,29 MS has ⲭ (a common scribal error for ⲭ).

6,29–31 The right side of the text reflects fragment placements made by Stephen
    Emmel on August 8, 1977, at the Coptic Museum, Cairo, which are not included in
    the facsimile edition. The fragments are those numbered 1 and 40 in the facsimile
    edition.

6,29–32 The left margin in the MS appears to have been shifted about one letter's
    width to the right, perhaps because of an imperfection in the sheet.

Eug-III:

77,23 T–S holds that the section found in *SJC* following ϩⲩⲡⲏⲣⲉⲥⲓⲁ is missing from
    Eug–III through homoioteleuton. However it seems more closely related to the
    Sondergut of *SJC* than to *Eug*.

NHC III 102,5–17 · BG 95,14–96,8

ⲁⲩϯ ⲛⲁϥ | ⲛ̄ⲟⲩⲛⲟϭ
ⲛ̄ⲉ3ⲟⲩⲥⲓⲁ ⲁϥⲣ̄ ⲣ̄ⲣⲟ | ⲉⲝⲙ̄
ⲡⲥⲱⲛⲧ̄ ⲛ̄ⲧⲙⲛ̄ⲧ2ⲏⲕⲉ | ⲁϥⲥⲱⲛⲧ̄
ⲛⲁϥ ⲛ̄2ⲉⲛⲛⲟⲩⲧⲉ | ⲙⲛ̄
2ⲉⲛⲁⲅⲅⲉⲗⲟⲥ ⟨ⲙⲛ̄⟩
2ⲉⲛⲁⲣⲭⲁⲅ ¹⁰ⲅⲉⲗⲟⲥ 2ⲉⲛⲧⲃⲁ
ⲉⲙⲛ̄ⲧⲟⲩ ⲏⲡⲉ | ⲉⲩϣⲙ̄ϣⲉ
ⲉⲃⲟⲗ 2ⲙ̄ ⲡⲟⲩⲟⲉⲓⲛ | ⲉⲧⲙ̄ⲙⲁⲩ ⲙⲛ̄
ⲡⲉⲡ̄ⲛ̄ⲁ̄ ⲛ̄ϣⲟ|ⲙⲛ̄ⲧ ⲛ̄2ⲟⲟⲩⲧ̄ ⲉⲧⲉ
ⲡⲁ ⲧⲥⲟ|ⲫⲓⲁ ⲡⲉ ⲧⲉϥⲥⲩⲛ2ⲩⲅⲟⲥ
ⲉ ¹⁵ⲃⲟⲗ ⲅⲁⲣ 2ⲙ̄ ⲡⲉⲉⲓⲛⲟⲩⲧⲉ
ⲁⲥ|ⲁⲣⲭⲉⲥⲑⲁⲓ ⲛ̄ϭⲓ
ⲧⲙⲛ̄⟨ⲧ⟩ⲛⲟⲩⲧⲉ | ⲙⲛ̄ ⲧⲙⲛ̄ⲧⲣ̄ⲣⲟ·

ⲁϥϯ ⲇⲉ ⲛⲁϥ ⲛ̄ⲛⲟⲩⲛⲟϭ ¹⁵
ⲛⲉ3ⲟⲩⲥⲓⲁ ⲁϥⲣ̄ ⲣ̄ⲣⲟ ⲉ2ⲣⲁⲓ | ⲉⲝⲛ
ⲛ̄ⲥⲱⲛⲧ ⲛ̄ⲧⲙⲛ̄ⲧ2ⲏ|ⲕⲉ ⲁϥⲥⲱⲛⲧ
ⲛⲁϥ ⲛ̄2ⲛ̄ⲛⲟⲩ|ⲧⲉ ⲙⲛ̄ 2ⲛ̄ⲁⲅⲅⲉⲗⲟⲥ
ⲙⲛ̄ 2ⲛ̄|ⲁⲣⲭⲓⲁⲅⲅⲉⲗⲟⲥ 2ⲛ̄ⲧⲃⲁ ⲉⲙⲛ̄   ⲕ̄ⲥ̄
ⲧⲉⲩ ⲏⲡⲉ ⲉⲩϣⲙ̄ϣⲉ
ⲉ|ⲃⲟⲗ 2ⲙ̄ ⲡⲟⲩⲟⲓ̈ⲛ ⲉⲧⲙ̄|ⲙⲁⲩ ⲙⲛ̄
ⲡⲉⲡ̄ⲛ̄ⲁ̄ ⲛ̄ϣⲙ̄ⲧ|2ⲟⲟⲩⲧ ⲉⲧⲉ ⲡⲁⲓ̈
ⲡⲉ ⲡⲁ ⲧ̄⁵ⲥⲟⲫⲓⲁ ⲧⲉϥϣⲃⲉⲉⲣⲉ

ⲉ|ⲃⲟⲗ ⲅⲁⲣ 2ⲙ̄ ⲡⲓⲛⲟⲩⲧⲉ
ⲁⲥ|ⲁⲣⲭⲉⲥⲑⲁⲓ ⲛ̄ϭⲓ ⲧⲙⲛ̄ⲧⲛⲟⲩ|ⲧⲉ
ⲙⲛ̄ ⲧⲙⲛ̄ⲧⲣ̄ⲣⲟ

He was given | great authority, and he ruled | over the creation of poverty. | He created gods | and angels <and> archangels, ¹⁰ myriads without number | for retinue from that Light | and the | tri-male Spirit, which is that of Sophia, | his consort.

¹⁵ For from this God originated | divinity | and kingdom.

| And he gave him great ¹⁵ authority, and he ruled | over the creations of poverty. | He created gods | and angels and | archangels, myriads without number for retinue **96** | from that Light | and the tri-male Spirit, | that is, that of ⁵ Sophia, his companion. | For from this God originated | divinity | and kingdom.

SJC-III:

102,7 Corr.: first ⲛ for ⲧ.

NHC V 6,31–7,8

Ẕ

ⲙⲛ̅ ⲛⲏ ⲉⲧⲟⲩⲏⲍ [ⲛ̅ⲥⲱⲟⲩ˙] | [ⲉⲧⲃ]ⲉ̣
[ⲡⲁⲓ̈] ⲁ̣ⲩ† ⲣⲁⲛ ⲉ[ⲣⲟϥ ϫⲉ ⲡⲛⲟⲩ]
[ⲧⲉ ⲛ̅ⲧⲉ ⲛⲓⲛⲟ ⲩⲧ]ⲉ̣ ⲡ̣[ⲓ ϫ ⲟ ⲉⲓⲥ
ⲛ̅ⲧ̣]ⲉ̣ | [ⲛⲓ ϫ ⲟ ⲉ ⲓⲥ ⲡⲓ ⲣ̅ ⲣ]ⲟ ⲛ̅ⲧ̣[ⲉ
ⲛⲓⲣ̅]ⲣⲱⲟⲩ˙ | [ⲁϥⲟⲩⲱⲛⲍ̅ ⲇⲉ ⲉ]ⲃⲟⲗ
ⲍ̅ⲙ [ⲡⲁ]ⲓ̈ ⲛ̅ϭⲓ ⲕⲉ|[7±]˳ⲟⲥ˙
ⲉⲧ̣[ⲉ] ⲟⲩⲡⲏⲅⲏ ⁵ [ⲡⲉ ⲛ̅ⲧⲉ ⲛⲏ
ⲉⲧ]ⲁⲩⲱϣ[ⲡ]ⲉ̣ ⲙⲛ̅ⲛ̅ⲥⲱϥ˙
| [ⲟⲩⲛ̅ⲧⲁϥ ⲇⲉ ⲛ̅ⲟ]ⲩⲛⲟⲩⲥ ⲙⲛ̅
ⲟⲩⲉⲛ|[ⲛⲟⲓⲁ]

ⲙⲛ̅ ⲟⲩⲱϣ˙ ⲟⲩⲙⲉⲉⲩⲉ ⲇⲉ | [ⲙⲛ̅]
ⲟⲩⲥⲃ̣[ⲱ] ⲙⲛ̅ ⲟⲩϣⲟϫⲛⲉ˙

NHC III 78,1–8

ⲛⲟⲩⲧⲉ ⲙ̣[ⲛ̅ ⲧⲙⲛ̅ⲧⲣ̅̅ⲣⲟ˙ ⲉ]ⲧⲃⲉ ⲡⲁⲓ̈
ⲁⲩ† | ⲣ̅ⲛ̣ϥ ϫⲉ ⲡⲛⲟⲩ[ⲧⲉ
ⲛ̅ⲛ̅ⲛⲟⲩ]ⲧ̣ⲉ˙ ⲡ̅ⲣ̅ⲣⲟ | ⲛ̅ⲣ̅ⲣⲱⲟⲩ˙
ⲡⲉⲍⲟ[ⲩⲉⲓⲧ̣ ⲛ̅]ⲣⲱⲙⲉ

| ⲧⲡⲓⲥⲧⲓⲥ ⲡⲉ ⲛ̅ⲛ̅[ⲉ]ⲧ̣ⲛⲁϣⲱⲡⲉ˙ ⁵
ⲙⲛ̅ⲛ̅ⲥⲁ ⲛⲁⲓ̈
ⲟⲩⲛ̅ⲧⲁϥ ⲛ̅ⲍⲏⲧ̅ϥ̅ ⲛ̅|ⲟⲩⲍⲓⲇⲓⲟⲛ
ⲛ̅ⲛⲟⲩⲥ ⲟⲩⲉⲛⲛⲟⲓⲁ˙

ⲛ̅|ⲑⲉ ⲉⲧⲉ ϥⲟ ⲛ̅ⲙⲟⲥ
ⲟⲩⲉⲛⲑⲩⲙⲏⲥⲓⲥ | ⲙⲛ̅
ⲟⲩ ϥ ⲣⲟⲛⲏⲥⲓⲥ ⲟⲩ ⲗ ⲟ ⲅ ⲓⲥ ⲙ ⲟⲥ

those that follow [them]. |
[Therefore he] was
called ["God

7   [of gods, Lord of] | [lords, King of]
kings." | [And] from [him appeared]
another | [. . .], who [is] the source
⁵ [of those who came] afterward. |
[Now he has] mind and [thought]

| and will, also thinking | [and
teaching] and counsel

[and kingdom]. Therefore he was | [78]
called "God of gods," "King | of
kings." First Man | is "Faith" for
those who will come ⁵ afterward.

He has, within, | a unique mind
(and) thought—just as | he is it
(thought)—(and) reflecting | and
considering, rationality

Eug-V:

7,3 Third superlinear stroke is in lacuna.

7,4 The trace immediately following the first lacuna is compatible with the tail of an ⲁ
or ⲙ.

Eug-III:

78,3–4 So restored by T–S (but superlinear stroke is omitted).

78,6–7 See endnote 5.

NHC III 102,17–103,1	BG 96,8–18

ετβε παϊ αγ|μογτε εροϥ xε	αγω ε|τβε παϊ αϥсмογ εροϥ ¹⁰
πνογτε ν|ννογτε· πῥρο	xε πνογτε ννΝογτε | αγω
νῥρωογ πε ²⁰ zογειτ νρωμε	πῥρο ννεῥωογ | πϣῥπ νρωμε

εγντaϥ μ|мaγ μπεϥ2ιΔιον	ογντaϥ | ммaγ 2рaϊ ν2нтϥ̄
ννογс | ν2рaϊ ν2нтϥ̄· мν̄	νογ|νογс επωϥ πε μμιν ¹⁵
ογεννοιa	ммοϥ мν̄ ογεννοιa
| ν̄θε ετϥ̄ο μμος	| ν̄τzε ετϥο μμος
ογφρονη|сιс ογενθγμηсις	ογ|ενθγмнсις мν̄
ογλογι|	ογφро|νнсις ογмεεγε
смос	

ρг

Therefore he | was called 'God of |	And therefore | he blessed himself ¹⁰
gods,' 'King of kings.' ²⁰ First Man	as 'God of gods' | and 'King of
	kings.' | First Man

has | his unique mind, | within, and	has, | within, a | mind, which is his
thought | —just as he is it	own, ¹⁵ and thought | —just as he is
(thought)— (and) considering, |	it (thought)— | (and) reflecting and
reflecting, rationality,	considering, | thinking

SJC-III:

102,23 See endnote 5.

SJC-BG:

96,9 αϥсмογ εροϥ, "he blessed himself": <αγμογτε> εροϥ, "he <was called>"
(T–S sugg.); <αγсмογ> εροϥ, "he <was blessed>" (T–S sugg.). In the context,
self-benediction does not seem inappropriate.

96,16 See endnote 5.

NHC V 7,8–18   NHC III 78,9–17

мм | [пн є]†д̂ⲓ x [м̄м] ογϣоⲭⲛⲉ
мм̄ ογϭⲟⲙ ¹⁰ [z]ⲉⲛⲙⲉⲗ[ⲟⲥ]
ⲛ̄ⲧⲉⲗⲓⲟⲥ · ⲁγⲱ ⲛ̄ⲛⲁ|ⲧⲙⲟ[γ·
ⲕⲁⲧ]ⲁ̣ ⲇⲉ †ⲁⲫⲑⲁⲣⲥⲓⲁ ⲉγ|ϣⲏϣ
ⲙⲛ̄ [ⲛ]ⲏ̣ ⲉ†ⲛⲉ ⲙ̄ⲙⲟⲟγ ⲉⲃⲟⲗ·
| ⲕ[ⲁⲧ]ⲁ̣ †ϭ[ⲟⲙ] ⲇⲉ
ⲥⲉϣⲃ̄ⲃⲓⲏⲟγ† ⲛ̄|ⲑⲉ ⲉⲧⲉ ⲟγⲱ†
ⲟγⲉⲓⲱ† ⲟγⲉ† ¹⁵ ⲟγϣⲏⲣⲉ· ⲁγⲱ
ⲡϣⲏⲣⲉ ⲉγⲉⲛⲛⲟⲓⲁ | †ⲉⲛⲛⲟⲓⲁ
<ⲁ>ⲉ ⲉⲥⲟγⲁⲧⲃ̄ ⲉⲛⲓⲕⲉϣⲱ |ⲝ̄ⲡ
ⲧⲏⲣⲟγ· ⲁγⲱ ⲛ̄ⲑⲉ ⲛ̄zⲣⲁ̈ⲓ zⲛ̄
ⲛⲓⲁⲧ̣|ⲭⲡⲟ· ⲉⲗⲉ†ⲙⲟⲛⲁⲥ

      | ⲙⲛ̄ ⲟγⲇγⲛⲁⲙⲓⲥ · ⲙⲉⲗⲟⲥ ⲛⲓⲙ
      ⲉ¹⁰ⲧϣⲟⲟ∏ zⲛ̄ⲧⲉⲗⲓⲟⲥ ⲛⲉ
      zⲛⲁⲑⲁⲛⲁ|ⲧⲟⲥ ⲛⲉ ⲕⲁⲧⲁ ⲙⲉⲛ
      ⲧⲁⲫⲑⲁⲣⲥⲓⲁ ⲥⲉ|ϣⲏϣ·
      ⲕⲁⲧⲁ ⲧϭⲟⲙ ⲟγⲛ̄ ⲟγⲇⲓⲁ|ⲫⲟⲣⲁ·
      ⲛ̄ⲑⲉ ⲛ̄ⲡϣⲓⲃⲉ ⲛ̄ⲟγⲉⲓⲱ† |
      ⲉγϣⲏⲣⲉ· ⲁγⲱ ⲟγϣⲏⲣⲉ
      ⲉγⲉⲛⲛⲟⲓⲁ ¹⁵ ⲁγⲱ ⲧⲉⲛⲛⲟⲓⲁ
      ⲉⲡϣⲱⲭ∏ ⲛ̄ⲑⲉ ⲛ̄|ⲧⲁⲉⲓϣⲣ̄∏
      ⲛ̄ⲭⲟⲟⲥ zⲛ̄ ⲛⲉⲛⲧⲁγⲭⲡⲟ|ⲟγ·
      ⲧⲙⲟⲛⲁⲥ ⲟ̂ ⲛ̄ϣⲟⲣ∏

—even | [that which] is over
counsel—
and power: ¹⁰ perfect and immortal
[attributes]. | Now [in respect to]
imperishableness, they are | [equal]
to [those] that resemble them. | But
[in respect to power], they are
different, just | as father differs from
¹⁵ son, and the son from thought, |
<and> the thought surpasses
everything else. | And in the (same)
way, among uncreated things, | the
monad

      | and power. All the attributes ¹⁰
      that exist are perfect and immortal. |
      In respect to imperishableness, they |
      are indeed equal.

      (But) in respect to power, there is a
      difference, | like the difference
      between father | and son, and son
      and thought, ¹⁵ and the thought and
      the remainder. As | I said earlier,
      among the things that were created, |
      the monad is first.

Eug-V:

7,10 First superlinear stroke is in lacuna. Punctuation: see 5,4n.

7,12 First word: see Emmel, 1979: 183 (line identified as 7,22 up).

7,16 ᴍs has ⲧ.

7,17 The stroke over ⲭ: see 6,6n. ⲭ is written in the left margin.

7,18 The F form of the nominal subject prefix of the present circumstantial is not
     found elsewhere in the codex; but see 29,6 for a similar form.

NHC III 103,1–10   BG 96,18–97,11

ⲟⲩϭⲟⲙ· ⲙⲉⲗⲟⲥ ⲛⲓⲙ ⲉⲩ|ϣⲟⲟⲡ̄   ⲙⲛ̄ | ⲟⲩϭⲟⲙ ⲙⲉⲗⲟⲥ ⲛⲓⲙ ⲉⲧ   [ϙ̄ⲍ̄]
ⲍⲛ̄ⲧⲉⲗⲓⲟⲛ ⲛⲉ ⲁⲩⲱ | [ϣⲟⲟⲡ ⲍⲛ̄ⲧⲉⲗ]ⲓ̣ⲟ̣ⲛ ⲛⲉ |
ⲍⲉⲛⲁⲑⲁⲛⲁⲧⲟⲛ ⲛⲉ ⲕⲁⲧⲁ ⲙⲉⲛ | ⲍⲛ̄|[ⲁⲧⲙⲟⲩ ⲛ]ⲉ̣ ⲕⲁⲧⲁ ⲙⲉⲛ |
ⲧⲁⲫⲑⲁⲣⲥⲓⲁ ⲥⲉϣⲏϣ·   ⲧⲙⲛ̄ⲧⲁⲧⲧⲁⲕⲟ ⲥⲉϣⲏϣ
ⲕⲁⲧⲁ ⲟⲩ⁵ϭⲟⲙ ⲥⲉϣⲟⲃⲉ· ⲛ̄ⲑⲉ | ⲕⲁⲧⲁ ⲇⲉ ⲧϭⲟⲙ ⲥⲉϣⲟ⁵ⲃⲉ ⲛⲑⲉ
ⲙ̄ⲡϣⲓⲃⲉ | ⲛ̄ⲟⲩⲉⲓⲱⲧ̄ ⲉⲩϣⲏⲣⲉ·   ⲙ̄ⲡϣⲓⲃⲉ ⲛⲟⲩ|ⲉⲓⲱⲧ ⲉⲩϣⲏⲣⲉ ⲙⲛ̄
<ⲁⲩⲱ ⲟⲩϣⲏⲣⲉ> ⲉⲩⲉⲛⲛⲟⲓⲁ · | ⲟⲩ|ϣⲏⲣⲉ ⲉⲩⲉⲛⲛⲟⲓⲁ ⲙⲛ̄
ⲁⲩⲱ ⲧⲉⲛⲛⲟⲓⲁ ⲉⲡϣⲱⲭⲡ̄ ⲛ̄ⲑⲉ | ⲟⲩ|ⲉⲛⲛⲟⲓⲁ ⲉⲡⲕⲉⲥⲉⲉⲡⲉ | ⲁⲩⲱ
ⲛ̄ⲛⲉⲛⲧⲁⲉⲓⲣ̄ ϣⲣ̄ⲡ̄ ⲛ̄ⲭⲟⲟⲩ ⲍⲛ̄ | ⲛⲑⲉ ⲛ̄ⲧⲁⲓ̈ⲭⲟⲟⲥ ⲛ̄¹⁰ϣⲟⲣⲡ
ⲛⲉⲛⲧⲁⲩⲭⲡⲟⲟⲩ ⲧⲙⲟⲛⲁⲥ   ⲧⲙⲟⲛⲁⲥ ⲍⲛ̄ ⲛ̄|ϣⲣ̄ⲡ̄ ⲛ̄ⲭⲡⲟ ⲁⲛ
ⲛ̄¹⁰ϣⲟⲣⲡ̄

103 power. All the attributes that exist | and | power. All the attributes that   **[97]**
are perfect and | immortal. In   exist are [perfect] (and) | [immortal].
respect to | imperishableness, they   In respect to | imperishableness, they
are indeed equal.   are indeed equal.

(But) in respect to ⁵ power, they are | But in respect to power, they are
different, like the difference | different, ⁵ like the difference
between father and son, <and son>   between | father and son, and | son
and thought, | and the thought and   and thought, and | thought and the
the remainder. As | I said earlier,   remainder. | Now, as I said ¹⁰
among | the things that were created,   earlier, the monad is not among the |
the monad is ¹⁰ first.   first creations.

SJC-III:

103,6 Erroneous omission noted by T–S.

SJC-BG:

97,10 ᴍꜱ has just one stroke over the last two letters.

97,10–11 ⲧⲙⲟⲛⲁⲥ . . . ⲁⲛ, "the monad . . . creations": T–S sees a textual corruption
    here and proposes that the text read ⲧⲙⲟⲛⲁⲥ ⲛ̄ϣⲟⲣⲡ or ⲧⲉ ⲧϣⲟⲣⲡ ⲍⲛ̄ ⲛ̄ϣⲟⲣⲡ
    ⲛ̄ⲭⲡⲟ, "the monad is the first among the first creations" (omitting ⲁⲛ). T–S may
    be correct, but see V par.

NHC V 7,18–28 | NHC III 78,17–24

ⲁⲩⲱ ϯⲁⲩⲁⲥ | ϣⲁϩⲣⲁⲓ̈
ⲉ[ⲛⲓⲁ]ⲉⲕⲁⲥˑ ⲛⲓⲁⲉⲕⲁⲥ ⲇⲉ 20
ⲥⲉⲣ̄ⲁⲣ<ⲭ>ⲓ ⲉϩⲣⲁⲓ ⲉⲭⲛ̄ |
ⲛⲓⲁⲛϣⲉˑ ⲛⲓⲁⲛϣⲉ ⲇⲉ
ⲥⲉⲣ̄ⲁⲣ<ⲭ>ⲉⲓ ⲉϩⲣⲁⲓ ⲉⲭⲛ̄ |
ⲛⲓⲁⲛϣⲟˑ ⲛⲓⲁⲛϣⲟ ⲇⲉ
ⲥⲉⲣ̄ⲁⲣ<ⲭ>ⲉⲓ | [ⲉ]ⲭⲛ̄ ⲛⲓⲁⲛⲧⲃⲁ ˑ
ⲡⲉⲓ̈ⲥⲙⲟⲧ ⲟⲛ ⲡⲉ | [ⲉⲧ]ϣⲟⲟⲡ ϩⲛ̄
ⲛⲓⲁⲧⲙⲟⲩˑ ϯⲙⲟⲛⲁⲥ 25 ⲇⲉ ⲙⲛ̄
ϯⲉ[ⲛ]ⲛⲟⲓⲁˑ ⲛⲁ ⲡⲓⲣⲱⲙ [ⲉ]
ⲛ̄|ⲛ[ⲁ]ⲧ[ⲙⲟⲩˑ] ⲛⲓⲙⲉⲉⲩⲉ ϣ[ⲱⲡⲉ]
| ⲉ<ⲛ>ⲇⲉⲕ[ⲁ]ⲥˑ ⲛⲓⲁⲛϣⲉ ⲇⲉ ⲛ[ⲉ
ⲛⲓⲥⲃⲟ]|ⲟⲩⲉˑ [ⲛⲓⲁⲛ]ϣ̣[ⲟ ⲇⲉ] ⲛⲉ

ⲥⲟⲩϩⲍ | ⲛ̄ⲥⲱⲥ ⲛ̄ϭⲓ ⲧⲁⲩⲁⲥ ⲙⲛ̄
ⲧⲉⲧⲣⲓⲁⲥ | ϣⲁϩⲣⲁⲓ̈ ⲉⲛⲣⲁⲙⲏⲧ
ⲛ̄ⲣⲁⲙⲏⲧ ⲇⲉ 20 ⲥⲉⲁⲣⲭⲓ ⲉⲭⲛ̄
ⲛ̄ⲣⲁϣⲉˑ ⲉⲣⲉⲛ̄ⲣⲁϣⲉ | ⲁⲣⲭⲓ ⲉⲭⲛ̄
ⲛ̄ⲣⲁϣⲟˑ ⲉⲣⲉⲛ̄<ⲣⲁ>ϣⲟˑ ⲁⲣ|ⲭⲓ
ⲉⲭⲛ̄ <ⲛ̄ⲣⲁ>ⲧⲃⲁˑ ⲡⲉⲥⲙⲟⲧ ⲡⲉ ⲡⲁⲓ̈
<ϩⲛ̄> | <ⲛ̄>ⲁⲑⲁⲛⲁⲧⲟⲥ ⲡⲉϩⲟⲩⲉⲓⲧ̄
ⲛ̄ⲣⲱ|ⲙⲉ ⲛ̄ⲧⲉⲉⲓϩⲉˑ ⲧⲉϥⲙⲟⲛⲁⲥ ⲧⲉ
(Coptic pages 79 and 80 are
missing.)

and the dyad | go up to [the] decads,
and the decads [20] rule the hundreds,
| and the hundreds rule | the
thousands, and the thousands rule |
the ten thousands. Again it is this
pattern | [that] exists among the
immortals: the monad [25] and the
thought are those things that belong
to [Immortal] Man. | The thinkings
[are] for | <the> decads, and the
hundreds are [the teachings,] | [and
the thousands] are the

The dyad | follows it, and the triad, |
up to the tenths. Now the tenths [20]
rule the hundredths; the hundredths |
rule the thousandths; the
thousand<th>s rule | the ten
thousand<th>s. This is the pattern
<among the> | immortals. First Man
| is like this: His monad

Eug-V:

7,19–22 See endnote 6.

7,20–22 MS has in each case x (a common scribal error for ⲭ).

7,24–25 "the monad . . . Man": see 7,6–7. Apparently mind, thought and will are
referred to. The punctuation in line 25 is a word separator but may also be
intended to replace a missing sentence pronoun.

7,26 Corr.: ϣⲟⲣⲡ̄, "first," is deleted at the beginning of the line by a dot over each
letter.

7,27 MS has ϯ (sing.).

Eug-III:

78,19–21 Tr translates the fractions as whole numbers without emending the text. See
endnote 6.

78,22 First emendation: MS has ⲛⲉ.

78,22–23 MS has ⲛ̄ϩⲛ̄, "*of* immortal*s*" (not emended by Tr, although his translation
reflects an emendation).

NHC V 7,28–8,8   NHC III

ⲛⲓϣⲟⲭⲛ [ⲉ·] | ⲛ[ⲓ]ⲁⲛⲧⲃⲁ [ⲇⲉ ⲛ]ⲉ
ⲛⲓ6ⲁⲙ · ⲛⲏ [ⲇⲉ ⲉⲧ]³⁰[ϣ]ⲱⲡⲉ
ⲉⲃ[ⲟⲗ ⲍⲛ̄] ⲛⲉ̣ⲧ̣[. . . . ⲥⲉ]|ϣⲟⲟⲡ̄
ⲙⲛ̄ ⲛⲉγⲁ[11±] | [ⲍ]ⲛ̣̄ⲛ ⲉϣ[ⲛ]
ⲛⲓⲙ [12±] | [. . .] . . [. .] ⲁ̣
ϣⲱ[10±]

[ⲏ̄]   ⲛ̄[7±] ⲁ̣ⲥⲟ[γⲱⲛ̄ ⲉⲃⲟⲗ ⲍⲙ̄] |
ⲡⲛⲟγ[ⲥ ⲛ̄]ⲧⲁⲣ[ⲭⲏ ⲛ̄6ⲓ †ⲉⲛⲛⲟⲓⲁ]
| ⲙⲛ̄ ⲛⲓⲙ [ⲉⲉ]γⲉ· ⲁ[γⲱ ⲉⲃⲟⲗ ⲍⲛ̄
ⲛⲓ]|ⲙⲉⲉγⲉ ⲛ̣[ⲓⲥ]ⲃⲱ· ⲉ[ⲃⲟⲗ ⲍⲛ̄
ⲛⲓⲥⲃⲱ] ⁵ ⲛⲓϣⲟⲭⲛ̣ [ⲉ·] ⲉⲃⲟ[ⲗ ⲍⲛ̄
ⲛⲓϣⲟⲭⲛⲉ] | ⲟγ6ⲟⲙ·
ⲙⲛ̄ⲛ̄ⲥⲁ [6]ⲉ ⲇⲉ ⲙ̄[ⲙⲉⲗⲟⲥ] |
ⲧⲏⲣⲟγ. ⲁ<ⲩ>ⲟγⲱⲛ̄ ⲉⲃ̣[ⲟ]ⲗ̣ ⲍⲛ̄
ⲛ̣[ⲉⲩ6ⲟⲙ] | ⲛ̄6ⲓ ⲡⲏ ⲧⲏⲣⲩ̣̄

counsels, | [and] the ten thousands
[are] the powers. [Now] those [who]
³⁰ come [from the . . .] | exist with
their [. . .] | [in] every aeon [. . .] |
[. . .]

[8]   [. . . In the beginning, thought] | and
thinkings [appeared from] mind, |
[then] teachings [from] | thinkings,
counsels ⁵ [from teachings], (and)
power [from] | [counsels].
And after all [the attributes,] | all
that [was revealed] | appeared from

Eug-V:

7,33 Corr.: γ deleted between ⲁ and ϣ by two superior dots.

8,4 ⲃⲱ: see Emmel, 1979: 183 (line identified as 8,30 up).

8,5 ⲉⲃ: see Emmel, 1979: 183 (line identified as 8,29 up).

8,7 Low dot probably indicates word separation; see 8,16n.

   ᴍs has γ (incorrect pl. pron.).

   ⲗ̣: see Emmel, 1979: 183 (line identified as 8,27 up).

NHC III 103,10–12   BG 97,11–14

<ⲛ>ⲑⲁⲏ ⲇⲉ ⲛ̄ⲛ̄ⲕⲁ ⲛⲓⲙ·   ⲛ̄ⲍⲁⲉ ⲇⲉ | ⲛ̄ⲕⲁ ⲛⲓⲙ ⲁⲩⲟⲩⲟⲛⲍ̄ⲟⲩ
ⲁⲩ|ⲟⲩⲱⲛⲍ ⲉⲃⲟⲗ ⲛ̄ϭⲓ | ⲉⲃⲟⲗ ⲍ̄ⲛ ⲧⲉⲩϭⲟⲙ ⲛ̄ϭⲓ |
ⲡⲉⲛⲧⲁⲩⲟⲩⲟⲛⲍ̄ϥ | ⲉⲃⲟⲗ ⲧⲏⲣϥ·   ⲡⲉⲛⲧⲁϥⲟ ⲩⲟⲛⲍ̄ϥ ⲧⲏⲣϥ

And after everything, | all that was   And finally he who | revealed it all |
revealed | appeared from his power.   revealed everything | from his
                                            power.

SJC-III:

103,11–12 "all … power": "all that was revealed from his power appeared" (T–S);
    less likely because of the Coptic punctuation and the parr.

SJC-BG:

97,11–14 "And … power": or "… he who wholly revealed himself …"; "But he
    brought to appearance the last (pl.) of all things from his power, namely, the one
    whom he brought to appearance completely" (T–S). The sentence appears to be
    corrupt; see parr.

NHC V 8,8–18   NHC III

ⲉⲧⲁⲩ[ⲟⲩ]ⲟ̣ⲛⲍ̄ϥ [ⲉⲃⲟⲗ] | ⲁⲩⲱ
ⲁ̣ϥ̣ⲟⲩⲱⲛⲍ̄ [ⲉⲃⲟⲗ] ⲍ̣ⲙ̄ ⲡⲏ̣
[ⲉⲧⲁⲩ]¹⁰ⲥⲟ<ⲛ>ⲧⲩ̣ ⲛ̄ϭⲓ ⲡ̣ⲏ
ⲉⲧⲁⲩⲙ̣[ⲟⲛⲕⲩ̄] ⲁⲩⲱ | ⲡⲏ ⲉⲧⲁⲩ†
ⲙⲟⲣⲫⲏ ⲛ[ⲁϥ ⲁ]ϥ̣ⲟ̣ⲩ̣ⲱⲛⲍ̄ | ⲉⲃⲟⲗ
ⲍ̄ⲙ̄ ⲡⲏ ⲉⲧⲁⲩ[ⲙⲟ]ⲛ̣[ⲕⲩ̄·] ⲡ̣ⲏ |
ⲉⲧⲁⲩ† ⲣⲁⲛ ⲉⲣⲟϥ· ⲁϥⲟⲩⲱⲛⲍ̄ |
ⲉⲃⲟⲗ ⲍ̄ⲙ̄ ⲡⲏ ⲉⲧⲁⲩ† ⲙⲟⲣⲫⲏ ⲛⲁϥ·
¹⁵ ⲉⲁ†ⲇⲓⲁⲫⲟⲣⲁ ⲛ̄ⲧⲉ ⲛ̣ⲏ
ⲉⲧⲁⲩⲭⲡⲟ|ⲟⲩ. ⲟⲩⲱⲛⲍ̄ ⲉⲃⲟⲗ ⲍ̄ⲙ̄
ⲡⲏ ⲉⲧⲁⲩ† ⲣ̣[ⲁⲛ] | ⲉⲣⲟϥ ⲭⲓⲛ
ⲧⲁⲣⲭⲏ ϣⲁ ⲁⲣⲏⲭ̣ϥ̄· ⲕⲁ̣ⲧ̣ⲁ̣ |
ⲟⲩϭⲟⲙ ⲛ̄ⲧⲉ ⲛⲓⲉⲱⲛ ⲧⲏ[ⲣ]ⲟⲩ·

[his powers.] | And [from] what
[was] ¹⁰ created, what was
[fashioned] appeared. And | what
was formed appeared | from what
was [fashioned.] | What was named
appeared | from what was formed, ¹⁵
while the difference among begotten
things | appeared from what was
[named], | from beginning to end, by
| power of all the aeons.

Eug-V:

8,8 ⲟ̣ⲛⲍ̄ϥ: see Emmel, 1979: 183 (line identified as 8,26 up).

8,9 ⲍ̣ⲙ̄: see Emmel, 1979: 184 (line identified as 8,25 up).

8,10 Last three letters and preceding superlinear stroke: see Emmel, 1979: 184 (line identified as 8,24 up). The stroke is visible in the MS. Emmel reports seeing a remnant of the letter under the stroke, but none is visible in a photo taken prior to removal of transparent tape.

8,11 ⲩ̣ⲱⲛⲍ̄: see Emmel, 1979: 184 (line identified as 8,23 up).

8,12 Final word: see Emmel, 1979: 184 (line identified as 8,22 up).

8,13 Final letter: see Emmel, 1979: 184 (line identified as 8,21 up).

8,16 Low dot after initial ⲟⲩ is not a stop; it makes clear word separation; cf. V 34,10.

NHC III 103,12–21

ⲉⲃⲟⲗ ⳥ⲛ̄ ⲧⲉϥϭⲟⲙ· | ⲁⲩⲱ ⲉⲃⲟⲗ
⳥ⲙ̄ ⲡⲉⲛⲧⲁⲩⲥⲟⲛⲧⲩ̄ | ⲁϥⲟⲩⲱⲛ⳥
ⲉⲃⲟⲗ ⲛ̄ϭ ⲓ ⲡⲉⲛⲧⲁⲩ ¹⁵ⲣ̄ⲡⲗⲁⲥⲥⲁ
ⲙ̄ⲙⲟϥ ⲧⲏⲣϥ· ⲉⲃⲟⲗ ⳥ⲙ̄ |
ⲡⲉⲛⲧⲁⲩⲣ̄ⲡⲗⲁⲥⲥⲁ ⲙ̄ⲙⲟϥ
ⲁϥ|ⲟⲩⲱⲛ⳥ ⲛ̄ϭ ⲓ ⲡⲉⲛⲧⲁϥϫⲓ
ⲙⲟⲣ|ⲫⲏ ⲉⲃⲟⲗ ⳥ⲙ̄ ⲡⲉⲛⲧⲁϥϫⲓ
ⲙⲟⲣⲫⲏ | ⲡⲉⲛⲧⲁⲩϯ ⲣⲁⲛ ⲉⲣⲟϥ
ⲉⲧⲃⲉ ⲡⲁⲓ̈ ²⁰ ⲁⲡϣⲓⲃⲉ ϣⲱⲡⲉ
ⲛ̄ⲛⲓⲁⲅⲉⲛⲛⲏ |ⲧⲟⲥ ϫⲛ̄ ⲛ̄ⲧⲁⲣⲭⲏ ϣⲁ
ⲁⲣⲏϫⲛⲟⲩ

BG 97,15–98,7

¹⁵ ⲁⲩⲱ ⲉⲃⲟⲗ ⳥ⲙ ⲡⲉⲛⲧⲁϥ|ⲥⲟⲛⲧϥ
ⲧⲏⲣϥ ⲁϥⲟⲩⲱⲛ⳥ | ⲉⲃⲟⲗ ⲛ̄ϭ ⲓ
ⲡⲉⲛⲧⲁⲩⲡⲗⲁⲥ|ⲥⲁ ⲙ̄ⲙⲟϥ ⲧⲏⲣϥ
ⲉⲃⲟⲗ | ⳥ⲙ ⲡⲉⲛⲧⲁⲩⲡⲗⲁⲥⲥⲁ ⲙ̄
ⲙⲟϥ ⲁϥⲟⲩⲱ[ⲛ⳥ ⲉⲃⲟⲗ ⲛϭ ⲓ] | **[ϥ̄ⲏ]**
ⲡⲉⲛⲧⲁϥϫⲓ ⲙⲟⲣⲫⲏ ⳥ⲙ |
ⲡⲉⲛⲧⲁϥϫⲓ ⲙⲟⲣⲫⲏ ⲡⲉ | ⲛ̄ⲧⲁⲩϯ
ⲣⲁⲛ ⲛⲁϥ ⲉⲃⲟⲗ ⳥ⲙ̄ ⁵ ⲡⲁⲓ̈ ⲁⲡϣⲓⲃⲉ
ϣⲱⲡⲉ ⲛ̄|ⲛⲓⲁ <ⲧ>ϫⲡⲟⲟⲩ ϫⲓⲛ
ⲧⲁⲣⲭⲏ ϣⲁ | ⲁⲣⲏϫⲛⲟⲩ

And from what | was created, | all
that was fashioned ¹⁵ appeared; from
| what was fashioned | appeared
what was formed; | from what was
formed, | what was named. Thus ²⁰
came the difference among the
unbegotten ones | from beginning to
end."

¹⁵ And from everything that he |
created, all that | was fashioned |
appeared; | from what was
fashioned,
appeared | what was formed; from | **[98]**
what was formed, | what was named.
From ⁵ this came the difference
among | the unbegotten things from
beginning to | end."

NHC V 8,18–28   NHC III

ⲡⲓⲣⲱ |ⲙⲉ ⲇⲉ ⲛ̄ⲁⲧⲙⲟⲩ ⲉϥⲙⲉϩ
ⲉⲃⲟⲗ ⲛ̄ⲛ̣[ⲉ]²⁰ⲟⲟⲩ ⲛⲓⲙ ˙
ⲛ̄ⲛⲁⲧⲧⲁⲕⲟ ⲙⲛ̄ ⲟⲩⲣⲁϣⲉ̣ |
ⲛ̄ⲛⲁⲧϣⲁⲭⲉ ⲙ̄ⲙⲟϥ˙
ⲉⲣⲉⲧⲉϥⲙⲛ̄ⲧⲣ̄|ⲣⲟ ⲧⲏⲣⲥ̄ ⲧⲉⲗⲏⲗ
ⲙ̄ⲙⲟⲥ ⲛ̄ϩⲏⲧⲥ̄ ϩⲛ̄ ⲟⲩ|ⲧⲉⲗⲏⲗ ⲛ̄ϣⲁ
ⲉⲛⲉϩ˙ ⲛⲏ ⲉⲧⲉ ⲙ̄ⲡ̣[ⲟⲩ]|ⲥⲱⲧⲙ̄
ⲉⲣⲟⲟⲩ ⲉⲛⲉϩ˙ ⲟⲩⲧⲉ
ⲙ̄[ⲡⲟⲩ]²⁵ⲥⲟ[ⲩ]ⲱⲛⲟⲩ ϩⲛ̄ⲛ ⲉ[ⲱ]ⲛ
ⲛⲓⲙ ⲉ[ⲧⲁϥ]|[ϣ]ⲱⲡⲉ ⲙⲛ̄ⲛ̄ⲥⲱ[ⲟ]ⲩ̣
[ⲙ]ⲛ̄ ⲛⲉϥⲕⲟ[ⲥ]|[ⲙⲟⲥ: ⲙⲛ̄ⲛ̄ⲥⲱϥ
ⲁⲥϣ[ⲱ]ⲡⲉ ⲛ̄ϭⲓ ⲕ̣[ⲉ]|[ⲁ]ⲣ̣ⲭⲏ ⲉⲃⲟⲗ
ϩ[ⲙ̄

Now Immortal Man | is full of every
²⁰ imperishable glory and ineffable |
joy. His whole kingdom | rejoices in
| everlasting rejoicing, those who
never | have been heard of or known
²⁵ in any aeon that | [came] after
[them and] its [worlds]. | Afterward
[another] | [principle] came from

NHC III 103,22–104,4   BG 98,7–13

| ṬOTE ΠΕϪΑϤ ΝΑϤ Ñϭ I
ΒΑΡΘΟΛΟ|ΜΑΙΟⳞ ϪΕ ΠⲰ Ⳟ
ΑⲨΟΝΟΜΑⲌΕ <ⲘⲘΟϤ> ⲌΙ

PΔ   ΠΕⲨΑ͞ΓΓΕΛ <I >ΟΝ ϪΕ ΠΡⲰΜΕ |
ΑⲨⲰ ΠϢΗΡΕ Ñ͞ΠΡⲰΜΕ ΠΕΕΙ|ϢΗΡΕ
ϭΕ ΟⲨΕΒΟΛ ⲌΝ̄ ΝΙΜ Ñ͞|ΜΟΟⲨ ΠΕ

ⲦⲞⲦⲈ ΠⲈϪⲀϤ | ⲚⲀϤ Ñϭ I
ΒⲀΡⲐⲞⲖⲞⲘⲀⲒ|ⲞⳞ ϪⲈ ΠⲰ Ⳟ
ⲀⲨⲘⲞⲨⲦⲈ ¹⁰ ⲈΡⲞϤ ⲌⲘ̄
ΠⲈⲨⲀⲄⲄⲈⲖⲒⲞⲚ | ϪⲈ ΠΡⲰⲘⲈ ⲀⲨⲰ
ΠϢⲎΡⲈ | Ñ͞ΠΡⲰⲘⲈ ΠⲒϢⲎΡⲈ
ⲞⲨⲈ|ⲂⲞⲖ ⲚⲀϢ Ñ͞ΜⲞⲞⲨ ΠⲈ

| Then Bartholomew | said to him:
"How (is it that) <he> was
designated in

104   the Gospel 'Man' | and 'Son of
Man'? | To which of | them, then, is
this Son related?" The

Then Bartholomew | said to him: |
"How (is it that) he was called ¹⁰ in
the Gospel | 'Man' and 'Son | of
Man'? | To which of them is the Son

NHC V 8,28–9,3　　　　　　　NHC III

ⲡ]ⲓ̣ⲣⲱ[ⲙⲉ] ⲛ̄ⲛⲁⲧⲙⲟⲩ[·] | ⲡ̣ⲏ ⲉⲧⲉ
ⲱⲁⲩϯ [ⲣⲁⲛ ⲉ]ⲣⲟϥ ⲭⲉ
ⲡⲓⲣⲉϥ ³⁰[ⲭⲡⲟ] ⲛ̄ⲭⲱⲕ ⲉ̣[ⲃⲟⲗ
ⲙ̄]ⲙⲟϥ ⲟⲩ[ⲁⲁϥ·] | [ⲛ̄ⲧⲉⲣⲉϥⲭⲓ
ⲡⲓϯ] ⲙⲉ̣ⲧⲉ̣ ⲛ̄ⲧⲉϥⲥⲩⲛ[ⲍⲩⲅⲟⲥ] |
[ϯⲛⲟϭ ⲛ̄ⲥⲟⲫⲓⲁ ⲁϥ]ⲟⲩⲱⲛ̄ⲍ̄ ⲉⲃ[ⲟⲗ
ⲙ̄]|[ⲡⲓϣⲟⲣⲡ̄ ⲙ̄ⲙⲓⲥⲉ ⲉⲧ]ⲙ̄ⲙⲁ[ⲩ]
ⲛ̄ⲍ[ⲟⲟⲩⲧ]

[ⲑ̄]　[ⲥⲍ̂ⲓⲙⲉ· ⲡⲏ ⲉⲧ]ⲉ̣ ϣⲁ̣[ⲩϯ ⲣ]ⲁⲛ |
　　　[ⲉⲣⲟϥ ⲭⲉ ⲡⲓϣⲏⲣⲉ] ⲛ̄ϣⲟⲣ[ⲡ̄]
　　　ⲙ̄ⲙⲓⲥⲉ | [ⲛ̄ⲧⲉ ⲡⲛⲟⲩⲧⲉ]·

Immortal [Man], | who is [called]
"Self-perfected ³⁰ [Begetter.]" |
[When he received the consent] of
his [consort,] | [Great Sophia, he]
revealed | [that first-begotten
androgyne,]

[9]　[who is called] | "First-begotten
[Son] | [of God]."

Eug-V:

8,33 Third superlinear stroke is in lacuna.

9,1 Corr.: ⲛ incorporates initial ϥ (cf. 2,18n.).

9,2 First superlinear stroke is in lacuna.

NHC III 104,4–16

ΠΕΧΑϤ ΝΑϤ Ν̄ϬΙ ⁵ ΠΕΤΟΥΑΑΒ· ΧΕ
†ΟΥѠѠ· ΕΤΡΕ|ΤΝ̄ΕΙΜΕ ΧΕ
ΠΕϨΟΥΕΙΤ Ν̄ΡѠ|ΜΕ ϢΑΥΜΟΥΤΕ
ΕΡΟϤ ΧΕ | ΠΡΕϤΧΠΟ ΠΝΟΥϹ
ΕΤΧΗΚ | ΕΒΟΛ ϨΙΤΟΟΤϤ̄ Μ̄ΜΙΝ
Μ̄ΜΟϤ ¹⁰ ΠΑΪ ΑϤΕΝΘΥΜΕΙ ΜΝ̄
ΤΝΟϬ Ν̄|ϹΟΦΙΑ ΤΕϤϹΥΝϨΥΓΟϹ
ΑϤΟΥ|ѠΝϨ ΕΒΟΛ Μ̄ΠΕϤϢΟΡΠ̄
Ν̄ΧΠΟ | Ν̄ϢΗΡΕ Ν̄ϨΟΟΥΤϹϨΙΜΕ
ΠΕϤ|ΡΑΝ Ν̄ϨΟΟΥΤ ϢΑΥΜΟΥΤΕ
Ε ¹⁵ΡΟϤ ΧΕ ΠΡѠΤΟΓΕΝΕΤѠΡ ·
Ν̄|ϢΗΡΕ Μ̄ΠΝΟΥΤΕ·

BG 98,13–99,9

ΠΕ|ΧΑϤ Ν̄ϬΙ ΠΕΤΟΥΑΑΒ ΧΕ ¹⁵
†ΟΥѠѠ ΕΤΡΕΤΝ̄ΕΙΜΕ | ΧΕ
ΠΕϨΟΥΕΙΤ Ν̄ΡѠΜΕ Ε|ΤΕ
ϢΑΥΧΟΟϹ ΕΡΟϤ ΧΕ ΠΡΕϤ|ΧΠΟ
ΠΝΟΥϹ ΝΑΥΤΟΤΕ
[ΛΙΟϹ ΠΑΙ ΑϤΕΝ]ΘΥΜΕΙ ΜΝ̄ | [Ϥ̄Θ̄]
ΤΕΕΙΝΟϬ ΝϹ]ΟΦΙΑ ΤΕϤ|Ϣ[ΒΕ]ΕΡ
ΑϤΟΥѠΝϨ ΕΒΟΛ |
Μ̄ΠΕϤΠΡΟΤ<Ο>ΓΕΝ<ΗΤΟϹ> ⁵
Ν̄ϢΗΡΕ Ν̄ϨΟΥΤϹϨΙΜΕ | ΠΑΪ ΕΤΕ
ΠΕϤΡΑΝ Ν̄ϨΟ|ΟΥΤ ΠΕ
ΠΡΟΤΟΓΕΝΕ|ΤѠΡ ΠϢΗΡΕ
Μ̄ΠΝΟΥ|ΤΕ

Holy One ⁵ said to him: "I want you | to know that First Man | is called | 'Begetter, Self-perfected | Mind.' ¹⁰ He reflected with Great | Sophia, his consort, and revealed | his first-begetten, | androgynous son. His | male name ¹⁵ is called 'First Begetter | Son of God';

related?" | The Holy One said: ¹⁵ "I want you to know | that First Man, who | is called | 'Begetter, Self-perfected Mind,' reflected with | [this Great]   **[99]** Sophia, his | companion, and revealed | his first-<begotten>, ⁵ androgynous son, | whose male name | is First Begetter, | Son of God,

---

SJC-BG:

98,18–99,1 T–S mistakes the last 7 letters of 98,18 for two words and divides thus: ΝΑΥ, "to them" and ΤΟΤΕ, "then." The latter word is made the beginning of a new sentence, which is continued by T–S on 99,1 with the questionable restoration of ΟΥΝ.

99,3 Alt. ϢΒΕΕΡ<Ε> (T–S; unnecessary since ϢΒΕΕΡ is also fem. [Kasser: 84]).

99,4 MS has ΠΡΟΤΕΓΕΝΕΤѠΡ , "First Begetter" (harmonization: see lines 7 and 14). T–S has only the first emendation, but translates as above, which is possible because of the ambiguity of the word (see LSJ, s.v.). It is difficult to believe, however, that that ambiguity was involved here.

NHC V 9,3–15　　　　　NHC III 81,1–5

теч[мн̄]тсꙅ҇ме | [хе †ϣорпе]
м̄мı[се] н̄софıа ⁵ [†мааγ
м̄птнр]ꝗ· ете ϣарезо|[ïне
моγте] ерос хе тагапн· |
[н̄точ де пı]ϣорп̄ м̄мıсе

еγн̄|[тач н̄тече]ꙅоγсıа евол
зм̄ | [пе]ч[еıωт·
ач]тамıо нач н̄оγ¹⁰наб
н̄[еωн] прос течмн̄тноб· |
е[чтамıо]нач н̄зенагге лос
| н̄на[н]тꙅа н̄нат† нпе ероγ
| езраï еγϣм̄ϣе·
паϣеï тнрꝗ | н̄нıагге лос
еϣаγмоγте еро¹⁵оγ хе

ачтам[ıо нач н̄зен]агге лос | 　　[па
зентв[а емн̄тоγ] нпе езоγн |
еγзγпнресıа·
пмннϣе тнрꝗ | н̄нагге лос
етм̄маγ ϣаγхо⁵ос ероγ хе

His female aspect | [is "First-]
begotten Sophia, ⁵ [Mother of the
Universe]," whom some | [call]
"Love." | [Now] First-begotten,

since he has | [his] authority from |
his [father],
created a ¹⁰ great [aeon] for his own
majesty,
| [creating] numberless myriads of |
angels | for retinue.
The whole multitude | of angels,
who are called

He created angels, | myriads 　　[81
[without] number, | for retinue. The
whole multitude | of those angels are
called

Eug-V:

9,10 First superlinear stroke is in lacuna.

9,12 First superlinear stroke is in lacuna.

For the remarkable reconstruction of the first word I am indebted to Bentley Layton.

NHC III 104,16–105,2   BG 99,9–100,1

ετε πεΧΣ πε

ΠΕϤΡΑΝ | ΝΣϨΙΜΕ ΤΣΟΦΙΑ   ΠΕϤ¹⁰ΡΑΝ ΜΜΝΤΣϨΙΜΕ ΠΕ
ΝΠΡΩΤΟ|ΓΕΝΕΤΙΡΑ ΤΜΑΑΥ   ΠΡΟ|ΤΟΓΕΝΕΤΕΙΡΑ ΤΣΟΦΙΑ |
ΜΠΤΗΡϤ· | ϢΑΡΕϨΟΕΙΝΕ ΜΟΥΤΕ   ΤΜΑΥ ΜΠΤΗΡϤ ΤΑΪ ΕΤΕ |
ΕΡΟΣ ²⁰ ΧΕ ΤΑΓΑΠΗ· ΝΤΟϤ ΔΕ   ϢΑΡΕϨΟΪΝ ΜΟΥΤΕ ΕΡΟΣ ΧΕ |
ΠϢΟΡΠ | ΝΧΠΟ   ΤΑΓΑΠΗ ΠΕΠΡΟΤΟΓΕΝΕ ¹⁵ΤΩΡ ΓΑΡ
ϢΑΥΜΟΥΤΕ ΕΡΟϤ ΧΕ | ΠΕΧΡΣ   ΕϢΑΥΜΟΥΤΕ | ΕΡΟϤ ΧΕ ΠΕΧΣ
ΕΥΝΤΑϤ ΝΤΕϨΟΥΣΙΑ | ϨΙΤΜ   ΕΟΥΝΤΕϤ | ΤΕϨΟΥΣΙΑ ϨΙΤΟΟΤϤ
ΠΕϤΕΙΩΤ   Μ|ΠΕϤΕΙΩΤ

ΑϤΤΑΜΙΟ | ΝΑϤ ΝΟΥΜΗΗϢΕ   ΑϤΤΑΜΙΟ ΝΑϤ | ΝΟΥΑΤΟ
ΝΑΓΓΕ   ΝΑΓΓΕΛΟΣ ΕΜΝ
ΡΕ   ΛΟΣ ΕΜΝΤΟΥ ΗΠΕ   ΤΟΥ ΗΠΕ Ε[ΥϨΥΠΗΡΕΣΙΑ]   [Ρ̄]
     ΕΥϨΥΠΗ|ΡΕΣΙΑ

his female | name, 'First | Begettress | who is Christ; his ¹⁰ female name is
Sophia, Mother of the Universe.' | First | Begettress, Sophia, | Mother
Some call her ²⁰ 'Love.' Now first- | of the Universe, | whom some call |
begotten is called | 'Christ.' Since   'Love.' For First Begetter,
he has authority | from his father,   ¹⁵ who is called | 'Christ,'
                                              since he has | authority from | his
                                              father,

he created | a multitude of angels   created | a multitude of angels
105 without number for retinue   without
                                              number for [retinue]   **[100]**

SJC-BG:

100,1 Restoration is T–S, alt. Others are: ε[ΥϢΜϢΕ] (correctly rejected by T–S as
too short); ε[ϨΟΥΝ ΕΥϢΜϢΕ] (T–S, alt.; a combination not found elsewhere in
BG). Meanings are similar in all cases.

NHC V 9,15–21

ⲧⲉⲕⲕⲗⲏⲥⲓⲁ ⲛ̅ⲛⲉⲧⲟⲩⲁⲁⲃ | ⲛ̣ⲏ
ⲉⲧⲉ ⲛ̅ⲟⲩⲟⲉⲓⲛ ⲙⲛ̅ ⲛⲓⲁⲧⲍⲁ ⲉⲓ | [ⲃ]ⲉ
<ⲛⲉ>· ⲛⲓⲁⲅⲅⲉⲗⲟⲥ ⲟⲩⲛ ⲉⲧⲙ̅ⲙⲁⲩ |
[ⲉ]ϣⲱⲡⲉ ⲉⲩϣⲁⲛϯ ⲡⲓ ⲉⲣⲛ̅
ⲛⲉⲩ | ⲉⲣ̣ⲏ̣ⲟⲩ·
ϣⲁⲣⲉⲛⲉⲩⲁⲥⲡⲁⲥⲙⲟⲥ · ²⁰ [ϣⲱⲡ]ⲉ
ⲛ̅ⲍⲉⲛⲁⲅⲅⲉⲗⲟⲥ ⲉⲩⲉⲓⲛⲉ |
[ⲙ̅ⲙⲟⲟⲩ·]

NHC III 81,5–10

ⲧⲉⲕⲕⲗⲏⲥⲓⲁ ⲛ̅ⲛⲉ | ⲧⲟⲩⲁⲁⲃ·
ⲛ̅ⲟⲩⲟⲉⲓⲛ ⲛ̅ⲁⲧⲍⲁⲉⲓⲃⲉⲥ |
ⲛⲉⲧⲙ̅ⲙⲁⲩ ϭⲉ ⲉⲩϣⲁⲛⲁⲥⲡⲁⲍⲉ |
ⲛ̅ⲛⲉⲩⲉⲣⲏⲟⲩ ϣⲁⲣⲉⲛⲉⲩⲁⲥⲡⲁⲥ |
ⲙⲟⲥ ϣⲱⲡⲉ ⲛ̅ⲍⲉⲛⲁⲅⲅⲉⲗⲟⲥ
ⲉⲩ ¹⁰ⲉⲓⲛⲉ ⲙ̅ⲙⲟⲟⲩ

---

¹⁵ "Assembly of the Holy Ones," |
are the lights and shadowless ones. |
Now when these angels | kiss each
other, | their embraces ²⁰ [become]
angels like | [themselves.]

---

⁵ "Assembly of the | Holy Ones, the
Shadowless Lights." | Now when
these greet | each other, their
embraces | become angels ¹⁰ like
themselves.

Eug-V:

9,21 MS has a blank of approx. 1 cm. between the lacuna and the subsequent word.

Eug-III:

81,5–6 "Assembly ... Lights" (similarly, Tr): "The church of the saints of light
without shadow" (K); ". . . of the holy lights . . ." (K, footnote).

ЄΒΟλ ᴢм̄ πЄπ͞ν͞а мν̄ πΟγ|ΟЄιν·	| ЄΒΟλ ᴢм̄ πЄ[π͞ν͞а мν πΟ]γ|Οϊν
πЄχаγ ναч ν̄ϭι νЄчма|ΘΗΤΗС	πЄχаγ ναч ν̄ϭι νЄч|маΘΗΤΗС
χЄ πχΟЄιс πЄΤЄϣаγ ⁵мΟγΤЄ	χЄ πЄχ͞с πЄι ⁵ω̄Τ ЄΤЄ
ЄрΟч χЄ πρωмЄ· Ογ|ωνᴢ ναν	ϣаγмΟγΤЄ ЄрΟч | χЄ πρωмЄ
ЄΤΒΗΗΤч̄· χЄκααс | ᴢωων	маΤсаΒΟν Є|рΟч χЄκααс ᴢωων
Єνα ЄιмЄ акριΒως Є|ΤΒЄ	Єν|νасΟγων πЄчЄΟΟγ
πЄчЄΟΟγ πЄχач ν̄`ϭι´	акρι|Βως πЄχач ν̄ϭι πΤЄλιΟс
πΤЄ|λιΟс ν̄сωΤΗρ· χЄ πЄΤЄ	¹⁰ ν̄сωΤΗρ χЄ πЄΤЄ

| from Spirit and Light." | His disciples | said to him: "Lord, reveal to us ⁵ about the one | called 'Man' that | we also may know his glory exactly." | The perfect | Savior said: "Whoever	| from [Spirit and] Light." | His | disciples said to him: "Christ, ⁵ teach us | about the Father, | who is called 'Man,' that we also may | know his glory exactly." | The perfect ¹⁰ Savior said: "Whoever

NHC V 9,21–25   NHC III 81,10–12

ⲡⲉⲩϣⲟⲣⲡ̄ ⲙ̄ⲙⲓⲥⲉ | [. . . . .   ⲡⲉⲡⲣⲱⲧⲟⲅⲉⲛⲉ |ⲧⲱⲣ· ⲛ̄ⲉⲓⲱⲧ·
ⲛ̄ⲉⲓ]ⲱⲧ ϣ[ⲁ]ⲅⲧ ⲣⲁⲛ̣ [ⲉⲣ]ⲟⲩ | [ⲭⲉ   ϣⲁⲩⲭⲟⲟⲥ ⲉⲣⲟⲩ | ⲭⲉ ⲁⲇⲁⲙ ⲡⲁ
. . . . .] . [.]ⲛ̣ⲟ̣[ⲅⲥ· ⲁ]ⲇⲁ[ⲙ ⲉⲧ]ⲉ   ⲡⲟⲩⲟⲉⲓⲛ·
| [ⲡⲓⲃⲁⲗ ⲙ̄ⲡⲟⲩⲟⲉⲓⲛ ⲡⲉ·] ⲡⲏ
[ⲉⲧⲁⲩ] ²⁵ [ⲉ̂ⲓ ⲉⲃⲟⲗ ⲍⲙ̄
ⲡⲟⲩⲟⲉⲓⲛ·]

Their first-begotten | [. . . father] is   First Begetter | Father is called |
called | [". . . Mind, Adam," who] | "Adam of the Light."
[is the Eye of Light,] who ²⁵ [came
from Light,]

Eug-V:

9,23 ᴍs has a stroke above the second lacuna.

Eug-III:

81,11 Corr.: an erased point between first ⲱ and ⲣ. The point following ⲣ is inexpli-
    cable, unless it, together with the erased point, was intended to signal the deletion
    of ⲣ.

NHC III 105,9–19   BG 100,10–101,6

ⲟⲩⲛⲧϥ̄ ¹⁰ ⲙⲁⲁϫⲉ ⲙ̄ⲙⲁⲩ ⲉⲥⲱⲧⲙ̄   ⲟⲩⲛ̄ⲧϥ̄ | ⲙⲁⲁϫⲉ ⲉⲥⲱⲧⲙ̄
ⲙⲁⲣⲉϥ|ⲥⲱⲧⲙ̄·   ⲙⲁⲣⲉϥ|ⲥⲱⲧⲙ̄
ⲡⲉⲡⲣⲱⲧⲟⲅⲉⲛⲉⲧⲱⲣ ⲛ̄ⲉⲓⲱⲧ   ⲡⲉⲡⲣⲟⲧⲟⲅⲉⲛⲉⲧⲱⲣ | ⲛ̄ⲉⲓⲱⲧ
ⲉϣⲁⲩϫⲟⲟⲥ ⲉⲣⲟϥ ϫⲉ ⲁⲇⲁⲙ· | ⲉϣⲁⲩⲙⲟⲩⲧⲉ ⲉⲣⲟϥ | ϫⲉ ⲁⲇⲁⲙ
[ⲡ]ⲃⲁⲗ ⲙ̄ⲡⲟⲩⲟⲉⲓⲛ ϫⲉ ⲛ̄ⲧⲁϥⲉⲓ   ⲡⲃⲁⲗ ⲙⲡⲟⲩⲟⲓ̈ⲛ ¹⁵ ⲉⲃⲟⲗ ϫⲉ ⲁϥⲉⲓ
ⲉ|[ⲃⲟ]ⲗ ⲍⲙ̄ ⲡⲟⲩⲟⲉⲓⲛ   ⲉⲃⲟⲗ ⲍⲙ ⲡⲟⲩ|ⲟⲓ̈ⲛ
                                      ⲧⲉϥⲙⲛ̄ⲧⲉⲣⲟ ⲇⲉ ⲧⲏⲣⲥ | ⲧⲁ
                                      ⲡⲟⲩⲟⲓ̈ⲛ ⲧⲉ
ⲉⲧⲣ̄ ⲟⲩⲟⲉⲓⲛ ¹⁵ [ⲙⲛ̄]   ⲉⲧⲣ̄ ⲟⲩⲟⲓ̈ⲛ | ⲙⲛ̄ ⲛⲉϥⲁⲅⲅⲉⲗⲟⲥ
ⲛⲉϥⲁⲅⲅⲉⲗⲟⲥ ⲉⲧⲟⲩⲁⲁⲃ·   ⲉⲧⲟⲩⲁ
ⲛ̄|ⲁⲧϣⲁϫⲉ ⲉⲣⲟⲟⲩ ⲛ̄ⲁⲧⲍⲁⲉⲓⲃⲉⲥ | [ⲁⲃ ⲛⲁⲧϣⲁϫⲉ] ⲉⲣⲟⲟⲩ | [ⲣ̄ⲁ]
ⲉⲩⲧⲉⲣⲡⲏ ⲉⲩⲙⲏⲛ ⲉⲃⲟⲗ ⲉⲩⲣⲁ|ϣⲉ   [ⲛⲁⲧⲍⲁⲓⲃⲉⲥ] ⲥⲉⲧⲉⲣⲡⲉ | ⲉⲩⲙⲏⲛ
ⲍⲛ̄ ⲧⲉⲩⲉⲛⲑⲩⲙⲏⲥⲓⲥ ⲛ̄ⲧⲁⲩ|ϫⲓⲧⲥ̄   ⲉⲃⲟⲗ ⲉⲩⲣⲉϣⲉ | ⲍⲛ̄
ⲛ̄ⲧⲛ̄ ⲡⲉⲩⲉⲓⲱⲧ   ⲧⲉⲩⲉⲛⲑⲩⲙⲏⲥⲓⲥ ⲛ̄⁵ⲧⲁⲩϫⲓⲧⲥ̄
                                      ⲛⲧⲟⲟⲧϥ ⲙ̄|ⲡⲉⲩⲉⲓⲱⲧ

has ¹⁰ ears to hear, let him | hear.   has | ears to hear, let him | hear.
First Begetter | Father is called   First Begetter | Father is called |
'Adam, | Eye of Light,' because he   'Adam, Eye of Light,' ¹⁵ because he
came | from shining Light,   came from Light.
                                          | And his whole kingdom | is of the
                                          shining Light,

¹⁵ [and] his holy angels, who are | and his holy angels, who are
ineffable | (and) shadowless, | ever   [ineffable] | (and) [shadowless], ever   [101]
rejoice with joy | in their reflecting, | rejoice | with joy | in their reflecting,
which they received from their   ⁵ which they received from | their
Father.   Father.

SJC-III:

105,14 Regarding the section in the parr. (added here by K) following ⲡⲟⲩⲟⲉⲓⲛ ,
    "Light," see BG 100,16–17n.

SJC-BG:

100,16–17 ⲧⲉϥⲙⲛ̄ⲧⲉⲣⲟ ... ⲧⲉ, "And ... Light" (omitting "shining"): T–S holds
    that this section is missing in *SJC*–III through homoioteleuton.

NHC V 9,25–10,2   NHC III 81,12–21

пιϣ[нре] | [ετερετεϥμ̄ν̄τ̄р̄рο   тм̄ν̄т̄р|ро ⲇⲉ м̄пϣнре м̄прⲱме

м]ⲉ2 т̣[нр̄ⲥ̄] | [ν̄оурⲁϣⲉ
ν̄ⲁⲧϣⲁ]ϫⲉ м̄м[оϥ] | [21±] |
[21±] ³⁰ [21±] | [21±] | [21±] | ⲉⲥ|мⲉ2 ν̄рⲁϣⲉ ν̄ⲁⲧ̇ϣⲁϫⲉ ⲉроϥ
[11± оуⲇⲉ м̄пⲉϥоу]   ¹⁵ мν̄ оуⲧⲉⲗнⲗ ⲉмⲉϥϣⲓⲃⲉ

[ī]   [ⲱν̄2 2ν̄ⲛ ⲉⲱ]ν ν̣[ⲓм ⲉⲧⲁуϣⲱпⲉ]   ⲉуⲧⲉр|пⲉ ⲉумнⲛ ⲉⲃоⲗ 2ν̄
    | мⲛ̄ⲛⲥⲱ[оу] мⲛ̄ [ⲛⲉуⲕоⲥмоⲥ·   оурⲁϣⲉ ν̄ⲁⲧ̇|ϣⲁϫⲉ ⲉроϥ ⲉ2рⲁ̈ⲓ
                                         ⲉⲭν̄ пⲉуⲉооу | ν̄ⲁⲧ̇ⲧⲁⲕо· пⲁ̈ⲓ
                                         ⲉⲧⲉ м̄поуⲥо|ⲧмⲉϥ ⲉⲛⲉ2 оуⲇⲉ
                                         м̄пⲉϥоуⲱν2 ²⁰ ⲉⲛⲁⲓⲱⲛ тнроу
                                         ν̄ⲧⲁуϣⲱпⲉ | мⲛ̄ ⲛⲉуⲕоⲥмоⲥ·

the [Son] | [whose whole kingdom   And the kingdom | of Son of Man

is] full | [of ineffable joy] | [. . .] | is | full of ineffable joy ¹⁵ and
[. . .] ³⁰ [. . .] | [. . .] | [. . .] | unchanging jubilation, (they) ever
[. . . nor has it been revealed]   rejoicing | in ineffable joy | over

[10]   [in all the aeons that came] | their imperishable | glory, which has
    afterward and [their worlds.] | never been heard nor has it been
                                         revealed ²⁰ to all the aeons that came
                                         to be | and their worlds.

Eug-V:

10,2 First superlinear stroke is in lacuna.

NHC III 105,19–106,6   BG 101,6–102,3

ТМⲚⲦⲢ²⁰РО ТНРⲤ ⲘⲠϢНРЕ ⲘⲠⲢⲰⲘⲈ | ⲠⲈⲦⲈϢⲀⲨⲘⲞⲨⲦⲈ ⲈⲢⲞϥ ϪⲈ Ⲡ|ϢНⲢⲈ ⲘⲠⲚⲞⲨⲦⲈ Ⲉ<Ⲥ>ⲘНⲌ ⲚⲢⲀ|ϢⲈ ⲚⲀⲦϢⲀϪⲈ ⲈⲢⲞϥ ⲚⲀⲦⲌⲀⲈⲒⲂⲈⲤ | ⲌⲒ ⲦⲈⲖНⲖ ⲈⲘⲈϥϢⲒⲂⲈ ⲈⲨⲢⲞⲞⲨⲦ ²⁵ ⲈⲌⲢⲀⲒ ⲈⲬⲘ ⲠⲈϥⲈⲞⲞⲨ ⲚⲀⲦⲦⲀⲔⲞ ⲈⲦⲈ ⲘⲠⲞⲨⲤⲞⲦⲘⲈϥ ⲈⲚⲈⲌ ϢⲀ | ⲦⲈⲚⲞⲨ ⲞⲨⲆⲈ ⲘⲠⲈϥⲞⲨⲰⲚⲌ | ⲈⲂⲞⲖ ⲌⲚ ⲚⲀⲒⲰⲚ ⲚⲦⲀⲨϢⲰⲠⲈ | ⲘⲚⲚⲤⲀ ⲚⲀⲒ ⲘⲚ ⲚⲈⲨⲔⲞⲤⲘⲞⲤ· ⁵ ⲀⲚⲞⲔ ⲚⲦⲀⲈⲒⲈⲒ ⲈⲂⲞⲖ ⲌⲒⲦⲚ ⲠⲀⲨ|ⲦⲞⲄⲈⲚНⲤ ⲘⲚ	ТМⲚⲦⲈⲢⲞ ⲆⲈ | ⲦⲀ ⲠϢНⲢⲈ ⲘⲠⲢⲰⲘⲈ | ⲦⲈ ⲈⲦⲈ ϢⲀⲨⲘⲞⲨⲦⲈ | ⲈⲢⲞϥ ϪⲈ ⲠⲈⲬⲤ ⲈⲤⲘⲈⲌ ¹⁰ ⲦНⲢⲤ ⲚⲢⲀϢⲈ ⲚⲀⲦϢⲀ|ϪⲈ ⲈⲢⲞϥ ⲚⲀⲦⲌⲀⲒⲂⲈⲤ | <ⲘⲚ> ⲞⲨⲦⲈⲖНⲖ ⲈⲘⲀϥϢⲒⲂⲈ | ⲈⲨⲦⲈⲢⲠⲈ ⲈⲨⲘНⲚ ⲈⲂⲞⲖ | ⲈⲌⲢⲀⲒ ⲈⲬⲘ ⲠⲈϥⲈⲞⲞⲨ ¹⁵ ⲚⲀⲦⲦⲀⲔⲞ ⲠⲀⲒ | ⲈⲦⲈ Ⲙ|ⲠⲞⲨⲤⲞⲦⲘⲈϥ ⲈⲚⲈⲌ ϢⲀ | ⲦⲈⲚⲞⲨ ⲞⲨⲆⲈ ⲘⲠⲈϥⲞⲨ|ⲰⲚⲌ ⲌⲚ <Ⲛ>ⲀⲒⲰⲚ ⲚⲦⲀⲨϢⲰ|ⲠⲈ ⲘⲚⲚⲤⲀ ⲚⲀⲈⲒ ⲘⲚ ⲚⲈⲨⲔⲞⲤ[ⲘⲞⲤ [ⲢⲂ] ⲀⲚⲞⲔ ⲠⲈⲚ]|ⲦⲀϥⲈⲒ ⲈⲂⲞ[Ⲗ ⲌⲘ ⲠⲀⲨⲦⲞⲄⲈ]|ⲚНⲤ ⲀⲨⲰ ⲈⲂⲞⲖ

ⲢⲤ (margin, left)

The whole kingdom ²⁰ of Son of Man, | who is called 'Son | of God,' is full of | ineffable and shadowless joy, | and unchanging jubilation, (they) rejoicing ²⁵ over his imperishable **106** glory, which has never been heard until | now, nor has it been revealed | in the aeons that came | afterward and their worlds. ⁵ I came from Self- | begotten and	Now the kingdom is | that of Son of Man, | who is called | 'Christ.' It is completely ¹⁰ full of ineffable | and shadowless joy, | <and> unchanging jubilation, | (they) ever rejoicing | over his imperishable ¹⁵ glory, which has | never been heard until | now, nor has it been revealed | in <the> aeons that came | afterward and their worlds. **[102]** | [I] came [from Self-begotten] | and from the

---

SJC-III:

105,22 MS has ϥ (incorrect gender, by attraction to ⲠϢНⲢⲈ, "Son"; not emended by T–S).

SJC-BG:

101,12 Alt.: <ⲌⲒ>ⲦⲈⲖНⲖ (T–S, alt.).

101,18 Alt.: ⲌⲚ ⲀⲒⲰⲚ <ⲚⲒⲘ>, "in <every> aeon" (T–S, alt.).

NHC V 10,2–6   NHC III 81,21–23

ⲙ︤ⲛ︦] | ⲛ̄ⲥⲱϥ ⲁ[ϥ]ϣⲱⲡⲉ̣ [ⲛ̄ϭⲓ . . .
ⲉⲃⲟⲗ] | ⳍⲙ︦ ⲡⲁⲓ̈ ⲉ̣[ⲧ]ⲉ ⲡϣⲏ[ⲣⲉ
ⲙ̄ⲡⲓⲣⲱⲙⲉ] ⁵ ⲡⲉ· ⲉⲁϥ[†] ⲙⲉⲧⲉ̣
[ⲙ̄ⲛ ⲧⲥⲟⲫⲓⲁ ⲧⲉϥ]|ⲥⲩⲛⲍⲩⲅⲟⲥ ·

ⲡϣⲏⲣⲉ ϭⲉ | ⲙ̄ⲡⲣⲱⲙⲉ
ⲁ̣ϥⲥⲩⲙⲫⲱⲛⲉⲓ ⲙ̄ⲛ | ⲧⲥⲟⲫⲓⲁ
ⲧⲉϥⲥⲩⲛⲍⲩⲅⲟⲥ

| Afterward [. . .] came from | him, [who] is Son [of Man.] ⁵ Having consented [with Sophia, his] | consort,

Then Son | of Man consented with | Sophia, his consort,

Eug-V:

10,3 Corr.: ⲁ over false start of another letter.

NHC III 106,6–17	BG 102,3–17

ⲡⲉ²ⲟⲩⲉⲓϯ ⲛ̄|ⲟⲩⲟⲉⲓⲛ ⲉⲧⲉ ⲙⲛ̄
ⲁⲣⲏⲭ⳥̄· ⲭⲉ | ⲉⲉⲓⲉⲙⲏⲛⲉⲩ ⲉ ⲛⲏⲧⲛ̄
ⲛ̄ⲛ̄ⲕⲁ | ⲛⲓⲙ · ⲡⲁⲗⲓⲛ ⲛⲉϥⲙⲁⲑⲏⲧⲏⲥ
¹⁰ ⲡⲉⲭⲁⲩ ⲭⲉ ⲙⲁⲧⲁⲙⲟⲛ ²ⲛ̄
ⲟⲩ|ⲱⲛ² ⲉⲃⲟⲗ ⲭⲉ ⲡⲱⲥ ⲉⲃⲟⲗ ²ⲛ̄
ⲛⲓ|ⲁⲧⲟⲩⲱⲛ² ⲉⲃⲟⲗ ⲁⲩⲉⲓ ⲉⲡⲉⲥⲏⲧ
| ²ⲓⲧⲛ̄ ⲡⲓⲁⲑⲁⲛⲁⲧⲟⲥ ⲉⲡⲕⲟⲥ|ⲙⲟⲥ
ⲉϣⲁ<ϥ>ⲙⲟⲩ ⲡⲉⲭⲉ ⲡⲧⲉ ¹⁵ⲗⲓⲟⲥ
ⲛ̄ⲥⲱⲧⲏⲣ· ⲭⲉ

ⲡϣⲏⲣⲉ ⲙ̄|ⲡⲣⲱⲙⲉ ⲁϥϥⲓ ⲙⲛ̄
ⲧⲥⲟⲫⲓⲁ ⲧⲉϥ|ⲥⲩⲛⲍⲩⲅⲟⲥ

---

²ⲙ ⲡⲉ|²ⲟⲩⲉⲓⲧ ⲛ̄ⲟⲩⲟⲓ̈ⲛ̄
ⲙⲡⲓⲁ ⁵ⲡⲉⲣⲁⲛⲧⲟⲛ ⲭⲉ
ⲉⲉⲓⲛⲁ ⲧⲥⲁ|ⲃⲉ ⲧⲏⲩⲧⲛ̄ ⲉⲛⲁⲓ̈
ⲧⲏⲣⲟⲩ | ⲡⲁⲗⲓⲛ ⲡⲉⲭⲁⲩ ⲛ̄ϭⲓ
ⲛⲉϥ|ⲙⲁⲑⲏⲧⲏⲥ ⲭⲉ ⲡⲉⲭ̄ⲥ̄
ⲙⲁ|ⲧⲥⲁⲃⲟⲛ ²ⲛ̄ⲛ ⲟⲩⲱⲛ² <ⲉⲃⲟⲗ
ⲭⲉ ⲡⲱⲥ> ⲉ ¹⁰ⲃⲟⲗ ²ⲛ̄ ⲛⲓⲁⲧⲟⲩⲱⲛ²
ⲛⲁ|ⲉⲓ ⲉⲧϣⲟⲟⲡ ⲉⲁ<ⲩ>ⲉⲓ
ⲉⲡⲉ|ⲥⲏⲧ ⲉⲃⲟⲗ ²ⲛ̄ ⲛⲓⲁⲧⲙⲟⲩ |
ⲉⲡⲕⲟⲥⲙⲟⲥ ⲉⲧⲉ ϣⲁϥ|ⲙⲟⲩ
ⲡⲉⲭⲁϥ ⲛ̄ϭⲓ ⲡⲧⲉⲗⲓ ¹⁵ⲟⲥ ⲛ̄ⲥⲱⲧⲏⲣ
`ⲭⲉ´
ⲡϣⲏⲣⲉ ⲙ̄|ⲡⲣⲱⲙⲉ ⲁϥⲥⲩⲙⲫⲱⲛⲓ ⲙⲛ̄
| ⲧⲥⲟⲫⲓⲁ ⲧⲉϥⲥⲩⲛⲍⲩⲅⲟⲥ |

First | Infinite Light that | I might reveal everything to you." | Again, his disciples said: ¹⁰ "Tell us clearly | how (it is that) they came down from the | invisibilities, | from the immortal (realm) to the world | that dies?" The perfect ¹⁵ Savior said:	| First Light of the ⁵ infinite that I might teach | you all these things." | Again, his disciples | said: "Christ, teach | us clearly <how> (it is) that ¹⁰ those who truly exist came down | from the invisibilities, | from the immortals, | to the world that | dies?" The perfect ¹⁵ Savior said:
"Son of | Man consented with Sophia, his	"Son of | Man consented with | Sophia, his consort

---

SJC-III:

106,10 "clearly": "through a revelation" (K).

106,13 Corr.: third ⲁ for erased ⲟ.

106,14 MS has ⲩ (incorrect pronoun number; not emended by T–S).

SJC-BG:

102,4–5 MS has stroke over the second ⲛ (line 4), which rightly belongs over the following ⲙ.

    Alt.: <ⲛ̄>ⲁⲡⲉⲣⲁⲛⲧⲟⲛ , *"infinite* light" (T–S sugg.).

102,11 MS has ϥ, "*he* came down" (translation line 10) (emendation is T–S sugg.); unemended, "those who truly exist" would be in apposition to "the invisiblities."

NHC V 10,6–18

ⲁϥ[ⲟⲩⲱⲛⲍ̄ ⲉⲃⲟⲗ] | ⲛ̄ⲟⲩⲛⲟϭ
ⲙ̄ⲫⲱⲥ[ⲧⲏⲣ ⲉϥⲉ ⲛ̄ⲍⲟ]|ⲟⲩⲧⲥϩⲓ̄ⲙⲉ·
ⲉⲧⲉ [ⲡⲉϥⲣⲁⲛ ⲛ̄ⲍⲟ]|ⲟⲩⲧ
ϣⲁⲩⲙⲟⲩ[ⲧⲉ ⲉⲣⲟϥ ϫ]ⲉ
ⲡ[ⲥⲱ]¹⁰ⲧⲏⲣ ⲡⲓⲣⲉϥϫⲡⲟ ⲛ̄ⲧ[ⲉ
ⲛⲓⲧⲏⲣ]ⲟⲩ· | ⲡⲉϥⲣⲁⲛ
ⲙ̄ⲙⲛ̄ⲧⲥϩⲓ̄ⲙ[ⲉ ϣⲁⲣⲉϩ]ⲟ|ⲉⲓⲛⲉ †
ⲣⲁⲛ ⲉⲣⲟⲥ ϫⲉ [ⲧⲡⲓⲥⲧⲓⲥ]
ⲧⲥ[ⲟ]|ⲫⲓⲁ·
ⲉⲧⲁⲡⲥⲱⲧⲏⲣ ⲟⲩⲛ † ⲙⲉⲧⲉ | ⲙⲛ̄
ⲧⲉϥⲥⲩⲛⲍⲩⲅⲟⲥ ⲧⲡⲓⲥⲧⲓⲥ · ¹⁵
ⲧⲥⲟⲫⲓⲁ· ⲁϥⲟⲩⲱⲛⲍ̄ ⲉⲃⲟⲗ
ⲛ̄ⲛⲟⲩⲁ[ⲛ]|ⲥⲟⲟⲩ ⲙ̄ⲡⲛⲓⲕⲏ̄ ⲉⲥⲉ
ⲛ̄ⲍⲟⲟⲩⲧ | ⲥϩⲓ̄ⲙⲉ· ⲉⲧⲉ ⲛ̄ⲣⲁⲛ
ⲛ̄ⲧⲉⲩⲙⲛ̄†[ⲍⲟ]|ⲟⲩⲧ ⲛⲁⲓ̈ ⲛⲉ·

he [revealed] | a great luminary,
[who is] androgynous (and) | whose
[male name] | is called
["Savior,] ¹⁰ Begetter of [All
Things"]. | Some call his
feminine | name "[Pistis] Sophia." |
Then when Savior consented with |
his consort, Pistis ¹⁵ Sophia, he
revealed | six spiritual beings, who
are androgynous, (and) | whose
masculine names | are these:

NHC III 81,23–82,12

ⲁϥⲟⲩ|ⲱⲛⲍ ⲉⲃⲟⲗ ⲛ̄ⲟⲩⲛⲟϭ
ⲛ̄ⲟⲩⲟⲉⲓⲛ
ⲛ̄ⲍⲟⲟⲩ† [ⲥϩⲓⲙⲉ· ⲡⲉϥⲣ]ⲁⲛ   [ⲡⲃ]
ⲙ̄ⲙⲛ̄†|ⲍⲟⲟⲩ† ϣⲁ<ⲩ>[ϫⲟⲟⲥ
ⲉⲣⲟϥ] ϫⲉ ⲡⲥⲱ|ⲧⲏⲣ ⲡⲣⲉϥϫⲡⲉ
ⲛ̄ⲕⲁ ⲛ[ⲓ]ⲙ ⲡⲉϥⲣⲁⲛ | ⲙ̄ⲙⲛ̄ⲧⲥϩⲓⲙⲉ
ϣⲁⲩϫⲟⲟⲥ ⲉⲣⲟϥ ϫⲉ ⁵ ⲧⲥⲟⲫⲓⲁ
ⲡⲁⲛⲅⲉⲛⲉⲧⲓⲣⲁ ϣⲁⲣⲉ|ϩⲟⲉⲓⲛ
ϫⲟⲟⲥ ⲉⲣⲟⲥ ϫⲉ ⲧⲡⲓⲥⲧⲓⲥ
| ⲡⲥⲱⲧⲏⲣ ϭⲉ ⲁϥⲥⲩⲙⲫⲱⲛⲉⲓ ⲙⲛ̄ |
ⲧⲉϥⲥⲩⲛⲍⲩⲅⲟⲥ ⲧⲡⲓⲥⲧⲓⲥ ⲥⲟⲫⲓⲁ |
ⲁϥⲟⲩⲱⲛⲍ ⲛ̄ⲥⲟⲟⲩ
ⲙ̄ⲡⲛⲉⲩⲙⲁ ¹⁰ⲧⲓⲕⲟⲛ ⲛ̄ⲍⲟⲟⲩⲧⲥϩⲓⲙⲉ
ⲉⲡⲧⲩ|ⲡⲟⲥ ⲡⲉ ⲛ̄ⲛⲉⲧⲍⲁⲧⲉⲩⲍⲏ·
ⲛ̄ⲍⲟⲟⲩ† | ⲛ̄ⲉⲩⲣⲁⲛ ⲛⲉ ⲛⲁⲓ̈

and | revealed a great androgynous
light.   [82]
[His] masculine name | is [called]
"Savior, | Begetter of
All Things." His feminine name | is
called ⁵ "Sophia, All-
Begettress." Some | call her
"Pistis." | Then Savior consented
with | his consort, Pistis Sophia, |
and revealed six androgynous
spiritual beings ¹⁰ who are the type |
of those who preceded them. | Their
male names are these:

Eug-III:

82,1 T–S restores only ⲡⲉϥⲣ.

82,2 MS has ϥ. Alt. ϣⲁⲣ[ⲉϩⲟⲓⲛ ϫⲟⲟϥ ϫ]ⲉ, "name [*is called*]" (?) (Tr; an unusual
locution in the context; see lines 5 and 6). All that remains of ϥ is the lower part of
the long vertical line, which would be compatible also with ⲣ or †.

NHC III 106,17–24

ⲁϥⲟⲩⲱⲛⲍ ⲉⲃⲟⲗ ⲛ̄|ⲟⲩⲛⲟϭ
ⲛ̄ⲟⲩⲟⲉⲓⲛ ⲛ̄ⲍⲟⲟⲩⲧ̄ | ⲥⲍⲓⲙⲉ ·
ⲡⲉϥⲣⲁⲛ ⲛ̄ⲍⲟⲟⲩⲧ̄ ²⁰ ϣⲁⲩⲙⲟⲩⲧⲉ
ⲉⲣⲟϥ ϫⲉ ⲡⲥⲱ|ⲧⲏⲣ ⲡⲣⲉϥϫⲡⲉ ⲛ̄ⲕⲁ
ⲛⲓⲙ · ⲡⲉϥ|ⲣⲁⲛ ⲛ̄ⲥⲍⲓⲙⲉ ⲡⲉ
ⲡⲁⲛⲅⲉⲛⲉⲧⲓ|ⲣⲁ ⲥⲟⲫⲓⲁ
ϣⲁⲣⲉⲍⲟⲉⲓⲛ ⲙⲟⲩⲧⲉ | ⲉⲣⲟⲥ ϫⲉ
ⲧⲡⲓⲥⲧⲓⲥ

BG 102,18–103,9

ⲁϥⲟⲩⲱⲛⲍ ⲉⲃⲟⲗ {ⲍ}ⲛ̄ⲛⲟⲩ|
[ⲛⲟϭ ⲛⲟⲩⲟⲉⲓⲛ] ⲛⲍⲟⲩⲧ|[ⲥⲍⲓⲙⲉ   [ⲣ̅ⲅ̅]
ⲧⲉ]ϥⲙⲛ̄ⲧⲍⲟ|ⲟⲩⲧ ⲙⲉⲛ
ⲉϣⲁⲩⲙⲟⲩ|ⲧⲉ ⲉⲣⲟⲥ ϫⲉ ⲡⲥⲱⲧⲏⲣ
⁵ ⲡⲣⲉϥϫⲡⲟ ⲛ̄ⲕⲁ ⲛⲓⲙ |
ⲧⲉϥⲙⲛ̄ⲧⲥⲍⲓ̈ⲙⲉ ⲇⲉ ϫⲉ | ⲥⲟⲫⲓⲁ
ⲡⲁⲛⲅⲉⲛⲏⲧⲉⲓ|ⲣⲁ ⲉⲧⲉ ϣⲁⲣⲉⲍⲟⲓ̈ⲛ
ⲙⲟⲩ|ⲧⲉ ⲉⲣⲟⲥ ϫⲉ ⲧⲡⲓⲥⲧⲓⲥ

| consort, and revealed | a great
androgynous light. | His male name
²⁰ is called 'Savior, | Begetter
of All Things.' His | female name is
'All-Begettress Sophia.' | Some call
her | 'Pistis.'

| and revealed a
[great] androgynous [light]. | His   **[103]**
maleness | is called | 'Savior, ⁵
Begetter of All Things'; | and his
femaleness is called | 'Sophia, All-
Begettress,' | whom some call |
'Pistis.'

SJC-BG:

102,18 Not emended by T–S ("appeared *in*"). I had earlier thought it best not to
emend [1975: 176, n.3], but the testimony of the other texts here, as well as the
evidence of scribal carelessness elsewhere in BG, have persuaded me otherwise.

NHC V 10,18–11,4

ⲡϣⲟⲣ︤ⲡ︥ ⲡⲉ ⲡ⟨ⲓ⟩ⲁ︤ⲧ︥|ⲭⲡⲟ ⟨ⲛ̄ⲉⲓⲱ︤ⲧ︥
ⲛ̄ⲛⲓ⟩ⲧⲏⲣⲟⲩ· ⲡⲙⲉ︤ⲍ︥ⲥⲛⲁⲩ [ⲡⲉ] ²⁰
ⲡⲓⲭⲡⲟ ⲉⲃⲟⲗ ⲙ̄ⲙⲟϥ·
ⲡⲓⲙ̣[ⲉ︤ⲍ︥ϣⲟⲙⲛ̄ⲧ] | ⲡⲉ ⲡⲏ
ⲉⲧⲁⲩⲭ̣ⲡⲟϥ[· ⲡⲙⲉ︤ⲍ︥ⲧⲟ]|ⲟⲩ [ⲡⲉ]
ⲡⲓⲭ ⲡ[ⲟ] ⲛ̄ⲧⲉ ⲡ[ϣⲟⲣ︤ⲡ︥·] |
ⲡⲙ̣[ⲉ︤ⲍ︥]ϯⲟⲩ [ⲡⲉ ⲡⲓⲭ ⲡⲟ ⲧⲏⲣ︤ϥ︥·
ⲡⲙⲉ︤ⲍ︥] | [ⲥⲟⲟⲩ] ⲡ[ⲉ 15±]
²⁵[. . . .] ⲛⲓⲣ̣ [ⲁⲛ
ⲛ̄ⲧⲉⲩⲙⲛ̄ⲧⲥⲍⲓ̂ⲙⲉ] | [ⲛⲁⲓ̈ ⲛⲉ·]
ϯ︤ⲍ︥[ⲟⲩⲉⲓⲧⲉ ⲡⲉ 6±] |
(6± lines lacking)
[ⲓ̄ⲁ̄] [12±] . [10±] | [13±] ϯ[ⲙⲉ︤ⲍ︥ϯⲉ
ⲡⲉ] | [ⲧⲁⲅⲁⲡⲏ ⲧⲥⲟϥ]ⲓ̣ⲁ·
ϯ[ⲙⲉ]︤ⲍ︥[ⲥⲟ ⲡⲉ] | [ⲧⲡⲓⲥⲧⲓⲥ
ⲧ]ⲥⲟϥⲓ[ⲁ·

NHC III 82,12–83,2

ⲡϣⲟⲣ︤ⲡ︥ ⲡⲉ ⲡⲁ|ⲅⲉⲛⲛⲏⲧⲟⲥ
ⲡⲙⲉ︤ⲍ︥ⲥⲛⲁⲩ ⲡⲉ ⲡⲁⲩ|ⲧⲟⲅⲉⲛⲛⲏⲧⲟⲥ
ⲡⲙⲉ︤ⲍ︥ϣⲟⲙⲛ︤ⲧ︥ ¹⁵ ⲡⲉ ⲡⲅⲉⲛⲉⲧⲱⲣ·
ⲡⲙⲉ︤ⲍ︥ϥⲧⲟⲟⲩ ⲡⲉ |
ⲡⲉⲡⲣⲱⲧⲟⲅⲉⲛⲉⲧⲱⲣ · ⲡⲙⲉ︤ⲍ︥ϯ|ⲟⲩ
ⲡⲉ ⲡⲁⲛⲅⲉⲛⲉⲧⲱⲣ · ⲡⲙⲉ︤ⲍ︥ⲥⲟⲟⲩ |
ⲡⲉ ⲡⲁⲣⲭⲓⲅⲉⲛⲉⲧⲱⲣ · ⲛ̄ⲣⲁⲛ ⲍⲱⲟⲩ |
ⲛ̄ⲛⲉⲍⲓⲟⲙⲉ ⲛⲉ ⲛⲁⲓ̈· ⲧϣⲟⲣ︤ⲡ︥ ⲡⲉ ²⁰
ⲡ̄ⲡⲁⲛⲥⲟⲫⲟⲥ ⲥⲟⲫⲓⲁ· ⲧⲙⲉ︤ⲍ︥ⲥⲛ̄ⲧⲉ
| ⲡⲉ ⲡⲁⲛⲙⲏⲧⲱⲣ· ⲥⲟⲫⲓⲁ·
ⲧⲙⲉ︤ⲍ︥ϣⲟ|ⲙ̄ⲧⲉ ⲡⲉ ⲡⲁⲛⲅⲉⲛⲉⲧⲓⲣⲁ
ⲥⲟⲫⲓⲁ·
| ⲧⲙⲉ︤ⲍ︥ϥⲧⲟⲉ ⲡⲉ
ⲧⲉⲡⲣⲱⲧⲟⲅⲉⲛⲉⲧⲓ |ⲣⲁ ⲥⲟⲫⲓⲁ·
ⲧⲙⲉ︤ⲍ︥ϯⲉ ⲧⲉ ⲧⲁⲅⲁⲡⲏ ⲥⲟ
ⲫⲓⲁ· ⲧⲙ̣[ⲉ︤ⲍ︥ⲥⲟⲉ ⲧⲉ ⲧⲡ]ⲓⲥⲧⲓⲥ   [ⲡⲅ
ⲥⲟ|ⲫⲓⲁ·

---

first, "Unbegotten | <Father of> All
Things"; second, ²⁰ "Self-begotten";
[third,] | "Begotten"; [fourth,] |
"Begotten of the [First";] | fifth,
["All-begotten"; sixth,] | [. . .] ²⁵
[. . .] the [feminine names] | [are
these: first, . . .] | (6± lines lacking)
[11] [. . .] | [. . . fifth,] | ["Love
Sophia"; sixth,] | ["Pistis] Sophia."

first, "Unbegotten"; | second, "Self-
| begotten"; third, ¹⁵ "Begetter";
fourth, | "First Begetter"; fifth, |
"All-Begetter"; sixth, | "Arch-
Begetter." Also the names | of the
females are these: first, ²⁰ "All-wise
Sophia"; second, | "All-Mother
Sophia"; third, | "All-Begettress
Sophia"; | fourth, "First Begettress |
Sophia"; fifth, "Love Sophia";
[sixth], "Pistis Sophia."   [83

Eug-V:

10,19 For restoration, see V 3,4.

NHC V 11,4–19

ο]ΥΝΤΑΥ ⁵ [ΔΕ ΝzΕΝΚΕΡ]ΑΝ· Ν[Η
Ε]ΤΑΪΤΑΑΥ | [ΝΗΤΝ ΝϢΟΡΠ·
Ε]ΒΟΛ ΔΕ zΜ ΠΙϯ ΜΕ|[ΤΕ ΝΤΑΥ]
ΕΤΑΥΡ ϢΟΡΠ ΝΧΟΟΥ· |
[ΑΥΟΥΩΝz̄] ΕΒΟΛ Ν̄6ι
zΕΝΕΝΝΟΙΑ | [zΝ zΕΝΕΩΝ] ΕΑΥΡ
ϢΟΡΠ Ν̄ΧΟΟΥ ¹⁰ ΕΒΟ[Λ ΔΕ zΝ]
ΝΙΕΝΝΟΙΑ ΝΙΜΕΕΥ Ε· | Ε[ΒΟΛ ΔΕ
zΝ] ΝΙΜΕΕΥΕ ΝΙCΒΟΟΥΕ· | ΕΒ[ΟΛ
ΔΕ zΝ] ΝΙCΒΟΟΥΕ ΝΙϢΟΧΝΕ· |
ΕΒΟΛ ΔΕ zΝ ΝΙϢΟΧΝΕ ΝΙΟΥΩϢ·
| ΕΒΟΛ ΔΕ zΝ ΝΙΟΥΩϢ ΝΕ
ΝΙϢΑΧ Ε·
¹⁵ ΟΥΝΤΑΥ ΔΕ Ν̄zΕΝΚΕΡΑΝ·
ΝΙΕΝ|ΝΟΙΑ ΔΕ ϢΑΥΜΟΥΤΕ
ΕΡΟΟΥ ΧΕ | ΝΙΝΟΥΤΕ· ΝΙΜΕΕΥ Ε
ΔΕ ΧΕ ΝΙ|[ΧΟ]ΕΙC· ΝΙCΒΩ ΝΕ
ΝΙΑΓΓΕΛΟC· | ΝΙϢΟΧΝΕ ΝΕ

NHC III 83,2–10

ΕΒ[ΟΛ zΝ ΤΕ]ΥCΥΝΦΩΝΗ|CΙC
Ν̄ΤΑΕΙΡ ϢΡΠ Ν̄ΧΟΟΥ ΑΥΟΥ|ΩΝz
zΝ ΝΑΙΩΝ ΕΤΚΗ ΕzΡΑΪ Ν̄6ι ⁵
Ν̄ΕΝΝΟΙΑ· ΕΒΟΛ zΝ <Ν̄>ΕΝΝΟΙΑ
ΝΕΝ|ΘΥΜΗCΙC ΕΒΟΛ zΝ
ΝΕΝΘΥΜΗCΙC | ΝΕΦΡΟΝΗCΙC
ΕΒΟΛ zΝ ΝΕΦΡΟΝΗ|CΙC
Ν̄ΛΟΓΙCΜΟC· ΕΒΟΛ zΝ
Ν̄ΛΟΓΙ|CΜΟC ΝΕΘΕΛΗCΙC· ΕΒΟΛ
zΝ ΝΕ¹⁰ΘΕΛΗCΙC Ν̄ΛΟΓΟC·

[And] they have ⁵ [other names,
which] I gave | [you earlier.]
Now from the consent | [of those]
who have just been mentioned, |
thoughts [appeared] | [in aeons] that
were mentioned earlier. ¹⁰ [And
from] thoughts, thinkings; | [and
from] thinkings, teachings; | [and
from] teachings, counsels; | and
from counsels, wills; | and from
wills are words.
¹⁵ Now they have other names.
Thoughts | are called | "gods";
thinkings, | "lords"; teachings are
"angels"; | counsels are

| [From the] consenting | of those I
have just mentioned, thoughts
appeared | in the aeons that exist. ⁵
From thoughts, reflectings; | from
reflectings, | considerings; from
considerings, | rationalities; from
rationalities, | wills; from ¹⁰ wills,
words.

Eug-III:

83,3–4 K omits "in" and incorrectly makes "aeons" the subject of "appeared" (followed by Tr).

83,5 Not emended by Tr, although his translation reflects the above emendation (so also K's translation). My translation omits the articles here and elsewhere in the list because it appears that inclusive collectivities are referred to.

NHC III   BG

NHC V 11,19–25

NHC III 83,10–16

ⲛⲓⲁⲅⲅⲉⲗⲟⲥ· †ⲛⲓⲟ ⲩ²⁰[ⲱ ϣ ⲛ]ⲉ
ⲛⲓϣⲁⲭⲉ· †
†ⲁⲛⲙⲛ̄†<ⲥⲛⲟⲟⲩⲥ> ⲓ̅ⲃ̅ | [ⲁⲉ] ⲛ̄ⲧⲉ
ⲛⲓ6ⲟⲙ ⲉⲧⲉ ⲁⲩⲣ̄ ϣⲟ|[ⲣ̄ⲡ̄
ⲛ̄]ⲭ[ⲟⲟ]ⲩ ⲉⲧⲁⲩⲉⲓⲣⲉ ⲛ̄ⲛⲟⲩ† |
[ⲙⲉⲧ]ⲉ· ⲁⲩⲟⲩⲱⲛⲍ̄ ⲉⲃⲟⲗ
ⲛ̄ⲛⲟⲩⲁⲛ|[ⲥⲟ ⲛ̄6ⲟⲙ ⲙ̄ⲡ̄ⲛ̄]ⲓⲕ̄ⲏ̄
ⲧⲟⲩⲉ[ⲓ] ⲧⲟⲩⲉ[ⲓ] ²⁵ [ⲙ̄]ⲙⲟⲟⲩ
ⲛ̄ⲑⲉ ⲉⲧ[ⲉ ⲛⲏ] ⲙ̄ⲙ[ⲛ̄ⲍ ⲟⲟⲩ†] |

ⲧⲙ̄ⲛ̄ⲧⲥ̄ⲛⲟⲟⲩⲥ | 6ⲉ ⲛ̄6ⲟⲙ
ⲛ̄ⲧⲁⲉⲓⲣ̄ ϣⲣ̄ⲡ ⲛ̄ⲭⲟⲟⲩ |
ⲁⲩⲥⲩⲙⲫⲱⲛⲉⲓ ⲙⲛ̄ ⲛⲉⲩⲉⲣⲏⲟⲩ |
ⲁⲩⲟⲩⲱⲛⲍ ⲉⲃⲟⲗ ⲛ̄6ⲓ ⲛ̄ⲍ ⲟⲟⲩⲧ
<ⲋ̄ ⲋ̄> | ⲛⲉ ⲍ ⲓⲟⲙⲉ <ⲋ̄ ⲋ̄>· ⲍⲱⲥⲧⲉ
ⲛ̄ⲥⲉⲣ̄ ϣ ⲩ ⲉ ¹⁵ⲥⲛⲟⲟⲩⲥ ⲛ̄ⲁ ⲩ ⲛ ⲁⲙⲓⲥ·
ⲧⲉ ϣ ⲩ ⲉ ⲥⲛⲟ |ⲟⲩⲥ ⲁⲩⲟⲩⲱⲛⲍ ⲉⲃⲟⲗ

"angels"; † [wills] ²⁰ [are] "words." †
[Now] when the | twelve powers
who have [just] | been [discussed]
achieved | [consent], each (pair)
revealed | [six spiritual powers]. ²⁵
Just as [the masculine (off-spring)]

Then the twelve | powers, whom I
just discussed, | consented with each
other. | <Six> males (each) (and)
<six> females (each) were revealed,
| so that there are seventy- ¹⁵ two
powers. Each one of the seventy-
two | revealed

Eug-V:

11,19–20 Some text has apparently dropped out: ⲛⲓϣⲁⲭⲉ , "words," is not another
name (11,15).

11,20 The numeral at the end of the line following the written number is probably a
scribal gloss, similar to those in *Apoc. Adam* (V,5) 80,9; 81,14; 82,4; 82,10.
Apparently interest in the gloss led the final copyist to overlook the second half of
the number.

11,23 Third letter after lacuna: see Emmel, 1979: 184.

Second superlinear stroke is in lacuna.

11,24 Emmel reconstructs]ⲡ̄ⲛ̄[ⲁ̄ⲧ̄]ⲓ̄ⲕ̄ⲏ̄ (1979: 184). An examination of the photographs leaves me unconvinced of any ink traces before ⲓ̄ⲕ̄ⲏ̄; moreover the abbreviation Emmel employs for πνευματική differs from that used in the one other place
in the codex where the word is found: 10,16.

11,25 Second and fifth letters after first lacuna: see Emmel, 1979: 184.

Eug-III:

83,13–14 MS has, in each case, ⲥ̄ ⲥ̄. Since ⲥ̄ is the numeral for 200, it is inappropriate
in the context. At some point in the transmission of the text stigmas (ς) were
apparently mistaken for sigmas (ⲥ). Not emended by Tr, although his translation
reflects an emendation (so also K).

Corr.: second ⲥ̄ (line 13) for erased ⲍⲓⲙⲉ .

NHC III   BG

NHC V 11,26–12,4   NHC III 83,16–20

[ⲛ̄]ⲧⲉ ⲛⲉⲩⲥⲟⲟ̣[ⲩ· ⲉⲩⲉ] ⲛ̄ⲥⲟⲟⲩ   ⲛ̄ⲥ̄ⲓ ⲧⲟⲩⲉⲓ ⲧⲟⲩ|ⲉⲓ ⲙ̄ⲙⲟⲟⲩ ⲛ̄ⲧⲟⲩ
ⲥ̣ⲟ̣[ⲟⲩ·] | [ⲍⲱ]ⲥ̣ⲧⲉ ⲛ̄[ⲏ ⲉⲧ]ⲱ̣ⲱⲡⲉ   ⲙ̄ⲡⲛⲉⲩⲙⲁⲧⲓ|ⲕⲟⲛ
ⲛ̄ⲥ̣[ⲓⲟⲙⲉ ⲙ̄]|[ⲡ̄ⲛ̄]ⲁ̣· ⲉⲩ[ⲉ   ⲉⲧⲉ ⲛⲁⲓ̈ ⲛⲉ ⲧⲱ̄ⲙ̄ⲧⲱⲉⲥⲉ
ⲛ̄ⲥⲟ]ⲥ̣[ⲟ· ⲁⲩⲱ ⲛⲁⲓ̈ ⲉⲧ]|ⲉ   ⲛ̄|ⲇⲩⲛⲁⲙⲓⲥ ⲡⲉⲩⲍⲱⲧⲣ̄ ⲧⲏⲣⲟⲩ ⲡⲉ
ⲛⲓⲁ [ⲛ̄ⲱ̣ϥⲉⲥⲛⲟⲟ ⲩⲥ ⲛ̄ⲧⲉ   20 ⲡⲟⲩⲱⲱ·
ⲛⲓⲁ]ⲩⲛ³⁰[ⲁⲙⲓⲥ ⲛⲉ ⲁⲩⲟⲩⲱⲛⲍ̄
ⲉⲃⲟⲗ 6±]
(2± lines lacking)

[ⲓ̄ⲃ̄] [. ⲛⲓⲁⲛⲱⲙ]ⲛ̄ⲧⲱ̣[ⲉⲥⲉ· ⲡⲉⲩⲍⲱⲧⲣ̄
ⲡⲉ] | [ⲡⲓⲟ ⲩⲱⲱ
ⲙ̄ⲡⲓ]ⲱⲧ̇· ⲡ̄[ⲏ ⲉⲧⲁϥⲟⲩⲟⲛⲍⲟⲩ] |
ϫⲉ ⲉⲩ[ⲉⲱ]ⲱⲡⲉ [ⲛ̄ⲍⲉⲛⲧⲩⲡⲟⲥ·] |
ⲡⲓⲣⲱⲙ[ⲉ ⲥ̄]ⲉ ⲛ̄ⲛ[ⲁⲧⲙⲟⲩ   ⲡⲁⲑⲁⲛⲁⲧⲟⲥ ⲥ̄ⲉ ⲛ̄ⲣⲱⲙⲉ |

| of the six (pairs) of them [are] six | five spiritual (powers), | which
each, | so [those who] are [female] | (together) are the three hundred sixty
[spirits are six each. And these] | | powers. The union of them all is ²⁰
[seventy-two] ³⁰ [powers revealed   the will.
. . .] | (2± lines lacking)

[12] [. . . the three hundred sixty. Their
union is] | [the will
of the Father, who revealed them] |
that they might become [types.]
| [Therefore our aeon]   Therefore our aeon came to be as the
                                                type

Eug-V:

11,26 Third letter after first lacuna: see Emmel, 1979: 184.

11,27 ⲱ: see Emmel, 1979: 184. Emmel reconstructs ⲉ̣ immediately after the first
    lacuna, but all that is visible is the top of the curve. Since a middle stroke, which
    usually extends to the right of the upper curve, is not visible, the more likely
    reconstruction is ⲥ.

12,1 First superlinear stroke is in lacuna.

12,2 See endnote 7.

Eug-III:

83,20 "will": see endnote 7.

NHC III   BG

NHC V 12,4–12   NHC III 83,21–84,4

ⲁⲡⲉⲛⲉⲱⲛ] ⁵ ϣⲱⲡⲉ
ⲙ̅ⲡⲉ⳽ⲧ[ⲩⲡⲟⲥ · ⲡⲓⲭⲣⲟⲛⲟⲥ] | ⲇⲉ
ⲉⲧⲁ⳽ϣⲱⲡⲉ ⲛ̅ⲟ[ⲩⲧⲩⲡⲟⲥ ⲛ̅]|ⲧⲉ
ⲡⲓϣⲟⲣⲡ̅ ⲛ̅ϫⲡⲟ ⲛ̅[ⲧⲉ⳽ ⲛ̅ϣⲏⲣⲉ·] |
ϯⲣⲟⲙⲡⲉ ⲇⲉ ⲁⲥϣ[ⲱⲡⲉ
ⲛ̅ⲟⲩⲧⲩⲡⲟⲥ] | ⲛ̅ⲧⲉ ⲡⲥ̅ⲣ̅·
ⲡⲓⲙⲛ̅ⲧ̅[ⲥⲛⲟⲟⲩ]ⲥ ⲇⲉ ¹⁰ ⲛ̅ⲛⲉⲃⲟⲧ̂ .
ⲁⲩϣⲱⲡ[ⲉ ⲛ̅ⲟⲩⲧⲩⲡ]ⲟⲥ | ⲛ̅ⲧⲉ
ϯⲙⲛ̅ⲧⲥⲛⲟⲟⲩ[ⲥ ⲛ̅ϭⲟⲙ ⲉⲧ]ⲁⲩ|ⲟⲩ
ⲱⲛⲍ̅ ⲉⲃⲟⲗ ⳽ⲙ̅ ⲡⲥ̅ⲣ̅· ⲛⲓⲁⲅⲅⲉⲗⲟⲥ |

ⲁ⳽ϣⲱⲡⲉ ⲛⲁ⳽ ⲛ̅ⲧⲩⲡⲟⲥ ⲛ̅ϭⲓ
ⲡⲉⲛ|ⲁⲓⲱⲛ · ⲡⲉⲭⲣⲟⲛⲟⲥ ⲁ⳽ϣⲱⲡⲉ
ⲛ̅|ⲧⲩⲡⲟⲥ ⲙ̅ⲡⲉⲡⲣⲱⲧⲟⲅⲉⲛⲉⲧⲱⲣ
ⲡⲉ⳽ϣⲏⲣ[ⲉ· ⲧⲉⲣⲟⲙⲡⲉ ⲁ]ⲥ⳽ϣⲱⲡⲉ   [ⲡ.
ⲛ̅|ⲧⲩⲡⲟⲥ ⲙ̅ⲡ[ⲥⲱⲧⲏⲣ·
ⲡⲙⲛ̅]ⲧ̅ⲥ̅ⲛⲟ|ⲟⲩⲥ ⲛ̅ⲉⲃⲟⲧ̂ ⲁⲩϣⲱⲡⲉ
ⲛ̅ⲧⲩⲡⲟⲥ | ⲛ̅ⲧⲙⲛ̅ⲧⲥ̅ⲛⲟⲟⲩⲥ ⲛ̅ϭⲟⲙ·

came to be ⁵ as the [type] of
[Immortal] Man. [Time] | came to
be as the [type of] | [his] first-
begotten [son.] | The year [came to
be as the type] | of Savior. The
twelve ¹⁰ months came to be [as the
type] | of the twelve [powers who] |
appeared from Savior. They are

| of Immortal Man. | Time came to
be as | the type of First Begetter,
his son. [The year] came to be as |
the type of [Savior. The] twelve |
months came to be as the type | of   [8⁴

Eug-V:

12,5 Superlinear stroke is in lacuna.

12,6 First superlinear stroke is in lacuna.

12,10 Low dot may indicate word separation (see 8,7 and 8,16).

12,12 Third superlinear stroke is in lacuna.

Eug-III:

83,21–22 K unaccountably does not translate the possessive article ⲡⲉⲛ- ("our"),
leaving instead a lacuna indicator. He also incorrectly makes "the immortal Man"
the subject of the sentence.

84,1 ⲁ⳽ϣ]ⲱⲡⲉ (Tr—incorrectly restored).

[ⲧⲉⲣⲟⲙⲡⲉ], ["the year"]: ["the all-begetter"] (ⲡⲁⲛⲅⲉⲛⲉⲧⲱⲣ) (K) (too long for
the lacuna).

84,2 "savior": not restored by K.

84,3 Corr.: ⲧⲩⲡⲟⲥ for ⲧⲟⲡⲟⲥ (erasure).

MS has the second superlinear stroke in lacuna.

NHC III   BG

NHC V 12,13–21

ⲚⲈ ⲠⲒⲰⲘⲚ̄ⲦⲰⲈⲤⲈ Ⲛ̄ⲌⲞⲞⲨ Ⲛ̄ⲦⲈ |
ⲦⲈⲢⲞⲘⲠⲈ · ⲀⲨⲰⲰⲠⲈ
Ⲛ̄ⲞⲨⲦⲨ ¹⁵ⲠⲞⲤ Ⲛ̄ⲦⲈ ⲦⲰⲘⲚ̄ⲦⲰⲈⲤⲈ
Ⲛ̄ϬⲞⲘ | ⲈⲦⲀⲨⲞⲨⲰⲚⲌ̄ ⲈⲂⲞⲖ ⲌⲘ̄
ⲠⲤⲰⲦⲎⲢ · | ⲚⲒⲀⲄⲄⲈⲖⲞⲤ ⲆⲈ
ⲈⲦⲀⲨϢⲰⲠⲈ ⲈⲂ[ⲞⲖ] | ⲌⲚ̄ ⲚⲀⲒ̈ ⲈⲨⲈ
Ⲛ̄ⲚⲀⲦⲦ ⲎⲠⲈ ⲈⲢⲞⲞⲨ[·] | ⲀⲨϢⲰⲠⲈ
Ⲛ̄ⲞⲨⲦⲨⲠⲞⲤ Ⲛ̄ⲦⲀ[Ⲩ] ²⁰ Ⲛ̄ϬⲒ
ⲚⲒⲌⲞⲞ Ⲩ ⲘⲚ̄ ⲚⲈⲨⲞⲨⲚⲞⲨ Ⲙ[Ⲛ̄] |
ⲚⲈⲨⲤⲞⲨⲤⲞⲨ·

NHC III 84,4–11

ⲠϢⲘⲦ ⁵{Ⲧ}ϢⲈⲤⲈ Ⲛ̄ⲦⲚ̄
ⲦⲈⲢⲞⲘ<Ⲡ>Ⲉ Ⲛ̄ⲌⲞⲞⲨ Ⲛ̄|ⲦⲀⲨϢⲰⲠⲈ
Ⲛ̄ⲦⲨⲠⲞⲤ Ⲛ̄ⲦϢⲘ̄ⲦϢⲈ|ⲤⲈ Ⲛ̄ϬⲞⲘ·
ⲚⲀⲒ̈ Ⲛ̄ⲦⲀⲨⲞⲨⲰⲚⲌ ⲈⲂⲞⲖ | ⲌⲘ̄
ⲠⲤⲰⲦⲎⲢ Ⲛ̄ⲀⲄⲄⲈⲖⲞⲤ Ⲛ̄ⲦⲀⲨ|ϢⲰⲠⲈ
ⲈⲂⲞⲖ ⲌⲚ̄ ⲚⲀⲒ̈ ⲈⲦⲈ ⲘⲚ̄ ⲎⲠⲈ ¹⁰
Ⲉ̅ⲢⲞⲞⲨ ⲀⲨϢⲰⲠⲈ ⲚⲀⲨ Ⲛ̄ⲦⲨⲠⲞⲤ |
Ⲛ̄ϬⲒ ⲚⲈⲨⲚⲞⲞⲨⲈ ⲘⲚ̄ ⲚⲈⲨⲤⲞⲨⲤⲞⲨ

| the angels. The three hundred sixty
days of | the year came to be as the
type ¹⁵ of the three hundred sixty
powers | who appeared from Savior.
| The days with their hours and |
moments came to be as the type of |
the angels who came from ²⁰ them
(the three hundred sixty powers),
since | they are numberless.

the twelve powers. The three ⁵
hundred sixty days of the year |
came to be as the type of the three
hundred | sixty powers who
appeared | from Savior. Their hours
| and moments came to be as the ¹⁰
type of the angels who came | from
them (the three hundred sixty
powers) (and) who are without
number.

Eug-V:

12,13 The absence of punctuation after ⲚⲈ may indicate that ⲚⲒⲀⲄⲄⲈⲖⲞⲤ ⲚⲈ, "They
are the angels," is a gloss (see par.), or it may mean that the scribe intended the
rendering "The angels are the three hundred sixty days of the year. They came to
be. . . ."

Eug-III:

84,5 MS has ⲦⲈⲢⲞⲘⲦⲈ. Tr emends this word but lacks the initial emendation.

NHC III 106,24–107,5 BG 103,10–17

ΝΕΤΝΗΟΥ ²⁵ ΤΗΡΟΥ ΕΖΟΥΝ
ΕΠΚΟΣΜΟΣ Ν̄
ΡΖ ΘΕ Ν̄ΟΥΤᾹ†ΛΕ ΕΒΟΛ ΖΜ̄
ΠΟΥΟΕΙΝ | ΕΒΟΛ ΖΙΤΟΟΤϤ Μ̄ΠΑΪ
ΕΥΤΝ̄ΝΟ|ΟΥ Μ̄ΜΟΟΥ ΕΠΚΟΣΜΟΣ
Μ̄Π̄ΠΑΝ|ΤΟΚΡΑΤΩΡ· ΧΕ ΕΥΕΖΑΡΗΖ
ΕΡΟΟΥ ⁵ ΕΒΟΛ ΖΙΤΟΟΤϤ· ΑΥΩ

¹⁰ ΟΥΟΝ ΝΙΜ ΕΤΝΗΥ ΕΠ|ΚΟΣΜΟΣ
ΑΥΤΝ̄ΝΟΟΥ|ΣΕ ΕΒΟΛ ΖΙΤΜ̄ ΠΑΕΙ
| Ν̄ΘΕ Ν̄ΝΟΥΤᾹ†ΛΕ ΕΒΟΛ | ΖΜ
ΠΟΥΟΪΝ ΕΠΚΟΣΜΟΣ ¹⁵
Μ̄ΠΠΑΝΤΟΚΡΑΤΩΡ †ΕΑ|ΡΕΖ ΕΡΟϤ
ΕΒΟΛ ΖΙΤΟΟΤϤ † | ΑΥΩ

107 All who come ²⁵ into the world, like a drop from the Light, | are sent by him | to the world of Almighty, | that they might be guarded ⁵ by him. And the

¹⁰ All who come into the | world have been sent | by him, | like a drop | from the Light, to the world ¹⁵ of Almighty, | † to guard it by him. † | And the

SJC-III:

107,1 Corr.: second ʌ for erased ρ; ᴢ for erased letter.

NHC V   NHC III

NHC III 107,5–14   BG 103,17–104,11

ⲁⲡⲥⲱⲛⲍ ⲛ|ⲧⲉϥⲃⲱϣⲉ ⲙⲟⲣϥ· ⲍⲙ   ⲧⲙⲣⲣⲉ ⲛⲧⲉϥⲃⲱϣⲉ | ⲁⲥⲙⲟⲣϥ ⲍⲙ
ⲡⲉⲧⲉⲍⲛⲉⲥ· | ⲛ̄ⲧⲥⲟⲫⲓⲁ ϫⲉ   ⲡⲟⲩⲱϣⲉ ⲛ̄
ⲉⲣⲉⲡⲍⲱⲃ <ⲛⲁⲟⲩⲱⲛⲍ> ⲉⲃⲟⲗ   ⲧⲥⲟⲫⲓⲁ [ϫⲉⲕⲁⲁⲥ ⲉⲣⲉⲡⲓ]|ⲍⲱⲃ   [ⲣ̄ⲇ̄]
ⲍⲓ|ⲧⲟⲟⲧⲩ̄ ⲙ̄ⲡⲕⲟⲥⲙⲟⲥ ⲧⲏⲣϥ̄   ⲛⲁⲟⲩ[ⲱⲛⲍ ⲉⲃⲟⲗ ⲙ]|ⲡⲕⲟⲥⲙⲟⲥ
ⲛ̄ⲧⲙⲛ̄<ⲧ>|ⲍⲏⲕⲉ ⲉⲧⲃⲉ   ⲧⲏⲣϥ ⲍⲛ ⲧⲙ[ⲛⲧ]|ⲍⲏⲕⲉ ⲉⲧⲃⲉ
ⲧⲉϥⲙⲛ̄ⲧⲭⲁⲥⲓ ⲍⲏⲧ̄ ¹⁰ ⲙⲛ̄   ⲧⲉϥⲙⲛ̄ⲧⲭⲁ⁵ⲥⲓ ⲍⲏⲧ ⲙⲛ̄
ⲧⲉϥⲙⲛ̄ⲧⲃⲗ̄ⲗⲉ· ⲙⲛ̄   ⲧⲉϥⲙⲛ̄ⲧⲃⲗ̄ⲗⲉ | ⲙⲛ̄
ⲧⲙⲛ̄ⲧ̄ⲁ|ⲧⲥⲟⲟⲩⲛ ϫⲉ ⲁ<ⲩ>ⲧ̄ ⲣⲁⲛ   ⲧⲉϥⲙⲛ̄ⲧⲁⲧⲥⲟⲟⲩⲛ ϫⲉ | ⲁⲩⲧ̄ ⲣⲁⲛ
ⲉⲣⲟϥ· ⲁⲛⲟⲕ | ⲇⲉ ⲛ̄ⲧⲁⲉⲓⲉⲓ̂ ⲉⲃⲟⲗ   ⲉⲣⲟϥ ⲁⲛⲟⲕ ⲇⲉ | ⲁ̈ⲉⲓ ⲉⲃⲟⲗ ⲍⲛ
ⲍⲛ̄ ⲛ̄ⲧⲟⲡⲟⲥ ⲙ̄|[ⲡ]ⲥ̣ⲁⲍⲣⲉ· ⲍⲙ̄   ⲛ̄ⲧⲟⲡⲟⲥ | ⲛⲧⲡⲉ ⲍⲣⲁ̈ ⲍⲙ ⲡⲟⲩⲱϣ
ⲡⲉⲧⲉⲍⲛⲉϥ ⲙ̄ⲡⲓⲛⲟϭ | [ⲛ̄ⲟ]ⲩⲟⲉⲓⲛ   ⲙ̄¹⁰ⲡⲛⲟϭ ⲛⲟⲩⲟ̈ⲛ ⲁ̄ⲃⲱⲗ
ⲛ̄ⲧⲁⲍⲉⲓ̂ ⲉⲃⲟⲗ ⲍⲙ̄ ⲡⲥⲱⲛⲍ   ⲙ̄|ⲡⲥⲱⲛ<ⲍ> ⲉⲧⲙ̄ⲙⲁⲩ

bond of | his forgetfulness bound   fetter of his forgetfulness | bound
him by the will | of Sophia, that the   him by the will of
matter might be <revealed> through   Sophia, [so that the] | matter might   **[104]**
it | to the whole world in poverty | be revealed [to] | the whole world in
concerning his (Almighty's)   poverty | concerning his
arrogance ¹⁰ and blindness and | the   (Almighty's) arrogance ⁵ and
ignorance that he was named. But I | blindness | and his ignorance that |
| came from the places | above by   he was named. But I | came from
the will of the great | Light, (I) who   the places | above by the will of ¹⁰
escaped from that bond;   the great Light; I have loosed | that
                                          <bond>;

SJC-III:

107,6 Corr.: second ⲍ for erased ⲛ.

107,7 So emended by T–S (in translation only) & K.

107,8 "in poverty": "as poverty" (K).

107,9 "concerning": "because of" (K).

107,11 MS has ϥ (active rather than passive: "*he* gave himself a name"; not emended by T–S or K). For the significance of a deity's being named, see 94,21–24, and parr.

107,13 T–S restores [ⲡⲥ].

107,14 "who": "which" (K) (great light? will?).

SJC-BG:

104,4 "concerning": "because of" (T–S).

104,6–7 See III 107, 11n.

104,11 MS has ⲧ, "that *creation*" (not emended by T–S).

N.B. the stroke rather than the expected dieresis in the last word; see also 115,11 and 123,16.

NHC V

NHC III

NHC III 107,15–22   BG 104,12–105,4

¹⁵ [ετ]ⲙ̅ⲙⲁⲩ ⲁⲉⲓⲥⲱⲗⲡ̅ ⲙ̅ⲫⲱⲃ   ⲁⲓ̈ⲥⲱⲗⲡ | ⲙ̅ⲫⲱⲃ ⲙ̅ⲡⲙ̅ⲍⲁⲟⲩ
ⲛ̅ⲛ̅|[ⲥ]ⲟⲟⲛⲉ ⲁⲉⲓⲧⲟⲩⲛⲟⲥϥ̅   ⲛ̅ⲥⲟⲛⲉ | ⲁⲓ̈ⲧⲟⲩⲛⲟⲥϥ ⲭⲉⲕⲁⲁⲥ
ⲭⲉⲕⲁⲁⲥ ⲉϥ|ⲛⲁϯ ⲕⲁⲣⲡⲟⲥ   ⲉϥⲉ|ϯ ⲕⲁⲣⲡⲟⲥ ⲉⲛⲁϣⲱϥ ⲉⲃⲟⲗ ¹⁵
ⲉⲛⲁϣⲱϥ ⲉⲃⲟⲗ | [ⲍ]ⲓ̣ ⲧⲟⲟϯ ⲛ̅ϭⲓ   ⲍⲓ̈ⲧⲟⲧ ⲛ̅ϭⲓ ϯⲧⲁ̅ϯⲗⲉ ⲉⲧⲙ̅|ⲙⲁⲩ
ⲡⲓⲧⲁ̅ϯⲗⲉ ⲉⲧⲙ̅ⲙⲁⲩ | ⲧⲁⲓ̈ ⲛ̅ⲧⲁⲩⲧⲛ̅ⲛⲟⲟⲩⲥ | ⲉⲃⲟⲗ
ⲡⲉⲛⲧⲁⲩⲧⲛ̅ⲛⲟⲟⲩϥ ⲍⲓⲧⲛ̅ ⲧⲥⲟⲫⲓⲁ   ⲍⲓ̈ⲧⲟⲟⲧⲥ ⲛ̅ⲧⲥⲟⲫⲓ|ⲁ ⲛ̅ϭⲭⲱⲕ
²⁰ ⲉϥⲉⲭⲱⲕ ⲉⲃⲟⲗ ⲁⲩⲱ   ⲛ̅ⲥⲧⲙ̅ϣⲱⲡⲉ
ⲛ̅ⲛⲉϥϣⲱⲱⲧ | ϭⲉ· ⲁⲗⲗⲁ   ϭⲉ [ⲛ̅]ϣⲧⲁ ⲁⲗⲗⲁ ⲉⲩⲉⲛⲁ|ⲍⲃⲉⲥ   [ⲣ̅ⲉ̅]
ⲉⲩⲛⲁⲛⲟⲍ <ⲃ>ϥ ⲉⲃⲟⲗ ⲍⲓⲧⲟ |ⲟ̅ϯ   ⲉⲃⲟⲗ ⲍⲓ̈ⲧⲟⲟⲧ ⲁ|ⲛⲟⲕ ⲡⲉ ⲡⲛⲟϭ
ⲡⲛⲟϭ ⲛ̅ⲥⲱⲧⲏⲣ ⲭⲉ   ⲛ̅ⲥⲱⲧⲏⲣ | ⲭⲉⲕⲁⲁⲥ

¹⁵ I have cut off the work of the | I have cut off | the work of the
robbers; I have wakened that drop | robber tomb; | I have wakened that
that was sent from Sophia, | that it | drop | that was sent ¹⁵ from Sophia,
might bear much fruit ²⁰ through me | that it | might bear much fruit |
and be perfected and not again be | through me and be perfected and not
defective but be <joined> through | again become
me, the Great Savior, that   defective but be joined | through   [105]
                                           me—I | am the Great Savior— | that

---

SJC-III:

107,15 MS has first superlinear stroke in lacuna.

    "cut off": "revealed" (K, apparently translating ϭⲱⲗⲡ instead of ⲥⲱⲗⲡ).

107,18 Regarding the gender of ⲧⲁ̅ϯⲗⲉ, see BG 104,13–105,2n. and Till's endnote (T–S: 328).

107,21 Not emended by T–S or K ("be separated"). T–S takes the word to refer to separation from material bonds. ⲛⲟⲍ⧫ is unattested elsewhere as stat. pron. of ⲛⲟⲩⲍⲉ, "separate." In view of the BG par. it seems, therefore, more likely that ⲛⲟⲍ⧫ should be emended as above. See BG 105,1–2n.

SJC-BG:

104,13–105,2 N.B., the pronouns referring to ⲧⲁϯⲗⲉ are masc., preceding its occurrence, and fem. following it. T–S suggests that the scribe copied his *Vorlage* until he came to the noun, which he took to be fem. (it occurs as either masc. or fem.). Subsequent pronouns therefore were changed (T–S: 328).

105,1–2 "be joined": less likely, "be fertilized" (T–S). T–S takes the verb to be different from, although similar in appearance to, ⲛⲟⲩⲍⲃ, "to yoke, be joined" (Crum: 243a). Crum also makes this distinction but expresses his uncertainty (243b). For the transitive use of ⲛⲟⲩⲍⲃ (2), meaning "to fertilize," Crum cites only the instance here, the grammatical object of which he mistakenly takes to be a female personage. For the concept of joining, see 122,5–123,1.

NHC V   NHC III

NHC III 107,22–108,12   BG 105,4–106,5

ερεπεϥ|εοου ναογωνζ εβολ·   ερεπεϥεο ⁵ογ ογωνζ εβολ χε
χεκααc | εγναтμαειε   εγ|ετμαϊε τκεcoφια | εβολ
τκεcoφια εβολ ζμ ²⁵ πεϭρωζ   ζμ πιϣτα ετ{ε}|<μμαγ χε
ετμμαγ χε ννενεc   ν>ненесϣн|ре ϭε ϣωпе νϣτα
ϣнре ϭε ϣωпе νϣτα αλλα | αλλα ¹⁰ εγεματε νногτιμн |
PH   εγναϯ ματε ζν τετιμн μν | μν ογεοογ νcεβωκ | εζραϊ ϣα
ογεοογ νcεβωκ εζραϊ ϣα   πεγειωτ αγ|ω νcεcoγων
πεγ|ειωϯ νcεcoγν νϣαχε   τεζϊн νν|ϣαχε μπογοειν
μπογ⁵οειν μμνϯζοογϯ ντωτν   ντω ¹⁵τν αγτννοογ θηγτν |
ν|λε νταγτννοογ θηγτν   εβολ ζϊτοοτϥ μπϣн|ре
ζι|τμ πϣнре νταγτννοογϥ· | νταγτννοογϥ χεκα|αc
χε ετετναχι ογοειν   ετετναχι ογοϊν ν
ντετν·|caζε θηνογ εβολ   τετνcaζε θηγ[τ]ν ε|βολ   [ΡϚ]
ντβϣε ν¹⁰неϳογcια αγω   ντβϣε ннеϳογ|cια
νcτμογωνζ | ϭε ετβε θηνογ   νcτμογωνζ ϭε ετ|βε θηγτν
νϭι τετριβн | ετχαζμ тн ετε   νϭι ϯτριβн ⁵ ετχαζμ τεβολ ζμ

his | glory might be revealed, so that   his glory ⁵ might be revealed, so that
| Sophia might also be justified in   Sophia | might also be | justified in
regard to that ²⁵ defect, that her   regard to <that> defect, | <that> her
108 sons might not again become   sons | <might not> again become
defective but | might attain honor   defective but ¹⁰ might attain honor |
and | glory and go up to their | and glory and go | up to their Father
Father and know the words of the   and | know the way of the | words of
masculine Light. And ⁵ you | Light. You ¹⁵ were sent | by the
were sent by | the Son, who was sent | Son, | who was sent that | you might
that you might receive Light and | receive Light and
remove yourselves from the   remove yourselves | from the   **[106]**
forgetfulness of ¹⁰ the authorities,   forgetfulness of the authorities, | and
and that it might not again come to   that it might not again come to
appearance | because of you,   appearance | because of you,
namely, the unclean rubbing | that is   namely, the unclean rubbing ⁵ that is

---

SJC-III:

108,11 "because of you": "for your sakes" (K).

SJC-BG:

105,8 MS has ΜΑϥϣΙΝΕ , "that *does not seek.*"

NHC V 12,21–23 NHC III 84,12–15

ⲛⲧⲉⲓ̈ⲍⲉ ⲟⲛ ⲛ[ⲏ ⲉ]|ⲧⲁⲩⲟⲩⲱⲛⲍ̄
ⲉⲃⲟⲗ· ⲁ·ϥⲧⲁⲙⲓⲟ ⲛ̄[ⲁϥ] | ⲛ̄ϭⲓ
ⲡⲉ·ⲅⲉⲓⲱⲧ̇ ⲡⲓⲣⲉϥϫⲡⲟ ⲛ̄[ⲛⲏ] |

| ⲛ̄ⲧⲉⲣⲟⲩⲱⲛⲍ ⲇⲉ ⲉⲃⲟⲗ ⲛ̄ϭⲓ
ⲛⲉⲛ|ⲧⲁⲉⲓ·ϣⲁ·ⲭ ⲉ ⲉⲣⲟⲟⲩ
ⲁ·ϥⲧⲁⲙⲓⲟ ⲛⲁ<ϥ> | ⲛ̄ϭⲓ
ⲡⲁⲛⲅⲉⲛⲉⲧⲱⲣ ⲡⲉ·ⲅⲉⲓⲱⲧ̇ ⲛ̄¹⁵ϣⲟⲣⲡ̄

Thus, again, | the father of those
who appeared, | Begetter of All
[Things], very soon created

| And when those whom I have
discussed appeared, | All-Begetter,
their father, very soon | created

Eug-III:

84,12 ⲛ̄ⲧⲉⲣⲟⲩ <ⲟⲩ>ⲱⲛⲍ (Tr; unnecessary emendation).

84,13 MS has ⲩ (correction of untranslated ethical dative): not emended by Tr, who
translates "for them" (so also K).

"their father, very soon": "their first father" (T–S, K & Tr).

NHC III 108,12–25 | BG 106,5–107,5

<table>
<tr><td>

ⲞⲨⲈⲂⲞⲗ ⲦⲈ | ⲌⲘ ⲠⲈⲔⲢⲰⳘ· ⲈⲦⲌⲀ
ⲌⲞⲦⲈ· ⲠⲈⲚ|ⲦⲀϤⲈⲒ ⲈⲂⲞⲗ ⲌⳘ
ⲠⲤⲀⲢⲔⲒⲚⲞⲤ Ⳙ ¹⁵ⲘⲞⲞⲨ ⲌⲰⳘ·
ⲈⲌⲢⲀⲒ ⲈⲬⲚ ⲦⲈⲨ|ⲠⲢⲞⲚⲞⲒⲀ · ⲦⲞⲦⲈ
ⲠⲈⲬⲀϤ ⲚⲀ[ϥ] | ⲚϬⲒ ⲐⲰⲘⲀⲤ ⲬⲈ
ⲠⲬⲞⲈⲒⲤ ⲠⲤⲰ|ⲦⲎⲢ ⲚⲈⲦⲞⲨⲀⲦⲂ̄
ⲈⲚⲠⲎⲞⲨⲈ ⲞⲨ|ⲎⲢ ⲚⲈ· ⲚⲈⲨⲀⲒⲰⲚ·
ⲠⲈⲬⲈ ⲠⲦⲈ ²⁰ⲗⲒⲞⲤ ⲚⲤⲰⲦⲎⲢ· ⲬⲈ
†ⲈⲠⲀⲒⲚⲞⲨ | ⳘⲘⲰⲦⲚ̄ ⲬⲈ
ⲦⲈⲦⲚ̄ϢⲒⲚⲈ Ⲛ̄ⲤⲀ | ⲚⲒⲚⲞϬ Ⲛ̄ⲀⲒⲰⲚ
ⲬⲈ ⲚⲈⲦⲚ̄ⲚⲞⲨ|ⲚⲈ ⲈⲨⲌⲚ̄
ⲚⲒⲀⲠⲈⲢⲀⲚⲦⲞⲚ

Ⲛ̄ⲦⲈ|ⲢⲞⲨⲰⲚⲌ ⲆⲈ Ⲛ̄ϬⲒ ⲚⲎ
Ⲛ̄ⲦⲀⲈⲒ ²⁵ϢⲀⲬⲈ ⲈⲢⲞⲞⲨ Ⲛ̄ϢⲞⲢⲠ̄
ⲀϤⲦⲤⲀ[ⲚⲞ]

</td><td>

Ⲡ|ⲔⲰⲌ ⲈⲦⲌⲀⲦⲚ̄ ⲦⲈⲚⲦⲀⲤ|ⲈⲒ ⲈⲂⲞⲗ

ⲌⳘ ⲠⲤⲀⲢⲔⲒⲚⲞⲤ | ⳘⲘⲞⲞⲨ ⲀⲨⲰ
ⲈⲦⲈⲦⲚⲈ|ⲌⲰⳘ ⲈⲬⲚ
ⲦⲈϤⲠⲢⲞⲚⲞ ¹⁰Ⲁ ⲦⲞⲦⲈ ⲠⲈⲬⲀϤ
ⲚⲀϤ Ⲛ̄ϬⲒ | ⲐⲰⲘⲀⲤ ⲬⲈ ⲠⲈⲬⲤ̄
ⲠⲤⲰ|ⲦⲎⲢ ⲞⲨⲎⲢ ⲚⲈ ⲚⲒⲀⲒⲰⲚ |
ⲈⲦⲞⲨⲞⲦⲂ̄ ⲈⲘⲠⲎⲨⲈ ⲠⲈ|ⲬⲀϤ Ⲛ̄ϬⲒ
ⲠⲦⲈⲗⲒⲞⲤ Ⲛ̄ⲤⲰ ¹⁵ⲦⲎⲢ ⲬⲈ
†ⲈⲠⲀⲒⲚⲞⲨ Ⳙ|ⲘⲰⲦⲚ̄ ⲬⲈ
ⲦⲈⲦⲚ̄ϢⲒⲚⲈ | ⲈⲦⲂⲈ ⲚⲒⲚⲞϬ ⲚⲀⲒⲰⲚ
| ⲬⲈ ⲚⲈⲦⲚ̄ⲚⲞⲨⲚⲈ ⲈⲨⲌⲢⲀ|ⲈⲒ ⲌⲚ̄
ⲚⲒⲀⲠⲈⲢⲀⲚⲦⲞⲚ
Ⲛ̄ⲦⲈⲢⲞⲨⲰⲚⲌ ⲆⲈ ⲚϬⲒ | Ⲣ̄Ⲍ̄
ⲚⲈⲚⲦⲀⲒ̈ⲬⲞⲞⲨ Ⲛ̄ϢⲞ|ⲢⲈⲠ· ⲀϤⲢ̄
ϢⲢ̄Ⲡ Ⲛ̄ⲦⲀⲘⲒ|Ⲟ ⲚⲀϤ Ⲛ̄ϬⲒ
ⲠⲀⲨⲦⲞⲄⲈⲚⲈ ⁵ⲦⲰⲢ ⲚⲈⲒⲰⲦ

</td></tr>
</table>

| from the fearful fire that | came from their fleshly part. ¹⁵ Tread upon their | malicious intent." Then Thomas said to [him]: | "Lord, Savior, | how many are the aeons of those | who surpass the heavens?" The perfect ²⁰ Savior said: "I praise | you (pl.) because you ask about | the great aeons, for your roots | are in the infinities. Now when | those whom I have discussed earlier were revealed, ²⁵ he [provided] | from the | envy that is with what | came from their fleshly part, | and (also) that you might | tread upon his malicious intent." ¹⁰ Then Thomas said to him: | "Christ, Savior, | how many are the aeons | that surpass the heavens?" The | perfect Savior said: ¹⁵ "I praise | you (pl.) because you ask | about the great aeons, | for your roots are | in the infinities. Now when | those whom I have discussed earlier were revealed, | Self-Begetter | Father very soon created |

107

SJC-III:

108,25 Bracketed letters are those presumed to be at the beginning of 109,1.

SJC-BG:

106,6 Alt. for line: <ⲔⲰⲌⲦ ⲈⲦⲌⲀ ⲌⲞⲦⲈ Ⲛ̄ⲦⲀϤ->, "the <*fearful fire that*> came . . ." (T–S sugg.); see *SJC*–III par.

106,11 ᴍꜱ has a large asterisk in the left margin.

106,14 ᴍꜱ has a large asterisk in the left margin.

NHC V 12,24–30

ⲧⲏⲣⲟⲩ ⲙ̄ⲙⲛ̄ⲧ̇ⲥⲛⲟⲟ[ⲩⲥ ⲛ̄ⲛⲉⲱⲛ] ²⁵
ⲛ̄ϣⲟⲣ[ⲡ̄] ⲉⲩ[ϣⲙ]ϣⲉ
ⲙ̄ⲡⲓⲙⲛ̄ⲧⲥⲛ[ⲟⲟⲩⲥ·]
| [ⲛ̄ⲧ̇]ⲍⲉ ⲛⲉⲓ[ⲉⲱⲛ· ⲡ]ⲟⲩⲁ̣ ⲡⲟⲩⲁ
ⲛ̄ⲛ̣[ⲏ] | ⲛ̄ⲧ̇ⲟ̄ⲃ ⲛ̄ⲥⲁ̣ⲙ
ⲉⲧⲁ[ⲩⲟⲩ]ⲱⲛⲍ̄ ⲉ̣[ⲃⲟⲗ] | [ⲛ̄ⲍ]ⲏⲧ[ϥ̄·
ⲟⲩⲛ̄ⲧⲁⲩ ⲛ̄ϯⲟⲩ] ⲛ̄ⲥⲧⲉ[ⲣⲉⲱⲙⲁ] |
[ⲍ]ⲛ̄ ⲛⲉ[ⲩⲡⲏⲟⲩⲉ ⲧⲏⲣⲟⲩ·]
ⲍⲱⲥⲧ[ⲉ] ³⁰ ⲛ̣[ⲥ]ⲉ̣ⲣ̄ ϣⲙⲛ̄ⲧ̇ϣⲉⲥⲉ
ⲛ̄ⲥⲧⲉⲣⲉⲱⲙⲁ . . .]
(2± lines lacking)

NHC III 84,15–85,3

ⲙ̄ⲙⲛ̄ⲧ̄ⲥⲛⲟⲟⲩⲥ ⲛ̄ⲁⲓⲱⲛ | ⲉⲍⲟⲩⲛ
ⲉⲧⲍⲩⲡⲏⲣⲉⲥⲓⲁ
ⲙ̄{ⲛ̄}ⲡⲙⲛ̄|ⲧ̄ⲥⲛⲟⲟⲩⲥ ⲛ̄ⲁⲅⲅⲉⲗⲟⲥ·
ⲁⲩⲱ ⲛ̄ⲍⲣⲁⲓ̈ | ⲍⲛ̄ ⲛⲁⲓⲱⲛ ⲧⲏⲣⲟⲩ
ⲛⲉⲩⲛ̄ ⲥⲟⲉ· ⲥⲟⲉ· ⲡⲉ· ⲍⲙ̄ ⲡⲟⲩⲁ
ⲡⲟⲩⲁ ⲙ̄ⲙⲟⲟⲩ ⲍⲱⲥⲧⲉ ²⁰ ⲛ̄ⲥⲉⲣ̄
ϣϥⲉⲥⲛⲟⲟⲩⲥ ⲙ̄ⲡⲉ ⲛ̄ⲧⲉ
ⲧⲉϣ|ϥⲉⲥⲛⲟⲟⲩⲥ ⲛ̄ⲥⲟⲙ ⲛⲁⲓ̈
ⲛ̄ⲧⲁⲩⲟⲩⲱⲛⲍ | ⲉⲃⲟⲗ ⲛ̄ⲍⲏⲧϥ̄· ⲁⲩⲱ
ⲍⲛ̄ ⲙ̄ⲡⲏⲟⲩⲉ | ⲧⲏⲣⲟⲩ ⲛⲉⲟⲩⲛ̄ ϯⲟⲩ
ϯⲟⲩ ⲛ̄ⲥⲧⲉ|ⲣⲉⲱⲙⲁ ⲍⲱⲥⲧⲉ ⲛ̄ⲥⲉⲣ̄
ϣⲙ̄ⲧϣⲉ
ⲥⲉ ⲛ̄ⲥⲧⲉ[ⲣⲉⲱⲙⲁ ⲛ̄]ⲧⲉ   [ⲡⲉ
ⲧϣⲙ̄ⲧϣⲉ|ⲥⲉ ⲛ̄ⲥⲟⲙ [ⲛⲁⲓ̈
ⲛ̄ⲧⲁⲩⲟ]ⲩⲱⲛⲍ ⲉⲃⲟⲗ | ⲛ̄ⲍⲏⲧⲟⲩ

| twelve [aeons] ²⁵ for [retinue] for the twelve (powers).
| So each of the [aeons] of | the seventy-two powers who appeared | [from him have five] firmaments | [in all their heavens], so ³⁰ [there are three hundred sixty firmaments . . .]
| (2± lines lacking)

¹⁵ twelve aeons | for retinue for the twelve | angels. And in | each aeon there were six (heavens), | so ²⁰ there are seventy-two heavens of the seventy-two | powers who appeared | from him. And in each of the heavens | there were five firmaments, | so there are (altogether) three hundred sixty [firmaments] of the three hundred | sixty powers that appeared | from them.   [85

Eug-V:

12,28 Fifth superlinear stroke is in lacuna.

12,30 MS has a superlinear stroke visible in the second lacuna above the letter that would have followed ⲥⲧⲉⲣⲉⲱⲙⲁ .

Eug-III:

84,16 Not emended by T–S, K or Tr ("*with* the twelve").

85,1 Tr restores as above but leave ⲛ̄ⲧⲉ untranslated ("[firmaments]. Three hundred") (similarly, K).

85,3 "from . . . firmaments": less likely, "from the firmaments. When they" (K & Tr).

NHC III

(Coptic pages 109 and 110 are
missing.)

BG 107,5–8

ⲙ̄ⲙⲛ̄ⲧⲥ|ⲛⲟⲟⲩⲥ ⲛ̄ⲁⲓⲱⲛ
ⲉⲩⲍⲏ|ⲡⲉⲣⲏⲥⲓⲁ ⲙ̄ⲡⲓⲙⲛ̄ⲧⲥ|ⲛⲟⲟⲩⲥ
ⲛⲁⲅⲅⲉⲗⲟⲥ

[5] twelve | aeons for retinue | for the
twelve | angels.

NHC V 13,1–7   NHC III 85,3–9

[ⲓ̄ⲅ̄] [9±] .[. ⲉⲧ]ⲁⲩⲣ̄ ϣⲟ||[ⲣⲡ̄ ⲛ̄ϫⲟⲟⲩ·
ⲛ̄ⲧⲉ]ⲣⲉⲛ[ⲓⲥⲧ]ⲉⲣⲉⲱⲙⲁ | [ϫⲱⲕ
ⲉⲃⲟⲗ· ⲁ]ⲩⲧ ⲣ̄[ⲁⲛ] ⲉⲣⲟⲟⲩ ϫⲉ |
[ⲧϯⲧⲝ̄ ⲙ̄ⲡⲏⲟⲩⲉ] ⲛ̄ⲛⲓⲱ̣ [ⲟⲣ]ⲡ̄
ⲛ̄ⲛⲉⲱⲛ·
5 [ⲛⲁⲓ̈ ⲇⲉ ⲧⲏⲣⲟⲩ ϩ]ⲉⲛⲧⲉⲗⲓⲟⲥ
ⲛⲉ ⲉⲛⲁ|[ⲛⲟⲩⲟⲩ ⲁⲩ]ⲱ ⲛ̄ϯϩⲉ
ⲁ̣ⲩⲟⲩⲱⲛⲍ̄ | [ⲉⲃⲟⲗ ⲛ̄ϭⲓ ⲡⲉ]ϣⲧⲁ
ⲛ̄ϯⲙⲛ̄ⲧⲥϩ̣ⲓ̈ⲙⲉ·

ⲛⲉⲥⲧⲉⲣⲉⲱⲙⲁ ⲛ̄ⲧⲉ|ⲣⲟⲩϫⲱⲕ
ⲉⲃⲟⲗ ⲁⲩⲧ ⲣ̄{ⲛ}ⲟⲩ ϫⲉ 5
ⲧϣⲙ̄ⲧϣⲉⲥⲉ ⲛ̄ⲡⲉ ⲉⲡⲣⲁⲛ
ⲛ̄ⲙ̄|ⲡⲏⲟⲩⲉ ⲉⲧϩⲁⲧⲉⲩϩⲏ·
ⲁⲩⲱ ⲛⲁⲓ̈ ⲧⲏ|ⲣⲟⲩ ⲥⲉϫⲏⲕ ⲁⲩⲱ
ⲛⲁⲛⲟⲩ ⲁⲩⲱ ⲛ̄ⲧⲉ|ⲉⲓϩⲉ ⲁϥⲟⲩⲱⲛϩ
ⲉⲃⲟⲗ ⲛ̄ϭⲓ ⲡϩⲩⲥⲧⲉ|ⲣⲏⲙⲁ
ⲛ̄ⲧⲙⲛ̄ⲧⲥ̄ϩⲓⲙⲉ·

[13] [. . . that] have | [just been
mentioned.
When] the firmaments | [were
complete,] they were [called] | [“The
Three Hundred Sixty Heavens] of
the [First] Aeons.”

5 [And all these] are perfect and |
[good. And] in this way [the] defect
| of femaleness appeared.

When the firmaments | were
complete, they were called 5 “The
Three Hundred Sixty Heavens,”
according to the name of the |
heavens that were before them.
And all these | are perfect and good.
And in this | way the defect | of
femaleness appeared.

Eug-V:

13,1 Superlinear stroke is in lacuna.

Eug-III:

85,4 Not emended by Tr.

85,8 Corr.: erased ⲓ at end of line.

85,9 Corr.: ⲏⲙⲁ for erasures.

NHC III   BG 107,8–108,1

ΝΑ|ϊ ΤΗΡΟΥ ΖΝΤΕΛΙΟΝ ΝΕ ¹⁰
ΑΥω ΝΑΝΟΥΟΥ ΕΒΟΛ |
ΖϊΤΟΟΤΟΥ Ν̄ΝΑϊ ΑϥΟΥ|ωΝΖ
ΕΒΟΛ ΝϬΙ ΠΕω|ΤΑ ΖΝ̄ ΤΕϹΖΙΜΕ
ΠΕΧΑ<ϥ> | ΝΑϥ ΧΕ ΟΥΗΡ ΝΕ
ΝΙ ¹⁵ΑΙωΝ ΧΙΝ ΝΙΑΠΕΡᾹ |ΤΟΝ
Ν̄ΤΕ ΝΙΑ ΤΜΟΥ ΠΕ|ΧΑϥ ΝϬΙ
ΠΤΕΛΙΟϹ ΝϹω|ΤΗΡ ΧΕ ΠΕΤΕ
ΟΥΝΤϥ | ΜΑΑΧΕ ΕϹωΤΜ̄ ΜΑΡΕϥ
ϹωΤΜ̄   Ρ̄Η̄

All | these are perfect ¹⁰ and good. |
Thus | the defect | in the female
appeared."
And <he> said | to him: "How many
are the ¹⁵ aeons of the immortals, |
starting from the infinities?" | The
perfect Savior said: | "Whoever has |
ears to hear, let him
hear.   **108**

SJC-BG:

107,13 T–S has ɣ, "they" (followed by K), but it is difficult to determine from the
photograph whether the scribe intended ɣ or ϥ. If the pl. was intended, this is the
only instance in the tractate where the questioner or questioners are not clearly
identified. If the sing., the questioner remains Thomas.

107,14–16 "How . . . infinities?": "How many aeons are there of the boundless ones
of the immortals?" (T–S).

107,17 MS has a large asterisk in the left margin.

NHC V 13,7–19

| [ⲁⲩⲱ ⲡⲓϣⲟⲣ]ⲡ̄ ⲛ̄ⲛⲉⲱⲛ ⲡⲁ
ⲡⲓⲣⲱ |ⲙⲉ ⲛ̄[ⲛⲁⲧⲙⲟ]ⲩ ⲡⲉ·
ⲡⲓⲙⲁϩⲥⲛⲁ ⲩ ¹⁰ ⲡ[ⲁ ⲡϣⲏⲣⲉ
ⲙ̄]ⲡⲣⲱⲙⲉ ⲡⲉ· ⲡⲏ ⲉⲧⲟⲩ|ⲙⲟⲩ[ⲧⲉ
ⲉ]ⲣ̣[ⲟ]ϥ ϫⲉ ⲡϣⲟⲣⲡ̄ ⲙ̄ⲙⲓⲥⲉ·

| ⲡⲓⲙⲁϩϣⲟⲙⲉⲧ̀ ⲡⲁ ⲡϣⲏⲣⲉ
ⲙ̄|ⲡϣⲏⲣⲉ ⲙ̄ⲡⲣⲱⲙⲉ ⲡⲉ· ⲡⲏ ⲉⲧⲉ |
ϣⲁⲩⲙⲟⲩⲧⲉ ⲉⲣⲟϥ ϫⲉ ⲡⲥⲱⲧⲏⲣ·
¹⁵ ⲡⲏ ⲇⲉ ⲉⲧⲁⲙⲁϩⲧⲉ ⲛ̄ⲛⲁⲓ̈ ⲡⲉ
ⲡⲓⲉⲱⲛ | [ⲙ̄ⲡⲓ]ⲁ̣ⲧⲣ̄ ⲣ̄ⲣⲟ ⲉϩⲣⲁⲓ̈
ⲉϫⲱϥ ⲛ̄ⲧⲉ | [ⲡⲛⲟⲩⲧ]ⲉ ⲛ̄ϣⲁ
ⲉⲛⲉϩ ⲙ̄ⲛ ⲡⲓⲁ ⲧⲛ̄|[ⲁⲣⲏϫϥ̄ ⲛ̄ⲧ]ⲉ
[ⲛⲓⲉ]ⲱ[ⲛ ⲛ̄]ⲧ̣ⲉ ⲛ̣ⲓ [ⲁ]ⲧⲙⲟⲩ | [ⲡⲏ

NHC III 85,9–18

ⲡⲉϩⲟⲩⲉⲓⲧ̀ ¹⁰ ϭⲉ ⲛ̄ⲁⲓⲱⲛ ⲡⲁ
ⲡⲁⲑⲁⲛⲁⲧⲟⲥ ⲛ̄ⲣⲱⲙⲉ | ⲡⲉ
ⲡⲙⲉϩⲥⲛⲁ ⲩ ⲛ̄ⲁⲓⲱⲛ ⲡⲁ ⲡϣⲏⲣⲉ |
ⲙ̄ⲡⲣⲱⲙⲉ ⲡⲉ ⲡⲉⲧⲉϣⲁⲩϫⲟⲟⲥ
ⲉ|ⲣⲟϥ ϫⲉ ⲡⲉⲡⲣⲱⲧⲟⲅⲉⲛⲉⲧⲱⲣ
ⲡⲉⲧⲉ | ϣⲁⲩⲙⲟⲩⲧⲉ ⲉⲣⲟϥ ϫⲉ
ⲡⲥⲱⲧⲏⲣ

¹⁵ ⲡⲉⲧⲉⲙⲁϩⲧⲉ ⲛ̄ⲛⲁⲓ̈ ⲡⲁⲓⲱⲛ
ⲡⲉⲧⲉ | ⲙ̄ⲛ ⲙ̄ⲛ̄ⲧⲣ̄ⲣⲟ ϩⲓϫⲱϥ ⲛ̄ⲧⲛ̄
ⲡϣⲁ | ⲉⲛⲉϩ ⲛ̄ⲛⲟⲩⲧⲉ
ⲛ̄ⲁⲡⲉⲣⲁⲛⲧⲟⲥ ⲡⲁⲓ|ⲱⲛ ⲛ̄ⲧⲉ
ⲛⲓⲁⲓⲱⲛ ⲛ̄ⲧⲛ̄ ⲛⲁⲑⲁⲛⲁⲧⲟⲥ |

| [Now the first] aeon is that | of [Immortal] Man. The second ¹⁰ is that [of Son of] Man, who is | called "First-begotten."
| The third is that of the son of | Son of Man, who is | called "Savior."
¹⁵ Now that which embraces these is the aeon | [of the] Unruled One, of | [the] Eternal [God] and the | [Infinite, (the aeon) of the aeons of] the immortals, | (the

The first ¹⁰ aeon, then, is that of Immortal Man. | The second aeon is that of Son of | Man, who is called | "First Begetter," (and) who | is called "Savior."

¹⁵ That which embraces these is the aeon | over which there is no kingdom, (the aeon) of the | Eternal Infinite God, the | aeon of the aeons of the immortals

---

Eug-V:

13,8 First superlinear stroke is in lacuna.

13,9 Superlinear stroke is in lacuna.

Eug-III:

85,15 "embraces" (so also Tr): "rules over" (K); see 73,6n.

85,16 Corr.: second ⲧ for partially inscribed and erased ⲛ.

85,17 "Eternal Infinite God" (similarly, K [footnote], & Tr): "divine, boundless Eternal One" (T–S); "eternal, divine unlimited" (K).

NHC III   BG 108,1–18

ⲡϣⲟⲣⲡ ⲛⲁⲓⲱ̄ | ⲡⲁ ⲡϣⲏⲣⲉ
ⲙ̄ⲡⲣⲱⲙⲉ | ⲡⲉ ⲡⲉⲧⲉ ϣⲁⲩⲙⲟⲩⲧⲉ |
ⲉⲣⲟϥ ϫⲉ ⲡⲣⲟⲧⲟⲅⲉⲛⲉ ⁵ⲧⲱⲣ ⲡⲉⲧⲉ
ϣⲁⲩⲙⲟⲩ|ⲧⲉ ⲉⲣⲟϥ ϫⲉ ⲡⲥⲱⲧⲏⲣ |
ⲡⲁ ⲓ̈ ⲛⲧⲁϥⲟⲩⲱⲛ̄ⲍ ⲉⲃⲟⲗ |
ⲡⲙⲉⲍⲥⲛⲁⲩ ⲛⲁⲓⲱⲛ ⲡⲁ | ⲡⲣⲱⲙⲉ
ⲉⲧⲉ ϣⲁⲩⲙⲟⲩ ¹⁰ⲧⲉ ⲉⲣⲟϥ ϫⲉ
ⲁⲇⲁⲙ ⲡⲃⲁⲗ | ⲙ̄ⲡⲟⲩⲟⲓ̈ⲛ

ⲡⲉⲧⲁⲙⲁⲍ|ⲧⲉ ⲛ̄ⲛⲁⲓ̈ ⲡⲓⲁⲓⲱⲛ ⲡⲉ |
ⲉⲧⲉ ⲙⲙ̄ ⲙⲛ̄ⲧⲣ̄ⲣⲟ ⲍⲓ̈|ϫⲱϥ ⲛ̄ⲧⲉ
ⲡⲓϣⲁ ⲉⲛⲉⲍ ¹⁵ ⲛⲁⲡⲉⲣⲁⲛⲧⲟⲛ
ⲛⲛⲟⲩ|ⲧⲉ ⲡⲓⲁⲩⲧⲟⲅⲉⲛⲏⲥ
{ⲛ̄}|ⲛⲁⲓⲱⲛ ⲛ̄ⲧⲉ ⲛⲓⲁⲓⲱⲛ |
ⲉⲧⲛ̄ⲍⲏⲧϥ ⲛ̄ⲛⲁⲧⲙⲟⲩ

The first aeon | is that of Son of
Man, | who is called | 'First
Begetter,' ⁵ who is called | 'Savior,'
| who has appeared. | The second
aeon (is) that of | Man, who is called
¹⁰ 'Adam, Eye | of Light.'

That which embraces | these is the
aeon | over which there is no
kingdom, | (the aeon) of the Eternal
¹⁵ Infinite God, | the Self-begotten
aeon | of the aeons | that are in it,
(the aeon) of the immortals,

SJC-BG:

108,11 "embraces": "rules" (T–S); see III 73,6n.

108,14–15 "Eternal, Infinite God": "eternal, divine Boundless" (T–S).

108,15 Corr.: an erased letter between the last two ⲛ's.

NHC V 13,19–27　　　　　　　　NHC III 85,19–86,5

ετⲛ̄ⲧⲡⲉ ⲛ̄ⲧⲙⲁⳅⳙⲙⲟⲩ]ⲛⲉ [20]
[ⲉⲧⲁⲥⲟⲩⲱⲛ̄ⳅ ⲉⲃⲟⲗ ⳅⲙ̄ ⲡⲓ]ⲭⲁⲟⲥ·

| [ⲡⲓⲣⲱⲙⲉ ⲇⲉ ⲛ̄ⲛⲁⲧ]ⲙⲟⲩ
ⲁϥⲟⲩ|[ⲱⲛ̄ⳅ ⲉⲃⲟⲗ ⲛ̄ⳅⲉⲛⲉⲱ]ⲛ ⲙ̣ⲛ̄
ⳅⲉⲛ|[ⲙⲛ̄ⲧⲣ̄ⲣⲱⲟⲩ ⲙⲛ̄ ⳅⲉ]ⲛ̣ⲅⲟ̣[ⲙ·] |
[ⲁϥⲧ ⲉⳅⲟⲩⲥⲓⲁ ⲛⲁⲩ] ⲧⲏⲣⲟⲩ [25]
[ⲉⲧⲁⲩⲟⲩⲱⲛ]ⳅ ⲉⲃⲟ[ⲗ] ⲛ̣̄ⳅⲏⲧϥ̄ |
[16±]ⲁⲩ[. .] | [13± ⲙ̄ⲡⲓ]ⲭⲁⲟ̣ⲥ·
(5± lines lacking)

ⲉⲧⲛ̄ⳅⲏⲧϥ̄· ⲡⲥⲁⲛⳅⲣⲉ
ⲛ̄ⲧⲙⲉⳅⳙ [20]ⲙⲟⲩⲛⲉ ⲛ̄ⲧⲁⳅⲟⲩⲱⲛⳅ
ⲉⲃⲟⲗ ⳅⲙ̄ ⲡ|ⲭⲁⲟⲥ

ⲛ̄ⲧⲟϥ ⲇⲉ ⲡⲁⲑⲁⲛⲁⲧⲟⲥ ⲛ̄ⲣⲱ|ⲙⲉ
ⲁϥⲟⲩⲱⲛⳅ ⲉⲃⲟⲗ ⲛ̄ⳅⲛ̄ⲁⲓⲱⲛ | ⲙⲛ̄
ⳅⲛ̄ⲅⲟⲙ ⲙⲛ̄ ⳅⲉⲛⲙⲛ̄ⲧⲣ̄ⲣⲟ | ⲁϥⲧ
ⲛ̄ⲧⲉⳅⲟⲩⲥⲓⲁ ⲛ̄ⲟⲩⲟⲛ ⲛⲓⲙ·
ⲛ̄ⲧⲁⲩⲟ̣[ⲩ]ⲱ̣[ⲛⳅ ⲉⲃⲟⲗ ⲛ̄]ⳅⲏⲧϥ̄· 　　　[ⲡⳅ]
ⲉ|ⲧⲣⲟⲩⲧⲁⲛⲟ̣ [ⲛ̄ⲛⲁⲓ̈ ⲉⲧⲟⲩⲁ]ⳙⲟⲩ
| ⳙⲁ ⲛⲉⳅⲟⲟⲩ ⲉⲧⲙ̄ⲡ<ⲥ>ⲁ̣ⳅ̣ⲣⲉ
ⲙ̄ⲡⲉⲭⲁ|ⲟⲥ ⲛⲁⲓ̈ ⲅⲁⲣ ⲁⲩⲥⲩⲙⲫⲱⲛⲓ
ⲙⲛ̄ <ⲛ>ⲉⲩ [5]ⲉⲣⲏⲟⲩ

aeon) [above the Eighth] [20] [that appeared in] chaos.

| who are in it, (the aeon) above the Eighth [20] that appeared in | chaos.

| [Now Immortal Man revealed] | [aeons] and [kingdoms] | [and powers] | [and gave authority to] all [25] [who appeared] from him | [. . .] | [. . . of] chaos. | (5± lines lacking)

Now Immortal Man | revealed aeons | and powers and kingdoms | and gave authority to everyone who [appeared from] him | to make [whatever they desire] | until the days that are above chaos. | For these consented with each other 　[86]

Eug-V:

13,22 First letter after lacuna: see Emmel, 1979: 185.

13,25 First letter after first lacuna: see Emmel, 1979: 185.

Eug-III:

85,19 "above": "the upper part of" (K & Tr).

85,20 "in" (so also T–S): "out of" (T–S, alt., K & Tr).

86,1 So restored by T–S, except that second ⳅ is in lacuna.

86,2 Alt.: [ⲟ ⲛ̄ⲛⲉⲧⲟⲩⲟⲩⲁ]ⳙⲟⲩ (T–S & Tr); the doubling of ⲟⲩ is uncharacteristic of the scribe (see 84,12; 89,4).

86,3 "that are above": "of the upper part" (Tr).

86,4 Not emended by Tr, although his translation, which follows K, reflects the above emendation.

NHC III   BG 108,19–109,15

| ⲚⲦⲀⲓ̈ⲭⲟⲟⲩ Ⲛ̄Ϣⲟⲣⲡ
ⲚⲦⲡⲉ Ⲛ̄ⲦⲘⲉⲍⲥⲁϢϥⲉ | ⲢⲐ̄
ⲚⲦⲀⲤⲟⲩⲰⲚⲍ ⲉⲂⲟⲗ ⲍⲚ̄ | ⲦⲤⲟⲫⲓⲁ
ⲉⲦⲉ ⲡⲉⲍⲟⲩⲓ̈Ⲧ | ⲚⲀⲓⲰⲚ ⲡⲉ
ⲚⲦⲟϥ ⲇⲉ ⲡⲓ ⁵ⲢⲰⲘⲉ ⲚⲀⲦⲘⲟⲩ
Ⲁϥⲟⲩ|ⲰⲚⲍ Ⲛ̄ⲍⲚ̄ⲀⲓⲰⲚ ⲉⲂⲟⲗ | ⲘⲚ̄
ⲍⲚ̄ϬⲟⲘ ⲘⲚ̄ ⲍⲘ̄ⲘⲚ̄|ⲦⲢ̄Ⲣⲟ ⲀⲨⲰ Ⲁϥⲧ
ⲚⲦⲉ|ⲌⲟⲨⲤⲓⲀ Ⲛ̄ⲚⲉⲦⲟⲨⲟⲚⲍ ¹⁰
ⲦⲎⲢⲟⲨ ⲚⲍⲎⲦϥ ⲭⲉ ⲉⲨⲉ|ⲉⲓⲣⲉ
Ⲛ̄ⲚⲉⲨⲟⲩⲰϢ ϢⲀ | ⲚⲓⲍⲀⲉ ⲉⲦⲉ
ⲚⲉⲦⲚⲦⲡⲉ | Ⲛⲉ Ⲙ̄ⲡⲉⲭⲀⲟⲥ ⲚⲀⲓ̈
ⲄⲀⲢ | ⲀⲨⲤⲨⲘⲫⲰⲚⲓ ⲘⲚ̄ Ⲛⲉⲩ ¹⁵ⲉⲣⲎⲨ

| whom I described earlier,   **109**
(the aeon) above the Seventh | that
appeared from | Sophia,
which is the | first aeon.
Now ⁵ Immortal Man revealed |
aeons | and powers and kingdoms |
and gave authority | to all who
appear ¹⁰ in him that they might |
exercise their desires until | the last
things that are above | chaos. For
these | consented with each ¹⁵ other

SJC-BG:

109,2 "from" (so also T–S, alt.): "in" (T–S).

109,3 "which": or "who" (presumably Sophia).

109,12 Corr.: a mostly erased letter (ⲍ?) after the first ⲧ, whose superlinear stroke
  remains.

NHC V 14,1–10 NHC III 86,5–15

ⲁⲩⲟⲩⲱⲛⲍ ⲉⲃⲟⲗ ⲙ̄ⲙⲛⲧ|ⲛⲟϭ ⲛⲓⲙ ·
ⲁⲩⲱ ⲉⲃⲟⲗ ⲍⲛ̄ ⲟⲩⲡ̄ⲛ̄ⲁ̄ |

[ⲓ̄ⲇ̄] [.] . . [. . .] . [12±] | [ⲍ]ⲛ̄   <ⲛ̄>ⲟⲩⲙⲏⲏϣⲉ ⲛ̄ⲟⲩⲟⲉⲓⲛ ⲉⲩ|ⲍⲁ
ⲉⲟ[ⲟⲩ] ⲏ̄ⲛⲁ[ⲧ̄ⲧ ⲏⲡⲉ ⲉⲣⲟⲟⲩ·] | ⲉⲟⲟⲩ ⲉⲙⲛ̄ⲧⲟⲩ ⲏⲡⲉ ⲛⲁⲓ̈ ⲛ̄|ⲧⲁⲩⲧ
ⲛⲏ ⲉⲧⲁ[ⲩⲧ] ⲡⲉⲩⲣ[ⲁⲛ ⲉⲣⲟⲟⲩ·   ⲣⲓⲛⲟⲩ ⲛ̄ⲧⲁⲣⲭⲏ
ⲛⲁⲓ̈] | ⲛ̄ⲧⲉ ⲧⲁ[ⲣⲭ]ⲏ̣ ⲙⲛ̄ [ⲧⲙⲏⲧⲉ   ⲉⲧⲉ ⲡⲉⲉⲓ ¹⁰ ⲡⲉ ⲧⲉⲍⲟⲩⲉⲓⲧⲉ
ⲙⲛ̄ ⲧ]⁵ⲁⲧ̄ⲣ̄ ⲍⲁⲏ [ⲉ]ⲧⲉ ⲡ[ⲭⲱⲕ   ⲧⲙⲏⲧⲉ <ⲙⲛ̄> ⲡⲭⲱⲕ
ⲉⲃⲟⲗ ⲡⲉ· | ⲉⲃⲟⲗ
ⲡⲉ]|ⲍⲟⲩⲉⲓⲧ̄ ⲛ̄ⲛⲉⲱ[ⲛ ⲙⲛ̄ ⲡⲓⲙⲉⲍ   ⲉⲧⲉ ⲡⲁⲓ̈ ⲡⲉ ⲡⲉⲍⲟⲩⲉⲓⲧ̄ ⲛ̄ⲁⲓ|ⲱⲛ
ⲥⲛⲁⲩ] | ⲙⲛ̄ ⲡⲓⲙⲉⲍϣⲟⲙ [ⲉⲧ·   ⲙⲛ̄ ⲡⲙⲉⲍⲥⲛⲁⲩ ⲙⲛ̄ ⲡⲙⲉⲍ|ϣⲟⲙⲛ̄ⲧ
ⲡⲉⲍⲟⲩⲉⲓⲧ̄] | ⲍⲙ̄ ⲡⲁⲓ̈ ⲁⲩⲧ ⲣⲁⲛ   ⲡⲉⲍⲟⲩⲉⲓⲧ̄ ⲁⲩⲧ ⲣⲛ̄ϥ | ⲭⲉ
ⲉ̣[ⲣⲟϥ ⲭⲉ ⲡⲓⲥⲁⲍ]|ⲣⲉ ⲛ̄ⲧⲉ   ⲧⲙⲛ̄<ⲧ>ⲟⲩⲁ ⲁ<ⲩⲱ>
ⲧ̄ⲙⲛ̄ⲧⲟⲩ[ⲁ ⲙⲛ̄ ⲡⲓⲙⲧⲟⲛ·   ⲧⲁⲛⲁⲡⲁⲩⲥⲓⲥ ⲉⲩ¹⁵ⲛ̄ⲧⲉ
ⲟ]ⲩ[ⲛ̄]¹⁰ⲧⲉ ⲡⲟⲩⲁ ⲡⲟⲩⲁ   ⲡⲟⲩⲁ ⲡⲟⲩⲁ

[14] [. . .] | [in glory (and) numberless.] | They [received] their [names, those] | of the [beginning] and [the middle and the] ⁵ unending, which [is the perfect, the] | first aeon [and the second] | and the third. [The first] | in it was called ["Above] | Unity [and Rest."] ¹⁰ Each one has

⁵ and revealed | every magnificence, even from spirit, | multitudinous lights | that are glorious and without number. These | received names in the beginning, that ¹⁰ is, the first, the middle, <and> the perfect; | that is, the first aeon and | the second and the third. | The first was called | "Unity and Rest." ¹⁵ Since each one

---

Eug-V:

14,2 Superlinear strokes are in lacuna.

Reconstruction: see 5,2.

14,4 Corr.: after first ⲉ, ⲛ is crossed out. The following ⲧ seems to be made from an initial ⲓ (i.e., the scribe first wrote ⲛⲓ [pl. art.]).

Eug-III:

86,7 MS has ⲙ̄ (not emended by Tr).

86,10 MS has ⲙ̄. Not emended by T–S or Tr, although Tr's translation, which follows K's ("the midst, the perfection"), reflects the emendation ⲧⲙⲏⲧⲉ {ⲙ̄}ⲡⲭⲱⲕ ⲉⲃⲟⲗ.

86,14 Tr lacks the first emendation but has the second.

NHC III   BG 109,15–110,8

ⲁ<ⲩ>ⲟⲩⲱⲛⲍ ⲉⲃⲟⲗ | ⲙⲙⲛⲧⲛⲟϭ
ⲛⲓⲙ ⲁⲩⲱ | ⲉⲃⲟⲗ ⲍⲙ ⲡⲉⲡⲛⲁ
ⲛⲟⲩ|ⲁⲧⲟ ⲛ̅ⲟⲩⲟⲓⲛ ⲉⲩⲍⲁ ⲉⲟ|ⲟⲩ
ⲉⲙⲛⲧⲉⲩ ⲏⲡⲉ ⲛⲁⲓ̈ ⲛ̅
ⲧⲁⲩⲙⲟⲩⲧⲉ ⲉⲣⲟⲟⲩ | ⲍⲛ̅ ⲧⲁⲣⲭⲏ   ⲣ̅ⲓ̅

ⲉⲧⲉ ⲡⲁⲉⲓ | ⲡⲉ ⲡⲉⲍⲟⲩⲉⲓⲧ ⲛⲁⲓⲱ̅ |
ⲙⲛ̅ <ⲡⲙⲉⲍ>ⲥⲛⲁⲩ ⲙⲛ̅
<ⲡⲙⲉⲍ>ϣⲟⲙⲛⲧ ⁵ ⲡⲉⲍⲟⲩⲉⲓⲧ
<ⲡⲉ> ⲉϣⲁⲩⲙⲟⲩ|ⲧⲉ ⲉⲣⲟϥ ϫⲉ
ⲧⲙⲛ̅ⲧⲟⲩⲁ | ⲁⲩⲱ ⲧⲁⲛⲁⲡⲁⲩⲥⲓⲥ |
ⲡⲟⲩⲁ ⲡⲟⲩⲁ

and revealed | every magnificence,
even | from spirit, | multitudinous
lights that are glorious | and without
number. These
were called | in the beginning,   **110**

that is, | the first aeon | and <the
second> and <the third>. ⁵ The first
<is> called | 'Unity | and Rest.' |
Each

SJC-BG:

109,15 MS has ϥ, "*he* revealed" (not emended by T–S).

110,4 Not emended by T–S ("and *two* and *three*"), although T–S recognizes that
     Eug–III par. has the better text.

110,5 Not emended by T–S. The gap in the sentence, remedied here by the insertion
     of a copula, may be caused by the omission of a line of text (see V par.).

NHC V 14,10–18

ⲡ[ⲉϥⲣⲁⲛ·] ⲉⲧⲣⲉⲩ|ϯ ⲣⲁⲛ ⲇⲉ ⲭⲉ
ⲧⲉⲕⲕ[ⲗⲏⲥⲓⲁ ⲙ̄]ⲡⲓ|ⲙⲉϩϣⲟⲙⲉⲧ
ⲛ̄ⲛⲉ[ⲱⲛ ⲉⲧ]ⲃⲉ | ⲡⲁϣⲁⲓ̈
ⲉⲧⲁϥⲟⲩⲱⲛϩ̄ ⲉⲃⲟⲗ ϩⲙ̄ | ⲡⲓⲟⲩⲁ·

ⲭⲉ ⲉⲩⲉⲥⲱⲟⲩϩ ⲧⲏⲣⲟⲩ

¹⁵ ⲉⲩⲙⲁ ⲉϩⲣⲁⲓ̈ ⲉⲟⲩⲁ ⲛ̄ⲥⲉϯ
ⲡⲉⲩ|ⲣⲁⲛ ⲭⲉ
ⲧⲉⲕⲕⲗⲏⲥⲓⲁ· ⲉⲃⲟⲗ | ϩⲛ̄
ϯⲉⲕⲕⲗⲏⲥⲓⲁ ⲉⲧϫⲟⲥⲉ ⲉⲛ[ⲓⲡⲉ·] |
ⲉⲧⲁⲥⲟⲩⲱⲛϩ̄ ⲉⲃⲟⲗ ⲛ̄ϭⲓ

NHC III 86,15–24

ⲙ̄ⲙⲁⲩ ⲡⲉϥ|ⲣⲁⲛ {ⲭⲉ}
ⲁⲩⲟⲛⲟⲙⲁⲍⲉ ⲛ̄ⲧⲉⲕⲕⲗⲏ|ⲥⲓⲁ
{ϩ}ⲙ̄ⲡ<ⲙⲉϩ>ϣⲟⲙⲛ̄ⲧ ⲛ̄ⲁⲓⲱⲛ {ⲭⲉ}
ⲉ|ⲃⲟⲗ ϩⲙ̄ ⲡⲓⲁⲧⲟ ⲛ̄ⲙⲏⲏϣⲉ
ⲛ̄ⲧⲁ|ϩⲟⲩⲱⲛϩ ⲉⲃⲟⲗ ϩⲙ̄ ⲡⲓⲟ ⲩⲁ
ⲛ̄ⲟⲩ ²⁰ⲁⲧⲟ ⲉⲧⲃⲉ ⲡⲁⲓ̈
ⲉⲣⲉⲡⲓⲙⲏⲏϣⲉ | ⲥⲱⲟⲩϩ

ⲛ̄ⲥⲉⲉⲓ ⲉⲩⲙⲛ̄ⲧⲟⲩⲁ· | ϣⲁⲩⲙⲟⲩⲧⲉ
ⲉⲣⲟⲟⲩ ⲭⲉ
ⲉⲕⲕⲗⲏ|ⲥⲓⲁ ⲉⲃⲟⲗ ϩⲛ̄ ϯⲉⲕⲕⲗⲏⲥⲓⲁ
ⲉⲧⲟⲩⲁⲧⲃ· | ⲉⲧⲡⲉ

ⲉⲧⲃⲉ ⲡⲉⲉⲓ ⲧⲉⲕⲕⲗⲏⲥⲓⲁ ⲛ̄|

[its (own) name.] And the naming |
[of] the third | [aeon] as "Assembly"
is [because of] | the multitude that
appeared in | the one, so that they all
might be gathered ¹⁵ together and |
named "Assembly," from | the
Assembly above the [heavens.] |
When the

has its (own) | name, the | <third>
aeon was designated "Assembly" |
from the great multitude that |
appeared in the multitudinous one. ²⁰
Therefore, when the multitude |
gathers and comes to a unity, | they
are called "Assembly," | from the
Assembly that surpasses | heaven.
Therefore, the Assembly of

Eug-III:

86,16–20 See endnote 8.

86,17 Not emended by Tr, although his translation reflects the second emendation, as
   does K's, which lacks the other two also; T–S does not have the first emendation;
   see endnote 8.

NHC III 111,1–3   BG 110,8–111,7

ⲟⲩⲛ̄ⲧⲁϥ | ⲡⲉϥⲣⲁⲛ ⲉⲃⲟⲗ ϫⲉ
ⲁⲩ ¹⁰<ⲟ>ⲛⲟⲙⲁⲍⲉ ⲛ̄ⲧⲉⲕⲕⲗⲏ|ⲥⲓⲁ
ⲙ̄ⲡ<ⲙⲉϩ>ϣⲟⲙⲛ̄ⲧ ⲛⲁⲓ|ⲱⲛ {ϫⲉ}
ⲉⲃⲟⲗ ϩⲙ ⲡ|ⲙⲏⲏϣⲉ ⲉⲧⲛⲁϣⲱϥ |
ⲛ̄ⲧⲁϥⲟⲩⲱⲛϩ ⲉⲃⲟⲗ ¹⁵ ϩⲛ̄ ⲟⲩⲁ
ⲁⲩⲁⲧⲟ ⲟⲩⲟⲛ|ϩⲟⲩ ⲉⲃⲟⲗ ⲉⲃⲟⲗ
ⲇⲉ | ϫⲉ ⲛⲓⲙⲏⲏϣⲉ ϣⲁⲩ

ⲣⲓⲁ   ⲛ̄ⲥⲉⲉⲓ̂ ⲉⲩⲙⲛ̄ⲧⲟⲩⲁ· ϣⲁⲛⲙⲟⲩ|ⲧⲉ   [ⲥ]ⲱⲟⲩϩ ⲉϩⲟⲩⲛ   ⲣⲓⲁ
       ⲉⲣⲟⲟⲩ ϫⲉ   ⲛ̄ⲥⲉⲣ ⲟⲩ|[ⲁ ⲉ]ⲧⲃⲉ ⲡⲁⲓ̈
              ⲉϣⲁⲩⲙⲟⲩ|[ⲧⲉ] <ⲉⲣⲟⲟⲩ> ϫⲉ
              ⲉⲕⲕⲗⲏⲥⲓⲁ ⲉⲃⲟⲗ | ⲇⲉ ϩⲛ
              ⲧⲉⲕⲕⲗⲏⲥⲓⲁ ⲉⲧⲙ̄⁵ⲙⲁⲩ ⲉⲧⲟⲩⲟⲧⲃ
              ⲉⲧⲡⲉ
       ⲧⲉⲕⲕⲗⲏⲥⲓⲁ ⲛ̄ⲧⲉ | ⲧⲙⲉϩϣⲙⲟⲩⲛⲉ· | ⲉⲧⲃⲉ ⲡⲁⲓ̈ ⲧⲉⲕⲕⲗⲏⲥⲓ|ⲁ

one has | its (own) name; for ¹⁰ the
<third> aeon | was designated
'Assembly' | from the | great
multitude that | appeared: ¹⁵ in one,
a multitude revealed themselves. |
Now because | the multitudes

111   and come to a unity, we call | them   gather and become one, | therefore   **111**
       <they> are called | 'Assembly,' |
       from that Assembly ⁵ that surpasses
'Assembly | of the Eighth.'   heaven. | Therefore the Assembly |
       <of>

SJC-III:

111,2 The section in the parr. immediately after ϫⲉ may be missing here through
homoioteleuton (so also T–S).

SJC-BG:

110,9–16 See endnote 8.

110,10 MS has ⲁ.

110,11 Not emended by T–S ("the *three* aeon*s*").

110,12 Not emended by T–S.

NHC V 14,18–30

ϯ[ⲉⲕⲕⲗⲏ]|ⲥⲓⲁ ⲛ̄ⲧⲉ ϯⲍⲟ[ⲅ]ⲇⲟⲁⲥ·
[ⲁⲩϯ ⲣⲁⲛ] [20] ⲉⲣⲟϥ·
ⲉⲩ[ⲍⲟⲟⲩϯⲥⲍ̂ⲓⲙⲉ ⲧⲉ· ⲕⲁ]|ⲧⲁ ⲑ̱[ⲉ
ⲛ̄ⲟⲩⲙⲉⲣⲟⲥ ⲛ̄ⲍⲟⲟⲩϯ ⲙ̄ⲛ̄] |
ⲟⲩⲙⲉⲣ[ⲟⲥ ⲛ̄ⲥⲍ̂ⲓⲙⲉ· ⲡⲓⲙⲉⲣⲟⲥ
ⲛ̄ⲍⲟ]|ⲟⲩⲧ ⲁⲩϯ [ⲣⲁⲛ ⲉⲣⲟϥ ⲭⲉ
ⲧⲉⲕ]|ⲕⲗⲏⲥⲓⲁ · [ⲡⲓⲙⲉⲣⲟⲥ ⲇⲉ
ⲛ̄ⲥⲍ̂ⲓⲙⲉ] [25] ⲭⲉ̱ [ⲍⲱⲏ ⲭⲉ
ⲉⲥⲛⲁⲟⲩⲱⲛⲍ̄ ⲉⲃⲟⲗ ⲭⲉ] | ⲁ̱ⲡⲱⲛⲍ̄
ϣ[ⲱ]ⲡ̱ⲉ̱ [ⲉⲃⲟⲗ ⲍⲛ̄ⲛ ⲟⲩ]|[ⲥⲍ̂ⲓ]ⲙⲉ
ⲛ̄[ⲛⲏ] ⲧⲏⲣ[ⲟⲩ· ⲛⲓⲣⲁⲛ ⲇⲉ] |
ⲧ̱ⲏ̱ⲣⲟⲩ [16±] | ⲙⲉ ⲛ̄ⲛ[17±] [30]
(3± lines lacking)

NHC III 87,1–12

ⲧⲙⲉⲍϣ[ⲙⲟⲩⲛⲉ· ⲁⲩⲟ]ⲩⲟ̱ⲛⲍⲥ   [ⲡⲍ
ⲉⲃⲟ̱[ⲗ] | ⲉⲩⲍⲁⲟⲩ[ϯⲥⲍ̂ⲓⲙⲉ· ⲁⲩ]ϯ
ⲣⲁⲛ ⲉⲣⲟⲥ | ⲉⲕ ⲙⲉⲣⲟⲥ ⲛ̄ⲍⲟⲟⲩⲧ̇
[ⲁ]ⲩⲱ ⲉⲕ ⲙⲉⲣⲟⲥ | ⲛ̄ⲥⲍ̂ⲓⲙⲉ·
ⲡ̄ⲍⲟⲟⲩⲧ̇ ⲁⲩϯ ⲣⲛ̄ϥ ⲭⲉ ⲉⲕ[5]ⲕⲗⲏⲥⲓⲁ
ⲧⲉⲥⲍ̂ⲓⲙⲉ ⲭⲉ ⲍⲱⲏ ⲭⲉ|ⲕⲁⲁⲥ
ⲉⲥⲛⲁⲟⲩⲱⲛⲍ ⲉⲃⲟⲗ ⲭⲉ ⲉⲃⲟⲗ | ⲍⲛ̄
ⲟⲩⲥⲍ̂ⲓⲙⲉ ⲁⲡⲱⲛⲍ ϣⲱⲡⲉ· ⲍⲛ̄ |
ⲛⲁⲓⲱⲛ ⲧⲏⲣⲟⲩ· ⲣⲁⲛ ⲛⲓⲙ
ⲉⲁⲩⲭⲓ|ⲧⲟⲩ ⲭⲓⲛ ⲛ̄ⲧⲁⲣⲭⲏ ⲉⲃⲟⲗ
ⲍⲙ̄ ⲡⲉϥ[10]ⲙⲉⲧⲉ ⲙⲛ̄ ⲧⲉϥⲉⲛⲛⲟⲓⲁ
ⲁⲩⲟⲩⲱⲛⲍ | ⲛ̄ⲅⲓ ⲛ̄ⲇⲩⲛⲁⲙⲓⲥ ⲛⲁⲓ̈
ⲛ̄ⲧⲁⲩϯ ⲣⲓ|ⲛⲟⲩ ⲭⲉ ⲛ̄ⲛⲟⲩⲧⲉ·

[Assembly] of the Ogdoad |
appeared, it [was named,] [20]
[because it was androgynous,
according to] | [a male portion and] |
a [female] portion. [The male] |
[portion] was [called] "Assembly," |
[and the female portion,] [25] ["Life,"
that it might be shown that] | life for
all [things came] | [from a female.
And] all | [the names . . .] | (3±
lines lacking)

the [Eighth was] revealed | as   [87]
[androgynous] and was named |
partly as male and partly | as female.
The male was called "Assembly," [5]
the female, "Life," that | it might be
shown that from | a female came the
life | in all the aeons. Every name
was received, | starting from the
beginning. From his [10] concurrence
with his thought, | the powers
appeared who were called | "gods";

Eug-V:

14,27 Circumflex is visible in MS. Superlinear stroke is not visible in MS.

Eug-III:

87,1 Tr restores second perfect.

87,2 Corr.: first ⲁ for erased ⲉ (transcribed as ⲟ by Tr). Tr restores ⲁⲩ]ϯ ⲣⲁⲛ, as above, but translates in the present, following K (similarly in line 4); T–S does not restore ⲁⲩ.

87,10 Corr.: ⲍ for an erased letter.

See endnote 9.

NHC III 111,3–15

ⲁⲥⲟⲩⲱⲛ︤ⲉ|ⲃⲟⲗ ⲉⲩⲍⲟⲟⲩⲧ︦ⲥⲍⲓⲙⲉ
ⲧⲉ· ⲁⲩⲧ ⲣⲁⲛ ⁵ ⲉⲣⲟⲥ ⲉⲕ ⲙⲉⲣⲟⲥ
ⲛ︥ⲍⲟⲟⲩⲧ︦ ⲁⲩⲱ | ⲉⲕ ⲙⲉⲣⲟⲥ
ⲛ︥ⲥⲍⲓⲙⲉ · ⲫⲟⲟⲩⲧ︦ ⲙⲉⲛ | ϣⲁⲩⲧ ⲣⲛ︤ϥ
ϫⲉ ⲧⲉⲕⲕⲗⲏⲥⲓⲁ · ⲧⲉ|ⲥⲍⲓⲙⲉ ⲁⲉ
ϣⲁⲩⲧ ⲣⲛ︦ⲥ ϫⲉ ⲍⲱⲏ | ϫⲉ
ⲉϥⲛⲁⲟⲩⲱⲛ︤ⲉ ⲉⲃⲟⲗ ϫⲉ ⲉⲃⲟⲗ ¹⁰
ⲍⲓⲧⲛ︥ ⲟⲩⲥⲍⲓⲙⲉ ⲁⲡⲱⲛ︤ⲉ ϣⲱⲡⲉ
ⲛ̄|ⲛⲓⲁⲓⲱⲛ︤ⲉ ⲧⲏⲣⲟⲩ ⲣⲁⲛ ⲁⲉ ⲛⲓⲙ
ⲁⲩ|ϫⲓⲧⲟ ⲩ ϫⲓⲛ ⲛ̄ⲧⲁⲣⲭⲏ ⲉⲃⲟⲗ
ⲅⲁⲣ ⲍⲙ̄ | ⲡⲉϥϫⲱⲛϥ ⲙⲛ̄
ⲧⲉϥⲉⲛⲛⲟⲓⲁ ⲁⲩⲟⲩ|ⲱⲛ︤ⲉ ⲉⲃⲟⲗ
ⲛ̄ϭⲓ ⲛ̄ϭⲟⲙ· ⲛ̄ϣⲟⲣⲡ̄ ⲛⲁ ⲓ̈ ¹⁵
[ⲛ̄ⲧ]ⲁⲩⲧ ⲣⲁⲛ ⲉⲣⲟⲟⲩ ϫⲉ ⲛⲟⲩⲧⲉ·

It appeared | as androgynous and
was named ⁵ partly as male and |
partly as female. The male | is
called 'Assembly,' while the |
female is called 'Life,' | that it might
be shown that from ¹⁰ a female came
the life for | all the aeons. And
every name was | received, starting
from the beginning. For from | his
concurrence with his thought, the
powers | very soon appeared who ¹⁵
were called 'gods';

BG 111,7–112,9

<ⲛ̄>ⲧⲙⲁⲍϣⲙⲟ ⲩⲛⲉ ⲛ̄|ⲧⲁⲩⲟⲩⲟⲛ︤ⲍ︥
ⲉⲃⲟⲗ ϫⲉ | ⲍⲟⲩⲧⲥⲍⲓⲙⲉ ⲁⲩⲧ ⲣⲁⲛ
ⲉ ¹⁰ⲣⲟⲥ ⲉⲕ ⲙⲉⲣⲟⲩⲥ ⲙ̄ⲙⲛ̄ⲧ|ⲍⲟⲟⲩⲧ
ⲁⲩⲱ ⲉⲕ ⲙⲉ|ⲣⲟⲩⲥ ⲙ̄ⲙⲛ̄ⲧⲥⲍⲓⲙⲉ |
ⲫⲟⲟⲩⲧ ⲙⲉⲛ ⲁⲩⲙⲟⲩⲧⲉ | ⲉⲣⲟϥ
ϫⲉ ⲉⲕⲕⲗⲏⲥⲓⲁ ⲧⲉ ¹⁵ⲥⲍⲓⲙⲉ ⲁⲉ
ⲁⲩⲙⲟⲩⲧⲉ ⲉ|ⲣⲟⲥ ϫⲉ ⲍⲱⲏ ϫⲉ
ⲉⲩⲉ|ⲟⲩⲟⲛ︤ⲍ︥ϥ ⲉⲃⲟⲗ ϫⲉ ⲉⲃⲟⲗ | ⲍⲛ̄
ⲧⲉⲥⲍⲓⲙⲉ ⲁⲡⲱⲛ︤ⲉ
ϣⲱⲡⲉ ⲛⲛⲓⲁⲓⲱⲛ [ⲧⲏ]|ⲣⲟⲩ ⲛⲣⲁⲛ   ⲣ̄ⲓ̄ⲃ̄
ⲁⲉ ⲧⲏⲣⲟⲩ [ⲁⲩ]|ϫⲓⲧⲟⲩ ⲛ̄ⲧⲟⲟⲧ︤ⲥ̄
ⲛ̄ⲧ[ⲁⲣ]|ⲭⲏ ⲉⲃⲟⲗ ⲅⲁⲣ ⲍⲛ̄
ⲧⲉϥⲉⲩ ⁵ⲁⲟⲕⲓⲁ ⲙⲛ̄ ⲧⲉϥⲉⲛⲛⲟⲓ |ⲁ
ⲁⲩⲣ̄ ϣⲣ̄ⲡ ⲛ̄ⲟⲩⲱⲛ︤ⲍ︥ ⲉⲃⲟⲗ <ⲛ̄ϭⲓ>
ⲛ̄ϭⲟⲙ ⲛⲁⲓ̈ ⲛ̄ⲧⲁⲩ|ⲙⲟⲩⲧⲉ ⲉⲣⲟⲟⲩ
ϫⲉ ⲛⲟⲩ|ⲧⲉ

the Eighth was | revealed as |
androgynous and was named ¹⁰
partly as masculine | and partly | as
feminine. | The male was called |
'Assembly,' ¹⁵ while the female was
called | 'Life,' that it might be |
shown that from | the female came
the life
for all the aeons. | And all the names   **112**
were | received from the beginning
(*or* principle). | For from his consent
⁵ with his thought, | the powers very
soon appeared | who were | called
'gods';

SJC-III:

111,13 See endnote 9.

SJC-BG:

111,7 Not emended by T–S.

112,4 See endnote 9.

NHC V 15,1–7   NHC III 87,12–18

[Ῑє] (Line 1 lacking)
| [. . . . . N̄ZєNNO]Y̧Ţ[є N̄]Ţє
NIN[OY]||[Tє·
NINOYTє ΔE N̄]Ţє N[INOY]Tє
a[Y]||[OYωN̄Z̄ єBOΛ]
{Z}N̄Zє[NN]Q̧YTє Z̄N̄ ⁵
[NєYMN̄TCABє·] NIN[O]YTє Δє |
[aYOYωN̄Z̄ єBO]Λ Z̄N̄ Ņ̣єYCBω· |
[N̄ZєNXOєIC N̄]Ţє ZєNXOєIC·

                                  N̄NOYTє Δє | єBOΛ Z̄N̄
                                  NєYΦPONHCIC aYOY|ωN̄Z єBOΛ
                                  N̄ZNNOYTє N̄NOY ¹⁵Tє· N̄NOYTє
                                  Δє єBOΛ Z̄N̄ NєY|ΦPONHCIC
                                  aYOYωN̄Z N̄ZN̄XO|єIC· N̄XOєIC
                                  Δє N̄N̄XOєIC єBOΛ | Z̄N̄

[15] (Line 1 lacking) | [. . . gods of] the
      [gods;]
      | [and the gods of the gods] |
      [revealed] gods in ⁵ [their wisdoms;]
      and the gods | [revealed] from their
      teachings | [lords of] lords; [and]

                                    and the gods | from their
                                    considerings revealed | divine gods;
                                    ¹⁵ and the gods from their |
                                    considerings revealed lords; | and
                                    the lords of the lords from

---

Eug-V:

15,4 MS has Z̄N̄, "in."

Eug-III:

87,14–15 N̄NOYTє, "divine": untranslated by K; the English translator's note in K
    suggests it may be a dittography; Tr renders "gods *of gods*."

NHC III 111,16–20   BG 112,9–16

| [Ⲛ]ⲚⲞⲨⲦⲈ ⲆⲈ ⲚⲚⲚⲞⲨⲦⲈ ⲈⲂⲞⲖ   ⲚⲚⲞⲨⲦⲈ ⲆⲈ ⲚⲚⲚⲞⲨ ¹⁰ⲦⲈ ⲈⲂⲞⲖ
ⲌⲚ ⲦⲈⲨ|ⲘⲚⲦⲤⲀⲂⲈ ⲀⲨⲞⲨⲰⲚⲌ   ⲆⲈ ⲌⲚ ⲦⲈ<Ⲩ>ⲪⲢⲞ|ⲚⲎⲤⲒⲤ
ⲚⲌⲈⲚⲚⲞⲨⲦⲈ | ⲈⲂⲞⲖ· <ⲚⲚⲞⲨⲦⲈ   ⲀⲨⲞⲨⲰⲚⲌ ⲈⲂⲞⲖ | <Ⲛ>ⲚⲚⲞⲨⲦⲈ
ⲆⲈ> ⲌⲚ ⲦⲈⲨⲘⲚⲦⲤⲀⲂⲈ ⲀⲨⲞⲨⲰⲚⲌ | {Ⲛ}ⲚⲚⲞⲨⲦⲈ | ⲚⲚϮ ⲆⲈ ⲈⲂⲞⲖ ⲌⲚ
ⲚⲌⲈⲚⲬⲞⲈⲒⲤ ⲈⲂⲞⲖ· ⲚⲬⲞⲈⲒⲤ ⲆⲈ   ⲦⲈⲨⲘⲚⲦ|ⲤⲀⲂⲈ Ⲁ<Ⲩ>ⲞⲨⲰⲚⲌ
Ⲛ²⁰[Ⲛ]ⲬⲞⲈⲒⲤ ⲀⲨⲞⲨⲰⲚⲌ ⲈⲂⲞⲖ   ⲈⲂⲞⲖ | ¹⁵ Ⲛ<Ⲭ̄>Ⲥ̄ Ⲛ<Ⲭ̄>Ⲥ Ⲛ<Ⲭ̄>Ⲥ̄
                                     ⲆⲈ ⲚⲚ<Ⲭ̄>Ⲥ̄ | ⲀⲨⲞⲨⲰⲚⲌ ⲈⲂⲞⲖ

| and [the] gods of the gods from | and the gods of the gods ¹⁰ from
their | wisdom revealed gods; | <and   <their> considering | revealed |
the gods> from their wisdom   <the> divine gods; | and the gods
revealed | lords; and the lords of ²⁰   from their wisdom | revealed ¹⁵ <the
the lords from their thinkings   lords> of <lords>; and the <lords> of
revealed lords;   the <lords> | <from> thinkings

SJC-III:

111,17–18 The first letter of each line has been lost from the MS but is preserved in old
     photographs. See Emmel, 1978: 204.

111,19–20 MS has first superlinear stroke in lacuna (line 19).

     At the beginning of each line T–S restores [ⲛ] and [ⲛ] respectively.

     Line 20 is not emended by T–S ("the lords of the lords revealed their thoughts of
     lords"). However T–S considers the correct reading to be found in *Eug*–III.

SJC-BG:

112,10 {ⲆⲈ} (T–S). Although untranslatable, ⲆⲈ does seem to have an emphasizing
     function here in Coptic, perhaps on analogy with its use with pronouns in Greek.

112,12–13 <Ⲛ>ⲚⲞⲨⲦⲈ ... ⲚⲚϮ, "<the> ... gods": "<the> gods. The divine gods"
     (T–S).

     Alt.: first emendation: <Ⲛ̄ⲌⲈ> (indefinite article) (T–S, alt.).

112,14 MS has ϥ (incorrect pronoun number).

112,15 MS has x for each emendation. Without the emendation the translation would
     be "Christs" here and on line 17 in each case (not emended by T–S, although the
     error is recognized). x for ⲭ is a common scribal error.

NHC V 15,7–20

ⲛⲓⲭ ⲟ‖[ⲉⲓⲥ ⲇⲉ ⲛ̄ⲛ]ⲓⲭⲟⲉⲓⲥ
ⲁⲩⲟⲩⲱⲛⲍ̄ | [ⲉⲃⲟⲗ ⲍⲛ
ⲛⲉ]ⲩϣⲟⲭⲛⲉ ⲛ̄ⲍⲉⲛⲭⲟ¹⁰[ⲉⲓⲥ ·
ⲁⲛⲓⲭⲟⲉⲓ]ⲥ ⲇⲉ ⲟⲩⲱⲛⲍ̄ ⲉⲃⲟⲗ | ⲍⲛ
[ⲛⲉⲩϭ ⲟⲙ] ⲛ̄ⲍⲉⲛⲁⲣⲭⲓⲁⲅⲅⲉⲗⲟⲥ · |
ⲛ[ⲓⲁⲣⲭⲓⲁⲅⲅ]ⲉⲗⲟⲥ ⲇⲉ ⲁⲩⲟⲩⲱⲛⲍ̄ |
ⲉⲃⲟⲗ ⲍ̄ⲛ ⲛⲉⲩϣⲁⲭⲉ
ⲛ̄ⲍⲉⲛⲁⲅⲅⲉ | ⲗⲟⲥ · ⲁⲩⲱ ⲉⲃⲟⲗ ⲍⲛ
ⲛⲁⲓ̈ ⲁⲩⲟⲩ¹⁵ⲱⲛⲍ̄ ⲉⲃⲟⲗ ⲛ̄ϭ ⲓ
ⲍⲉⲛⲉⲓⲇ ⲟⲥ ⲙⲛ̄ | ⲍⲉⲛⲥⲭⲏⲙⲁ ⲙⲛ̄
ⲍⲉⲛⲙⲟⲣⲫⲏ | ⲙⲛ̄ ⲛⲓⲉⲱⲛ ⲧⲏⲣⲟⲩ
ⲙⲛ̄ ⲛⲉⲩⲕⲟⲥ‖[ⲙⲟⲥ·] ⲟⲩⲛ̄ⲧ̣[ⲉ]
ⲛ̣ⲓⲁⲧⲙⲟⲩ ⲧⲏⲣⲟⲩ | [ⲛ̄ⲧⲉ ⳁⲟⲩⲥⲓⲁ
ⲉⲃⲟⲗ ⲍ̄ⲛ ⲧ̀ϭ]ⲟ̣ⲙ ⲙ̄ⲡⲓ²⁰[ⲣⲱⲙⲉ

the | [lords of the] lords revealed |
[from their] counsels lords; ¹⁰ and
[the lords] revealed | from [their
powers] archangels; | and the
[archangels] revealed | from their
words angels; | and from them
appeared ¹⁵ shapes and | structures
and forms | and all the aeons and
their worlds. | All the immortals
have | [authority from the power] of
²⁰ [Immortal Man

NHC III 87,18–88,7

ⲛⲉⲩⲗⲟⲅⲟⲥ ⲁⲩⲟⲩⲱⲛⲍ ⲉⲃⲟⲗ |
ⲛ̄ⲍⲛ̄ⲭⲟⲉⲓⲥ · ⲛ̄ⲭⲟⲉⲓⲥ ⲇⲉ ⲉⲃⲟⲗ ⲍⲛ̄
²⁰ ⲛⲉⲩϭ ⲟⲙ ⲁⲩⲟⲩⲱⲛⲍ ⲉⲃⲟⲗ
ⲛ̄ⲍⲉⲛ|ⲁⲣⲭⲁⲅⲅⲉⲗⲟⲥ·
ⲛⲁⲣⲭⲁⲅⲅⲉⲗⲟⲥ ⲁⲩ|ⲟⲩⲱⲛⲍ ⲉⲃⲟⲗ
ⲛ̄ⲍⲉⲛⲁⲅⲅⲉⲗⲟⲥ ⲉ|ⲃⲟⲗ ⲍⲛ̄ <ⲛ>ⲁⲓ̈
ⲁⲧⲍⲓⲇⲉⲁ ⲟⲩⲱⲛⲍ·
ⲍⲓ· ⲥⲭⲏⲙ̣[ⲁ ⲍⲓ̈ ⲙⲟⲣⲫⲏ] ⲉϯ ⲣⲁⲛ | [ⲡⲓ⊦
ⲉⲛⲓⲁⲓ [ⲱⲛ ⲧⲏⲣⲟⲩ ⲙⲛ̄]
ⲛⲉⲩⲕⲟ|ⲥⲙⲟⲥ· ⲛⲁ[ⲑ]ⲁ̣ⲛⲁⲧⲟⲥ
ⲧⲏⲣⲟⲩ ⲛ̄ⲧⲁ|ⲉⲓⲣ̄ ϣⲡ̄ ⲛ̄ⲭⲟⲟⲩ
ⲉⲩⲛ̄ⲧⲟⲩ ⲧⲉ⁵ⳁⲟⲩⲥⲓⲁ ⲧⲏⲣⲟⲩ
ⲉⲃⲟⲗ ⲍⲛ̄ ⲧϭ ⲟⲙ ⲙ̄|ⲡⲓⲁⲑⲁⲛⲁⲧⲟⲥ
ⲛ̄ⲣⲱⲙⲉ ⲙⲛ̄ ⲧⲥⲟ|ⲫⲓⲁ

| their words revealed lords; | and
the lords from ²⁰ their powers
revealed | archangels; the archangels
| revealed angels; from | <them> the
semblance appeared
with structure [and form] for naming   [8:
| [all] the aeons [and] their worlds. |
All the immortals, whom | I have
just described, have authority—all of
them— ⁵ from the power of |
Immortal Man and Sophia,

Eug-V:

15,13 First superlinear stroke is in lacuna.

Eug-III:

87,21 "archangels" (2): +"<out of their words> (K).

87,22 Corr.: at the end of the line the letters ⲃⲟⲗ are erased.

87,23 MS has ⲧⲁⲓ̈, "her" or "this" (not emended by K or Tr).

88,2–3 Lacuna in line 3, so restored by T–S.

     "their worlds. All the immortals" (so also T–S): "all their immortal worlds" (K &
Tr).

NHC III 111,20–112,7   BG 112,16–113,15

<ż>ν̄ ΝΕΥΜΕΙΟΥΕ Ν̄ΖΕΝΧΟΕΙϹ ·   <ζΝ̄> ʿ ζʹ Μ̄ΜΕΙΕΥΕ Ν̄<Χ̄>Ϲ̄ Ν̄<Χ̄>Ϲ̄
Ν̄ΧΟΕΙϹ ΔΕ ζΝ̄ | ΤΕΥϬΟΜ   ΔΕ ΕΒΟΛ
ΑΥΟΥωΝζ ΕΒΟΛ   ζΝ̄ ΤΕΥϬΟΜ Α<Υ>ΟΥωΝζ | ΡΙΓ̄
Ν̄ΖΕΝΑΡ|[Χ Α]Γ̄ΓΕΛΟϹ·   [Ε]ΒΟΛ Ν̄ζΝ̄ΑΡΧΙΑΓΓΕ| [ΛΟ]Ϲ
ΝΑΡΧΑΓΓΕΛΟϹ ΕΒΟΛ | [ζ]Ν   ΝΑΡΧΙΑΓΓΕΛΟϹ ΔΕ | [ΕΒ]ΟΛ ζΝ̄
ΝΕΥΛΟΓΟϹ ΑΥΟΥωΝζ ΕΒΟΛ Ν̄   ΝΕΥΛΟΓΟϹ Α<Υ>⁵[Ο]ΥωΝζ ΕΒΟΛ
ΡΙΒ ζΕΝΑΓΓΕΛΟϹ ΕΒΟΛ ζΝ̄ ΝΑΪ   Ν̄ζΝ̄ΑΓ|ΓΕΛΟϹ ΑΥω ΕΒΟΛ ζΝ̄
ΑζΕΝ|ζΙΔΕΑ ΟΥωΝζ ζΙ ϹΧΗΜΑ ζΙ   ΝΑ|ΕΙ <ζΕΝζΙΔΕΑ Α>ΥΟΥωΝζ
ΜΟΡ|ΦΗ ζΙ ΡΑΝ ΕΝΙΑΙωΝ ΤΗΡΟΥ | Ε|ΒΟΛ ζΙ ϹΧΗΜΑ ζΪ ΜΟΡ|ΦΗ ζΪ
Μ̄Ν ΝΕΥΚΟϹΜΟϹ· Ν̄ΑΘΑΝΑΤΟϹ ⁵   ΡΑΝ ΕΝΙΑΙωΝ ΤΗ¹⁰ΡΟΥ Μ̄Ν
ΔΕ Ν̄ΤΑΕΙΧΟΟΥ Ν̄ϢΟΡπ̄ ΟΥΝ̄|ΤΑΥ   ΝΕΥΚΟϹΜΟϹ | ΝΙΑΤΜΟΥ ΔΕ
ΕζΟΥϹΙΑ ΤΗΡΟΥ ΕΒΟΛ ζΜ̄ | Ν̄ΤΑΪϢΑ|ΧΕ ΕΡΟΟΥ ΝϢΟΡπ
ΠΙΑΘΑΝΑΤΟϹ Ν̄ΡωΜΕ † ΠΕΤΕ   ΟΥ Ν̄|ΤΟΥ ΕζΟΥϹΙΑ ΕΒΟΛ ζΝ̄ |
                                         ΤϬΟΜ Μ̄ΠΙΑΤΜΟΥ Ν̄¹⁵ΡωΜΕ ΠΕΤΕ

| and the lords from | their power   revealed <lords>; | and the <lords>
revealed archangels; | the archangels   from their power revealed | **113**
| from their words revealed angels;   archangels; | and the archangels |
112 from them | semblances appeared   from their words ⁵ revealed angels; |
with structure and form | and name   and from them | <semblances>
for all the aeons | and their worlds.   appeared | with structure and form |
And the immortals, ⁵ whom I have   and name for all the aeons ¹⁰ and
just described, all have | authority   their worlds. | And the immortals,
from | Immortal Man, † who   whom I have | just described, have |
                                            authority from | the power of
                                            Immortal ¹⁵ Man, who

---

SJC-BG:

112,16 Not emended by T–S ("the <lords> of the <lords> revealed <lord>-thoughts").
However T–S considers that the correct reading is found in *Eug*–III.

112,17 MS has x for both emendations (not emended by T–S).

113,1 MS has ϥ (incorrect pronoun number).

113,4 MS has ϥ (incorrect pronoun number).

113,7 MS has ΑΪΝΑΥ Ε, "I saw that structure ... appeared"; T–S plausibly suggests
that the translator of the Greek misunderstood ἰδέα and thought it meant, "I saw,"
but T–S does not emend the text. In the T–S translation, however, "<semblances
(ἰδέα)>" is inserted before "structure," while "I" and "saw" remain as the subject
and verb!

NHC V 15,20–16,2

ⲚⲚⲀⲦⲘⲞⲨ ⲈϮ ⲢⲀⲚ] ⲈⲢⲞⲞⲨ· |
[ⲦⲤⲞⲫⲒⲀ ⲀⲨϮ ⲢⲀⲚ ⲈⲢⲞⲤ ⲬⲈ]
ⲦⲤⲒⲄⲎ | [ⲬⲈ ⲀⲤⲬⲰⲔ
ⲚⲦⲈⲤⲘⲚⲦⲚⲀ]ϭ ⲦⲎⲢⲤ̄ | [ⲌⲚ̄
ⲞⲨⲈⲚⲐⲨⲘⲎⲤⲒⲤ ⲀⲬⲚ̄] ϢⲀⲬⲈ |
[19±]ⲀⲨ
(8± lines lacking)

[ⲓ̄ⲋ̄] [12± ⲈⲞⲞⲨ ⲚⲚⲀϮ]|[ϣ]ⲀⲬⲈ
[ⲘⲘ]ⲞⲞ[Ⲩ· ⲚⲎ ⲈⲦⲈ

to name] them. | [Sophia they called]
"Silence," | [because she perfected
her] whole [majesty] | [by reflecting
without] a word. | [. . .] 25 (8± lines
lacking)

[16] [. . . ineffable] | [glory, who

NHC III 88,7–19

ⲦⲈϤⲤⲨⲚⲌⲨⲄⲞⲤ ⲦⲀⲒ̈ ⲚⲦⲀⲨ|ⲬⲞⲞⲤ
ⲈⲢⲞⲤ ⲬⲈ ⲤⲒⲄⲎ· ⲚⲦⲀⲨϮ ⲢⲚ̄Ⲥ | ⲬⲈ
ⲤⲒⲄⲎ ⲬⲈ ⲚⲌⲢⲀⲒ̈ ⲌⲚ̄
ⲞⲨⲈⲚⲐⲨⲘⲎ ¹⁰ⲤⲒⲤ ⲀⲬⲚ̄ ϢⲀⲬⲈ
ⲀⲤⲬⲰⲔ ⲚⲦⲈⲤ|ⲘⲚⲦⲚⲞϭ
ⲚⲀⲫⲐⲀⲢⲤⲒⲀ ⲈⲨⲚⲦⲀⲨ |
ⲚⲦⲈⲌⲞⲨⲤⲒⲀ ⲀⲨⲦⲤⲀⲚⲞ ⲚⲀⲨ ⲚϭⲒ |
ⲠⲞⲨⲀ ⲠⲞⲨⲀ ⲘⲘⲞⲞⲨ ⲚⲌⲈⲚⲚⲞϭ |
ⲘⲘⲚ̄ⲦⲢ̄ⲢⲰⲞⲨ ⲌⲚ̄ ⲘⲠⲎⲞⲨⲈ ⲦⲎ¹⁵ⲢⲞⲨ
ⲚⲀⲐⲀⲚⲀⲦⲞⲤ ⲘⲚ ⲚⲈⲨⲤⲦⲈ|ⲢⲈⲰⲘⲀ
ⲌⲚ̄ⲐⲢⲞⲚⲞⲤ ⲌⲈⲚⲢ̄ⲠⲈ | ⲠⲢⲞⲤ
ⲦⲈⲨⲘⲚ̄ⲦⲚⲞϭ
ⲌⲞⲒ̈ⲚⲈ ⲘⲈⲚ | ⲌⲚ̄ ⲘⲘⲀ ⲚϢⲰⲠⲈ ⲘⲚ
ⲌⲈⲚⲌⲀⲢ|ⲘⲀ ⲈⲨⲌⲀ ⲈⲞⲞⲨ

| his consort, who was | called
"Silence," (and) who was named |
"Silence" because by reflecting ¹⁰
without speech she perfected her |
own majesty. Since the
imperishabilities had | the authority,
each provided | great | kingdoms in
all the immortal heavens ¹⁵ and their
firmaments, | thrones, (and) temples,
| for their own majesty.
Some, indeed, | (who are) in
dwellings and in chariots, | being in

Eug-V:

16,2–3 Reconstruction: see 8,23–24.

Eug-III:

88,10 See endnote 10.

88,11 See endnote 11.

88,12 "provided": "created" (K, translating ⲦⲀⲘⲒⲞ instead of ⲦⲤⲚⲀⲞ; followed by
Tr, who does not emend).

88,17–19 "Some . . . glory": "some indeed dwelling-places and chariots unspeakably
glorious" (K, who overlooks ⲌⲚ̄, "in," & Tr).

NHC III 112,8–17	BG 113,15–114,9

<table>
<tr><td>

| ϣⲁⲩⲙⲟⲩⲧⲉ ⲉⲣⲟϥ ϫⲉ ⲧⲥⲓⲅⲏ ϫⲉ
| ⲉⲃⲟⲗ ⲍⲛ ⲟⲩⲉⲛⲑⲩⲙⲏⲥⲓⲥ ⲁϫⲛ ¹⁰
ϣⲁϫⲉ ⲁⲥϫⲱⲕ ⲉⲃⲟⲗ ⲛ̄ϭⲓ
ⲧⲉⲥ|ⲙⲛ̄ⲧⲛⲟϭ ⲧⲏⲣⲥ̄ †
ⲛ̄ⲁⲫⲑⲁⲣⲥⲓⲁ ⲉⲩ|ⲛ̄ⲧⲁⲩ ⲅⲁⲣ
ⲛ̄ⲧⲉϫⲟⲩⲥⲓⲁ ⲁⲩⲧⲁⲙⲓⲟ | ⲛⲁⲩ
ⲛ̄ⲟⲩⲛⲟϭ ⲛ̄ⲙⲛ̄ⲧⲣ̄ⲣⲟ ⲛ̄ϭⲓ | ⲡⲟⲩⲁ
ⲡⲟⲩⲁ ⲙ̄ⲙⲟⲟⲩ ⲍⲛ̄
ⲧⲙⲉⲍϣ ¹⁵ⲙⲟⲩⲛⲉ· ⲁⲩⲱ
ⲍⲉⲛⲑⲣⲟⲛⲟⲥ ⲙ[ⲛ̄] | ⲍⲉⲛⲣ̄ⲡⲉ·
ⲍⲉⲛⲥⲧⲉⲣⲉⲱⲙⲁ ⲡⲣⲟⲥ |
ⲛⲉⲩⲙⲛ̄ⲧⲛⲟϭ |

</td><td>

| ϣⲁⲩⲙⲟⲩ|ⲧⲉ ⲉⲣⲟϥ ϫⲉ ⲡⲕⲁⲣⲱϥ
<ⲉⲃⲟⲗ ϫⲉ> | ⲍ̈ⲓ̈ⲧⲛ̄
ⲟⲩⲉⲛⲑⲩⲙⲏⲥⲓⲥ | ⲁϫⲛ̄ ϣⲁϫⲉ
ⲧⲉϥⲙⲛ̄ⲧ
ⲛⲟϭ ⲧⲏⲣⲥ ⲁϥϫⲟⲕⲥ ⲉ̣|ⲃⲟⲗ   ⲣ̄ⲓ̄ⲇ
ⲛ̄ⲁⲧⲧⲁⲕⲟ ⲉⲩ[ⲛ̄]|ⲧⲟⲩ ⲧⲉϫⲟⲩⲥⲓⲁ
ⲁⲩⲧ[ⲁ]|ⲙⲓⲟ ⲛⲁⲩ ⲛ̄ⲛⲟⲩⲛⲟ[ϭ
ⲙ]⁵ⲙⲛ̄ⲧⲣ̄ⲣⲟ ⲡⲟⲩⲁ ⲡⲟⲩⲁ ⲍ̣[ⲛ̄] |
ⲧⲉϥⲍⲟⲅⲇⲟⲁⲥ ⲙⲛ̄
ⲡⲉϥ|ⲥⲧⲉⲣⲉⲱⲙⲁ <ⲙ>ⲛ̄
ⲍⲛ̄ⲑⲣⲟ|ⲛⲟⲥ ⲙⲛ̄ ⲍⲛ̄ⲣ̄ⲡⲉ ⲡⲣⲟⲥ |
ⲛⲉⲩⲙⲛ̄ⲧⲛⲟϭ |

</td></tr>
<tr><td>

| is called 'Silence' | because by
reflecting without ¹⁰ speech all her
own majesty was perfected. † | For
since the imperishabilities had | the
authority, each created | a great
kingdom | in the Eighth ¹⁵ and (also)
thrones and | temples (and)
firmaments for | their own majesties.

</td><td>

is called | 'Silence,' <because> | by
reflecting | without speech
he perfected all his own majesty. |
Since the imperishables had | the
authority, they created | a great ⁵
kingdom. Each one is [in] | his
ogdoad with his | firmament <and>
thrones | and temples for | their own
majesties.

114

</td></tr>
</table>

SJC-III:

112,10 See endnote 10.

112,11 See endnote 11.

112,16 ⲡⲣⲟⲥ: ⲡⲣⲟ[ⲥ] (T–S).

SJC-BG:

113,16 Not emended by T–S.

113,18–114,1 See endnote 10.

114,2 See endnote 11.

114,4 Alt. {ⲛ̄}ⲛⲟⲩ (T–S; unnecessary in view of examples in 78,16 and 95,14).

114,7 Not emended by T–S ("his firmament *of* thrones," although T–S translates "his firmament, thrones," i.e., as though the ⲛ̄ before ⲍⲛⲑⲣⲟⲛⲟⲥ were deleted).

NHC V 16,2–6	NHC III 88,19–23

ⲙ̅ⲡⲟⲩ]‖[ⲥ]ⲱⲧⲙ̅ [ⲉⲣ]ⲟⲟⲩ [ⲛ̅ϣⲁ
ⲉⲛⲉⲍ·ⲍⲱⲥ] | ⲛⲉⲩϣ [ⲭⲟ]ⲟⲩ
ⲛ̅[ⲛⲓ ⲫⲩⲥⲓⲥ ⲧⲏⲣⲟⲩ·]

ⲛ̅ⲁⲧϣⲁⲭⲉ ⲉⲣⲟⲟⲩ ²⁰ ⲛⲁⲓ̈ ⲉⲙⲛ̅
ϭϭⲟⲙ ⲉⲭⲟⲟⲩ ⲍⲙ̅ ⲫⲩ|ⲥⲓⲥ ⲛⲓⲙ·

---

⁵ ⲁⲩⲧⲁⲙⲓⲟ ⲇⲉ ⲛ[ⲁⲩ
ⲛ̅ⲍⲉⲛⲥⲧⲣⲁ ⲧⲓⲁ] | ⲛ̅ⲧⲉ
ⲍⲉⲛⲁⲣⲭⲓⲁⲅ̣ [ⲅⲉⲗⲟⲥ ⲙⲛ̅

ⲁⲩⲧⲥⲁⲛⲟ ⲛⲁⲩ ⲛ̅ⲍⲉⲛ|ⲥⲧⲣⲁⲧⲓⲁ
ⲛ̅ⲁⲅⲅⲉⲗⲟⲥ ⲍⲉⲛⲧⲃⲁ ⲉ|ⲙⲛ̅ⲧⲟⲩ
ⲏⲡⲉ ⲉⲍⲟⲩⲛ ⲉⲩⲍⲩⲡⲏ

have] | [never been heard of, since] |
they cannot [be sent] into [any
creature.]

ineffable glory ²⁰ and not able to be
sent into any creature,

---

⁵ Now they created [hosts] | of
archangels [and]

| provided for themselves | hosts of
angels, myriads | without number,
for retinue

Eug-V:

16,4 "sent": see endnote 12.

Eug-III:

88,20 "and . . . creature": less likely, "which cannot be described in any condition" (K
& Tr [similar]).

"sent": See endnote 12.

88,21 "provided": "created" (K, translating ⲧⲁⲙⲓⲟ instead of ⲧⲥⲁⲛⲟ; followed by
Tr, who does not emend).

NHC III 112,17–113,5   BG 114,9–115,7

ⲚⲀⲒ ⲄⲀⲢ ⲦⲎⲢⲞⲨ | ⲀⲨϢⲰⲠⲈ ϩⲒⲦⲚ   ⲚⲀⲒ ⲄⲀⲢ ¹⁰ ⲦⲎⲢⲞⲨ ⲀⲨϢⲰⲠⲈ ϩⲘ |
ⲠⲈⲦⲈϩⲚⲈ | ⲦⲘⲀⲀⲨ ⲘⲠⲦⲎⲢϤ· ⲦⲞⲦⲈ   ⲠⲞⲨⲰϢ ⲚⲦⲘⲀⲨ ⲘⲠⲦⲎ|ⲢϤ ⲦⲞⲦⲈ
ⲚⲀ²⁰ⲠⲞⲤⲦⲞⲖⲞⲤ ⲈⲦⲞⲨⲀⲀⲂ   ⲚⲀⲠⲞⲤⲦⲞⲖⲞⲤ | ⲈⲦⲞⲨⲀⲀⲂ
ⲠⲈⲬⲀⲨ | ⲚⲀϤ ⲬⲈ ⲠⲬⲞⲈⲒⲤ   ⲠⲈⲬⲀⲨ ⲚⲀϤ | ⲬⲈ ⲠⲈⲬⲤ ⲠⲤⲰⲦⲎⲢ
ⲠⲤⲰⲦⲎⲢ· | ⲀⲬⲒ ⲚⲈⲦϩⲚ ⲚⲒⲀⲒⲰⲚ   ⲚⲈⲦ¹⁵ϩⲚ ⲚⲒⲀⲒⲰⲚ ⲞⲨⲞⲚϩⲞⲨ |
ⲈⲢⲞⲚ ⲬⲈ | ⲦⲀⲚⲀⳠⲔⲎ ⲚⲀⲚ ⲦⲈ   ⲚⲀⲚ ⲈⲂⲞⲖ ⲈⲠⲒ ⲦⲀⲚⲀⲄ|ⲔⲎ ⲈⲢⲞⲚ
ⲈⲦⲢⲈⲚϢ[Ⲓ]|ⲚⲈ ⲚⲤⲰⲞⲨ ⲠⲈⲬⲈ   ⲦⲈ ⲈϢⲒⲚⲈ | ⲚⲤⲰⲞⲨ ⲠⲈⲬⲀϤ ⲚϬⲒ
ⲠⲦⲈⲖⲒⲞⲤ Ⲛ   ⲠⲦⲈ
ⲢⲒⳠ ⲤⲰⲦⲎⲢ ⲬⲈ ⲈϢϪⲈ <Ⲉ>ⲦⲈⲦⲚϢⲒⲚⲈ   [Ⲗ]ⲒⲞⲤ ⲚⲤⲰⲦⲎⲢ ⲬⲈ ⲈϢ|[Ⳝ]ⲉ   ⲢⲒⲈ
     | ⲚⲤⲀ ϩⲰⲂ ⲚⲒⲘ· ⲦⲚⲀⲬⲞⲞⲨ ⲈⲢⲰⲦⲚ   ⲦⲈⲦⲚϢ ⲚⲤⲀ | [ϩⲰ]Ⲃ ⲚⲒⲘ
                                    ⲦⲚⲀⲬⲞⲞⲨ Ⲉ|[Ⲣⲱ]ⲦⲚ

     | ⲀⲨⲦⲀⲘⲒⲞ ⲚⲀⲨ ⲚϨⲈⲚⲤⲦⲢⲀⲦⲒⲀ   ⲀⲨⲦⲀⲘⲒⲞ ⲚⲀⲨ Ⲛ⁵ϩⲚⲤⲦⲢⲀⲦⲒⲀ
     Ⲛ|ⲀⲄⲄⲈⲖⲞⲤ ϩⲈⲚⲦⲂⲀ ⲈⲘⲚⲦⲞⲨ   ⲚⲀⲄⲄⲈⲖⲞⲤ | ϩⲚⲦⲂⲀ ⲈⲘⲚⲦⲞⲨ ⲎⲠⲈ
     ⲎⲠⲈ ⁵ ⲈⲨϢⲘ̅ϢⲈ ⲘⲚ ⲚⲈⲨⲈⲞⲞⲨ   ⲈⲨ|ϢⲘ̅ϢⲈ ⲘⲚ ⲞⲨⲈⲞⲞⲨ

For these all | came by the will | of   For these ¹⁰ all came by | the will of
the Mother of the Universe." Then ²⁰   the Mother of the Universe." | Then
the Holy Apostles said | to him: the Holy Apostles | said to him: |
"Lord, Savior, | tell us about those   "Christ, Savior, ¹⁵ reveal to us those
who are in the aeons, | since it is   who are in the aeons, | since it is
necessary for us to ask | about   necessary | for us to ask about |
them." The perfect   them." The perfect

113 Savior said: "If you ask | about   Savior said: "If | you ask about | **115**
anything, I will tell you.   anything, I will tell | you.
| They created hosts of | angels,   They created ⁵ hosts of angels, |
myriads without number ⁵ for retinue   myriads without number for | retinue
and their glory. They   and glory. And

SJC-III:

113,1 MS has ⲁ (not emended by T–S).

NHC V 16,6–17

ⲌⲈⲚ]|ⲀⲄⲄⲈⲖⲞⲤ ⲚⲦⲈ ⲌⲈⲚⲦ̲[ⲂⲀ
Ⲛ̄Ⲁⲧ̄ⲧ̄] | ⲎⲠⲈ ⲈⲢⲞⲞⲨ ⲈⲨ[Ⲱ̄Ⲙ̄Ⲱ̄Ⲉ
Ⲙ̄Ⲛ ⲞⲨ]|ⲈⲞⲞⲨ Ⲙ̄Ⲛ
ⲌⲈⲚⲠⲀ[ⲢⲐⲈⲚⲞⲤ Ⲙ̄Ⲛ] ¹⁰ ⲌⲈⲚⲠ̄Ⲛ̄Ⲁ̄ˑ
ⲈⲨⲈ Ⲛ̄Ⲟ̲[ⲨⲞⲈⲒⲚ | Ⲛ̄ⲚⲀⲧ̄|ⲰⲀⲬⲈ
Ⲙ̄ⲘⲞⲞⲨˑ Ⲙ[Ⲛ̄ⲦⲞⲨ Ⲍ̂Ⲓ Ⲥ]Ⲉ | ⲄⲀⲢ
ⲌⲀⲦⲞⲞⲦⲞⲨˑ ⲞⲨ[Ⲧ]ⲉ̲
[ⲞⲨ]Ⲙ̄Ⲛ̄ⲧ̄|Ⲁⲧ̄ϬⲞⲘˑ ⲀⲖⲖⲀ ⲞⲨⲰ̄Ⲱ̄
ⲞⲨⲀⲈⲦⲨ̄ | ⲠⲈˑ
ⲀⲨⲰ Ⲱ̄ⲀϤⲰ̄ⲰⲠⲈ Ⲛ̄ⲦⲈⲨⲚⲞⲨˑ
¹⁵ ⲀⲨⲰ Ⲛ̄ⲦⲈⲒ̈Ⲍ̄Ⲉ ⲀϤⲬⲰⲔ ⲈⲂⲞⲖ
Ⲛ̄Ϭ[Ⲓ] | ⲠⲈⲰⲚ Ⲙ̄Ⲛ ⲦⲠⲈ Ⲙ̄Ⲛ
ⲠⲒⲤⲦⲈⲢⲈⲰ |ⲘⲀ Ⲛ̄ⲦⲈ ⲠⲢⲰⲘⲈ

NHC III 89,1–8

ⲢⲈⲤⲒⲀ Ⲙ̄Ⲛ ⲞⲨⲈⲞⲞⲨ ⲈⲦⲒ   [ⲠⲐ]
ⲌⲈⲚⲠⲀⲢⲐ̲ [Ⲉ]|ⲚⲞⲤ <Ⲙ̄>Ⲡ̄Ⲛ̄Ⲁ̄
ⲚⲞⲨⲞⲈⲒⲚ Ⲛ̄ⲀⲦⲰ̄ⲀⲬⲈ | ⲈⲢⲞⲞⲨˑ
Ⲙ̄Ⲙ̄Ⲛ̄ ⲌⲒⲤⲈ Ⲙ̄ⲘⲀⲨ ⲌⲀⲦⲎ|ⲞⲨ Ⲙ̄Ⲛ
Ⲙ̄Ⲛ̄ⲦⲀⲦϬⲞⲘˑ ⲀⲖⲖⲀ ⲞⲨⲰ̄Ⲱ̄Ⲉ ⁵
Ⲙ̄ⲘⲀⲦⲈ ⲠⲈˑ

Ⲱ̄ⲀϤⲰ̄ⲰⲠⲈ Ⲛ̄ⲦⲈⲨ|ⲚⲞⲨ
Ⲛ̄ⲦⲈⲈⲒⲌ̄Ⲉ ˑ ⲀⲨⲬⲰⲔ ⲈⲂⲞⲖ Ⲛ̄ϬⲒ |
ⲚⲀⲒⲰⲚ Ⲙ̄Ⲛ ⲚⲈⲨⲠⲈˑ Ⲙ̄Ⲛ
ⲚⲈⲤⲦⲈⲢⲈ |ⲰⲘⲀ Ⲙ̄ⲠⲈⲞⲞⲨ

| angles, (hosts) of [numberless] |
myriads for [retinue and] | glory,
even [virgins and] ¹⁰ spirits, who are
ineffable | [lights]. For [they have
no sickness] | nor weakness, | but it
is only will, | and it comes to be in
an instant. ¹⁵ And thus was
completed | the aeon, with (its)
heaven and firmament, | of Immortal
Man

and glory, even virgin | spirits, the   [89]
ineffable lights. | They have no
sickness | nor weakness, but it is
only will: ⁵ it comes to be in an
instant. | Thus were completed | the
aeons with their heavens and
firmaments | for the glory

Eug-V:

16,8 Stroke over Ⲙ is visible.

16,10 Third superlinear stroke is in lacuna.

   ⲧ: see Emmel, 1979: 185 (line identified as extant line 9).

16,11 End of line: see Emmel, 1979: 185 (line identified as 16, extant line 10);
   Emmel's restoration is too short for the lacuna.

Eug-III:

89,1–2 "even ... lights": less likely, in view of V 16,9–11, "indescribable virgin
   spirits of light" (K & Tr).

89,2 MS has Ⲛ̄ (not emended by Tr).

89,6 "Thus" could be taken with the preceding sentence (noted by T–S).

89,8 "for": "of" (T–S, but "perhaps 'for'"; K & Tr).

NHC III 113,5–12   BG 115,7–18

ⲁⲩⲧⲁ|ⲙⲓⲟ ⲛ̄ⲍⲉⲛⲡⲁⲣⲑⲉⲛⲟⲥ
ⲙ̄ⲡⲛ̄ⲁ̄ ⲛ̄|ⲟⲩⲟⲉⲓⲛ ⲛ̄ⲁⲧⲱⲁⲭⲉ
ⲉⲣⲟⲟⲩ ⲛ̄ⲁ\<ⲧ\>|`ⲱ´{ⲉ}ⲓⲃⲉ ⲉⲙⲛ̄
ⲍⲓⲥⲉ ⲅⲁⲣ ⲙ̄ⲙⲁⲩ | ⲍⲁⲧⲏⲟⲩ ⲁⲩⲱ
ⲙ̄ⲛ̄ ⲙⲛ̄ⲧⲁⲧϭⲟⲙ ¹⁰ ⲁⲗⲗⲁ ⲟⲩⲱⲱ
ⲡⲉ

ⲁⲩ|ⲧⲁⲙⲓⲟ ⲇⲉ ⲛ̄ⲍⲙ̄ⲡⲁⲣⲑⲉ|ⲛⲟⲥ
ⲙ̄ⲡⲛ̄ⲁ̄ ⲛⲟⲩⲟ̈ⲓⲛ ⲛ̄ ¹⁰ⲁⲧⲱⲁⲭⲉ
ⲉⲣⲟⲟⲩ ⲁⲩⲱ ⲛ̄|ⲁⲧⲍⲁⲓ̄ⲃⲉⲥ ⲙⲛ̄
ⲍⲓ̈ⲥⲉ ⲅⲁⲣ | ⲍⲁⲧⲏⲩ ⲟⲩⲧⲉ ⲙⲛ̄
ⲁⲧϭⲟⲙ | ⲁⲗⲗⲁ ⲟⲩⲱⲱⲉ ⲙⲙⲁⲧⲉ
ⲡⲉ

| ⲁⲩⲱ ⲛⲧⲉⲩⲛⲟⲩ ⲁⲩⲱⲱ ¹⁵ⲡⲉ
ⲛ̄ⲧⲍⲉ ⲁⲩⲭⲱⲕ ⲛϭⲓ | ⲛ̄ⲁⲓⲱⲛ ⲙⲛ̄
{ⲛ}ⲙ̄ⲡⲏⲩⲉ | ⲙⲛ̄ <ⲛ>ⲉⲥⲧⲉⲣⲉⲱⲙⲁ
ⲙ̄|ⲡⲉⲟⲟⲩ ⲙⲡⲓⲣⲱⲙⲉ ⲛⲁⲧ

ⲁⲛⲁⲓⲱⲛ ⲭⲱⲕ ⲉ|ⲃⲟⲗ ⲛ̄ⲧⲉⲉⲓⲍⲉ ⲍⲛ̄
ⲟⲩϭⲉⲡ`ⲏ´ ⲙⲛ̄ ⲙ̄ⲡⲉ | ⲙⲛ̄
ⲛⲉⲥⲧⲉⲣⲉⲱⲙⲁ ⲍⲙ̄ ⲡⲉⲟⲟⲩ |

created | virgin spirits, the |
ineffable and unchangeable lights. |
For they have no sickness | nor
weakness, ¹⁰ but it is will.

Thus the aeons were completed |
quickly with the heavens | and the
firmaments in the glory

they | created virgin | spirits, ¹⁰ the
ineffable and shadowless | lights.
For there is no sickness | among
them nor weakness, | but it is only
will, | and they came to be in an
instant. ¹⁵ Thus were completed the
aeons | with the heavens | and the
firmaments for | the glory of
Immortal Man

SJC-III:

113,8 Corr.: `ⲱ´ for marked out ⲑⲁ; ⲥ marked out after second ⲉ (see 97,18 for
     similar correction); uncorrected, the text agrees with the BG par.

113,11 Corr.: first ⲙ for erased letter.

SJC-BG:

115,15 "Thus" could be taken with the preceding sentence (noted by T–S).

115,17 MS has ⲡ, "*the* firmament" (not emended by T–S).

     "for": "of" (T–S, but "perhaps 'for'").

NHC V 16,17–28   NHC III 89,8–18

ⲛⲛⲁⲧⲙⲟⲩ [ⲙⲛ̄] | ⲧⲉϥⲥⲟⲫⲓⲁ ⲉⲧ[ⲉ
ⲟⲩⲛ̄ⲧⲁϥ ⲛ̄ⲍⲏ]|ⲧϥ̄ ⲛ̄ⲧ̣[ⲉ]ⲥ̣[ⲙⲟⲧ̇
ⲛ̄ⲉⲱⲛ ⲛⲓⲙ ⲙⲛ̄ ⲕⲟ]²⁰ⲥⲙ[ⲟⲥ ⲛⲓⲙ
ⲙⲛ̄ ⲛⲏ ⲉⲧⲁⲩϣⲱⲡⲉ] | ⲛ̄ⲥⲱ[ⲟⲩ
ⲉⲧⲣⲉⲩⲧⲥⲁⲛⲟ ⲛ̄ⲛⲓⲧⲩ]|ⲡⲟⲥ
ⲉⲃⲟ̣[ⲗ ⲍⲙ̄ ⲡⲙⲁ ⲉⲧⲙ̄ⲙⲁⲩ] | ⲍⲛ̄
ⲙ̄ⲡ[ⲏⲟⲩⲉ ⲙ̄ⲡⲓⲭⲁⲟⲥ ⲙⲛ̄
ⲛⲉⲩ]|[ⲕ]ⲟⲥⲙ[ⲟⲥ· ⲁⲩⲱ ⲧⲉϥⲩⲥⲓⲥ
5±] ²⁵ [ⲧ]ⲏⲣ[ⲥ̄

17±] | [21±] | [21±] | [21±] |

[and] | his Sophia, [which has in] | it
the [pattern of every aeon and] ²⁰
[every world and those that came] |
afterward, [in order to provide the
types] | [from there] | in the
[heavens of chaos and their] |
worlds. [And all natures . . .]

²⁵ [. . .] | [. . .] | [. . .] | [. . .] |

ⲙ̄ⲡⲁⲑⲁⲛⲁⲧⲟⲥ | ⲛ̄ⲣⲱⲙⲉ ⲙⲛ̄
ⲧⲥⲟⲫⲓⲁ ⲧⲉϥⲥⲩⲛ ¹⁰ⲍⲩⲅⲟⲥ ⲡⲙⲁ
ⲉⲧⲁ<ϥϣⲱⲡ ⲉⲣⲟϥ ⲛ̄ⲧⲉⲥⲙⲟⲧ
ⲛ̄>ⲉⲱⲛ ⲛⲓⲙ ⲙⲛ̄ | ⲛⲉⲩⲕⲟⲥⲙⲟⲥ
ⲙⲛ̄ ⲛⲉⲛⲧⲁⲩϣⲱ|ⲡⲉ ⲙⲛ̄ⲛ̄ⲥⲁ ⲛⲁⲓ̈
ⲉⲧⲣⲟⲩⲧⲥⲁⲛⲟ ⲛ̄|ⲛ̄ⲧⲩⲡⲟⲥ ⲙ̄ⲡⲙⲁ
ⲉⲧⲙ̄ⲙⲁⲩ ⲛⲉⲩ|ⲉⲓⲛⲉ ⲍⲛ̄ ⲙ̄ⲡⲏⲟⲩⲉ
ⲙ̄ⲡⲉⲭⲁⲟⲥ ⲙⲛ̄ ¹⁵ ⲛⲉⲩⲕⲟⲥⲙⲟⲥ·
ⲧⲉϥⲩⲥⲓⲥ ⲇⲉ ⲧⲏⲣⲥ̄
| ⲉⲃⲟⲗ ⲍⲙ̄ ⲡⲁⲑⲁⲛⲁⲧⲟⲥ ⲭⲓⲛ
ⲙ̄ⲡⲁ|ⲅⲉⲛⲛⲏⲧⲟⲥ
ϣⲁ ⲡϭⲱⲗⲡ̄ ⲉⲃⲟⲗ ⲙ̄|ⲡⲉⲭⲁⲟⲥ ⲍⲙ̄

of Immortal | Man and Sophia, his
consort: ¹⁰ the area which
<contained the pattern of> every
aeon and | their worlds and those
that came | afterward, in order to
provide | the types from there, their |
likenesses in the heavens of chaos
and ¹⁵ their worlds. And all natures
|
from the Immortal One, from
Unbegotten
| to the revelation of | chaos, are in

Eug-V:

16,25 The superlinear stroke is visible, since a large portion of it is over ⲣ (not an
     unusual position for a final stroke in this tractate).

Eug-III:

89,10 Corr.: ⲧ for erasure; corr.: ⲱⲛ for ⲟ; a letter has been marked out between ⲉⲱⲛ
     and ⲛⲓⲙ ; not emended by K or Tr, although both note (as does T–S) that the
     sentence is incomplete as it stands.

89,12 Corr.: third ⲛ for ⲓ̈.

     "provide": "create" (K, translating ⲧⲁⲙⲓⲟ instead of ⲧⲥⲁⲛⲟ; followed by Tr,
     who does not emend).

89,14 ⲙ̄ⲡⲉⲭⲁⲟⲥ, "of chaos": ⲙ<ⲛ̄> ⲡⲉⲭⲁⲟⲥ, "<and> chaos" (T–S, "probably").

89,18 "are": omitted by T–S, K & Tr, for all of whom the predicate begins in line 21
     ("ever delight themselves . . .").

NHC III 113,13–21   BG 115,18–116,13

ⲘⲠⲀⲐⲀⲚⲀⲦⲞⲤ ⲚⲢⲰⲘⲈ· ⲘⲚ
ⲦⲤⲞⲪⲒⲀ ⲦⲈ·ⲤⲨⲚⲌⲨⲄⲞⲤ ⲠⲘⲀ
ⲚⲦⲀⲨⲬⲒ ¹⁵ ⲤⲘⲞⲦ ⲘⲘⲀⲨ Ⲛ·Ⲓ
ⲀⲒⲰⲚ ⲚⲒⲘ ⲌⲒ ⲔⲞ·[Ⲥ]ⲘⲞⲤ ⲘⲚ
ⲚⲈⲚⲦⲀⲨ·ⲰⲠⲈ ⲘⲚⲚ·ⲤⲀ ⲚⲀ·
ⲈⲂⲞⲖ ⲚⲌ̄ⲎⲦⲨ̄ ⲈⲠⲈⲨⲦⲀⲘⲒⲞ
ⲚⲌⲈⲚⲈⲒⲚⲈ ⲌⲚ̄ ⲘⲠⲈ ⲘⲠⲈⲬⲀⲞⲤ
ⲘⲚ ⲚⲈⲨⲔⲞⲤⲘⲞⲤ· ⲦⲈⲪⲨⲤⲒⲤ ⲆⲈ ²⁰
ⲦⲎⲢⲤ

ⲬⲒⲚ ⲘⲠⲞⲨⲰⲚⲌ ⲘⲠⲈⲬⲀⲞⲤ | ⲈⲂⲞⲖ

ⲘⲞⲨ ⲘⲚ ⲦⲤⲞⲪⲒⲀ   Ⲣ̄Ⲓ̄Ⲋ
ⲦⲈ[Ⲩ]·ⲤⲨⲚⲌⲨⲄⲞⲤ ⲠⲘⲀ Ⲛ̄[ⲦⲀⲨ]·ⲬⲒ
ⲦⲨⲠⲞⲤ ⲈⲂⲞⲖ Ⲛ̄[ⲌⲎⲦⲨ] | Ⲛ·Ⲓ ⲀⲒⲰⲚ
ⲚⲒⲘ ⲌⲒ Ⲕ[ⲞⲤ]⁵ⲘⲞⲤ <ⲘⲚ̄>
Ⲛ̄ⲦⲀⲨⲰⲠⲈ ⲘⲚ̄|ⲚⲚ̄ⲤⲀ ⲚⲀ· ⲀⲨⲬⲒ
ⲦⲨ|ⲠⲞⲤ ⲈⲂⲞⲖ ⲌⲘ ⲠⲘⲀ Ⲉ|ⲦⲘ̄ⲘⲀⲨ
ⲈⲦⲀⲘⲒⲞ <Ⲛ̄>Ⲛ<ⲈⲨ>|ⲈⲒⲚⲈ ⲘⲠⲎⲨⲈ
Ⲙ{Ⲛ̄}ⲠⲈ¹⁰ⲬⲀⲞⲤ ⲘⲚ̄ ⲚⲈⲨⲔⲞⲤⲘⲞⲤ
| ⲪⲨⲤⲒⲤ ⲆⲈ ⲚⲒⲘ

ⲬⲒⲚ Ⲙ̄|ⲠⲞⲨⲰⲚⲌ ⲘⲠⲈⲬⲀⲞⲤ | ⲈⲂⲞⲖ

| of Immortal Man and Sophia, | his consort: the area from which ¹⁵ every aeon and world | and those that came afterward | took (their) pattern for their creation | of likenesses in the heavens of chaos | and their worlds. And all natures,

and Sophia, his | consort: the area [from which] | every aeon and world | <and> those that came afterward ⁵ took (their) types. | They took (their) types | from there | to create <their> | likenesses for the heavens <of> ¹⁰ chaos and their worlds. | And all natures,   **116**

²⁰ starting from the revelation of chaos, | are

starting from | the revelation of chaos, | are

SJC-III:

113,16 Lacuna so restored by T–S.

113,18 Alt.: Ⲙ<Ⲛ̄> ⲠⲈⲬⲀⲞⲤ, "<and> chaos" (T–S, "probably").

SJC-BG:

116,5 Not emended by T–S.

   MS has final superlinear stroke in lacuna.

116,8–9 On line 8, MS has a large diple followed by ⲚⲀ at the end of the line (not emended by T–S). On line 9, T–S does not emend but divides the first four letters, ⲈⲒ ⲚⲈ, and translates the whole, "in order to create. These are: the heavens and chaos" (see explanatory n., T–S: 273). The lack of clear meaning, the parallels, and the unusualness of ⲦⲀⲘⲒⲞ without an object make the T–S solution unacceptable. The problem may have been caused by an error of hearing.

116,12 ⲠⲬⲀⲞⲤ, "chaos": <ⲠⲬⲢⲒⲤⲦⲞⲤ >, "<Christ>" (Schenke, 1962: 275, n. 57).

NHC V 16,29–17,9

[21±] [30] [21±] | [8± ⲉⲩⲣⲁϣⲉ
ⲉⲩⲙⲏⲛ]
[ⲓⲍ̄] [ⲍ̄ⲙ ⲡⲉⲩⲉⲟⲟⲩ· ⲛ̄ⲛⲁⲧ]ϣⲓⲃ̣[ⲉ] |
[ⲙ̄ⲛ ⲡⲓⲙ̄ⲧⲟⲛ ⲛ̄ⲛ]ⲁ†[† ϣ]ⲓ̣ ⲉⲣⲟ[ϥ·]
| [ⲛⲏ ⲉⲧⲉ ⲙ̄ⲛ ϣ]ϭⲟⲙ ⲛ̄[ⲟⲩ]ϣⲁⲭⲉ
| [ⲉⲭⲱ ⲙ̄ⲙⲟⲟⲩ]· ⲛ̄ⲥⲉ̣[ⲥⲟ]ⲩⲱⲛⲟⲩ
[5] [ⲍ̄ⲛ ⲛⲓⲉⲱⲛ ⲧⲏⲣ]ⲟⲩ ⲉⲧⲁⲩϣⲱⲡⲉ
| [ⲙⲛ̄ⲛ̄ⲥⲁ] ⲛ̣[ⲁ ⲓ̈] ⲙⲛ̄ ⲛⲉⲩϭⲟⲙ·
| [7±] ⲍ̄ⲱ ⲉⲣⲱⲧⲛ̄ ϣⲁ ⲡⲉⲓ̈ⲙⲁ
| [ⲛⲏ ⲇⲉ ⲧⲏ]ⲣ̣ⲟ̣[ⲩ] ⲉ̣ⲧⲁⲩⲣ̄ ϣⲟⲣⲡ̄ |
ⲛ̄[ⲭⲟⲟⲩ ⲛⲏⲧ]ⲛ̄· ⲁⲓ̈ϣⲁⲭⲉ ⲙ̄ⲙⲟⲟⲩ

NHC III 89,18–90,6

ⲡⲟⲩⲟⲉⲓⲛ ⲉⲧⲣ̄ ⲟⲩⲟⲉⲓⲛ· |
ⲛ̄ⲁⲧⲍⲁⲉⲓⲃⲉⲥ ⲙⲛ̄ ⲟⲩⲣⲁϣⲉ
ⲛ̄ⲁⲧϣⲁ[20]ⲭⲉ ⲉⲣⲟϥ ⲙⲛ̄ ⲟⲩⲧⲉⲗⲏⲗ
ⲛ̄ⲛⲁⲧⲭⲟ|ⲟϥ ⲉⲩⲧⲉⲣⲡⲉⲥⲑⲁⲓ
ⲉⲩⲙⲏⲛ ⲉⲃⲟⲗ | ⲉⲍⲣⲁ ⲓ̈ ⲉⲭⲙ̄
ⲡⲉⲩⲉⲟⲟⲩ ⲉⲧⲉ ⲙⲉϥ|ϣⲓⲃⲉ ⲙⲛ̄
ⲧⲁⲛⲁⲡⲁⲩⲥⲓⲥ ⲉⲧⲉ ⲙⲁⲩ|ϣⲓⲧⲥ̄
ⲧⲁ ⲓ̈ ⲉⲧⲉ ⲙⲛ̄ ϣϭⲟⲙ ⲉϣⲁⲭⲉ |
ⲉⲣⲟⲥ ⲟⲩⲇⲉ ⲛ̄ⲛⲉⲩⲉϣⲛⲟⲉⲓ |
ⲙ̄ⲙⲟⲥ ⲛ̄ⲍⲣⲁ ⲓ̈ ⲍ̄ⲛ ⲛⲁⲓⲱⲛ ⲧⲏ|ⲣⲟⲩ
ⲛ̄ⲧⲁⲩϣⲱⲡⲉ ⲙⲛ̄ ⲛⲉⲩϭⲟⲙ
| ⲁⲩⲱ ⲍ̄ⲱ ϣⲁ ⲡⲉⲉⲓⲙⲁ·
ⲛⲁ ⲓ̈ ⲇⲉ ⲧⲏ[5]ⲣⲟⲩ ⲛ̄ⲧⲁⲉⲓⲣ̄ ϣⲟⲣⲡ̄
ⲛ̄ⲭⲟⲟⲩ ⲛⲁⲕ | ⲁⲉⲓⲭⲟⲟⲩ

ϥ

[. . .] [30] [. . .] | [. . . ever
rejoicing]
[17] [in their unchanging glory] | [and the
unmeasured rest,] | [which cannot be
described] | or [known] [5] [among all
the aeons] that came to be |
[afterward] and their powers.

| [. . .] this much is enough for you.
| [Now all] that has just been | [said
to you,] I spoke

the light that shines without shadow
| and (in) ineffable joy [20] and
unutterable jubilation. | They ever
delight themselves | on account of
their glory that does not change | and
the rest that is not measured, | which
cannot be described
or conceived | among all the aeons |
that came to be and their powers.
| But this much is enough.
Now all [5] I have just said to you, | I
said

90

NHC III 113,21–114,7   BG 116,13–117,10

ⲍⲙ̄ ⲡⲟⲩⲟⲉⲓⲛ ⲉⲧⲣ̄ ⲟⲩⲟⲉⲓⲛ ⲉ|ⲧⲉ	ⲍⲙ ⲡⲓⲟⲩⲟⲓ̈ⲛ ⲉ|ⲧⲣ̄ ⲟⲩⲟⲓ̈ⲛ
ⲙⲛ̄ⲧϥ̄ ⲍⲁⲉⲓⲃⲉⲥ ⲙⲛ̄ ⲟⲩⲣⲁϣⲉ |	ⲛⲁⲧⲍⲁⲓ̈ⲃⲉⲥ ¹⁵ ⲉⲩⲍⲙ ⲡⲣⲁϣⲉ

ⲍⲙ̄ ⲡⲟⲩⲟⲉⲓⲛ ⲉⲧⲣ̄ ⲟⲩⲟⲉⲓⲛ ⲉ|ⲧⲉ
ⲙⲛ̄ⲧϥ̄ ⲍⲁⲉⲓⲃⲉⲥ ⲙⲛ̄ ⲟⲩⲣⲁϣⲉ |
ⲉ̄ⲛⲉⲩⲉϣ ϣⲁϫⲉ ⲉⲣⲟϥ ⲙⲛ̄
ⲟⲩ|ⲧⲉⲗⲏⲗ ⲛ̄ⲁⲧϫⲟⲟϥ ⲉⲩⲙⲏⲛ
ⲉⲃⲟⲗ ²⁵ ⲉⲩⲣⲟⲟⲩⲧ̄ ⲉⲍⲣⲁⲓ̈ ⲉⲭⲛ̄
ⲡⲉⲩⲉⲟⲟⲩ

ⲡⲓⲁ ⲛ̄ⲁⲧϣⲓⲃⲉ ⲙⲛ̄ ⲧⲁⲛⲁⲡⲁⲩⲥⲓⲥ
ⲛ̄ⲁ|ⲧϣⲓⲧⲥ̄ ⲧⲁⲓ̈ ⲉⲧⲉ ⲛ̄ⲛⲉⲩⲉϣ
ϣⲁ|ϫⲉ ⲉⲣⲟⲥ ⲍⲛ̄ ⲛⲁⲓⲱⲛ ⲧⲏⲣⲟⲩ
ⲛ̄ⲧⲁⲩ|ϣⲱⲡⲉ ⲙⲛ̄ⲛ̄ⲥⲁ ⲛⲁⲓ̈ ⲙⲛ̄
ⲛⲉⲩ⁵ⲃⲟⲙ ⲧⲏⲣⲟⲩ·

ⲛⲁⲓ̈ ⲇⲉ ⲧⲏⲣⲟⲩ ⲛ̄|ⲧⲁⲉⲓϫⲟⲟⲩ
ⲉⲣⲱⲧⲛ̄ ⲛ̄ϣⲟⲣⲡ̄ ⲁⲉⲓ|ϫⲟⲟⲩ

ⲍⲙ ⲡⲓⲟⲩⲟⲓ̈ⲛ ⲉ|ⲧⲣ̄ ⲟⲩⲟⲓ̈ⲛ
ⲛⲁⲧⲍⲁⲓ̈ⲃⲉⲥ ¹⁵ ⲉⲩⲍⲙ ⲡⲣⲁϣⲉ
ⲛ̄ⲛⲁⲧ|ϣⲁϫⲉ ⲉⲣⲟϥ ⲙⲛ̄ ⲡⲧⲉ|ⲗⲏⲗ
ⲛⲁⲧⲭⲟⲟϥ ⲉⲩ|ⲧⲉⲣⲡⲉ ⲉⲩⲙⲏⲛ
ⲉⲃⲟⲗ
[ⲉ]ⲍⲣⲁⲓ̈ ⲉⲭⲙ ⲡⲉⲩⲉⲟⲟⲩ | **ⲡⲓⲍ**
[ⲛ]ⲁ̣ⲧϣⲓⲃⲉ ⲙⲛ̄ ⲡⲉⲩⲙ̄|[ⲧⲟ]ⲛ
ⲛⲁⲧϣⲓⲧϥ̄ ⲛⲁⲓ̈ ⲉ|[ⲧⲉ] ⲛⲉⲩϣ
ϣⲁϫⲉ ⲉⲣⲟ⁵[ⲟ]ⲩ ⲍⲛ ⲁⲓⲱⲛ ⲛⲓⲙ
ⲛ̄|ⲧⲁⲩϣⲱⲡⲉ ⲙⲛ̄ⲛ̄ⲥⲁ | ⲛⲁⲓ̈ ⲙⲛ̄
ⲛⲉⲩⲃⲟⲙ ⲧⲏ|ⲣⲟⲩ

ⲛⲁⲓ̈ ⲛ̄ⲧⲁⲓ̈ϫⲟⲟⲩ ⲛ̄|ϣⲟⲣⲡ̄
ⲁⲓ̈ϫⲟⲟⲩ ⲛⲏ¹⁰ⲧⲛ̄

---

in the Light that shines without
shadow | and joy that cannot be
described | and | unutterable
jubilation. They ever ²⁵ delight
themselves on account of their
unchanging glory

114 and the immeasurable rest, | which
cannot be described | among all the
aeons that | came to be afterward
and all their ⁵ powers.
Now all that | I have just said to you,
I | said

in the Light | that shines without
shadow, ¹⁵ being in the ineffable joy
| and the unutterable | jubilation. |
They ever delight themselves
on account of their unchanging |
glory and their immeasurable | rest,   **117**
which | cannot be described ⁵ among
all the aeons that | came to be
afterward | and all their powers.

| These things that I have just | said,
I said to you

SJC-III:

113,21 "are in": "from" (T–S; for T–S the predicate begins in lines 24–25, "ever delight themselves . . .").

SJC-BG:

116,13–15 "are . . . being": "from the light . . . are" (T–S).

116,17–18 Corr.: ϣⲓ erased at the end of line 17; ⲧ for partly erased ⲡ at the beginning of line 18; originally ϣⲓⲡⲉ , "be ashamed."

NHC V 17,10–18

¹⁰ ⲛ̄ⲑⲉ̣[ⲉ ⲉⲛⲉⲩ]ⲛ̄ ϭⲟⲙ
ⲛ̄ⲧⲉⲧⲛ̄ϣⲟⲡⲟⲩ | ⲉ[ⲣⲱⲧⲛ̄ ⲧⲏ]ⲣⲟⲩ
ϣⲁⲛⲧⲉⲡⲓϣⲁϫⲉ | ⲛ̄ⲛⲁ[ϯϯ ⲥ]ⲃⲱ
ⲛⲁϥ ϣⲁⲛⲧⲉϥⲡⲣ̄ⲣⲉ | ⲉⲃⲟⲗ ⲍⲛ
ⲑⲏⲩⲧⲛ̄· ⲁⲩⲱ ϥⲛⲁ|ⲃⲱⲗ ⲛⲏⲧⲛ̄
ⲛ̄ⲛⲁⲓ̈ ⲍⲛ̄ ⲟⲩⲅⲛⲱⲥⲓⲥ · ¹⁵ ⲛ̄ⲛⲟⲩⲟⲧⲉ
ⲉⲥⲧⲃ̄ⲃⲏⲟⲩϯ·
ⲟⲩⲟⲛ | ⲅⲁⲣ ⲛⲓⲙ ⲉⲧⲉ ⲟⲩⲛ̄ⲧⲁϥ
ⲥⲉⲛⲉⲟⲩ|ⲱⲍ [ⲙ̄ⲡⲁⲓ̈] ⲛ̣̄ⲍⲟⲩⲟ :
| [ⲉⲩⲅⲛⲱⲥⲧ]ⲟ̣[ⲥ]

¹⁰ in [such a way that] you might
preserve it | [all], until the word that
need not be taught | comes forth |
among you, and it will | interpret
these things to you in knowledge ¹⁵
that is one and pure.
| For [to] everyone who has, | more
will be added.
| [EUGNOSTOS]

NHC III 90,6–12

ⲕⲁⲧⲁ ⲑⲉ ⲉⲧⲕⲛⲁϣ | ⲧⲱⲟⲩⲛ
ⲙ̄ⲙⲟⲥ· ϣⲁⲛⲧⲉⲡⲓⲁⲧ· | ϯ ⲥⲃⲱ
ⲟⲩⲱⲛⲍ ⲉⲃⲟⲗ· ⲛ̄ⲍⲏⲧⲕ· | ⲁⲩⲱ ⲛⲁⲓ̈
ⲧⲏⲣⲟⲩ ϥⲛⲁⲭⲟⲟⲩ ⲉ ¹⁰ⲣⲟⲕ ⲍⲛ̄
ⲟⲩⲣⲁϣⲉ ⲙⲛ̄ ⲟⲩⲥⲟⲟⲩⲛ |
ⲉϥⲧⲟⲩⲃⲏⲟⲩ

ⲉⲩⲅⲛⲱⲥⲧⲟⲥ ⲡⲙⲁ|ⲕⲁⲣⲓⲟⲥ

in the way you might | accept, until
the one who need not be taught |
appears among you, | and he will
speak all these things to you ¹⁰
joyously and in | pure knowledge.

| EUGNOSTOS, THE BLESSED

Eug-V:

17,11 Translation: see 5,22–23.

17,14 Punctuation: see 5,4n.

17,17 Stroke over ⲙ is visible.

17,17–18 Decorative diples and a line to the margin follow the full stop. Decorative
marks are also visible on the next line to the right of what remains of the title. The
left side of that line is in lacuna.

17,18 A small mark appears on the *Facsimile Edition–V* page to the upper left of the
omicron. An ultraviolet examination of the original by James M. Robinson in
December, 1980, failed to show any indication of ink.

It seems likely that the title contained only ⲉⲩⲅⲛⲱⲥⲧⲟⲥ . It is only one line long
(there is no decoration for a second line), and the practice of the scribe elsewhere
in the codex is to center titles so there is about as much decoration on the right side
as on the left. If that held true here, the space between the left and right decorations would have allowed only one word of nine letters, not two words, as in
Eug–III.

Eug-III:

90,11 MS has a *paragraphus cum corone* in the left margin just below the line. The
end of the text is decorated, as is the title, with diples and lines.

NHC III 114,7–8   BG 117,10–12

ϢⲀⲚⲦⲈⲦⲚ̄ⲢⲞⲨ ⲞⲨⲞⲈⲒⲚ ⲌⲘ̄ | ϢⲀⲚⲦⲈⲦⲚ̄Ⲣ ⲞⲨⲞⲒ̈Ⲛ | ⲌⲘ̄ ⲠⲞⲨⲞⲈⲒⲚ
ⲠⲞⲨⲞⲈⲒⲚ Ⲛ̄ⲌⲞⲨⲞ ⲈⲚⲀⲒ̈·   ⲀⲨⲱ Ⲛ̄ⲌⲞⲨ|Ⲟ ⲈⲚⲀⲒ̈

that you might shine in | Light more   ¹⁰ that you might shine | in Light
than these."   even more | than these."

SJC-III:

114,7 See endnote 13.

SJC-BG:

117,10 See endnote 13.

Since *Eug* concludes on p. 166, both facing pages will be used for the remainder of *SJC*, beginning with p. 170.

NHC III 114,8–25

пехас | нач ӣбι марιгаммн
хе пхо ¹⁰еιс етоуаав·
некмаθнтнс ӣ|тагеι των ӊ
еуна етωн ӊ еу|нар оу
ӣпееιма · пехач нау | ӣбι
птелιос ӣсωтнр· хе †оу|ωϣ
етретӣеιме хе тсофιа ¹⁵
тмаау ӣптнрч·
аγω тсγнгγ|гос аср̄ гнас
гιтоо т̄с ӣмιṇ | ӣмос етренаï
ϣωпе ах̄м | песгооут г̄м
петегнач де | ӣпеιωт ӣптнрц̄·
хе ерепец ²⁰агаθон оуωнг
евол ӣатме|оуе ероц·
ачтамιо ӣпееιка |тапетасма
оутωоу ӣнια |θанатос аγω
оутωоу ӣне|ӣтаγϣωпе

BG 117,12–118,10

пехас нач ӣ|бι марιгам хе
пехс̄ | етоуаав некмаθн ¹⁵тнс
ӣтагеι των ӊ | еунавωк етωн
| н еγр оу ӣпιма пе|хач нау
ӣбι птелιос
ӣсωтнр хе †оуω[ϣ] | [р̄]ιн̄
етретӣеιме хе т̣[со]|фιа
тмау ӣнιпт [нрч]

| наоуωнг пецаг̣а [θон] ⁵ евол
ецеоуωнг ев̣[ол] | мӣ пецна
мӣ тецмӣ̣т̣|атхι табсе нсωс
ац|тамιо мпιкатапе|тасма
оуте нιатмоу ¹⁰ аγω оуте

Mary said | to him: "Holy Lord, ¹⁰
where did your disciples | come
from and where are they going and
(what) should they | do here?" | The
perfect Savior said to them: "I want |
you to know that Sophia, ¹⁵ the
Mother of the Universe
and the consort, | desired by herself |
to bring these to existence without |
her male (consort). But by the will |
of the Father of the Universe,
that his ²⁰ unimaginable goodness
might be revealed, | he created that
curtain | between the immortals |
and those | that came

Mary said to | him: "Holy | Christ,
where did your ¹⁵ disciples come
from and | where will they go | and
what should they do here?" | The
perfect
Savior said: "I want | you to know   [1]18
that Sophia, | the Mother of the
totalities—

| will reveal his goodness, ⁵ and it
will be revealed | with his mercy and
his untraceable | nature. He |
created the curtain | between the
immortals ¹⁰ and those

NHC III 114,24–25   BG 118,10–119,11

ⲘⲚⲚⲤⲀ ⲚⲀⲒ ²⁵ ⲬⲈ
ⲈⲢⲈⲠⲀⲔⲞⲗⲞⲨⲐⲞⲚ ⲀⲔⲞⲗⲞⲨ[ⲐⲈⲒ]
(Coptic pages 115 and 116 are
missing.)

ⲚⲈⲚⲦⲀⲨⲰ|ⲠⲈ ⲘⲚⲚⲤⲀ ⲚⲀⲒ
ⲬⲈⲔⲀ|ⲀⲤ ⲈⲢⲈⲠⲈⲦⲎⲠ ⲈⲰⲰ|ⲠⲈ
ⲈϤⲈⲞⲨⲀϨϤ
ⲚⲤⲀ ⲀⲒ|ⲰⲚ ⲚⲒⲘ ⲀⲨⲰ ⲠⲈⲬⲀⲞⲤ ¹⁵
ⲬⲈ ⲈϤⲈ<ⲞⲨ>ⲰⲚϨ ⲚϬⲒ ⲠⲈⲰ|ⲦⲀ
ⲚⲦⲈⲤϨⲒⲘⲈ ⲚⲤⲰⲰ|ⲠⲈ
ⲈⲢⲈⲦⲈⲠⲗⲀⲚⲎ † ⲚⲘ̄|ⲘⲀⲤ ⲚⲀⲒ ⲀⲈ
ⲚⲦⲀⲨⲰ
ⲠⲈ ⲚⲔⲀⲦⲀⲠⲈⲦⲀⲤⲘⲀ | ⲚⲚⲞⲨⲠⲚ̄Ⲁ̄   Ⲣ̄Ⲑ
ⲈⲂⲞⲗ ϨⲚ <Ⲛ̄>ⲀⲒ|ⲰⲚ Ⲛ̄ⲦⲠⲈ
Ⲛ̄Ⲛ̄ⲀⲠⲞⲢ|ⲢⲞⲒⲀ ⲚⲞⲨⲞⲒ̈Ⲛ ⲚⲐⲈ
Ⲛ̄⁵ⲦⲀⲒ̈ⲬⲞⲞⲤ Ⲛ̄ⲰⲞⲢⲠ ⲞⲨ|ⲦⲀ̄†ⲗⲈ
ⲈⲂⲞⲗ ϨⲘ̄ ⲠⲞⲨ|ⲞⲈⲒⲚ ⲘⲚ̄ ⲠⲈⲠⲚ̄Ⲁ̄
ⲈⲀⲤⲈⲒ | ⲈϨⲢⲀⲒ̈ ⲈⲘⲘⲈⲢⲞⲤ Ⲙ̄ⲠⲒ|ⲦⲚ̄
ⲚⲦⲈ ⲠⲠⲀⲚⲦⲞⲔⲢⲀ ¹⁰ⲦⲰⲢ
Ⲙ̄ⲠⲈⲬⲀⲞⲤ ⲬⲈⲔⲀ|ⲀⲤ

afterward, ²⁵ that the consequence
might follow

that came | afterward, that | what has
to be | might follow
every aeon | and chaos, ¹⁵ that the
defect of the female | might
<appear>, and it might come about
that | Error would contend with |
her. And these became
the curtain | of spirit. From <the>
aeons | above the emanations | of
Light, as ⁵ I have said already, a |
drop from Light | and Spirit came |
down to the lower regions | of
Almighty ¹⁰ in chaos, that

119

SJC-III:

114,24 T–S restores Ⲭ[.] at the end of the line, but the remains are more likely those
of a diple.

114,25 Bracketed letters are presumed to be at the beginning of 115,1 (so restored by
T–S).

SJC-BG:

118,15 Not emended by T–S or K ("might *live*"). Emendation is T–S sugg.; for support, see 107,11–12.

118,16–18 "and it . . . her": "and she engage in a struggle with Error" (an admittedly
free translation by T–S); "and she (Sophia) might come to be, since Error fights
with her" ("literal" rendering by T–S in n.); "and she (female) exist, Error contend-
ing with her" (K).

NHC III   BG 119,11–120,11

ⲉ<ⲩ>ⲉⲟⲩⲱⲛⲍ ⲛ̄ⲛⲉⲩ|ⲡⲗⲁⲥⲙⲁ
ⲉⲃⲟⲗ ⲍⲛ̄ ⲧⲧⲁ̄|ⲧⲗⲉ ⲉⲧⲙ̄ⲙⲁⲩ
ⲉⲩⲧⲁ|ϫⲟ ⲛⲁϥ ⲡⲉ
ⲡⲁⲣⲭⲓⲅⲉⲛⲉ ¹⁵ⲧⲱⲣ ⲉⲧⲉ
ϣⲁⲩⲙⲟⲩⲧⲉ | ⲉⲣⲟϥ ϫⲉ
ⲓ̈ⲁⲗⲇⲁⲃⲁⲱⲑ̄ | ⲧⲧⲁ̄ⲧⲗⲉ ⲉⲧⲙ̄ⲙⲁⲩ
ⲁⲥ|ⲟⲩⲱⲛⲍ ⲛ̄ⲛⲉⲩⲡⲗⲁⲥⲙⲁ | ⲉⲃⲟⲗ
ⲍⲓ̈ⲧⲙ̄ ⲡⲛⲓϥⲉ ⲉⲩ
ⲯⲩⲭⲏ ⲉⲥⲟⲛⲍ ⲁⲥⲍⲱ6ⲃ | ⲁⲥⲛ̄ⲕⲟⲧⲕ   ⲣ̄ⲕ̄
ⲉⲃⲟⲗ ⲍⲛ̄ ⲧⲃ̄|ϣⲉ ⲛⲧⲉⲯⲩⲭⲏ
ⲛⲧⲉⲣⲉⲥ|ⲍⲙⲟⲙ ⲉⲃⲟⲗ ⲍⲙ ⲡⲛⲓϥⲉ ⁵
ⲛ̄ⲧⲉ ⲡⲛⲟ6 ⲛⲟⲩⲟⲉⲓⲛ | ⲛ̄ⲧⲉ
ⲫⲟⲟⲩⲧ ⲁⲩⲱ ⲁϥⲙⲉ|ⲉⲩⲉ
ⲉⲍⲙ̄ⲙⲉⲉⲩⲉ ⲉⲩ|ϫⲓ ⲣⲁⲛ ⲧⲏⲣⲟⲩ
ⲛ̄6ⲓ ⲛⲉⲧ|ⲍⲙ̄ ⲡⲕⲟⲥⲙⲟⲥ
ⲙⲡⲉⲭⲁ ¹⁰ⲟⲥ ⲁⲩⲱ ⲛⲕⲁ ⲛⲓⲙ
ⲉⲧⲛ̄|ⲍⲏⲧϥ ⲍⲓ̈ⲧⲟⲧϥ ⲙⲡⲓⲁ ⲧⲙ`ⲟ´ⲩ |

| their molded forms might appear |
from that drop, | for it is a judgment
| on him, Arch-Begetter, ¹⁵ who is
called | 'Yaldabaoth.' | That drop
revealed | their molded forms |
through the breath, as a
living soul. It was withered | and it   **120**
slumbered in the ignorance | of the
soul. When it | became hot from the
breath ⁵ of the Great Light | of the
Male, and it took | thought, (then) |
names were received by all who |
are in the world of chaos ¹⁰ and all
things that are in | it through that

SJC-BG:

119,11 MS has ϥ, "that *he* might reveal their" (not emended by T–S or K).

119,19 "as": "in" (T–S & K).

NHC III　　　　　　　　BG 120,11–121,10

ⲉⲧⲙ̅ⲙⲁⲩ ⲛ̅ⲧⲉⲣⲉⲡⲛⲓ |ϥⲉ ⲛⲓϥⲉ
ⲉⲍⲟⲩⲛ ⲉⲣⲟϥ | ⲛⲁⲓ̈ ⲇⲉ
ⲛ̅ⲧⲉⲣⲟⲩϣⲱⲡⲉ ¹⁵ ⲍⲙ ⲡⲟⲩⲱϣ
ⲛ̅ⲧ<ⲙⲁ>ⲁⲩ | {ⲛ̅}ⲧⲥⲟⲫⲓⲁ
ϫⲉⲕⲁⲁⲥ ⲛ̅ⲍⲃ̅|ⲥⲱ ⲉⲧⲙ̅ⲡⲓⲙⲁ
ⲉϥⲉⲍⲟⲣ
ⲙⲁⲍⲉ ⲙⲙⲟⲟⲩ ⲛ̅ϭⲓ ⲡⲓ|ⲁⲧⲙⲟⲩ　　　　ⲣ̅ⲕ̅ⲅ̅
ⲛ̅ⲣⲱⲙⲉ ⲉⲩⲧⲁ|ϫⲟ ⲛⲁⲩ ⲛⲛⲓⲥⲟⲛⲉ
ⲁⲩⲱ | ⲁ<ϥ>ⲁⲥⲡⲁⲍⲉ ⲛ̅ⲧⲉⲡⲛⲟⲏ ⁵
ⲉⲃⲟⲗ ⲍⲙ̅ ⲡⲛⲓϥⲉ ⲉⲧⲙ̅|ⲙⲁⲩ
ⲉⲩⲯⲩⲭⲓⲕ ⲟⲥ ⲇⲉ | ⲡⲉ
ⲉⲙⲡⲉϥϣϭⲙϭⲟⲙ ⲉ|ϣⲱⲡ ⲉⲣⲟϥ
ⲛ̅ⲧϭⲟⲙ ⲉⲧⲙ̅|ⲙⲁⲩ ϣⲁⲛⲧϥ̅ϫⲱⲕ
ⲛ̅ϭⲓ ¹⁰ ⲡⲁⲣⲓⲑⲙⲟⲥ ⲙ̅ⲡⲉⲭⲁⲟⲥ |

| Immortal One, when the breath |
blew into him. | But when this came
about ¹⁵ by the will of Mother |
Sophia—so that Immortal Man |
might piece together
the garments there | for a judgment |　　**121**
on the robbers— | <he> then
welcomed the blowing ⁵ of that
breath; | but since he was soul-like, |
he was not able to take | that power
for himself | until ¹⁰ the number of
chaos should be complete,

SJC-BG:

120,14 "this": lit. "these" (rendered as above by T–S but not by K); see III 70,2n.

120,15 MS has ⲛ̅ⲧⲙ̅ⲙⲁⲩ; alt.: <ⲉ>ⲧⲙ̅ⲙⲁⲩ, "by *that* will of Sophia" (T–S, alt.).

120,16–121,3 Apparently a gloss on lines 14–15 that has crept into the text. It represents an ascetic interpretation of the will of Sophia; i.e., she brought all this about so that nakedness might be covered and the robbers (who use sex to enslave the soul) might therefore be rebuked (cf. Gen 3:21).

121,2–3 "for a jugment on the robbers" (so also Schenke in T–S: 340, & K): less likely, "while (or "whereby") the robbers were condemned for them" (T–S).

121,4 MS has ⲩ, "they" (emended as above by Schenke in T–S: 340; not emended by T–S or K).

NHC III 117,1–6   BG 121,11–122,16

ⲉϥϣⲁⲛϫⲱⲕ ⲇⲉ ⲛϭⲓ ⲡ`ⲟ´ⲩ|ⲟⲉⲓϣ
ⲉⲧⲏⲡ ⲍⲓ̈ⲧⲙ ⲡⲛⲟϭ | ⲛⲁⲅⲅⲉⲗⲟⲥ
ⲁⲛⲟⲕ ⲇⲉ ⲁⲉⲓ|ⲧⲥⲁⲃⲉ ⲑⲩⲧⲛ̄
ⲉⲡⲣⲱⲙⲉ ¹⁵ ⲛⲁⲧⲙⲟⲩ ⲁⲩⲱ ⲁⲓ̈ⲃⲱⲗ
ⲉ|ⲃⲟⲗ ⲛ̄ⲛ̄ⲥⲛⲟⲟⲩⲍ ⲛ̄ⲛ̄ⲥⲟ|ⲟⲟⲛⲉ
ⲛⲥⲁ ⲛⲃⲟⲗ ⲙ̄ⲙⲟϥ | ⲁⲓ̈ⲍⲱϣϥ
ⲛⲙ̄ⲡⲩⲗⲏ ⲛ̄ⲧⲉ
ⲛⲓⲁ ⲧⲛⲁⲉ ⲙ̄ⲡⲉⲩⲙ̄ⲧⲟ | ⲉⲃⲟⲗ   ⲣ̄ⲕ̄ⲃ̄
ⲁⲓ̈ⲑⲃ̄ⲃⲓⲟ ⲛⲧⲉⲩ|ⲡⲣⲟⲛⲟⲓⲁ ⲁⲩϫⲓ
ϣⲓⲡⲉ | ⲧⲏⲣⲟⲩ ⲁⲩⲧⲱⲟⲩⲛ ⲉ⁵ⲃⲟⲗ
ⲍⲛ̄ ⲧⲉⲩⲃ̄ϣⲉ ⲉⲧ|ⲃⲉ ⲡⲁⲓ̈ ϭⲉ ⲁⲓ̈ⲉⲓ
ⲉⲡⲙⲁ | ϫⲉⲕⲁⲁⲥ ⲉⲩⲉⲛⲟⲩⲍⲃ̄ ⲙⲛ̄ |
ⲡⲓⲡⲛⲁ̄

PIZ ⲉⲧⲙ̄ⲙⲁⲩ ⲙⲛ̄ ⲡⲛⲓϥⲉ ⲛ̄ⲥⲉϣⲱ|ⲡⲉ   ⲉⲧⲙ̄ⲙⲁⲩ ⲙⲛ̄ | ⲡⲛⲓϥⲉ ⲁⲩⲱ
ⲙ̄ⲡⲉⲥⲛⲁⲩ ⲛ̄ⲟⲩⲁ ⲛ̄ⲑⲉ ⲟⲛ ϫⲓⲛ | ⲉⲩⲉϣⲱ¹⁰ⲡⲉ ⲙ̄ⲡⲉⲥⲛⲁⲩ ⲉⲩⲁ
ⲛ̄ϣⲟⲣⲡ̄ ϫⲉ ⲉⲧⲉⲧⲛⲁϯ ⲕⲁⲣⲡⲟⲥ | ⲛⲟⲩ|ⲱⲧ ⲕⲁⲧⲁ ⲑⲉ ϫⲓⲛⲛ̄ ϣⲟ|ⲣⲡ
ⲉⲛⲁϣⲱϥ ⲛ̄ⲧⲉⲧⲛ̄ⲃⲱⲕ ⲉⲍⲣⲁⲓ̈ ϣⲁ ⁵   ⲭⲉⲕⲁⲥ ⲉⲧⲉⲧⲛⲁϯ | ⲕⲁⲣⲡⲟⲥ
ⲡⲉⲧϣⲟⲟⲡ̄ ϫⲓⲛ ⲛ̄ϣⲟⲣⲡ̄ ⲍⲛ̄   ⲉⲛⲁϣⲱϥ ⲛ̄|ⲧⲉⲧⲛ̄ⲃⲱⲕ ⲉⲍⲣⲁⲓ̈
ⲟⲩ|ⲣⲁϣⲉ ⲛ̄ⲁⲧϣ[ⲁ]ϫⲉ ⲉⲣⲟϥ ⲙⲛ̄   ⲉⲡⲉⲧ ¹⁵ϣⲟⲟⲡ ϫⲓⲛⲛ̄ ϣⲟⲣⲉⲡ | ⲙⲛ̄

| (that is,) when the time |
determined by the great | angel is
complete. Now I have taught | you
about Immortal ¹⁵ Man and have
loosed | the bonds of the robbers |
from him. I have broken the
gates of
the pitiless ones in their presence. | I   **122**
have humiliated their | malicious
intent, and they all have been
shamed | and have risen ⁵ from their
ignorance. Because | of this, then, I
came here, | that they might be
joined with | that Spirit
and | Breath, and might ¹⁰ from two
become a single one, | just as from
the first, | that you might yield |
much fruit | and go up to Him Who
Is ¹⁵ from the Beginning,

117 that [. . .] and Breath, and might |
from two become one, just as from |
the first, that you might yield much
fruit | and go up to ⁵ Him Who Is
from the Beginning, in | ineffable
joy and

NHC III 117,6–18　　　　　　BG 122,16–123,15

ογεοογ | μν ο[γταειο μν
ο]γϩμοτ ῆτε | [π]ε[ιωτ
ῆπτηρϥ] πετcοογν | [ϭε
ῆπειωτ ϩῆ ογϭν]ωcιc
ῆκα¹⁰[θαρον παϊ ϥναχω]ρι
επιωτ | [ῆϥῆτον ῆμοϥ ϩῆ]
παγεννη|[τοc ῆειωτ
πετcοο]γν δε ῆ|[μοϥ ϩῆ
ογϣωω]†̣ εϥναχω||[ρι επϣωωτ
αγ]ω ταναπαγcιc ¹⁵
[ῆμεϩϣμο γ]νε· πετcοογν |
[δε ῆπεπ̄ν̄ᾱ ῆαθ]α̣νατοc ῆτε |
[π]ο̣γ̣ο̣ε̣ι̣ν ϩῆ τcιγη ϩιτῆ
τενθγ|[μ]η̣cιc μν τεγδοκια

ογραϣε νατϣαχε | εροϥ μν
ογεοογ μν | ογταϊο μν
ογχαριc
ῆτε πειωτ ῆπτηρϥ | πετcοογν　р̄к̄γ̄
ϭε ῆπιωτ | ϩν ογcοογν
εϥογααβ | εϥναβωκ ϣα πειωτ
⁵ αγω εϥεῆτον ῆμοϥ | ϩμ
πιατχποϥ νειωτ | πετcοογν
δε ῆμοϥ | ϩν ογϣτα εϥεϣωπε
| ϩῆ πεϣτα νϥ̄<μ>τον ῆ¹⁰μοϥ
ϩῆ τμεϩϣμογνε | πετcοογν
δε ῆπιπ̄ν̄ᾱ | νατμογ ετε
πογοϊν | πε ϩν ογκαρωϥ ϩιτῆ |
τενθγμηcιc μν τεγ¹⁵δοκια

glory | and [honor and] grace of |
[the Father of the Universe].
Whoever, [then], knows | [the Father
in pure] knowledge ¹⁰ [will depart]
to the Father | [and repose in]
Unbegotten | [Father]. But
[whoever knows] | [him defectively]
will depart | [to the defect] and the
rest ¹⁵ [of the Eighth. Now]
whoever knows | Immortal [Spirit] |
of Light in silence, through reflecting
| and consent

| with ineffable joy | and glory and |
honor and grace
of the Father of the Universe. |
Whoever, then, knows the Father | in
pure knowledge | will go to the
Father ⁵ and repose | in Unbegotten
Father. | But whoever knows him |
defectively will dwell | in the defect
and repose ¹⁰ in the Eighth. | Now
whoever knows Immortal Spirit, |
who is Light, | in silence, through |
reflecting and consent ¹⁵ in truth,

SJC-III:

117,9 T–S restores only ΓΝ].

117,10 T–S restores only [θαρον] and [χω].

117,12 T–S restores only [τοc.

117,14 T–S restores only [ρι.

117,16 T–S restores only αθ].

117,18 εγδοκια , "consent": "the *eudokia* (= the decree)" (K) (?). See endnote 9.

SJC-BG:

123,12–13 "Light, in silence" (so also Schenke in T–S: 340): "Light in silence" (T–S).

123,14–15 T–S leaves both ενθγμηcιc and εγδοκια untranslated. See endnote 9.

NHC III 117,18–118,6   BG 123,15–124,15

 zꞢ тмнє | маречєıнє наї
Ꞣzєнсумвоλон 20 Ꞣтє
пıаzоратон аүω єчнаϣω|пє
Ꞣоүоєıн zꞟ пєꟺ︤ꟾꟺа︥ Ꞣтсıгн |
пєтсооүн ꞟпϣнрє ꞟпрω|[м]ẹ
zꞢ оүсооүн мꞢ оүагапн |
маречєıнє нєⲉ̂ı ·
Ꞣоүсумвоλон

PIH {N}Ꞣтє пϣнрє ꞟпрωмє нꞟ̣хω|рı
єнма мꞢ нєтzꞢ тмєzϣмоү|нє
єıс zннтє аєıоүωнz нн тꞢ |
ꞟпрєн ꟺ︤пıтєλıос поүωϣє 5
тнрꟺ Ꞣтмаүн ꞢꞢаггєλос
єтоү|ааⲃ· хє єчнахωк євоλ

                    zнн оүмнє ма|речєıнє наї
                    ꞢzꞢсум|воλон нтє пıатнаү
                    є|роч аүω єчєϣωпє | ноүоⲓ̈н
                    zꟺ пєꟺ︤ꟾꟺа︥ ꟺ
                    пкарωч пєтсооүн | ꞟпϣнрє   PKA
                    ꞟпрωмє | zн оүсооүн мꞢ
                    оүа|гапн маречєıнє на 5єı
                    нноүсумвоλон | ꟺпϣнрє
                    ꟺпрωмє | аүω єчнаϣωпє
                    ꟺ|пма єтꟺмаү мꞢ нєт|zꞢ
                    тмєzϣмоүнє єıс 10 zннтє
                    аⲓ̈тсєⲃє тнү<т>Ꞣ | єпран
                    ꟺпıтєλıос | поүωϣє тнрꟺ
                    ꞢꞢаг|гєλос єтоүааⲃ мꞢ |
                    тмаүн хєкаас єч 15єхωк

in the truth, | let him bring me signs
20 of the Invisible One, and he will
become | a light in the Spirit of
Silence. | Whoever knows Son of
Man | in knowledge and love, | let
him bring me a sign

118 of Son of Man, that he might depart |
to the dwelling-places with those in
the Eighth. | Behold, I have revealed
to you | the name of the Perfect One,
the whole will 5 of the Mother of the
Holy Angels, | that the masculine
[multitude]

let him | bring me signs of | the
Invisible One, | and he will become |
a light in the Spirit of
Silence. Whoever knows | Son of
Man | in knowledge and love, | let
him bring 5 me a sign | of Son of
Man, | and he will dwell there | with
those | in the Eighth. Behold, 10 I
have taught you | the name of the
Perfect One, | the whole will of the
holy angels | and | the Mother, that
15 the male   **124**

SJC-III:

117,20 MS has first superlinear stroke in lacuna.

118,1 So emended by T–S.

118,2 Corr.: first м for erased letter.

118,5 Corr.: first N for erased letter.

118,6 Corr.: ч for incomplete and erased N.

SJC-BG:

124,15 Alt. word division: хωкꟺ ꟺпıма , "that the … might *wash* there" (Carl
Schmidt as reported in T–S).

NHC III 118,6–17

ⲙ̄ⲡⲉ|ⲉⲓⲙⲁ ⲛ̄ϭⲓ ⲡⲙⲏ[ⲛϣⲉ
ⲙ̄ⲙ]ⲛ̄ⲧⲍⲟ|ⲟⲩⲧ̄ ϫⲉ ⲉⲩ[ⲉⲟⲩⲱⲛⲍ ⲍ̄ⲛ
ⲛⲓⲁⲓ]ⲱ[ⲛ] | ⲉⲃⲟⲗ ⲛ̄ϭⲓ
[ⲛⲓⲁⲡⲉⲣⲁⲛⲧⲟⲛ ⲁⲩⲱ] ¹⁰
ⲛⲉⲛⲧⲁⲩϣ[ⲱⲡⲉ ⲍ̄ⲛ ⲧⲙⲛ̄ⲧⲣⲙⲙⲁⲟ]
| ⲛ̄ⲛⲁⲧϫⲓ ϭⲉ[ⲭⲙⲉ ⲛ̄ⲥⲱⲥ ⲛ̄ⲧⲉ
ⲡⲛⲟϭ] | ⲛ̄ⲁⲍⲟⲣⲁ̣[ⲧⲟⲛ ⲙ̄ⲡ̄ⲛ̄ⲁ̄ ϫⲉ
ⲉⲩⲉϫⲓ] | ⲧⲏⲣⲟⲩ ⲉⲃⲟⲗ [ⲍ̄ⲙ
ⲡⲉ̣ϥⲁⲅⲁⲑⲟⲛ] | ⲙⲛ̄ ⲧⲙⲛ̄ⲧⲣⲙ[ⲙⲁⲟ
ⲛ̄ⲧⲉⲩⲁⲛⲁⲡⲁⲩ]¹⁵ⲥⲓⲥ ⲉⲧⲉ ⲙⲛ̄
ⲙⲛ̄[ⲧⲣ̄ⲣⲟ ⲍⲓϫⲱⲥ· ⲁ̣]ⲛⲟⲕ
ⲛ̄ⲧⲁⲉⲓⲉⲓ̂ [ⲉⲃⲟⲗ ⲍ̄ⲙ ⲡϣⲟⲣⲡ̄
ⲛ̄]|ⲧⲁⲩⲧⲛ̄ⲛⲟⲟⲩϥ· ϫⲉ

BG 124,15–125,12

ⲙ̄{ⲙ}ⲡⲓⲙⲁ ⲛ̄ϭⲓ | ⲡⲙⲏⲛϣⲉ
ⲛⲍⲟⲟⲩⲧ | ϫⲉ ⲉⲩⲉⲟⲩⲱⲛⲍ ⲉⲃⲟⲗ |
ⲍ̄ⲛ ⲛⲓⲁⲓⲱⲛ ⲧⲏⲣⲟⲩ ⲭⲓⲛ
ⲛⲓⲁⲡⲉⲣⲁⲛⲧⲟⲛ ϣⲁⲍⲣⲁ|ⲉⲓ   ⲣ̄ⲕ̄ⲉ̄
ⲉⲛⲉⲛⲧⲁⲩϣⲱⲡⲉ | ⲍ̄ⲛ ⲧⲙⲛ̄ⲧⲣ̄ⲙⲙⲁⲟ
ⲛ̄ⲛⲁⲧ|ϫⲓ ⲧⲁϭⲥⲉ ⲛ̄ⲥⲱⲥ ⲛ̄ⲧⲉ
ⲡⲛⲟϭ ⁵ ⲛ̄ⲛⲁⲧⲛⲁⲩ ⲉⲣⲟϥ ⲙ̄ⲡ̄ⲛ̄ⲁ̄ |
ϫⲉ ⲉⲩⲉϫⲓ ⲧⲏⲣⲟⲩ ⲉⲃⲟⲗ | ⲍ̄ⲛ
ⲧⲉϥⲙⲛ̄ⲧⲁⲅⲁⲑⲟⲥ ⲙⲛ̄ |
ⲧⲙⲛ̄ⲧⲣ̄ⲙⲙⲁⲟ <ⲛ̄ⲧⲉ ⲡⲉⲩⲙⲁ
ⲛ̄ⲙⲧⲟⲛ> ⲉⲧⲉ ⲙⲛ̄ | ⲙⲛ̄ⲧⲣ̄ⲣⲟ
ⲍⲓϫⲱ<ϥ> {ⲛ̄ⲧⲉ ⲡⲉⲩ¹⁰ⲙⲁ ⲛ̄ⲙⲧⲟⲛ}
ⲁⲛⲟⲕ ⲇⲉ ⲛ̄|ⲧⲁⲉⲓ ⲉⲃⲟⲗ ⲍ̄ⲙ
ⲡⲉⲍⲟⲩⲓ̈ⲧ | ⲛ̄ⲧⲁⲩⲧⲛ̄ⲛⲟⲟⲩϥ ϫⲉ

| may be completed here, | that there
[might appear, in the aeons,] | [the
infinities and] ¹⁰ those that [came to
be in the] untraceable | [wealth of
the Great] | Invisible [Spirit, that
they] all [might take] | [from his
goodness,] | even the wealth [of their
rest] ¹⁵ that has no [kingdom over it].
I | came [from First] Who | Was
Sent, that

multitude may be | completed here, |
that they might appear | in all the
aeons, from
the infinities to | those that came to
be | in the untraceable wealth | of
the Great ⁵ Invisible Spirit, | that
they all might take | from his
goodness, even | the wealth <of their
place of repose> that has no |
kingdom over it. ¹⁰ And I | came
from First | Who Was Sent,

125

SJC-III:

118,7 Alt.: ⲙ̄]ⲡ (T–S; incorrect restoration made on the basis of the visible superlinear
  stroke and the cross stroke).

118,8 "there [. . . aeons]": "[they may reveal aeons]" (K).

118,9 Lacuna not restored by K.

118,11 T–S restores only [ⲭⲙⲉ.

118,12 T–S restores only [ⲁⲧⲟⲥ (incorrect gender for ⲡ̄ⲛ̄ⲁ̄).

118,14 T–S restores only ⲛⲧⲉⲩⲁⲛⲁⲡⲁ ⲩ].

118,15 T–S restores only [ⲛ̄ⲧⲣ̄ⲣⲟ ⲍⲓϫⲱⲥ .

SJC-BG:

125,8 Not emended by T–S.

125,9 ms has ⲥ (not emended by T–S).

125,9–10 Bracketed words not deleted by T–S.

NHC III 118,17–119,6   BG 125,12–126,12

ⲉⲉⲓⲛⲁⲟ ⲩⲱⲛ[ⲍ] | ⲛⲏⲧⲛ̄ ⲉⲃⲟⲗ   ⲉⲉⲓ|ⲉⲟⲩⲱⲛⲍ ⲉⲃⲟⲗ ⲛⲏⲧⲛ̄
ⲙ̄ⲡⲉⲧϣⲟⲟⲡ̄ ⲭⲛ̄ ⲛ̄|ϣⲟⲣⲡ̄ ⲉⲧⲃⲉ   ⲙ̄|ⲡⲉⲧϣⲟⲟⲡ ⲭⲓⲛⲛ̄ ϣⲟ ¹⁵ⲣⲡ̄ ⲉⲧⲃⲉ
ⲧⲙⲛ̄ⲧⲭⲁⲥⲓ ⲍⲏⲧ̄ ²⁰   ⲧⲙⲛⲧⲭⲁⲥⲓ | ⲍⲏⲧ
ⲙ̄ⲡⲁⲣⲭⲓⲅⲉⲛⲉⲧⲱⲣ · ⲙⲛ   ⲙⲡⲁⲣⲭⲓⲅⲉⲛⲉⲧⲱⲣ | ⲙⲛ̄
ⲛⲉⲩⲁⲅ|ⲅⲉⲗⲟⲥ ⲭⲉ ⲥⲉⲭⲱ ⲙ̄ⲙⲟⲥ   ⲛⲉⲩⲁⲅⲅⲉⲗⲟⲥ ⲭⲉ ⲥⲉ|ⲭⲱ ⲙ̄ⲙⲟⲥ
ⲉⲣⲟⲟⲩ | ⲭⲉ ⲍⲉⲛⲛⲟⲩⲧⲉ ⲛⲉ·   ⲉⲣⲟⲟⲩ ⲭⲉ | ⲍⲛⲛⲟⲩⲧⲉ ⲛⲉ ⲁⲛⲟⲕ
ⲁⲛⲟⲕ ⲇⲉ | ⲛ̄ⲧⲁⲉⲓⲉ̂ⲓ · ⲉⲥⲁⲍⲱⲟⲩ   ⲇⲉ
ⲛ̄ⲧⲉⲩⲙⲛ̄ⲧ|ⲃⲁ̄ⲗⲉ· ⲭⲉ ⲉⲉⲓⲛⲁⲭ ⲱ   ⲛ̄ⲧⲁⲓ̈ⲉ̂ⲓ ⲉⲥⲟⲟⲍⲉ ⲙ̄ⲙⲟ|ⲟⲩ ⲉⲃⲟⲗ   ⲣ̄ⲕ̄ⲋ̄
ⲛ̄ⲟⲩⲟⲛ ⲛⲓⲙ ²⁵ ⲙ̄ⲡⲛⲟⲩⲧⲉ ⲉⲧⲍⲓⲭⲙ̄   ⲇⲉ ⲍⲛ̄ ⲧⲉⲩⲙⲛ̄|ⲧⲃⲁ̄ⲗⲉ ⲭⲉ
ⲡⲧⲏⲣϥ·   ⲉⲉⲓⲉⲧⲥⲁⲃⲉ | ⲟⲩⲟⲛ ⲛⲓⲙ
ⲣ̄ⲓ̄ⲑ̄ ⲛ̄ⲧⲱⲧⲛ̄ ϭⲉ ⲍⲱⲙ ⲉⲍⲣⲁⲓ̈ ⲉⲭⲛ̄   ⲉⲡⲛⲟⲩⲧⲉ ⁵ ⲉⲧⲍⲓⲭⲙ̄ ⲡⲧⲏⲣϥ
ⲛⲉⲩ|ⲙ̄ⲍⲁⲟⲩ ⲧⲉⲩⲡⲣⲟⲛⲟⲓⲁ   ⲛ̄ⲧⲱ|ⲧⲛ̄ ϭⲉ ⲍⲱⲙ ⲉⲍⲣⲁⲓ̈ ⲉⲭⲛ̄ |
ⲙⲁⲑⲃ|ⲉⲓⲟⲥ ⲁⲩⲱ ⲡⲉⲩⲛⲁⲍⲃ̄   ⲛⲉⲩⲙ̄ⲍⲁⲟⲩ ⲁⲩⲱ ⲛ̄ⲧⲉ|ⲧⲛ̄ⲑⲉⲃ̄ⲃⲓⲟ
ⲟⲩⲟϭⲡϥ· | ⲁⲩⲱ ⲡⲱⲓ̈ ⲙⲁⲧⲟⲩⲛⲟⲥϥ   ⲛ̄ⲧⲉⲩⲡⲣⲟ|ⲛⲟⲓⲁ ⲛ̄ⲧⲉⲧⲛ̄ⲍⲱϣϥ
ⲁⲉⲓϯ ⁵ ⲛⲏⲧⲛ̄ ⲛ̄ⲧⲉⲍⲟⲩⲥⲓⲁ ⲛ̄ⲛⲕⲁ   ⲙ̄ ¹⁰ⲡⲉⲩⲛⲁⲍⲃⲉϥ ⲁⲩⲱ
ⲛⲓⲙ · | ⲍⲱⲥ ϣⲏⲣⲉ ⲛ̄ⲧⲉ ⲡⲟⲩⲟⲉⲓⲛ   ⲛ̄ⲧⲉ|ⲧⲛ̄ⲧⲟⲩⲛⲟⲥ ⲙ̄ⲡⲉⲧⲉ | ⲡⲱⲉⲓ

I might reveal | to you Him Who Is   that I | might reveal to you | Him
from | the Beginning, because of the   Who Is from the Beginning, ¹⁵
arrogance ²⁰ of Arch-Begetter and   because of the arrogance | of Arch-
his angels, | since they say about   Begetter | and his angels, since they
themselves that | they are gods. And | say about themselves that | they are
I | came to remove them from their   gods. And I
blindness | that I might tell everyone   came to remove them | from their
²⁵ about the God who is above the   blindness | that I might teach |
universe.   everyone about the God ⁵ who is
119 Therefore, tread upon their | above the universe. | Therefore,
graves, humiliate their malicious intent | and   tread upon | their graves and |
break their yoke | and arouse my   humiliate their malicious intent | and
own. I have given ⁵ you authority   break their ¹⁰ yoke and | arouse
over all things | as Sons of Light,   whoever | is mine. For I have given

                                            126

SJC-III:

118,18–19 See endnote 14.

SJC-BG:

125,14–15 See endnote 14.

NHC III 119,6–16

ⲭⲉ ⲉⲧⲉ|ⲧⲛⲁϩⲱⲙ ⲉϩⲣⲁⲓ̈ ⲉⲭⲛ̄
ⲧⲉⲩϭⲟⲙ· ϩⲁ | [ⲛ]ⲉ̣ⲧ̣ⲛ̄[ⲟ]ⲩⲉⲣ̣ⲏⲧⲉ·
ⲛⲁⲓ̈ ⲛⲉ ⲛ̄ⲧⲁϥ|[ⲭⲟⲟⲩ ⲛ̄ϭⲓ]
ⲡ[ⲙⲁⲕⲁ]ⲣⲓⲟⲥ ⲛ̄ⲥⲱⲧⲏⲣ· ¹⁰ [ⲁϥⲣ̄
ⲁⲧⲟⲩⲱⲛϩ ⲛ̄ⲥⲁ ⲛⲃⲟ]ⲗ ⲛⲁⲩ· ⲧⲟⲧⲉ
| [ⲙ̄ⲙⲁⲑⲏⲧⲏⲥ ⲧⲏⲣⲟⲩ ⲁⲩϣ]ⲱⲡⲉ
ϩⲛ̄ ⲟⲩ|[ⲛⲟϭ ⲛ̄ⲧⲉⲗⲏⲗ
ⲛ̄ⲁⲧ]ϣ̣[ⲁ̣]ⲭⲉ ⲉⲣⲟϥ ϩⲙ̄ | [ⲡⲉⲡ̄ⲛ̄ⲁ̄
ⲭⲓⲛ] ⲡⲉϩⲟⲟⲩ ⲉⲧⲙ̄ⲙⲁⲩ |
[ⲁⲛⲉϥⲙⲁⲑⲏⲧ]ⲏⲥ ⲁⲣⲭⲉⲥⲑⲁⲓ
ⲉⲧⲁϣⲉ¹⁵[ⲟⲉⲓϣ ⲙ̄ⲡⲉⲩⲁ̣]ⲅ̣ⲅⲉⲗⲓⲟⲛ
ⲙ̄ⲡⲛⲟⲩ|[ⲧⲉ ⲡⲉⲡ̄ⲛ̄ⲁ̄ ⲛ̄ⲁ]ⲫⲑⲁⲣⲧⲟⲛ

BG 126,12–127,8

ⲡⲉ ⲁⲓ̈ϯ ⲅⲁⲣ ⲛⲏ|ⲧⲛ̄ ⲛ̄ⲧⲉⲝⲟⲩⲥⲓⲁ
ⲛ̄ⲅⲕⲁ | ⲛⲓⲙ ϩⲱⲥ ϣⲏⲣⲉ ⲛ̄ⲧⲉ
ⲡ`ⲟ´ⲩ ¹⁵ⲟ̈ⲓⲛ ⲉϩⲱⲙ ⲉⲭⲛ̄
ⲧⲉⲩ|ϭⲟⲙ ϩⲛ̄ ⲛⲉⲧⲛ̄ⲟⲩⲣⲏⲧⲉ | ⲛⲁⲓ̈
ⲁϥⲭⲟⲟⲩ ⲛ̄ϭⲓ ⲡⲙⲁ|ⲕⲁⲣⲓⲟⲥ
ⲛ̄ⲥⲱⲧⲏⲣ ⲁϥⲣ̄
ⲁⲧⲟⲩⲱⲛ[ϩ] ⲛ̄ⲥⲁ ⲛⲃⲟⲗ ⲙ̄|ⲙⲟⲟⲩ   ⲣ̄[ⲕ̄]·
ⲁⲩϣⲱⲡⲉ ϩⲛ̄ ϩⲛ̄|ⲛⲟϭ ⲛ̄ⲣⲁϣⲉ
ⲛⲁⲧϣⲁⲭⲉ | ⲉⲣⲟⲟⲩ ϩⲙ̄ ⲡⲓⲡ̄ⲛ̄ⲁ̄
ⲭⲓⲛ ⁵ ⲡⲉϩⲟⲟⲩ ⲉⲧⲙ̄ⲙⲁⲩ ⲁⲩⲣ̄ |
ⲁⲣⲭⲉⲥⲑⲁⲓ ⲛ̄ϭⲓ ⲛⲉϥⲙⲁ|ⲑⲏⲧⲏⲥ
ⲉⲧⲁϣⲉⲟⲉⲓϣ | ⲙ̄ⲡⲉⲩⲁⲅⲅⲉⲗⲓⲟⲛ

| that you might tread upon their power with | [your] feet." These are the things [the] blessed | Savior [said,] ¹⁰ [and he disappeared] from them. Then | [all the disciples] were in | [great, ineffable joy] in | [the spirit from] that day on. | [And his disciples] began to preach ¹⁵ [the] Gospel of God, | [the] eternal, imperishable [Spirit].

you | authority over all | things as Sons of Light ¹⁵ to tread upon their | power with your feet." | These are the things the blessed | Savior said, and he disappeared from them. | And they were in | great, ineffable joy | in the spirit from ⁵ that day on. And his | disciples began | to preach | the Gospel of

1[2]

SJC-III:

119,7 Corr.: ⲩ for erased ϥ.

119,10 T–S restores only ⲉⲃⲟⲗ.

119,11 T–S restores only ϣ].

119,13–14 See endnote 15.

119,14 Lacuna so restored by T–S.

119,16 The neuter form of the adjective makes restoration of ⲡⲉⲓⲱⲧ ⲛ̄ⲁ]ⲫⲑⲁⲣⲧⲟⲛ, "imperishable [Father]," following BG (so restored by K), unlikely if not impossible (so also T–S). T–S suggests ⲡⲉⲓⲱⲧ ⲛ̄ⲛⲁ]ⲫⲑⲁⲣⲧⲟⲛ, "Father of the] imperishable things," or ⲛ̄ⲧⲙ̄ⲛ̄ⲧⲣ̄ⲣⲟ ⲛ̄ⲁ]ⲫⲑⲁⲣⲧⲟⲛ, "[of the] imperishable [Kingdom]." Support for my reconstruction: 117,16.21; 118,12.

SJC-BG:

126,16 MS has a *paragraphus* in the left margin just below the line of the text.

127,1–12 MS has extensive decorations in both margins and surrounding the title.

127,4–5 See endnote 15.

NHC III 119,16–18	BG 127,8–12

ⲚϢⲀ | [ⲉ]ⲚⲉⲌ ⲌⲀⲘⲎⲚ:
ⲦⲤⲟⲫⲓⲀ ⲚⲒⲎⲤ̅

ⲘⲠⲚˋⲟˊⲨ|Ⲧⲉ ⲠⲉⲓⲰⲦ ⲚϢⲀ ⲉⲚⲉⲌ
Ⲛ̅¹⁰ⲚⲀⲦⲦⲀⲔⲟ ϢⲀ ⲚⲓⲉⲚⲉⲌ |
ⲦⲤⲟⲫⲓⲀ Ⲛ̅|ⲒⲎⲤ̅ ⲠⲉⲬⲢⲤ̅

| Amen. | THE SOPHIA
OF JESUS

God, | the eternal Father, ¹⁰
imperishable forever. | THE
SOPHIA OF | JESUS CHRIST

SJC-III:

119,17 Lacuna so restored by T–S.

119,17–18 MS has diple and line decorations at the end of the text proper and surrounding the title.

ENDNOTES

1.　III 91,1–2 || BG 78,1–2 "Divination" (derived from μαντεία): less likely, "Place of Harvest Time" (T–S) or "Place of Ripeness" (Pu & K). See Till's note, T–S: 327. The word division ма ӣ, assumed by T–S, Pu & K, is not supported by the scribe of either III or BG. The former omits the expected stroke over the ɴ, and in BG the scribe treats ɴ as though it were a part of ма by using the conventional stroke over а at the end of the line in place of the ɴ. The spelling мантн may reflect an Ionic form (μαντηίη) and may have been an attempt to archaize. Μαντεία is related to joy, as here, in Plat. *Tim.* 71d.

2.　III 70,21 оүпетнп ещωпе, "fate" || III 93,3 (do.) || BG 81,10–11 оүтеѳонт, "fate": The par. in V, of which Till was unaware (T–S: 327), makes clear that "fate" is the correct translation, both here and where теѳонт recurs (III 71,4 [тетzант]; III 93,15–16 [do.]; BG 82,7). Crum says that zонт is a qualitative of unknown meaning, citing only the instance in BG (691b). Till considers that it might be an unattested qualitative of zωн, "bid, command" (Crum: 688a) but expresses his uncertainty (T–S: 327). It is more likely a qualitative of zωнт, "approach," where the form zант (found in III) is attested (Crum: 691b). Its basic meaning then would be "that which comes," or the like (so also K & Tr). The use of the fem. article probably reflects ἡ εἱμαρμένη.

3.　III 73,14 || III 96,10 || BG 87,4–5 T–S suggests, probably correctly, that behind the differences among these texts lies confusion over γένος and γενόμενος.

4.　V 6,15–17 || III 77,11–13 || III 101,20–22 || BG 95,6–8 The lack of the term ономасіа (ран), "designation" ("name"), in either version of *SJC*, while it is present in both versions of *Eug,* shows that the haplography probably occurred in the text of *SJC* rather than *Eug.* And further, since the Greek text used by both *SJC* translators was, in all probability, uniform (see Introduction, sec. X), and the Coptic texts are so different, we are probably justified in thinking that the translators met the problem in the Greek independently and attempted to deal with it each in his own way in their translations. (It is possible that subsequent Coptic copyists were involved, but that seems less likely in view of the fact that *both* texts deal with the problem, suggesting that it could not easily be overlooked by a translator.) If that was the case, then those attempts provide us with some evidence about the two Coptic translators of *SJC*.

The translator of *SJC*–III seems to be more conservative (e.g., he preserves the correct person and number of the, for him, lost subject), but he makes a clumsy and basically meaningless connection with the preceding sentence. The translator of *SJC*–BG is more daring, conceiving of the idea that the passage was a reference to the intiial appearance of the gnostic race, which would mean that it was engendered by Immortal Man. Unfortunately, in taking that position, he has ignored a preceding statement that the gnostic race appeared prior to Immortal Man (III 99,13–19 || BG 91,17–92,9).

5.   III 78,6–7 || III 102,23 || BG 96,16 ⲛ̄ⲑⲉ ⲉⲧⲉ ϥ̄ⲟ ⲛ̄ⲙⲟⲥ (and the like), "just as he is it (thought)": Appears to be a gloss (n.b. its absence in V). The point seems to be that First Man not only *has* thought but *is* thought. That is perhaps based on an identification of his feminine aspect, the Great Sophia (see III 104,10–11 & parr.), with hypostasized thought. T–S renders "just as he is" (connection with preceding and following is not clear); K, "just as he is a reflection"; Tr, "thought as he is" (?).

6.   V 7,19–22 || III 78,19–21 In V there are whole numbers, while III has fractions. The former version is probably to be preferred since it is the more difficult reading, i.e., it is easier to imagine larger fractions (e.g., tenths) ruling over smaller fractions (e.g., hundredths), then smaller whole numbers (e.g., tens) ruling over larger ones (e.g., hundreds). N.B. that the last two numbers were left unchanged in III.

7.   V 12,2 || III 83,20 "will": less likely, "interval" (Crum: 501b).

8.   III 86,16–20 ⲁⲩⲟⲛⲟⲙⲁⲍⲉ ... ⲛ̄ⲟⲩⲁⲧⲟ, "the ... multitude" || BG 110,9–16: "they called the church in the third aeon 'the multitude from the multitude, which the multitude caused to appear from the one'" (K [III]; similarly Tr); "the 'church of the three aeons' was spoken of, because, from the crowd that came to appearance in (or 'from') one, a multitude was revealed" (T–S [BG]); "the church of the three aeons was furnished with names ..." (Schenke in T–S: 340 [BG]). The problem of III 86,16–17 and BG 110,9–12, reflected in the variety of translations above (n.b. the similarity of the texts), may go back to the Greek where the distinction between the designation and the designee may not have been clear grammatically. That the designation is "Assembly" or "Church," however, is evident from III 86,22 and BG 111,3. And that one of the aeons *is* the designee is clear from III 86,14–16 and BG 110,8–9. As to the omission of the ordinal prefixes, see 110,4 for additional examples of the error in BG. In III, lines 11–13 make clear the error (for omission of numeral prefixes, see 78,21–22). Both texts appear to have been adjusted in minor ways in hopes of making sense out of what was received, but the result was to make a difficult situation worse. The text of V, lacking those adjustments, seems closer to the original. Since the original can be discerned, I have chosen to edit *Eug*-III and SJC-BG accordingly.

For ⲡⲓⲟⲩⲁ ⲛ̄ⲟⲩⲁⲧⲟ, "the multitudinous one" (III 86,19–20), T–S has "one as a multitude"; K & Tr omit a translation of ⲛ̄ⲟⲩⲁⲧⲟ, although Tr leaves the text unemended.

9. III 87,10 ⲙⲉⲧⲉ, "concurrence" ‖ III 111,13 ⲭⲱⲛϥ, "concurrence" ‖ BG 112,4 ⲉⲩⲁⲟⲕⲓⲁ, "consent": "good will" (Tr [*Eug*–III]); "good pleasure" (K [*Eug*–III]); untranslated (T–S [BG]). Basic for understanding ⲉⲩⲁⲟⲕⲓⲁ here, as well as the Coptic words used to translate it, is the observation of LSJ that εὐδοκία can be equivalent to εὐδόκησις when used of God. Thus it can mean "consent, concurrence." See also *TDNT* (2), 1964: 750 (Schrenk).

10. III 88,10 ‖ III 112,10 ‖ BG 113,18–114,1 The fem. pronouns in III 88,10 refer to Sophia (contra T–S). It appears that the reference to Sophia was dropped at an early stage from *SJC* and that the BG version (with masc. pronouns) reflects a more careful adjustment to that fact than does *SJC*–III.

11. III 88,11 ‖ III 112,11 ‖ BG 114,2 Should ⲁⲫⲑⲁⲣⲥⲓⲁ (*Eug*–III & *SJC*–III) or ⲁⲧⲧⲁⲕⲟ (BG) be translated with the preceding ⲙⲛⲧⲛⲟϭ, "majesty," as an adjective (as though a genitive) (so also K & Tr [*Eug*–III]) or in an identity relationship ("as imperishability") (so T–S [*Eug*–III & *SJC*–III])? Or should they be taken with the following ⲉⲩⲛⲧⲟⲩ, "had," as the plural subject, as I have done (so also T–S [BG])? My decision is based on the clear-cut nature of the case in BG and the difficulty of relating ⲁⲫⲑⲁⲣⲥⲓⲁ (in *Eug*–III & *SJC*–III) satisfactorily to ⲙⲛⲧⲛⲟϭ.

12. V 16,4 ‖ III 88,20 "sent": or "sown" (ⲭⲟ, Crum: 752a).

13. III 114,7 ‖ BG 117,10 "that you might shine" (so also T–S): "until you shine" (K).

14. III 118,18–19 ‖ BG 125,14–15 "Him Who Is from the Beginning": "that which is from the beginning" (T–S, D & K).

15. III 119,13–14 ‖ BG 127,4–5 "from that day on. And his": "From that day (on) his" (T–S, Pu, D & K).

WORD INDICES

Words in the Coptic Words index are ordered according to Crum's *Coptic Dictionary*. Nouns are indicated simply by gender designation (m. or f.), where that is clear. Where it is not, nn. is used. Verbs are indicated by v. ⁺ designates the qualitative form of the Coptic verb. Definitions are omitted as unnecessary in view of the translations to which the entries refer. Where a word or phrase is split between two lines in the text, only the first line is indicated. In the Greek Loan Words index the Coptic form of Greek loan words is not shown when the Coptic and Greek are identical in spelling; in this connection, a Greek rough breathing mark and a Coptic ⲍ are considered identical.

Omissions from the Coptic Words index because of frequency of occurrence and minor grammatical and lexical interest include the conjuctions ⲁⲩⲱ and ⲙⲛ̄, demonstratives (except ⲉⲧⲙ̄ⲙⲁⲩ), possessive pronouns, the preposition ⲍⲛ̄ (except in combinations), and ⲛ̄ϭⲓ. Omissions from the Greek Loan Word index include the conjunctions ἀλλά, γάρ, δέ and μέν. From the Proper Nouns index are omitted all proper nouns constructed from verbs or attributives (except ⲉⲩⲅⲛⲱⲥⲧⲟⲥ and ⲭⲣⲓⲥⲧⲟⲥ). Those are fully indexed in the other word indices.

COPTIC WORDS

ⲁⲙⲟⲩ: See ⲉ̂ⲓ .

ⲁⲙⲁⲍⲧⲉ v. V 3,8.9; 13,15. III 73,6.8. BG 86,15; 108,11. ⲉⲙⲁⲍⲧⲉ III 85,15; 96,1.[2]. BG 86,13.

ⲁⲛ- (collective numeral indicator) V 7,20.21.22twice.23.27.[28].[29]; 9,[12]; 10,[15]; 11,<20>.[23].[29]; 12,[1].

ⲁⲛ negative particle V 1,12.16; 3,10.[18].23; 4,7.9.15.25.[28]. III 70,16.22; 72,7; 74,2.18; 75,12; 92,22; 93,4; 95,2; 98,18.23; 99,13. BG 78,13; 81,5.12; 85,1; 89,19; 91,16; 97,11. ⲉⲛ III 91,11. BG 90,16.

ⲁⲛⲟⲕ pron. III 93,8.10; 94,14; 96,18; 97,23; 106,5; 107,11; 118,[15].22. BG 81,17.19; 83,19; 87,13; 89,7; 102,[1]; 104,7; 105,2; 121,13; 125,10.19.

ⲁⲣⲏⲝ⳹ nn. V 8,17. III 73,14; 95,7; 96,11; 97,12; 103,21; 106,7. BG 87,<5>; 98,7. ⲁⲧⲁⲣⲏⲝ⳹ III 72,14. BG 81,18; 87,7. ⲁⲧⲛ̄ⲁⲣⲏⲝ⳹ V 5,25; 13,[17]. ⲙⲛ̄ ⲁⲣⲏⲝ⳹ BG 88,12.

ⲁⲧⲟ m. V 5,[6]. III 86,18.19. BG 91,18; 99,19; 109,18; 110,15. ˈ

ⲁϣ interrog. pron. BG 98,13. ⲁϣ ⲙ̄ⲙⲓⲛⲉ V 1,8. III 92,12. ⲛ̄ⲁϣ ⲛ̄ⲍⲉ III 98,11. ⲟⲩⲁϣ ⲛ̄ⲍⲉ BG 80,11. ⲉϣ ⲛ̄ⲍⲉ III 70,7.

ⲁϣⲁⲓ m. V 14,13. ⲁϣⲉ̈ⲓ V 9,13.

ⲁⲝⲛ̄ prep. V 15,[23]. III 88,10; 112,9; 114,17. BG 113,18.

ⲃⲱⲕ v. BG 117,16. ⲃⲱⲕ ϣⲁ- BG 123,4. ⲃⲱⲕ ⲉⲃⲟⲗ ⲍⲛ̄ III 76,12. ⲃⲱⲕ ⲉⲃⲟⲗ ⲍⲓⲧⲛ̄- V 3,[31]. ⲃⲱⲕ ⲉⲍⲣⲁⲓ̈ ⲉ- BG 122,14. ⲃⲱⲕ ⲉⲍⲣⲁⲓ̈ ϣⲁ- III 108,3; 117,4. BG 105,11.

ⲃⲁⲗ V 9,[24]. III 105,13. BG 100,14; 108,10.

ⲃⲱⲗ v. V 17,14. BG 104,10. ⲃⲱⲗ ⲉⲃⲟⲗ BG 121,15. ⲣⲉϥⲃⲱⲗ nn. BG 94,16. ⲃⲟⲗ m.: ⲉⲃⲟⲗ ⲛ̄- BG 98,12. ⲉⲃⲟⲗ ⲭⲉ BG 100,15; 110,9.16. ⲃⲟⲗ and ⲉⲃⲟⲗ are otherwise listed with the verb or preposition in conjunction with which they occur.

ⲃⲁ̄ⲗⲉ nn.: ⲙⲛ̄ⲧⲃⲁ̄ⲗⲉ III 107,10; 118,23. BG 104,5; 126,2.

ⲉⲃⲟⲧ m. V 12,10. III 84,3.

ⲉⲛⲉⲍ m.: ϣⲁ ⲉⲛⲉⲍ III 85,16. BG 108,14. ⲉⲛⲉⲍ adj.: ⲛ̄ϣⲁ ⲉⲛⲉⲍ V 8,23; 13,17; 16,[3]. III 119,[16]. BG 127,9. ϣⲁ ⲁⲛⲏⲍⲉ III 71,19; 95,11. ϣⲁ ⲉⲛⲉⲍ V 2,14.15. III 94,15.16. BG 84,2.3; 85,16. ϣⲁ ⲛⲓ- ⲉⲛⲉⲍ BG 127,10. ⲉⲛⲉⲍ adv. V 5,17; 8,24. III 76,8; 81,19; 100,13; 106,1. BG 93,9; 101,16.

ⲉⲣⲏⲩ nn.: ⲛⲉⲩⲉⲣⲏⲟⲩ V 1,[15]; 9,18. III 81,8; 83,12; 86,4. BG 87,2; 109,14.

ⲉⲥⲏⲧ m.: ⲙ̄ⲡⲉⲥⲏⲧ III 77,8. See further ⲉⲓ.

ⲉⲧⲃⲉ- prep. V 3,[25]; 14,[12]. III 91,3.6; 92,4; 97,3; 107,9; 108,11; 118,19. BG 78,3.7; 80,1; 88,2; 104,4; 106,3; 125,15. ⲉⲧⲃⲉ ⲡⲁⲓ̈ V 1,15; 5,12; 6,[32]. III 70,15; 78,[1]; 86,20; 92,21; 102,17; 103,19. BG 81,4; 96,8; 111,[2].6; 122,5. ⲉⲧⲃⲉ ⲡⲉⲉⲓ- III 86,24. ⲉⲧⲃⲉ ⲟⲩ III 92,1; 96,16 twice. BG 79,15.16; 87,9.11. ⲉⲧⲃⲏ(ⲛ)ⲧ⳽ V 2,6. III 71,11; 105,6.

ⲉⲟⲟⲩ m. V 5,[2].10.15; 8,[19]; 14,[2]; 16,[1].9; 17,[1]. III 75,16; 76,6; 81,17; 86,8; 88,19; 89,1.8.22; 97,10; 99,17; 100,6.11; 105,8.25; 107,23; 108,3; 113,5.12.25; 117,6. BG 88,10; 92,3.17; 93,6; 100,8; 101,14; 105,4.11; 109,18; 115,7.18; 117,1; 122,17.

ⲉϣⲭⲉ conj. III 113,1. BG 115,[1].

ⲉⲓ v. III 114,11. BG 117,15. ⲉⲓ ⲉ- V 2,[2]. III 73,17; 86,21; 90,18; 97,17; 111,1; 118,23. BG 88,19; 122,6; 126,1. ⲉⲓ ⲉⲃⲟⲗ ⲍⲛ̄ V 9,[25]. III 93,8; 96,19; 105,[13]; 107,12.14; 108,14; 118,[16]. BG 81,17; 83,15; 87,13; 100,15; 102,[2]; 104,8; 106,7; 125,11. ⲉⲓ ⲉⲃⲟⲗ ⲍⲓⲧⲛ̄- III 106,5. ⲉⲓ ⲉⲡⲉⲥⲏⲧ III 106,12. BG 102,11. ⲉⲓ ⲉⲍⲟⲩⲛ III 71,8. ⲉⲓ ⲉⲍⲟⲩⲛ ⲙ̄ⲡⲃⲟⲗ ⲛ̄- III 71,6. ⲉⲓ ⲉⲍⲣⲁⲓ̈ ⲉ- BG 77,11; 119,7. ⲁⲙⲏⲉⲓⲧⲛ̄ imperat. III 98,13. BG 90,4. For qualitative, see ⲛⲏⲩⳁ.

ⲉⲓⲁⲗ f. III 75,5; 99,3. BG 91,6.

ⲉⲓⲙⲉ v.: ⲉⲓⲙⲉ ⲭⲉ III 70,3; 92,7; 100,21; 104,6; 114,14. BG 93,17; 98,15; 118,2. ⲙ̄ⲙⲉ ⲭⲉ V 1,[4]. ⲉⲓⲙⲉ ⲛⲁ⳽ V 2,[12]. ⲉⲓⲙⲉ ⲉ- (ⲉⲣⲟ⳽) V 4,16. BG 80,5. ⲙ̄ⲙⲉ ⲉⲣⲟ⳽ V 4,25. ⲉⲓⲙⲉ ⲉⲧⲃⲉ- III 105,7.

ⲉⲓⲛⲉ v. (carry): ⲉⲓⲛⲉ ⲛⲁ⳽ III 117,19. BG 123,16; 124,4. ⲉⲓⲛⲉ ⲛⲉ⳽ III 117,24.

ⲉⲓⲛⲉ v. (resemble) V 4,18; 9,20. III 77,5; 81,10; 99,4. BG 91,7. ⲓⲛⲉ BG 85,13. ⲓⲛⲉ ⲉⲃⲟⲗ V 7,12. ⲉⲓⲛⲉ m. V 5,[31]. III 72,16; 75,6; 76,20; 89,14; 91,12; 95,9; 99,5; 100,4; 101,5; 113,18. BG 78,15.16; 84,18; 85,3; 91,8; 92,15; 94,5; 116,9. ⲁⲧⳁ ⲉⲓⲛⲉ ⲉⲣⲟ⳽ V 2,[16].[17].[26].

ειρε v. V 11,22. III 91,7. BG 78,8; 109,11. ρ̄- V 12,[30]. III 83,14;
    84,20.24; 114,12. BG 117,17. See further καζ, ϣωρπ̄, ζογο. ααϥ III
    71,3; 93,14. BG 82,6. ε⁺ V 2,6.<16>.23; 4,26; 5,[26]; 6,[2]; 10,[7].16;
    11,[26].[28]; 12,18; 16,10. ο⁺ III 70,5; 78,7.17; 92,10; 102,23. BG
    96,16.
ειϊωρζ v. III 72,12; 95,6. ειωρζ ν̄ca- BG 85,6.
εις interj.: εις ζηητε III 118,3. BG 124,9.
ειωτ m. V 7,14; 9,[9].[22]. III 74,22.23; 76,17; 78,13; 84,14; 97,15;
    98,23.<24>; 99,6; 101,1.22; 103,6; 104,23; 105,19; 108,4; 117,[9]. BG
    88,16; 90,16.17; 91,10; 95,8; 97,6; 99,18; 100,4; 101,6; 105,12; 123,4;
    127,9. ιωτ V 4,10.11; 6,[19]; 12,[2]. III 77,13; 117,10. BG 123,2.
    αγεννητος ν̄(ε)ιωτ III 75,22; 96,13; 98,20; 99,9; 100,1; 117,[11].
    BG 90,12; 91,13. ατχπο(ϥ) ν̄ειωτ V 10,<18–19>. BG 87,7; 123,6.
    αγτογενετωρ ν̄ειωτ BG 107,4. αγτογενης ν̄ειωτ III 101,19.
    BG 95,3. αγτοφγης ν̄αγτοκτιστος ν̄ειωτ BG 94,1. ειωτ εβολ
    ν̄μοϥ V 6,[20]. (ε)ιωτ ν̄πτηρϥ̄ V 3,[4]. III 73,2; 95,18; 114,19;
    117,[8]. BG 86,5; 123,1. ειωτ πιρεϥχ πο ν̄νη θρογ V 12,[23]. ιωτ
    ν̄ρεϥχποϥ ογααϥ V 4,[20]. ιωτ πεταϥχπο ν̄μοϥ ογααϥ V
    5,[25]. πρω(or ο)τογενετωρ ν̄(ε)ιωτ III 81,10; 105,11. BG 100,12.
    ϣ(ο)ρπ̄ ν̄ειωτ or ν̄ειοτε V 4,10.[13]; 6,11. BG 91,3.9.
ειτν̄ m.: ν̄πιτν̄ ν̄τε- BG 119,8.

κε- adj. V 2,4; 5,12.21; 7,3.16; 8,[27]; 11,[5].15. III 71,9; 76,13; 97,8;
    107,24. BG 88,7; 105,6. κεογα V 2,[20]. III 72,2.6; 94,24. BG
    84,12.17. κοογε pl. V 1,[20].21. III 70,19.20; 93,[1].2. BG 81,8.10.
    See further ceeπε.
κω v.: κη⁺ εζραϊ V 3,[30]; 5,5. III 74,14; 75,19; 83,4. See further ρο.
κιμ v. BG 88,9. κιμ m. III 92,16. BG 80,15. ατκιμ III 97,9.
κρωμ m. III 108,13.
καζ m. III 92,9. BG 80,7; 81,15. See further χπο.
κωζ m. BG 106,6.

λααγ indef. pron. V 1,[23]; 3,[5].10. III 73,3; 74,8; 95,22. BG 86,10. (ν̄)μν̄
    λααγ III 71,24; 73,7; 94,2.21; 96,2. BG 83,1; 84,9; 86,15.

μα m. V 14,15. III 75,20; 89,10; 113,14; 118,2. BG 92,10; 116,2.7; 125,<8>.
    πιμα BG 122,6. πμα ετμ̄μαγ V 16,[22]. III 89,13. BG 124,8.
    ν̄π(ι)μα BG 117,17; 120,17; 124,15. ν̄πεειμα III 93,10; 114,12;
    118,6. μα ν̄ϣωπε III 88,18. See further τη, ζω.
μα- (imperat. of †): See ταμο, τcβο, τογνος, εβ̄βιο.
με f. V 1,12.[24]; 6,10. BG 80,17; 83,2. μηε III 70,11.12; 71,1; 74,12; 77,7
    twice; 92,18; 93,7.12; 94,2.4; 117,18. BG 81,17; 82,3; 83,4; 123,15.
    μν̄τμε V 4,9; 6,12. See further νογτε.
μογ v. V 3,[24]. III 71,13; 74,7; 91,16; 93,24; 98,9; 106,14. BG 79,3; 82,18;
    89,20; 102,14. μοογτ⁺ V 2,8. νετμοογτ⁺ BG 77,10. μογ m.:
    ατμογ V 2,[6].7; 6,[4]; 7,[10].24; 13,[18]; 15,18. III 94,15. BG 82,17;

84,1; 97,[2]; 102,12; 107,16; 108,18; 113,11; 118,9; 120,11; 123,12. See
further ρωμε.

ⲙⲁⲁⲍ m.: ⲁⲧⲣ̄ ⲙⲁⲁⲍ V 6,[12].

(ⲙ̄)ⲙⲛ̄- (negation of existence) V 2,13; 4,[26]. III 70,24; 93.6.15; 95,7;
106,7; 113,9. BG 81,15; 85,13; 115,11.12. ⲙ̄ⲙⲛ̄- ⲙ̄ⲙⲁⲩ III 89,3; 113,8.
ⲙⲛ̄ⲧ(ⲉ)⳽ V 4,[23]; 16,[11]. III 71,22; 72,23; 94,19; 97,12. BG
84,7.10.14. (ⲙ̄)ⲙⲛ̄ⲧⲁ⳽ III 71,20; 72,1.3.16; 94,17.22; 95,9.16. BG 92,15.
ⲙⲛ̄ⲧⲁ⳽ ⲙ̄ⲙⲁⲩ BG 84,3; 86,2. See further ⲁⲣⲏⲭ⳽, ⲗⲁⲁⲩ, ⲣ̄ⲣⲟ, ⲱⲡ,
ⲍⲁⲉⲓⲃⲉⲥ , ϭⲟⲙ.

ⲙ̄ⲙⲓⲛ ⲙ̄ⲙⲟ⳽ III 70,19; 71,2; 72,7.13.21; 75,3; 93,1.13; 95,1; 97,5; 99,2.4.7;
104,9; 114,16. BG 81,8; 82,4; 84,18; 88,4; 91,4.7; 96,14.

ⲙⲓⲛⲉ f.: See ⲁϣ.

ⲙⲟⲩⲛ v.: ⲙⲏⲛ† V 5,14; 16,[31]. BG 93,4. ⲙⲏⲛ† ⲉⲃⲟⲗ III 72,15.18; 76,4;
81,16; 89,21; 95,8; 100,9; 105,17; 113,24. BG 85,12; 101,3.13; 116,18.

ⲙⲟⲩⲛⲕ v.: ⲙⲟⲛⲕ⳽ V 8,[10].[12].

ⲙ̄ⲡϣⲁ v.: ⲙ̄ⲡϣⲁ ⲛ̄- III 93,18. BG 82,10.

ⲙⲟⲩⲣ v.: ⲙⲟⲣ⳽ III 107,6. BG 103,18. ⲙⲣ̄ⲣⲉ f. BG 103,17.

ⲙⲓⲥⲉ m. ϣⲟⲣⲡ̄ ⲙ̄ⲙⲓⲥⲉ V 8,[33]; 9,7.21; 13,11. ϣⲟⲣⲡⲉ ⲙ̄ⲙⲓⲥⲉ V 9,[4].
ϣⲏⲣⲉ ⲛ̄ϣⲟⲣⲡ̄ ⲙ̄ⲙⲓⲥⲉ V 9,[2]. ⲁⲧⲙⲓⲥⲉ V 3,2; 5,8. ⲁⲧⲙⲓⲥⲓ V 2,16.

ⲙⲏⲧ cardinal number: ⲣⲁⲙⲏⲧ III 78,19 twice. ⲙⲛ̄ⲧ- in the following cardinal
number: ⲙⲛ̄ⲧⲥⲛⲟⲟⲩⲥ V 12,[9].[11].[24].[25]. III 83,10; 84,2.4.15.16;
90,16. BG 77,12; 107,5.7. ⲁⲛ ⲙⲛ̄ⲧⲥⲛⲟⲟⲩⲥ V 11,<20>.

ⲙⲁⲧⲉ v.: ⲙⲁⲧⲉ ⲛ̄- BG 105,10. ⲙⲁⲧⲉ m. † ⲙⲁⲧⲉ ⲛ̄- III 101,10. † ⲙⲁⲧⲉ
ⲍⲛ̄- III 108,2. † ⲙⲉⲧⲉ ⲙⲛ̄- V 1,[15]; 10,[5].13. † ⲙⲉⲧⲉ ⲛ̄- BG 94,13. †
ⲙⲉⲧⲉ m. V 8,[31]; 11,[6].[22]. ⲙⲉⲧⲉ ⲙⲛ̄- III 87,10.

ⲙⲁⲧⲉ: ⲙ̄ⲙⲁⲧⲉ adv. III 89,5. BG 115,13.

ⲙⲏⲧⲉ f. V 14,[4]. III 86,10. ⲍⲛ̄ ⲧⲙⲏⲧⲉ V 2,[7]. III 71,12; 93,23. BG 82,17.

ⲙⲟⲩⲧⲉ v.: ⲙⲟⲩⲧⲉ ⲉⲣⲟ⳽ BG 110,1. ⲙⲟⲩⲧⲉ ⲉ- (ⲉⲣⲟ⳽) ⲭⲉ V 3,[3];
9,[6].14; 10,[9]; 11,16; 13,[11].14. III 75,17; 85,14; 86,22; 91.1.19;
95,17; 99,17.24; 102,1.18; 104,7.14.19.21; 105,5.21; 106,20.23; 111,1;
112,8. BG 78,1; 79,7; 86,4; 92,5.12; 98,9; 99,13.15; 100,5.13; 101,8;
103,3.8; 108,3.5.9; 110,5; 111,13.15; 112,8; 113,15; 119,15. ⲙⲟⲩⲧⲉ
ⲭⲉ BG 111,[2].

ⲙ̄ⲧⲟ m.: ⲙ̄ⲧⲟ ⲉⲃⲟⲗ BG 122,1. ⲙ̄ⲧⲟ ⲉⲃⲟⲗ prep. BG 91,11. ⲣⲉϥⲙ̄ⲧⲟ ⲙ̄- V
4,[21].

ⲙ̄ⲧⲟⲛ v.: ⲙ̄ⲧⲟⲛ ⲙ̄ⲙⲟ⳽ ⲍⲛ̄- (ⲛ̄ⲍⲏⲧ⳽) III 76,3; 100,8; 117,[11]. BG 93,2;
123,5.<9>. ⲙ̄ⲧⲟⲛ m. V 5,13; 14,[9]; 17,[2]. BG 117,[2]; 125,<8>.

ⲙⲁⲩ nn.: ⲉⲧⲙ̄ⲙⲁⲩ V 2,13; 4,[2]; 6,[3]; 8,[33]; 9,17. III 71,18; 73,8; 75,1;
76,22; 77,24; 81,4.7; 94,14; 96,3; 98,25; 99,22.23; 101,7.10; 102,12;
107,[15].18.25; 117,1; 119,13. BG 84,1; 86,16; 91,2; 92,10; 94,7.8.12;
96,2; 104,11.15; 111,4; 116,7; 119,13.17; 120,12; 121,5.8; 122,8; 127,5.
See further ⲙⲁ, (ⲙ̄)ⲙⲛ̄-, ⲟⲩⲟⲛ.

ⲙⲁⲁⲩ f. III 118,5. BG 120,15; 124,14. ⲙⲁⲁⲩ ⲙ̄ⲡⲧⲏⲣϥ̄ V 9,[5]. III 104,18;
112,19; 114,15. ⲙⲁⲩ ⲙ̄ⲡⲧⲏⲣϥ̄ BG 99,12; 114,11. ⲙⲁⲩ ⲛ̄ⲛⲓⲡⲧⲏⲣϥ̄ BG
118,[3].

ⲙⲉⲉⲩⲉ v. V 4,[28]; 5,[30]. BG 79,15; 80,9. ⲙⲉⲩⲉ V 1,9. ⲙⲉⲟⲩⲉ III 92,2.
ⲙⲉⲉⲩⲉ ⲉ- BG 120,6. ⲙⲉⲉⲩⲉ m. V 3,[11]; 7,7.26; 8,[3].4; 11,10.11.17.
BG 86,19; 96,18; 112,16; 120,7. ⲙⲉⲟⲩⲉ III 111,20. ⲁⲧⲙⲉⲟⲩⲉ ⲉⲣⲟⳅ III
114,20.

ⲙⲏⲏϣⲉ m. V 3,[21]. III 74,5; 75,13.19; 81,3; 86,7.18.20; 98,7; 99,14.22;
104,24; 118,[7]. BG 89,18; 110,13.17; 124,16.

ⲙⲟⲩϣⲧ v. V 4,[2]. III 74,14.

ⲙⲟⲩⲍ v.: ⲙⲉⲍ⁺ V 9,[26]. III 81,14; 100,6. BG 101,9. ⲙⲏⲍ⁺ III 105,22. BG
92,17. ⲙⲉⲍ⁺ ⲉⲃⲟⲗ V 5,10.28; 8,19. ⲙⲏⲍ⁺ ⲉⲃⲟⲗ III 76,[1]. ⲙⲁⲍ- and
ⲙⲉⲍ- in ordinal numbers; see ⲥⲛⲁⲩ, ⲥⲟⲟⲩ, ⲥⲁϣϥ̄, †ⲟⲩ, ϣⲙⲟⲩⲛ,
ϣⲟⲙⲛ̄ⲧ, ϥⲧⲟⲟⲩ.

ⲙⲍⲁⲁⲩ m.: ⲙⲍⲁⲟⲩ III 119,2. BG 104,12; 126,7.

ⲙⲁⲁϫⲉ m. III 97,21; 98,21; 105,10. BG 89,5; 90,13; 100,11; 107,19.

ⲛⲁ m. BG 118,6. ⲁⲧⲛⲁⲉ BG 122,1.

ⲛⲁ v.: ⲛⲁ ⲉ- III 114,11.

ⲛⲏⲩ⁺ ⲉ- BG 103,10. ⲛⲏⲟⲩ⁺ ⲉⲃⲟⲗ V 4,11. ⲛⲏⲟⲩ⁺ ⲉⲍⲟⲩⲛ ⲉ- III 106,24.

ⲛ̄ⲕⲁ m.: ⲛ̄ⲕⲁ ⲛⲓⲙ III 72,10; 73,21; 82,[3]; 95,4; 98,1; 103,10; 106,8.21;
119,5. BG 85,5; 87,15; 89,9; 120,10. Ⳍⲕⲁ ⲛⲓⲙ BG 97,12; 103,5; 126,13.

ⲛ̄ⲕⲟⲧⲕ v. BG 120,2.

ⲛⲓⲙ interrog. pron. V 1,7. III 70,7; 92,12; 104,3. BG 80,10.

ⲛⲓⲙ indef. pron. V 2,12; 5,10.19; 7,32; 8,20.25; 10,[1]; 16,[19].[20]. III 70,3;
71,17; 72,12; 78,9; 86,6; 87,8; 88,21; 89,10; 91,15; 94,8; 95,6; 97,15;
100,6.15; 103,1; 111,11; 113,15. BG 85,7; 88,17; 92,18; 96,19; 109,16;
116,4.11; 117,5; 118,14. See further ⲛ̄ⲕⲁ, ⲛⲁⲩ, ⲟⲩⲁ, ⲟⲩⲟⲛ, ⲟⲩⲟⲉⲓϣ,
ⲍⲱⲃ.

ⲛⲁⲛⲟⲩ- v. III 85,7. ⲛⲁⲛⲟⲩⳅ V 13,[5]. BG 107,10.

ⲛⲟⲩⲛⲉ f. III 108,22. BG 106,18.

ⲛⲟⲩⲧⲉ m. V 1,7; 3,26; 6,[26]; 9,[3]; 11,17; 13,[17]; 15.[2] twice. [3]
twice.[4].[5]. III 70,6; 74,11; 77,20; 87,12 twice.14 twice.15; 92,11;
100,2; 102,8.15; 111,15.16 twice.17.<18>; 118,22; 119,[15]. BG 80,10;
92,13; 95,17; 96,6; 112,8.9 twice.12 twice; 125,19; 127,8. ⲛ̄† BG
112,13. ⲁⲧϫⲡⲟϥ ⲛ̄ⲛⲟⲩⲧⲉ BG 88,15. ⲁⲩⲧⲟⲅⲉⲛⲏⲥ ⲛ̄ⲛⲟⲩⲧⲉ III 97,14.
ⲛⲟⲩⲧⲉ ⲉⲧⲍⲓϫⲙ̄ ⲡⲧⲏⲣϥ̄ III 118,25. BG 126,4. ⲛⲟⲩⲧⲉ ⲛ̄ⲛⲟⲩⲧⲉ III
78,[2]; 102,18. BG 96,10. ⲛⲟⲩⲧⲉ ⲛ̄ⲧⲉ ⲛ̄ⲛⲟⲩⲧⲉ V 6,[32]. ⲛⲟⲩⲧⲉ
ⲛ̄ⲧⲁⲗⲏⲑⲉⲓⲁ III 71,10. ⲛⲟⲩⲧⲉ ⲛ̄ⲧⲉ ⲧⲙⲉ V 2,[3]. ⲛⲟⲩⲧⲉ adj. III
85,17; 87,14; 99,6. BG 91,10; 108,15. ⲙⲛ̄ⲧⲛⲟⲩⲧⲉ V 2,14; 6,16.[29].
III 77,12.24; 101,21; 102,16. BG 95,7; 96,7. See further ϣⲏⲣⲉ.

ⲛ̄ⲧⲟⲥ pron. V 6,11. III 98,15. BG 90,7.

ⲛ̄ⲧⲱⲧⲛ̄ pron. III 93,16; 108,5; 119,1. BG 82,9; 105,14; 126,5.

ⲛ̄ⲧⲟⲟⲩ pron. III 73,12; 76,3; 96,7; 100,8. BG 87,1; 93,2.

ⲛ̄ⲧⲟϥ pron. V 2,[22]; 4,18; 9,[7]. III 71,18; 75,23; 85,21; 94,10; 99,5; 100,4;
104,20. BG 83,13; 91,8; 92,16; 109,4.

ⲛ̄ⲧⲟϥ conj. V 3,9.

ⲚⲀⲨ v. III 72,11; 95,6. BG 85,2. ⲚⲀⲨ ⲉⲣⲟ⸗ III 72,8; 75,3; 95,2; 99,2. BG 85,7; 91,4. ⲁⲧⲚⲀⲨ ⲉⲣⲟ⸗ BG 123,17; 125,5.

ⲚⲀⲨ m.: Ⲛ̄ⲚⲀⲨ Ⲛⲓⲙ III 76,1.

ⲚⲀⲱⲉ- v.: ⲚⲀⲱⲱ⸗ III 97,18; 107,17; 117,4. BG 89,2; 104,14; 110,13; 122,13.

Ⲛⲓϥⲉ v.: Ⲛⲓϥⲉ ⲉⲍⲟⲩⲚ ⲉⲣⲟ⸗ BG 120,13. Ⲛⲓϥⲉ m. III 117,1. BG 119,19; 120,4.12; 121,5; 122,9.

Ⲛⲟⲩⲍⲃ̄ v.: Ⲛⲟⲩⲍⲃ̄ ⲙⲚ̄- BG 122,7. Ⲛⲟⲍⲃ⸗ III 107,<21>. ⲚⲀⲍⲃⲉ⸗ BG 105,1. Ⲛⲟⲩⲍⲃ̄ m. III 101,18. ⲚⲀⲍⲃ̄ III 119,3. ⲚⲀⲍⲃⲉ BG 126,10.

ⲚⲀⲍⲧⲉ v.: ⲚⲀⲍⲧⲉ ⲉ- V 3,[29].

ⲚⲟϬ adj. V 2,23; 5,[31]; 8,[32]; 10,7. III 76,21; 77,16.17; 81,24; 88,13; 91,13; 94,14; 97,2; 101,5.16; 102,3.6; 104,10; 106,18; 107,13.22; 108,22; 112,13; 118,[11]; 119,[12]. BG 78,16; 83,19; 87,20; 94,6; 95,1.12.14; 99,[2]; 103,[1]; 104,10; 105,3; 106,17; 114,[4]; 120,5; 121,12; 125,4; 127,3. ⲚⲀϬ V 6,22.25; 9,10. ⲙⲚ̄ⲧⲚⲟϬ V 3,6; 9,10. III 73,5; 77,17; 86,5; 88,11.17; 95,23; 102,5; 112,11.17. BG 86,11; 95,13; 109,16; 113,18; 114,9. ⲙⲚ̄ⲧⲚⲀϬ V 6,23; 15,[22].

ⲟⲚ adv. V 7,23; 12,21. III 77,5; 117,2. BG 93,9.

ⲟⲉⲓⲱ nn.: ⲧⲀⲱⲉ ⲟⲉⲓⲱ III 119,[14]. BG 127,7.

ⲡⲉ f. V 14,[17]; 16,16. III 84,20; 85,5; 86,24; 89,7; 113,11.18. BG 111,5. ⲡⲏⲩⲉ pl. BG 106,13; 115,16; 116,9. ⲡⲚⲟⲩⲉ pl. V 12,[29]; 13,[4]; 16,[23]. III 108,18. Ⲛ̄ⲧⲡⲉ V 4,6. BG 104,9. Ⲛ̄ⲧⲡⲉ Ⲛ̄- V 13,[19]. BG 109,1.12; 119,3.

ⲡⲉⲓ f.: † ⲡⲓ ⲉⲣⲚ̄- V 9,18.

ⲡⲉⲓⲣⲉ v.: ⲡ̄ⲣ̄ⲣⲉ ⲉⲃⲟⲗ V 5,[21]. ⲡ̄ⲣ̄ⲣⲉ ⲉⲃⲟⲗ ⲍⲚ̄- V 17,12. ⲡ̄ⲣ̄ⲣⲉ m.: ⲡ̄ⲣ̄ⲣⲉ ⲉⲃⲟⲗ ⲙ̄ⲙⲟ⸗ V 5,[8]. ⲡⲓⲣⲉ ⲉⲃⲟⲗ ⲙ̄ⲙⲟ⸗ V 5,[20].

ⲡⲉⲭⲉ- v.: ⲡⲉⲭⲉ- ⲭⲉ III 92,3; 98,12; 100,19; 106,14; 108,19; 112,24. ⲡⲉⲭⲀ⸗ BG 79,18; 83,4. ⲡⲉⲭⲀ⸗ ⲭⲉ III 91,21; 94,4; 95,19; 96,17; 98,1; 105,8; 106,10. BG 79,9; 80,4; 86,6.8; 87,8.12; 89,9; 90,3; 93,15; 98,13; 100,9; 102,7.14; 106,13; 107,16; 114,18. ⲡⲉⲭⲀ⸗ ⲚⲀ⸗ ⲭⲉ III 92,1.6; 93,24; 95,21; 96,14; 98,9; 100,16; 103,22; 104,4; 105,3; 108,16; 112,20; 114,8.12. BG 79,14; 82,19; 89,20; 93,12; 98,7; 100,3; 106,10; 107,13; 114,13; 117,12.17.

ⲣⲟ m.: ⲕⲀⲣⲱϥ m. BG 113,16; 123,13; 124,1. ⲣⲀ- in fractions: III 78,19 twice.20 twice.21 twice.<22>.

ⲣⲱⲙⲉ m. V 1,[4]; 2,8; 3,22.[24]; 6,[2].20. III 70,3; 71,13; 72,4.5; 74,5; 76,23; 77,23; 92,8; 93,8.24; 98,7; 99,22; 100,18; 101,7.9; 104,1; 105,5. BG 81,14; 82,18; 84,15.16; 89,18; 92,9; 93,15; 98,11; 100,6; 108,9. ⲁⲑⲀⲚⲀⲧⲟⲥ Ⲛ̄ⲣⲱⲙⲉ III 77,10; 83,20; 85,10.21; 88,6; 89,8; 101,20; 112,7; 113,13. ⲁⲧⲙⲟⲩ Ⲛ̄ⲣⲱⲙⲉ BG 94,12; 95,5; 113,14; 121,2. ⲣⲱⲙⲉ Ⲛ̄(Ⲛ)ⲁⲧⲙⲟⲩ V 6,15; 7,[25]; 8,18.[28]; 12,[4]; 13,[8].[21]; 15,[20]; 16,17. BG 109,5; 115,18; 121,14. ⲣⲱⲙⲉ ⲡ- ⲟⲅ Ⲛ̄ⲀⲩⲧⲟⲡⲀⲧⲱⲣ III 77,14;

102,1. BG 95,9. ϣⲣⲡ̅ ⲛ̅ⲣⲱⲙⲉ BG 96,12. ⳅⲟⲩⲉⲓⲧ ⲛ̅ⲣⲱⲙⲉ III 78,[3].23;
102,20; 104,6. BG 94,9; 98,16. ⳅⲟⲩⲉⲓⲧ ⲛ̅ⲣⲱⲙⲉ ⲛ̅ⲛⲁⲑⲁⲛⲁⲧⲟⲥ BG
94,9. ⲣⲙ̅ⲙⲁⲟ m.: ⲙⲛ̅ⲧⲣⲙ̅ⲙⲁⲟ III 97,2; 118,[10].[14]. BG 88,1; 125,3.8.
See further ϣⲏⲣⲉ, ⳅⲱⲧⲃ̅.

ⲣⲟⲙⲡⲉ f. V 12,8.14. III 84,[1].<5>.

ⲣⲁⲛ m. V 4,15; 6,16; 10,[8].11.17.[25]; 11,[5].15; 14,[10].[27]. III 72,1.2;
76,24; 77,3; 82,[1].3.12.18; 85,5; 86,16; 87,8; 94,22.23; 102,4;
104,14.16; 106,19.22; 111,11; 112,3. BG 84,11.12; 95,12; 99,6.10;
110,9; 112,2; 113,9; 124,11. ⲣⲉⲛ III 118,4. † ⲣⲁⲛ ⲉ- (ⲉⲣⲟ⳽) V
8,13.[16]; 14,[3].[19]; 15,[20]. III 87,2; 88,1; 103,19; 111,4. BG 104,7;
111,9. † ⲣⲁⲛ ⲉ- (ⲉⲣⲟ⳽) ⲭⲉ V 4,9.[19]; 5,[3].7; 6,[5].[9].[19].[32];
8,[29]; 9,[1].[22]; 10,12; 13,[3]; 14,[8].[23]; 15,[21]. III 107,11; 111,15.
† ⲣⲁⲛ ⲛⲁ⳽ BG 98,4. † ⲣⲁⲛ ⲭⲉ V 14,11.15. † ⲡⲛ̅⳽ ⲭⲉ III 78,1; 85,4;
86,13; 87,4; 88,8; 111,7.8. † ⲡⲓⲛ⳽ III 86,9. † ⲡⲓⲛ⳽ ⲭⲉ III 87,11. ⲭⲓ ⲣⲁⲛ
BG 120,8. ⲁⲧ† ⲣⲁⲛ ⲉⲣⲟ⳽ III 72,3. ⲁⲧ† ⲣⲁⲛ ⲛⲁ⳽ BG 84,13.

ⲣ̅ⲡⲉ m. III 88,16; 112,16. BG 114,8.

ⲣ̅ⲣⲟ m.: ⲣ̅ⲣⲟ ⲛ̅ⲛⲉⲣⲱⲟⲩ BG 96,11. ⲣ̅ⲣⲟ ⲛ̅ⲣ̅ⲣⲱⲟⲩ III 78,2; 102,19. ⲣ̅ⲣⲟ ⲛ̅ⲧⲉ
ⲛⲓⲣ̅ⲣⲱⲟⲩ V 7,[2]. ⲙⲛ̅ⲧⲣ̅ⲣⲟ V 6,[17].[30]; 8,21; 9,[26]. III 77,13;
78,[1]; 81,12; 85,23; 101,22; 102,17; 105,19; 112,13. BG 95,7; 96,8;
109,7; 114,5. ⲙⲛ̅ⲧⲉⲣⲟ BG 100,16; 101,6. ⲙⲛ̅ⲧⲣ̅ⲣⲱⲟⲩ pl. V 5,[5];
13,[23]. III 88,14. ⲙⲛ̅ⲧⲣ̅ⲣⲁⲓ̈ pl. III 75,19. ⲣ̅ ⲣⲣⲟ ⲉⳅⲣⲁⲓ̈ ⲉⲭⲛ̅- (ⲉⲭⲱ⳽)
V 6,[25]. III 77,18. BG 95,15. ⲣ̅ ⲣ̅ⲣⲟ ⲉⲭⲛ̅- III 102,6. ⲁⲧⲣ̅ ⲣ̅ⲣⲟ ⲉⳅⲣⲁⲓ̈
ⲉⲭⲱ⳽ V 5,[4].[6]; 13,16. ⲙⲛ̅ ⲙⲛ̅ⲧⲣ̅ⲣⲟ ⳅⲓⲭⲱ⳽ III 75,18.20; 85,16;
99,19.23; 118,[15]. BG 92,6.11; 108,13; 125,8.

ⲣⲟⲉⲓⲥ v. BG 89,8. ⲣⲏⲥ† III 97,23.

ⲣⲟⲟⲩϣ m. V 1,[11].

ⲣⲁϣⲉ v.: ⲣⲁϣⲉ ⳅⲛ̅- V 5,14. III 70,2; 76,5; 100,10; 105,17. BG 93,4. ⲣⲉϣⲉ
ⳅⲛ̅- BG 101,3. ⲣⲁϣⲉ m. V 8,20; 9,[27]. III 76,2.5; 81,14.16; 89,19;
90,10; 91,2; 100,7.10; 105,22; 113,22; 117,6. BG 78,2; 93,1.4; 101,10;
116,15; 122,16; 127,3. ⲣⲉϣⲉ V 5,11.

ⲥⲁ m. III 72,12; 95,6. BG 85,7. ⲛ̅ⲥⲁ (ⲛ̅)ⲃⲟⲗ ⲛ̅- (ⲙ̅ⲙⲟ⳽) V 2,[4]. III
119,[10]. BG 121,17. ⲙⲛ̅ⲛ̅ⲥⲁ- (-ⲥⲱ⳽) V 4,[29].[31]; 6,18; 8,6.27;
10,[2]. III 75,12; 90,14; 99,13. BG 77,9; 91,17. See further ⳅⲣⲁⲓ̈.

ⲥⲁⲃⲉ m. V 1,10. BG 80,12. ⲥⲁⲃⲉⲉⲩⲉ pl. III 70,8; 92,14. ⲙⲛ̅ⲧⲥⲁⲃⲉ V
15,[5]. III 111,17.18; BG 86,19; 112,13. ⲙⲛ̅ⲧⲥⲁⲃⲏ III 93,15. ⲥⲃⲱ f. V
3,12; 7,[8]; 8,[4] twice; 11,18; 15,6. ⲥⲃⲟⲟⲩⲉ pl. V 7,[27]; 11,11.12.
ⲁⲧ† ⲥⲃⲱ III 90,7. ⲁⲧ† ⲥⲃⲱ ⲛⲁ⳽ V 17,[12].

ⲥⲱⲃⲉ v. III 92,1. BG 79,14.

ⲥⲱⲗⲡ v. III 107,15. BG 104,11.

ⲥⲙⲏ f. V 2,4.[4]. III 70,23; 71,7.9; 93,5. BG 81,13.

ⲥⲙⲟⲩ v.: ⲥⲙⲟⲩ ⲉⲣⲟ⳽ ⲭⲉ BG 96,9.

ⲥⲙⲟⲧ m. V 1,14; 2,[22]; 4,[19].[22]; 7,23; 16,[19]. III 78,22; 89,<12>;
91,14. BG 79,1. ⲭⲓ ⲥⲙⲟⲧ ⲙ̅ⲙⲟ⳽ III 113,14.

ⲥⲟⲛ m. III 77,6.

ⲥⲟⲟⲛⲉ m. III 101,15; 107,[16]. BG 94,18; 121,16. ⲥⲟⲛⲉ BG 104,12; 121,3.

ⲥⲱⲛⲧ̄ v.: ⲥⲱⲛⲧ̄ ⲛⲁⲍ V 6,[26]. III 77,19; 102,8. BG 95,17. ⲥⲟⲛⲧⲍ V 8,<10>. III 103,13. BG 97,16. ⲥⲱⲛⲧ̄ nn. V 2,[19]. III 72,2.5; 77,19; 94,23; 102,7. BG 84,<12>.17; 95,16.

ⲥⲛⲁⲩ cardinal number III 117,2. BG 122,10. ⲙⲉⲍⲥⲛⲁⲩ V 10,19; 14,[6]. III 82,13; 85,11; 86,12. BG 108,8; 110,<4>. ⲙⲉⲍⲥⲛ̄ⲧⲉ III 82,20. ⲙⲁⲍⲥⲛⲁⲩ V 13,9. ⲓ̄ⲃ̄ V 11,20. See further ⲙⲏⲧ, ⲥⲁⲱϥ.

ⲥⲱⲛⲍ m. III 107,5.14. BG 104,<11>. ⲥⲛⲟⲟⲩⲍ pl. BG 121,16.

ⲥⲟⲡ m. ⲍⲓⲟⲩⲥⲟⲡ III 91,2.

ⲥⲉⲉⲡⲉ m.: ⲕⲉⲥⲉⲉⲡⲉ BG 97,8.

ⲥⲱⲣⲙ̄ v. V 3,[22]. III 98,8. BG 89,18.

ⲥⲱⲧⲙ̄ v. III 97,22; 98,21.22; 105,10.11. BG 89,5; 90,14 twice; 100,11.12; 107,19; 108,1. ⲥⲱⲧⲙ̄ ⲉ- (ⲉⲣⲟⲍ) V 8,24; 16,[3]. III 97,21. BG 89,6. ⲥⲱⲧⲉⲙ ⲉⲣⲟⲍ V 5,17. ⲥⲟⲧⲙⲉⲍ III 76,8; 81,18; 100,13; 106,1. BG 93,9; 101,16.

ⲥⲱⲧⲡ v.: ⲥⲁⲧⲡ⁺ ⲉ- V 2,[23]. III 72,11. ⲥⲟⲧⲡ⁺ ⲉ- III 95,5. BG 85,6.

ⲥⲟⲟⲩ cardinal number V 11,[26]. III 82,9. ⲥⲟⲟⲩ ⲥⲟⲟⲩ V 11,[26]. ⲥⲟⲉ ⲥⲟⲉ III 84,18. ⲥⲟ ⲥⲟ V 11,[28]. ⲋ̄ⲋ̄ III 83,<13>.<14>. ⲙⲉⲍⲥⲟⲟⲩ V 10,[23]. III 82,17. ⲙⲉⲍⲥⲟⲉ III 83,[1]. ⲙⲉⲍⲥⲟ V 11,[3]. ⲁⲛⲥⲟⲟⲩ V 10,[15]. ⲁⲛⲥⲟ V 11,[23].

ⲥⲟⲟⲩⲛ v. V 4,15. III 93,17. BG 82,10. ⲥⲟⲟⲩⲛ ⲛ̄- (ⲙ̄ⲙⲟⲍ) V 3,[23]; 6,[12]. III 93,10; 117,8.[12].15.22. BG 81,19; 89,19; 123,2.7.11; 124,1. ⲥⲟⲩⲛ̄- III 74,6; 98,8.11; 108,4. ⲥⲟⲩⲱⲛ- BG 90,2; 100,8; 105,13. ⲥⲟⲩⲱⲛⲍ V 2,10; 5,18; 8,[25]; 17,[4]. III 71,15; 94,6. BG 83,7.12. ⲥⲟⲟⲩⲛ m. III 74,20; 76,13; 90,10; 93,18; 117,23. BG 82,11; 123,3; 124,3. ⲱ(ⲟ)ⲣⲡ̄ ⲛ̄ⲥⲟⲟⲩⲛ III 96,12. BG 87,6. ⲍⲟⲩⲉⲓⲧ ⲛ̄ⲥⲟⲟⲩⲛ III 73,15. ⲁⲧⲥⲟⲩⲱⲛⲍ V 5,9. ⲙⲛ̄ⲧⲁⲧⲥⲟⲟⲩⲛ III 107,10. BG 104,6.

ⲥⲟⲩⲥⲟⲩ m. V 12,21. III 84,11.

ⲥⲁⲱϥ cardinal number: ⲥⲁⲱϥⲉ III 90,17. BG 77,13. ⲱϥⲉⲥⲛⲟⲟⲩⲥ III 83,14.15; 84,20 twice. ⲙⲉⲍⲥⲁⲱϥⲉ BG 109,1. ⲁⲛⲱϥⲉⲥⲛⲟⲟⲩⲥ V 11,[29]. ⲟ̄ⲃ̄ V 12,27.

ⲥⲱⲱϥ v.: ⲥⲟⲟϥ⁺ III 93,14.

ⲥⲱⲟⲩⲍ v. V 14,14. III 86,21; 91,2. ⲥⲱⲟⲩⲍ ⲉⲍⲟⲩⲛ BG 111,[1].

ⲥⲟⲟⲍⲉ v.: ⲥⲟⲟⲍⲉ ⲙ̄ⲙⲟⲍ ⲉⲃⲟⲗ ⲍⲛ̄- BG 126,1. ⲥⲁⲍⲉ- ⲉⲃⲟⲗ ⲛ̄- III 108,9. BG 106,1. ⲥⲁⲍⲱⲍ ⲛ̄- III 118,23.

ⲥⲍⲓⲙⲉ f. and adj. V 14,[22].[24].[27]. III 87,4.5.7; 90,18; 104,17; 106,22; 111,6.8.10. BG 77,13; 107,13; 111,15.18; 118,16. ⲍⲓⲟⲙⲉ pl. V 11,[27]. III 82,19; 83,14. ⲙⲛ̄ⲧⲥⲍⲓⲙⲉ V 6,[7]; 9,[3]; 10,[11].[25]; 13,7. III 77,[3]; 82,4; 85,9. BG 99,10; 103,6; 111,12. See further ⲍⲟⲟⲩⲧ.

ⲥⲟϭ m.: ⲙⲛ̄ⲧⲥⲟϭ III 71,4.

ⲧⲁⲉⲓⲟ m. III 117,[7]. ⲧⲁⲓ̈ⲟ BG 122,18.

† v.: †- III 107,17; 117,3. BG 104,14; 122,12. † ⲛ̄- (ⲛⲁⲍ) V 6,[24]; 8,[11].14; 13,[24]. III 77,17; 85,24; 93,19; 102,5; 119,4. BG 95,14;

109,8; 126,12. † ⲙ̄ⲙⲟⲋ ⲛⲁⲋ III 91,22. BG 79,11. † ⲛ̄ⲙⲙⲁⲋ III 77,7.8.
BG 118,17. † ⲟⲩⲃⲉ- III 74,9. † ⲉⲍⲣⲁⲓ̈ ⲉⲭⲱⲋ V 6,14. ⲧⲁⲁⲋ ⲛⲁⲋ V
11,[5]. BG 82,11. ⲧⲟ⁺ ⲛⲁⲋ III 93,17. BG 82,9. ⲡⲉⲩ† III 97,[1]. BG
87,19. See further ⲉⲓⲛⲉ , ⲙⲁⲧⲉ, ⲡⲉⲓ, ⲣⲁⲛ, ⲥⲁⲃⲉ, ⲧⲟⲛⲧⲛ̄, ⲟⲩⲱ, ⲱⲡ,
ⲱⲓ.

ⲧⲃⲁ cardinal number V 6,[27]; 16,[7]. III 77,21; 81,[2]; 88,22; 102,10; 113,4.
BG 95,19; 115,6. ⲁⲛⲧⲃⲁ V 7,23.[29]; 9,[12]. <ⲣⲁ>ⲧⲃⲁ III 78,22.

ⲧⲃ̄ⲃⲟ v.: ⲧⲟⲩⲃⲏⲟⲩ⁺ III 90,11. ⲧⲃ̄ⲃⲏⲟⲩⲧ⁺ V 17,15.

ⲧⲁⲕⲟ v. III 71,21; 73,22; 74,2; 94,18; 98,[2].5. BG 84,6; 89,11.14. ⲧⲁⲕⲟ
m. V 3,16. III 73,22.23; 98,2.4. BG 89,11.12. ⲁⲧⲧⲁⲕⲟ V 5,10; 8,20. III
81,18; 98,6; 105,25. BG 85,10; 89,3.6.15; 101,15; 114,2; 127,10.
ⲙⲛ̄ⲧⲁⲧⲧⲁⲕⲟ III 98,5. BG 88,11.16; 89,14.17; 92,18; 97,3.

ⲧⲉⲗⲏⲗ v.: ⲧⲉⲗⲏⲗ refl. V 8,22. ⲧⲉⲗⲏⲗ m. V 5,15; 8,23. III 76,7; 81,15;
89,20; 100,12; 105,24; 113,24; 119,[12]. BG 93,7; 101,12; 116,16.

ⲧⲁ̄ⲧⲁ̄ v.: ⲧⲁ̄†ⲗⲉ m. or f. III 107,1.18; BG 103,13; 104,15; 119,6.12.17.

ⲧⲁⲙⲓⲟ v. III 113,5; 114,21. BG 115,8; 116,8; 118,8. ⲧⲁⲙⲓⲟ ⲛⲁⲋ V
9,9.[11]; 12,[22]; 16,[5]. III 77,16; 81,[1]; 84,13; 102,3; 104,23; 112,12;
113,3. BG 95,11; 99,18; 107,3; 114,[3]; 115,4. ⲧⲁⲙⲓⲟ m. III 113,17.

ⲧⲁⲙⲟ v.: ⲧⲁⲙⲉ- BG 82,1. ⲧⲁⲙⲟⲋ V 4,[5]. ⲙⲁⲧⲁⲙⲟ imperat. III 94,3. BG
83,3. ⲙⲁⲧⲁⲙⲟⲋ ⲭⲉ III 106,10.

ⲧⲙⲁ(ⲉ)ⲓⲟ v.: ⲧⲙⲁⲉⲓⲉ- III 107,24. ⲧⲙⲁⲓ̈ⲉ- BG 105,6.

ⲧⲱⲛ interrog. adv. III 114,11. BG 117,15. ⲉⲧⲱⲛ III 114,11. BG 117,16.

ⲧⲁⲛⲟ v. III 86,[2].

ⲧⲛ̄ⲛⲟⲟⲩ v.: ⲧⲛ̄ⲛⲟⲟⲩ ⲉ- III 107,2. ⲧⲛ̄ⲛⲟⲟⲩⲋ III 93,22; 101,13; 108,7;
118,17. BG 82,16; 105,17; 125,12. ⲧⲛ̄ⲛⲟⲟⲩⲋ ⲍⲓⲧⲛ̄- III 107,19; 108,6.
ⲧⲛ̄ⲛⲟⲟⲩ ⲉⲃⲟⲗ ⲍⲓⲧⲛ̄- (ⲍⲓⲧⲟⲟ ⲧⲋ) BG 103,11; 104,16; 105,15.

ⲧⲟⲛⲧⲛ̄ v.: † ⲧⲟⲛⲧⲛ̄ BG 80,15. † ⲧⲁⲛⲧⲛ̄ III 92,16. † ⲧⲁⲛⲧⲛ̄ ⲉ- III 70,10.
ⲧⲟⲛⲧⲛ̄ m. BG 80,16. ⲧⲁⲛⲧⲛ̄ III 70,11; 92,17.

ⲧⲏⲣⲋ adj. V 1,4; 3,[8].14.15 twice; 5,[6].13; 6,8; 7,17; 8,7.8.[18].22;
9,13.[26]; 10,19.[23]; 12,[29]; 13,[5].24; 14,14.[27].28; 15,17.18.22;
16,[4].[25]; 17,[5].[8].[11]. III 70,15; 73,9.12.14; 75,20; 76,3.10; 77,19;
81,3.20; 83,19; 84,18.23; 85,6; 87,8; 88,[2].3.5.14; 89,15; 90,2.4.9;
91,23; 92,8.21; 96,4.8.10; 99,15.23; 100,8; 103,12.15; 105,20; 106,25;
107,8; 111,11; 112,3.6.11.17; 113,20; 114,3.5 twice; 118,5.13; 119,[11].
BG 79,13; 80,5; 81,3; 86,17; 87,1.5; 92,2; 93,2.11; 97,14.16.18; 100,16;
101,10; 102,6; 104,3; 107,9; 109,10; 112,[1].2; 113,9; 114,1.10; 117,7;
120,8; 122,4; 124,12.18; 125,6. ⲡⲧⲏⲣϥ̄ V 3,8; 5,24. III 72,11; 73,7
twice.13; 76,15; 91,4; 92,5; 95,5; 96,2.9; 100,22; 114,15. BG 78,4; 80,2;
85,6; 86,14 twice; 87,3; 93,19. ⲛⲓⲧⲏⲣⲟ ⲩ V 10,[10]. See further ⲉⲓⲱⲧ,
ⲙⲁⲁⲩ, ⲛⲟⲩⲧⲉ, ⲭⲟⲉⲓⲥ .

ⲧⲱⲣⲉ f. occurring in the following prepositions: ⲛ̄ⲧⲛ̄- III 84,5; 85,16.18.
ⲍⲓⲧⲛ̄- III 71,8; 92,20; 101,12.18; 104,23; 106,13; 112,18. BG 81,3; 95,3;
119,19; 123,13. ⲍⲁⲧⲛ̄- V 1,[20]. BG 106,6. ⲍⲓⲧⲟ (ⲟ)ⲧⲋ V 1,[19]. III
70,19; 72,13; 92,24; 95,7; 97,5; 99,7; 104,9; 107,7; 114,16; 117,17. BG
81,7; 99,17; 120,11. ⲉⲃⲟⲗ ⲍⲓⲧⲛ̄- V 2,[3]; 3,10.[31]. III 93,7; 101,9;

111,9. BG 81,14; 94,11.15; 95,4; 113,<16>. ⲉⲃⲟⲗ ⲍⲓⲧⲟ (ⲟ)ⲧϥ V 1,[14];
4,[12]. III 70,14; 71,1; 76,13; 77,9.23; 93,12; 94,3.11; 107,2.5.[17].21.
BG 82,3; 83,3.14.18; 85,8; 88,3.14; 103,16; 104,14; 105,2; 107,10.

ⲧⲥⲁⲃⲟ v.: ⲧⲥⲁⲃⲉ- ⲉ- BG 102,5; 121,14; 126,3. ⲧⲥⲉⲃⲉ- ⲉ- BG 87,14;
124,10. ⲧⲥⲁⲃⲟϥ ⲉⲣⲟϥ III 91,18. BG 79,6. ⲧⲥⲁⲃⲟϥ ⲭⲉ III 74,17.
ⲙⲁⲧⲥⲁⲃⲟϥ imperat. BG 102,8. ⲙⲁⲧⲥⲁⲃⲟϥ ⲉⲣⲟϥ BG 100,6.

ⲧⲥⲁⲛⲟ v. V 16,[21]. III 89,12; 108,[25]. ⲧⲥⲁⲛⲟ ⲛ̄- (ⲛⲁϥ) III 88,12.21.

ϯⲟⲩ cardinal number V 12,[28]. III 83,17. ϯⲟⲩ ϯⲟⲩ III 84,23. ⲙⲉⲍϯⲟⲩ V
10,[23]. III 82,16. ⲙⲉⲍϯⲉ V 11,[2]. III 82,24.

ⲧⲟⲟⲩ m. III 90,19; 91,18. BG 77,16; 79,7.

ⲧⲁ(ⲟ)ⲩⲟ v.: ⲧⲁⲟⲩⲟϥ BG 94,16.

ⲧⲱⲟⲩⲛ v.: ⲧⲱⲟⲩⲛ ⲙ̄ⲙⲟϥ III 90,7. ⲧⲱⲟⲩⲛ ⲍⲁⲣⲟϥ BG 79,3. ⲧⲱⲟⲩⲛ
ⲉⲃⲟⲗ ⲍⲛ̄- III 90,15. BG 77,9; 122,4.

ⲧⲟⲩⲛⲟⲥ v. BG 126,11. ⲧⲟⲩⲛⲟⲥϥ III 107,16. BG 104,13. ⲙⲁⲧⲟⲩⲛⲟⲥϥ
imperat. III 119,4.

ⲧⲱϣ v. V 2,[11]. ⲧⲟϣϥ ⲉ- III 101,17. BG 95,1.

ⲧⲁϣⲉ-: See ⲟⲉⲓϣ.

ⲧⲁⲍⲟ v.: ⲧⲁⲍⲉ- III 70,11; 92,17. BG 80,17. ⲁⲧⲧⲁⲍⲟϥ III 72,14; 95,8. BG
85,11. ⲧⲁⲍⲟ m.: ⲧⲉⲍⲟ ⲉⲣⲁⲧϥ V 1,12.

ⲑⲃ̄ⲃⲓⲟ v. BG 122,2; 126,8. ⲙⲁⲑⲃⲉⲓⲟ imperat. III 119,2.

ⲧⲁⲭⲟ nn.: ⲧⲁⲭⲟ ⲛⲁϥ BG 119,13; 121,2.

ⲧⲁϭⲥⲉ f.: ⲁⲧϭⲓ ⲧⲁϭⲥⲉ ⲛ̄ⲥⲱϥ BG 86,1; 125,3. ⲙ̄ⲛⲧⲁⲧϭⲓ ⲧⲁϭⲥⲉ ⲛ̄ⲥⲱϥ
BG 118,6. Cf. ϭⲉⲭⲙ̄, with which ⲧⲁϭⲥⲉ is parallel.

ⲟⲩ interrog. pron. V 4,16. III 92,3; 114,12. BG 79,18; 117,17. See further
ⲉⲧⲃⲉ-.

ⲟⲩⲁ cardinal number and indef. pron. V 14,14.15. III 72,15.16.18; 74,12;
86,19; 117,2. BG 81,11; 85,12; 110,15. ⲟⲩⲉ̂ⲓ III 70,24; 71,<5>; 93,6.
ⲟⲩⲉⲓⲉ BG 82,8. ⲟⲩⲁ ⲛⲓⲙ III 71,23. ⲡⲟⲩⲁ ⲡⲟⲩⲁ V 12,[26]; 14,10. III
84,19; 86,15; 88,13; 112,14. BG 110,8; 114,5. ⲧⲟⲩⲉⲓ ⲧⲟⲩⲉⲓ V
11,[24]. III 83,16. ⲙ̄ⲛⲧⲟⲩⲁ V 14,[9]. III 86,14.21; 111,1. BG 110,6. ⲣ̄
ⲟⲩⲁ BG 111,[1]. See further ⲕⲉ-, ⲟⲩⲱⲧ.

ⲟⲩⲁⲁϥ refl. adj. V 1,[19]; 2,13.22; 5,9.20.22; 6,7; 8,[30]. III 71,18; 72,13.
BG 83,13. ⲟⲩⲁⲁⲧϥ III 94,10; 95,7.14; 97,7. ⲟⲩⲁⲉⲧϥ V 16,13. ⲙⲁⲩⲁⲁϥ
BG 85,9.18; 88,6. See further ⲉⲓⲱⲧ.

ⲟⲩⲱ nn.: ϯ ⲟⲩⲱ ⲉⲃⲟⲗ V 5,[26].

ⲟⲩⲟⲉⲓⲛ m. V 4,[25]; 5,[28]; 6,[1].[3]; 9,16.[24].[25]; 16,[10]. III 76,18.22;
81,6.12.24; 86,7; 89,2.18; 91,13; 93,9; 94,13; 99,11; 101,2.6; 102,11;
105,2.13.14; 106,7.18; 107,1.[14]; 108,4.8; 113,7.21; 114,8; 117,17.21.
BG 78,17; 94,3.7; 103,[1]; 105,14; 117,11; 119,6; 120,5. ⲟⲩⲟⲉ̈ⲓⲛ BG
81,18; 83,16; 91,15; 96,2; 100,[2].14.15.17; 102,4; 103,14; 104,10;
105,18; 108,11; 109,18; 115,9; 116,13; 119,4; 123,12.19. ⲣ̄ ⲟⲩⲟⲉⲓⲛ V
5,[29]; 6,[1]. III 76,18; 89,18; 101,2; 105,14; 113,21; 114,7. BG 94,3. ⲣ̄
ⲟⲩⲟⲉ̈ⲓⲛ BG 100,17; 116,14; 117,10. See further ϣⲏⲣⲉ.

ⲟⲩⲟⲛ (affirmation of existence): ⲟⲩⲛ̄- V 6,23. III 73,18; 74,12; 78,12;

84,18.23; 97,18. ογⲛ̄- ⲙ̄ⲙⲟⲋ III 97,21. BG 90,13. ογⲛ̄ⲧⲉ- V 14,[9];
15,[18]. ογⲛ̄ⲧⲉ- ⲙ̄ⲙⲁγ III 86,14. ογⲛ̄ⲧ(ⲉ)ⲋ III 72,1.4; 88,4; 98,21.
BG 84,17; 99,16; 100,10; 107,18; 113,12; 114,[2]. ογⲛ̄ⲧ(ⲉ)ⲋ ⲙ̄ⲙⲁγ III
105,9. BG 89,4. ογⲛ̄ⲧⲁⲋ V 2,[22]; 5,13; 6,13; 7,[6]; 9,[7]; 11,[4].15;
12,[28]; 16,[18]; 17,16. III 71,21.23.24; 72,6; 78,5; 88,11; 94,18.20.
21.23.24; 104,22; 112,5.11. BG 84,5.8.9.11.15; 110,8. ογⲛ̄ⲧⲁⲋ ⲙ̄ⲙⲁγ
III 96,22; 102,20. BG 87,17; 96,12. See further ϭⲟⲙ.
ογⲟⲛ indef. pron. III 70,22; 93,4. ογⲟⲛ ⲙ̄ⲙⲟⲋ BG 81,16. ογⲟⲛ ⲛⲓⲙ V
2,[5].[23].[24]; 17,15. III 71,11.20; 85,24; 94,17.20; 118,24. BG 84,4.7;
103,10; 126,4. ογⲁⲛ ⲛⲓⲙ III 71,23.
ογⲛⲟγ f. V 12,20. ογⲛⲟⲟγⲉ pl. III 84,11. ⲛ̄ⲧⲉγⲛⲟγ V 16,14. III 76,21;
89,5; 101,6. BG 94,7; 115,14. ⲛ̄ⲧⲟγⲛⲟγ V 6,[2]. ⲧⲉⲛⲟγ III 70,5;
92,10; 94,9.13; 100,16; 106,2. BG 80,8; 83,12.17; 93,12; 101,17. †ⲛⲟγ
V 1,6.
ογⲱⲛ(ⲉ)ⲍ v. V 6,[3]; 9,[33]. III 73,4; 76,15; 82,9; 83,3; 87,10.16.23; 91,10;
95,20; 99,20; 100,22; 101,7; 103,17; 108,10.24; 112,2. BG 86,7; 93,18;
101,17; 106,3; 107,1; 118,<15>; 119,11. ογⲟⲛ̄ⲍⲋ V 12,[2]. BG 97,14.
ογⲟⲛ̄ⲍ† V 3,[6]; 4,[3].[4].[6].7. BG 86,11; 109,9. ογⲁⲛ̄ⲍ† III 73,17;
97,17; 98,14. ογⲱⲛ̄ⲍ ⲉ- (ⲉⲣⲟⲋ) III 81,19. BG 78,11. ογⲱⲛ̄ⲍ ⲛⲁⲋ
ⲉⲃⲟⲗ III 98,16; 118,[17]. BG 90,8. ογⲟⲛⲍⲋ ⲛⲁⲋ ⲉⲃⲟⲗ BG 114,15.
ογⲱⲛ̄ⲍ ⲉⲃⲟⲗ V 3,5; 4,[18].[22].[29]; 5,[24]; 6,15.21; 8,[1].[7].[9].11.
13.16.[32]; 10,[6].15; 11,[8].23.[30]; 12,12.16.22.[27]; 13,[6].[20].
[21].[25]; 14,13.18.[25]; 15,[4].[6].[8].10.12.14. III 71,9; 75,5.12; 76,23;
77,11.15; 81,23; 83,13.16; 84,7.12.21; 85,[2].8.20.22; 86,[1].5.18;
87,6.13.18.20.22; 90,8; 95,22; 96,17; 97,[2]; 98,25; 99,3.6.13; 100,19;
101,20; 102,2; 103,11.14; 104,11; 106,2.17; 107,23;
111,9.13.17.18.20.22.24; 114,20; 118,[8]. BG 86,10; 87,11.20; 88,13;
91,1.6.18; 93,14; 95,6.10; 97,16; 98,[1]; 99,3; 102,18; 105,5; 107,11;
108,7; 109,5.15; 110,14; 112,6.11.14.16; 113,[1].[5].7; 118,[5]; 119,18;
124,17. ογⲱⲛ̄ⲍ ⲉⲃⲟⲗ ⲉ- III 111,3. ογⲱⲛ̄ⲍ ⲉⲃⲟⲗ ⲛ̄- (ⲛⲁⲋ) III
107,<7>. BG 104,[2]; 125,13. ογⲱⲛ̄ⲍ ⲉⲃⲟⲗ ⲍⲛ̄- (ⲛ̄ⲍⲏⲧⲋ) V 7,[3]. BG
92,8; 94,8; 97,12; 109,2. ογⲱⲛ̄ⲍ ⲉⲃⲟⲗ ⲍⲓⲧⲛ̄- III 97,13. ογⲱⲛⲍ- ⲉⲃⲟⲗ
BG 118,4. ογⲟⲛⲍⲋ ⲉⲃⲟⲗ V 8,[8]. III 87,[1]; 103,11. BG 91,8; 110,15;
111,8.17. ογⲟⲛ̄ⲍ† ⲉⲃⲟⲗ III 74,18; 98,18.19. BG 88,19; 90,6.11.
ογⲁⲛ̄ⲍ† ⲉⲃⲟⲗ III 73,4; 74,16.19; 75,[1]; 95,23. ογⲱⲛ̄ⲍ ⲉⲃⲟⲗ m. III
106,10; 113,20. BG 102,<9>; 116,12. ⲁⲧογⲱⲛ̄ⲍ V 4,[3]. BG 102,10.
ⲁⲧογⲱⲛ̄ⲍ ⲉⲃⲟⲗ III 98,13; 106,12. BG 90,5.10. ⲣ̄ ⲁⲧογⲱⲛ̄ⲍ ⲛ̄ⲥⲁⲃⲟⲗ
ⲛⲁⲋ III 119,[10]. ⲣ̄ ⲁⲧογⲱⲛ̄ⲍ ⲛ̄ⲥⲁ ⲛ̄ⲃⲟⲗ ⲙ̄ⲙⲟⲋ BG 126,[18].
ογⲟⲡ v.: ογⲁⲁⲃ† BG 81,7; 123,3. ⲉⲧογⲁⲁⲃ† V 9,15. III 81,5; 91,5.9;
104,5; 105,15; 112,20; 114,10; 118,5. BG 78,5.10; 98,14; 100,[18];
114,13; 117,14; 124,13.
ογⲏⲣ interrog. pron. III 108,18. BG 106,12; 107,14.
ογⲣⲟⲧ v.: ⲣⲟογⲧ† ⲉⲍⲣⲁï ⲉⲝⲛ̄- III 105,24; 113,25.
ογⲉⲣⲏⲧⲉ f. III 119,[8]. ογⲣⲏⲧⲉ BG 126,16.
ογⲱⲧ adj.: ογⲟⲧⲉ V 17,15. ογⲁ ⲛ̄ογⲱⲧ BG 122,10.

ογτε- prep. III 73,19; 97,19. BG 118,9.10. ογτωϩ III 114,22.23. BG 89,2.

ογ(ω)ωτε v.: ογωτ- v. V 7,14. ογετ- V 7,14.

ογωτb̄ v.: ογατb̄⁺ ε- V 7,16. III 72,10; 86,23; 95,4; 108,18. ογοτb̄ ε- BG 85,4; 106,13; 111,5.

ογοειϣ m. V 4,[26]. BG 121,11. ῆογοειϣ ΝΙΜ V 2,9; 4,16.[27].

ογωϣ v. V 1,3; 3,[29]; 4,14. III 92,7; 100,20; 104,5; 114,13. BG 80,4; 88,3; 93,17; 98,15; 118,[1]. ογεϣ- III 74,13. ογαϣϩ III 86,[2]. ογωϣ m. V 7,7; 11,13.14.[19]; 12,[2]; 16,13. III 83,20; 113,10. BG 104,9; 109,11; 114,11; 120,15. ογωϣε III 89,4; 118,4. BG 103,18; 115,13; 124,12.

ογωϩ v. V 17,16. ογωϩ ετοοτϩ III 97,24. BG 89,8. ογαϩϩ ῆca- BG 118,13. ογΗϩ⁺ ῆcωϩ V 6,[31]. III 78,17.

ογχαι m. III 101,11. BG 94,14.

ογωϭπ v.: ογοϭπϩ III 119,3.

ωβϣ v.: (ε)βϣε f. III 101,12; 107,6; 108,9. BG 94,15; 103,17; 106,2; 120,2; 122,5.

ωΝϩ v.: οΝϩ⁺ BG 120,1. ωΝϩ m. V 14,26. III 87,7; 111,10. BG 111,18.

ωπ v.: Ηπ⁺ ε- III 71,1; 98,19. Ηπ⁺ ϩιτῆ- BG 121,12. πετΗπ⁺ εϣωπε III 70,21; 93,3. BG 118,12. Ηπε f.: Μῆ Ηπε εροϩ III 84,9. Μῆτ(ε)ϩ Ηπε III 75,16; 77,22; 81,2; 86,8; 88,22; 99,17; 102,10; 105,1; 113,4. BG 92,4; 95,19; 99,19; 109,19; 115,6. ατ⁺ Ηπε εροϩ V 5,[2]; 9,12; 12,18; 14,[2]; 16,[7]. Μῆτατ⁺ Ηπε εροϩ V 6,[28]. ατχι Ηπε εροϩ V 4,[1].

ωϣ v.: ωϣ εβολ III 97,19. BG 89,4.

ϣ- v. III 90,6; 91,15; 94,2. BG 79,3; 83,2. Ναϩ ϣ- (non-literary form) III 91,14. BG 79,1. (ῆ)Νεϩ ϣ- V 16,4. III 113,23; 114,2. See further ϭοΜ.

ϣα- prep. V 4,[2]; 8,17. III 70,5; 73,14; 74,15; 86,3; 89,17; 92,10; 94,9; 96,11; 98,14; 100,16; 101,14; 103,21; 106,1. BG 80,8; 83,12; 87,5; 90,5; 93,12; 98,6; 101,16; 109,11. ϣα ϩογΝ ε- V 1,6. ϣαϩρα(ε)ι ε- V 7,19. III 78,19. BG 125,1. See further εΝεϩ, ϩαε.

ϣε cardinal number: ϣμῆτϣεce V 12,13.15.[30]. ϣμ̄τϣεce III 83,18; 84,4.6.24; 85,1.5. αΝϣε V 7,20.21.27. ραϣε III 78,20 twice. αΝ-ϣμῆτϣεce V 12,[1]. τϩ̄ V 13,[4].

ϣι v.: ϣιτϩ III 76,7; 89,24; 100,13. BG 93,8. ατϣιτϩ III 72,21; 95,14; 114,1. BG 85,19; 117,3. ατ⁺ ϣι εροϩ V 5,16; 17,[2].

ϣο cardinal number: αΝϣο V 7,22 twice.[28]. ραϣο III 78,21 twice.

ϣιβε v. III 76,7; 81,15; 89,23; 95,10; 100,12; 105,24. BG 85,15; 93,6; 101,12. ϣοβε⁺ III 103,5. BG 97,4. ϣb̄βιΗογτ V 7,13. ϣιβε m. III 78,13; 97,18; 103,5.20. BG 97,5; 98,5. ατϣιβε V 5,15; 17,[1]. III 72,17; 113,7; 114,1. BG 117,2.

ϣβΗρ m. V 6,[23]. ϣβεερε f. BG 94,19; 96,5. ϣβεερ BG 99,[3].

ϣωκ m. V 6,20.

ϣΜΜο nn. and adj. BG 85,4. ϣΜΜω III 72,9; 95,4.

ϣΜογΝ cardinal number: ΜεϩϣΜογΝε III 85,19; 87,[1]; 111,3; 112,14; 117,[15]; 118,2. BG 123,10; 124,9. ΜαϩϣΜογΝε V 13,[19]. BG 111,7.

ϢΟΜΝ̄Τ cardinal number V 1,14. III 92,19. ϢΟΜΤΕ V 2,[4]. III 70,13.23;
71,7; 93,5. BG 81,12. ϢΟΜΝ̄ΤΕ BG 81,2. ΜΕϨϢΟΜΝ̄Τ V 10,[20]. III
82,14; 86,12.<17>. BG 110,<4>.<11>. ΜΕϨϢΟΜΤΕ III 82,21. ΜΕϨ-
ϢΟΜΕΤ V 14,[7].[11]. ΜΑϨϢΟΜΕΤ V 13,12. See further ϢΕ, ϨΟΟΥΤ.
ϢΜ̄ϢΕ m. V 6,[28]; 9,13; 12,[25]; 16,[8]. III 102,11; 113,5. BG 96,1; 115,7.
ϢΙΝΕ v. BG 105,8. ϢΙΝΕ ΕΤΒΕ- BG 106,16. ϢΙΝΕ Ν̄ϹΑ- (Ν̄ϹΩϤ) V 1,[7].
III 70,6; 92,3.11; 108,21; 112,[23]; 113,1. BG 79,17; 80,9; 114,17;
115,2.
ϢΩΠ v.: ϢΩΠ Ε- (ΕΡΟϤ) Ν̄- V 2,15.[18].[19]. III 89,<10>. BG 121,8. ϢΟΠϤ
ΕΡΟϤ V 17,[10]. III 91,16.
ϢΙΠΕ m.: ΧΙ ϢΙΠΕ BG 122,3.
ϢΩΠΕ v. V 10,3; 16,14. III 76,20; 81,20; 89,5; 90,3; 96,16; 111,10; 112,18;
114,17; 119,[11]. BG 87,4.10; 115,14; 118,16. ϢΟΟΠ⁺ V 4,13; 7,31. III
73,18; 78,10; 103,2. BG 83,6; 89,2; 97,[1]; 102,11. ϢΩΠΕ Ε- V 7,[26].
ϢΩΠΕ ΜΝ̄Ν̄ϹΑ- (-ϹΩϤ) V 7,[5]; 8,[26]; 10,[1]; 17,[5]. III 78,4; 89,11;
97,16; 106,3; 113,16; 114,4.24. BG 88,18; 101,18; 116,5; 117,6; 118,10.
ϢΩΠΕ Ν̄- V 5,[31]; 9,[20]; 11,[27]; 12,[3].5.6.[8].[10].14.19. III 74,2;
81,9; 83,22; 84,1.3.6; 98,6; 101,5; 103,20; 108,1; 117,20. BG 98,5;
104,18; 105,9; 112,1; 118,18; 123,18; 124,7. ϢΩΠΕ Ν̄- Ε- BG 122,9.
ϢΩΠΕ Ν̄- (ΝΑϤ) Ν̄- III 83,21; 84,10; 117,1. ϢΩΠΕ Ν̄ϹΩϤ V 16,[20].
ϢΩΠΕ ϨΝ̄- (Ν̄ϨΗΤϤ). III 87,7; 118,[10]. BG 94,6; 114,10; 120,14; 123,8;
125,2; 127,2. ϢΩΠΕ ϨΑΤΝ̄- V 1,[20].[22]. ϢΟΟΠ⁺ Ν̄- V 3,[14]. BG
89,15. ϢΟΟΠ⁺ ϨΝ̄- (Ν̄ϨΗΤϤ) V 1,12; 2,[7]; 3,7; 5,[27]; 6,24; 7,24. III
71,12; 73,6.15; 95,24. BG 86,12. ϢΩΠΕ ΕΒΟΛ ϨΝ̄ (Ν̄)- V 3,[16]; 7,[30];
8,[27]; 12,[17]; 14,[26]. III 73,21.22.23; 74,3; 84,9; 98,[1].3.4. BG
89,10.12.13. ϢΟΟΠ⁺ ΕΒΟΛ ϨΝ̄- BG 89,16. ΕΤϢΟΟΠ⁺ V 2,8. III 71,13;
94,5; 96,21. BG 83,5; 87,16. ΕΤϢΟΟΠ⁺ ΧΙΝ Ν̄ϢΟΡ(Ε)Π III 117,5;
118,18. BG 91,12; 122,14; 125,14. (Ρ̄) ΑΤϢΩΠΕ V 3,17.[18]; 4,[26].
ΕϢΩΠΕ conj. V 9,[18]. III 74,12. See further ΜΑ, ΩΠ.
ϢΠΗΡΕ nn.: Ρ̄ ϢΠΗΡΕ III 91,23. BG 79,12.
ϢΗΡΕ m. V 1,[1]; 5,[8].12; 7,15 twice; 9,[2].[25]; 12,[7]; 13,12. III 75,22;
78,14 twice; 84,[1]; 100,1; 103,6.<6>; 104,3.13; 108,1.7. BG 97,6.7;
98,12; 99,5; 105,8.16. ϢΗΡΕ Μ̄ΠΝΟΥΤΕ III 100,3; 104,16; 105,22. BG
99,8. ϢΗΡΕ Ν̄ΤΕ ΠΝΟΥΤΕ BG 92,14. ϢΗΡΕ Μ̄Π(Ι)ΡΩΜΕ V 10,[4];
13,[10].13. III 81,13.21; 85,11; 104,2; 105,20; 106,15; 117,[22]; 118,1.
BG 98,11; 101,7; 102,15; 108,2; 124,2.6. ϢΗΡΕ Ν̄ΤΕ ΠΟΥΟ(Ε)ΙΝ III
119,6. BG 126,14. See further ΜΙϹΕ.
ϢΩΡΠ v.: ϢΡ̄Π Ν̄- III 71,8; 78,16. ϢΟΡΠ nn. and adj. V 10,18; 13,[4].[8]. III
77,12; 82,12.19; 91,11; 118,[16]. BG 78,13; 108,1. Ϣ(Ο)Ρ̄Π Ν̄ΧΠΟ V
12,7. III 104,12.20. BG 97,11. ΧΠΟ Ν̄ΤΕ ΠϢΟΡΠ V 10,[22]. Ν̄ϢΟΡ(Ε)Π
adv. V 4,[25]; 6,16; 11,[6]; 12,[25]. III 78,17; 84,14; 101,21; 103,9;
108,25; 111,14; 112,5; 114,6. BG 81,13; 95,6; 97,9; 107,2; 108,19;
113,12; 117,8; 119,5. Ν̄ϢΟΡΠ Ν̄- V 4,[22]. ΧΙΝ Ν̄ϢΟΡ(Ε)Π III
73,<14>; 96,10; 101,17; 117,2. BG 95,2; 122,11. Ρ̄ ϢΟΡΠ Ε- V 4,[24]. Ρ̄
ϢΟΡΠ Ν̄- V 11,7.9.[21]; 13,[1]; 17,8. Ρ̄ ϢΡ̄Π Ν̄- III 70,23; 74,10; 83,3.11;

88,4; 90,5; 93,5; 103,8. BG 107,3; 112,6. See further ⲉⲓⲱⲧ, ⲙⲓⲥⲉ, ⲣⲱⲙⲉ, ⲥⲟⲟⲩⲛ, ϣⲱⲡⲉ.

ϣⲱⲱⲧ v. III 107,20. ϣⲱⲱⲧ m. III 72,23; 95,16; 117,[13].[14]. ⲁⲧϣⲱⲱⲧ III 72,17; 95,11. ϣⲧⲁ m. V 13,[7]. III 108,1. BG 86,2; 105,1.7.9; 107,12; 118,15; 123,8.9. ⲁⲧϣⲧⲁ BG 85,15.

ϣⲟⲩⲟ v.: ϣⲟⲩⲉⲓⲧ⁺ III 71,3.

ϣⲱϣ v.: ϣⲏϣ⁺ III 78,12; 103,4. BG 97,3. ϣⲏϣ⁺ ⲙⲛ̄- (ⲛ̄ⲙ̄ⲙⲁ⸗) V 7,[12]. III 99,12. BG 87,2. ϣⲏϣ⁺ ⲟⲩⲃⲛ- V 4,[28]. III 75,11. BG 91,16. ϣⲏϣ⁺ (ⲍ)ⲛ̄- V 6,10. ϣⲱϣ m. V 4,[23].

ϣϭⲓϭ m. III 70,6; 92,11.

ϣⲁⲭⲉ v.: ϣⲁⲭⲉ ⲉⲣⲟ⸗ III 70,13; 84,13; 89,24; 91,14; 92,19; 108,25; 113,23; 114,2. BG 79,2; 113,11; 117,4. ϣⲁⲭⲉ ⲙ̄ⲙⲟ⸗ V 17,9. ϣⲁⲭⲉ ⲙⲛ̄- (ⲛ̄ⲙ̄ⲙⲁ⸗) III 97,23. BG 89,7. ϣⲁⲭⲉ m. V 3,[30]; 5,[23].[27]; 11,14.20; 15,13.23; 17,[3].11. III 74,9.13; 88,10; 108,4; 112,10. BG 105,14; 113,18. ⲁⲧϣⲁⲭⲉ ⲉⲣⲟ⸗ V 3,[3]; 5,[11].[29]. III 71,14; 76,2.5.19; 81,14.16; 88,19; 89,2.19; 94,5; 100,7.10; 101,3; 105,16.23; 113,7; 117,[6]; 119,[12]. BG 83,6; 93,1.5; 94,4; 101,[1].10; 115,10; 116,15; 122,16; 127,3. ⲁⲧϣⲁⲭⲉ ⲙ̄ⲙⲟ⸗ V 2,[9]; 8,21; 9,[27]; 16,[1].10. ϭⲓⲛϣⲁⲭⲉ III 70,14.

ϣⲟⲭⲛⲉ m. V 3,12.13; 7,8.9.[28]; 8,[5] twice; 11,12.13.19; 15,[9].

ϣⲱⲭⲡ m. V 7,16. III 78,15; 103,7.

ϥⲓ v.: ϥⲓ ⲙⲛ̄- III 106,16.

ϥⲧⲟⲟⲩ cardinal number: ⲙⲉϥⲧⲟⲟⲩ V 10,[21]. III 82,15. ⲙⲉϥⲧⲟⲉ III 82,23.

ⲍⲁ- prep. III 75,10.16; 82,11; 85,6; 86,8; 88,19; 99,17; 119,7. BG 92,3; 109,18. See further ⲧⲱⲣⲉ, ⲍⲏ.

ⲍⲁⲉ nn. BG 109,12. ⲍⲁⲏ III 71,24; 94,21; 103,10. BG 84,9. ⲛ̄ⲍⲁⲉ ⲛ̄- BG 97,11. ϣⲁ ⲍⲁⲉ BG 94,17. ⲁⲧⲣ̄ ⲍⲁⲉ V 4,[13]. ⲁⲧⲣ̄ ⲍⲁⲏ V 14,5.

ⲍⲉ v.: ⲍⲉ ⲉ- (ⲉⲣⲟ⸗) III 70,8; 92,13. BG 80,12; 83,2; 90,11.

ⲍⲉ f. III 92,19. BG 81,2. ⲛ̄ⲑⲉ ⲛ̄- V 3,[24]; III 72,7; 75,4; 78,13; 91,13; 103,5; 106,25. BG 97,5; 103,13. ⲛ̄ⲑⲉ V 4,17; 7,13.17; 11,25; 17,[10]. III 78,6.15; 91,17; 95,1.2; 102,23; 103,7; 117,2. BG 85,1.2; 89,17; 119,4. ⲛ̄ⲧⲍⲉ BG 96,16. ⲛ̄ϯⲍⲉ V 12,[26]; 13,6. BG 115,15. ⲛ̄ⲧⲉ(ⲉ)ⲓⲍⲉ V 12,21; 16,15. III 73,20; 78,24; 85,7; 89,6; 113,11. ⲛ̄ⲧⲉϥⲍⲉ BG 79,5. ⲕⲁⲧⲁ ⲑⲉ V 14,[20]. III 90,6. BG 122,11. See further ⲁϣ.

ⲍⲏ f.: ⲍⲁⲑⲏ ⲛ̄- V 3,4; 5,24. III 73,3; 76,15; 95,22; 100,22. ⲍⲁⲧⲉ⸗ (ⲉ)ⲍⲏ III 75,10; 82,11; 85,6; 99,11. BG 91,15. ⲍⲁⲧⲉⲍⲏ BG 86,10; 93,18.

ⲍⲓ- prep. III 72,12; 77,13; 88,1.[1]; 91,2; 95,6; 97,10; 99,16; 100,7; 101,21.22; 103,23; 105,24; 112,2 twice.3; 113,15. BG 78,2; 79,7; 88,10; 92,18 twice; 95,7; 113,8 twice.9; 116,4. See further ⲧⲱⲣⲉ, ⲭⲱ⸗.

ⲍⲓⲏ f. BG 105,13.

ⲍⲟ m. V 4,[21]. BG 91,12.

ⲋⲱ v.: ⲋⲱ ϣⲁ ⲡⲉ(ⲉ)ⲓⲙⲁ V 3,[25]; III 74,7; 76,11; 90,4. ⲋⲱ ⲉⲣⲟϥ ϣⲁ ⲡⲉⲓ̈ⲙⲁ V 17,7.

ⲋⲱⲱϥ pron. III 105,7. BG 100,7. ⲋⲱϥ III 82,18. ⲋⲱⲧϥ III 99,21.

ⲋⲱⲃ m. III 107,7.15. BG 104,2.12. ⲋⲱⲃ ⲛⲓⲙ III 91,7; 96,20; 113,2. BG 78,7; 115,[3].

ⲋⲁⲉⲓⲃⲉⲥ f.: ⲁⲧⲋⲁ(ⲉ)ⲓⲃⲉⲥ III 81,6; 89,19; 105,16.23. BG 101,[2].11; 115,11; 116,14. ⲁⲧⲋⲁⲉⲓⲃⲉ V 9,[16]. ⲙⲛ̄ⲧϥ ⲋⲁⲉⲓⲃⲉⲥ III 113,22.

ⲋⲱⲃⲥ v.: ⲋⲃ̄ⲥⲱ f. BG 120,16.

ⲋⲕⲟ v.: ⲋⲏⲕⲉ adj.: ⲙⲛ̄ⲧⲋⲏⲕⲉ III 101,15; 102,7; 107,8. BG 94,18; 95,16; 104,[3].

ⲋⲱⲙ v.: ⲋⲱⲙ ⲉⲝⲛ̄- BG 106,9; 126,15. ⲋⲱⲙ ⲉⲋⲣⲁⲓ̈ ⲉⲝⲛ̄- III 108,15; 119,1.7. BG 126,6.

ⲋⲙⲟⲙ v. BG 120,4.

ⲋⲙⲟⲧ m. III 97,12; 117,7. ⲣ̄ ⲋⲙⲟⲧ ⲛⲁϥ V 4,14.

ⲋⲟⲩⲛ m.: ⲉⲋⲟⲩⲛ ⲉ- III 77,22; 81,2; 84,16; 88,23. See further ϣⲁ-.

ⲋⲱⲛ v.: ⲋⲏⲛⲧ ⲉ- III 93,7.

ⲋⲟ(ⲉ)ⲓⲛⲉ indef. pron. V 4,[27]; 9,[5]; 10,[11]. III 88,17; 104,19. ⲋⲟ(ⲉ)ⲓⲛ III 82,6; 106,23. BG 99,13; 103,8. ⲋⲟⲉⲓⲛⲉ ⲛ̄ⲋⲏⲧϥ III 70,16; 92,22. ⲋⲟⲓ̈ⲛ ⲛ̄ⲋⲏⲧϥ BG 81,5. ⲋⲟⲓ̈ⲛⲉ ⲉⲃⲟⲗ ⲛ̄ⲋⲏⲧϥ V 1,[17].

ⲋⲛⲉ- nn. and v.: ⲉⲋⲛⲁϥ ⲉ- III 94,10. ⲉⲧⲉⲋⲛⲉ- III 112,18. ⲉⲧⲉⲋⲛⲉϥ III 107,6.13. ⲉⲧⲉⲋⲛⲁϥ III 114,18. BG 83,14. ⲣ̄ ⲋⲛⲁϥ III 97,5; 114,16.

ⲋⲱⲛⲧ v.: ⲧⲉⲧⲋⲁⲛⲧ III 71,4; 93,16. ⲧⲉⲑⲟⲛⲧ BG 81,11; 82,7.

ⲋⲱⲡ v.: ⲋⲏⲡⲧ V 4,[1]; 6,13. III 74,15. ⲋⲏⲡⲧ ⲛ̄ⲋⲏⲧϥ III 97,3.

ⲋⲣⲁⲓ̈ m.: ⲋⲣⲁⲓ̈ ⲋⲛ̄- (ⲛ̄ⲋⲏⲧϥ) V 4,[4]; 5,13.18. BG 78,14; 91,5; 96,13; 104,9. ⲋⲣⲁⲉⲓ ⲋⲛ̄- BG 106,18. ⲉⲋⲣⲁⲓ̈ ⲉ- V 6,[28]; 9,13; 14,15. ⲉⲋⲣⲁⲓ̈ ⲉⲝⲛ̄- V 7,20.21. III 76,6; 81,17; 89,22. BG 101,14; 117,[1]. ⲛ̄ⲋⲣⲁⲓ̈ ⲋⲛ̄- (ⲛ̄ⲋⲏⲧϥ) V 4,17; 5,[5]; 7,17. III 75,4.18; 84,17; 88,9; 90,2; 99,[3]; 101,18; 102,22. BG 95,2. ⲥⲁ(ⲛ)ⲋⲣⲉ m. V 14,[8]; III 85,19. ⲙ̄ⲡ<ⲥ>ⲁⲋⲣⲉ ⲛ̄- III 86,3. ⲙ̄ⲡⲥⲁⲋⲣⲉ III 107,[12]. See further ϣⲁ-.

ⲋⲁⲣⲉⲋ v.: ⲋⲁⲣⲏⲋ ⲉⲣⲟϥ III 107,4. ⲁⲣⲉⲋ ⲉⲣⲟϥ BG 103,15.

ⲋⲓⲥⲉ m.: ⲋⲓⲥⲉ ⲋⲁⲧⲟⲟⲧⲟⲩ V 16,[11]. ⲋⲓⲥⲉ ⲋⲁⲧⲏ(ⲟ)ⲩ III 89,3; 113,8. BG 115,11.

ⲋⲏⲧ m.: See ⲝⲓⲥⲉ .

ⲋⲟⲧⲉ f.: ⲣ̄ ⲋⲟⲧⲉ III 91,24. BG 79,13. ⲋⲁ ⲋⲟⲧⲉ adj. III 108,13.

ⲋⲱⲧⲃ̄ v.: ⲋⲉⲧⲃ̄ ⲣⲱⲙⲉ V 3,[24].

ⲋⲱⲧⲡ m. V 6,24.

ⲋⲱⲧⲣ̄ m. V 12,[1]. III 83,19.

ⲋⲟⲟⲩ m. V 12,13.20. III 84,<5>; 86,3; 119,13. BG 127,5.

ⲋⲟⲟⲩ v. BG 82,5.

ⲋⲟⲩⲟ m.: ⲛ̄ⲋⲟⲩⲟ V 17,17. III 70,9; 92,14. ⲛ̄ⲋⲟⲩⲟ ⲉ- III 72,10; 114,8. BG 117,11. ⲣ̄ ⲋⲟⲩⲉ- V 3,[19].

ⲋⲟⲩ(ⲉ)ⲓⲧ nn. V 14,6.7. III 76,14; 78,[3].23; 85,9; 86,11.13; 93,21; 94,12; 106,6. BG 82,15; 83,16; 102,4; 109,3; 110,3.5; 125,11. ⲋⲟⲩⲉⲓⲧⲉ V 10,[26]. III 86,10. See further ⲣⲱⲙⲉ, ⲥⲟⲟⲩⲛ.

ⲋⲟⲟⲩⲧ m. and adj. V 10,[8]; 14,[21].[22]. III 82,11; 83,13; 87,3.4; 104,14;

106,19; 111,5.6; 114,18. BG 99,6; 111,13; 120,6; 124,16. ϣⲟⲙⲛ̄ⲧ
ⲛ̄ⲍⲟⲟⲩⲧ III 102,12. ϣⲙ̄ⲧⲍⲟⲟⲩⲧ BG 96,3. ⲍⲟⲟⲩⲧⲥⲍⲓⲙⲉ V 6,[4];
8,[33]; 10,[7].16; 14,[20]. III 76,24; 82,[1].10; 101,8; 104,13; 106,18;
111,4. ⲍⲁⲟⲩⲧⲥⲍⲓⲙⲉ III 87,[2]. ⲍⲟⲩⲧⲥⲍⲓⲙⲉ BG 94,11; 99,5; 103,[1];
111,9. ⲙⲛ̄ⲧⲍⲟⲟⲩⲧ V 6,[5]; 10,[17]; 11,[25]. III 77,[1]; 82,1; 108,5;
118,[7]. BG 103,2; 111,10.
ⲍⲱϣϥ v. BG 121,18; 126,9.
ⲍⲁⲍⲧⲛ- prep.: ⲍⲁⲧⲏ⳽: See ⲍⲓⲥⲉ .
ⲍⲱⲟ̄ⲃ v. BG 120,1.

ⲭⲓ v. BG 85,3. ⲭⲓ- V 8,[31]. III 103,17.18; 108,8. BG 98,2.3; 105,18. ⲭⲓⲧ⳽
III 72,8; 87,8; 95,3; 111,12. ⲭⲓ ⲉ- V 1,[23]. ⲭⲓ ⲉⲃⲟⲗ ⲍⲛ̄- (ⲛ̄ⲍⲏⲧ⳽) III
118,[12]. BG 116,[3].6; 125,6. ⲭⲓⲧ⳽ ⲛ̄ⲧⲛ̄- (ⲛ̄ⲧⲟⲟⲧ⳽) III 105,19. BG
101,5; 112,3. See further ⲣⲁⲛ, ⲥⲙⲟⲧ, ⲧⲁⲃⲥⲉ, ⲱⲡ, ϣⲓⲡⲉ, ⲃⲉⲭⲙ̄.
ⲭⲟ v.: ⲭⲟ⳽ ⲛ̄- V 16,[4], ⲭⲟ⳽ ⲍⲛ̄- III 88,20.
ⲭⲱ v.: ⲭⲟⲟ⳽ V 2,[5]; 11,7.9.[22]; 13,[2]. III 70,24; 71,8; 74,10; 78,16;
83.3.11; 88,4; 90,6; 93,6; 103,8; 112,5; 114,7; 119,[9]. BG 81,13; 97,9;
107,2; 108,19; 117,8; 119,5; 126,17. ⲭⲱ ⲙ̄ⲙⲟ⳽ V 17,[4]. ⲭⲱ ⲙ̄ⲙⲟⲥ ⲭⲉ
V 1,[18]. III 92,23; 97,20. BG 81,6. ⲭⲱ ⲙ̄ⲙⲟⲥ ⲉ- (ⲉⲣⲟ⳽) ⲭⲉ III 70,17;
77,4; 118,21. BG 125,18. ⲭⲱ ⲛ̄- (ⲛⲁ⳽) III 93,11; 96,20; 118,24. ⲭⲟⲟ⳽
ⲉ- (ⲉⲣⲟ⳽) III 90,9; 113,2; 114,6. BG 115,[3]. ⲭⲟⲟ⳽ ⲉⲣⲟ⳽ ⲭⲉ BG
90,16. ⲭⲟⲟ⳽ ⲛ̄- (ⲛⲁ⳽) V 1,13; 17,[9]. III 90,5. BG 117,9. ⲭⲟⲟⲥ ⲉⲣⲟ⳽
ⲭⲉ III 73,2; 74,22; 75,21; 77,[1].14; 81,4.11; 82,[2].4.6; 85,12; 88,8;
98,23; 105,12. BG 81,1; 98,17. ⲭⲟⲥ ⲉⲣⲟ⳽ ⲭⲉ BG 95,8. ⲁⲭⲓ- ⲉⲣⲟ⳽
imperat. III 112,22. ⲁⲧⲭⲟⲟ⳽ III 89,20; 113,24. BG 116,17.
ⲭⲱ⳽ m. occurring in the following prepositions: ⲉⲭⲛ̄- (ⲉⲭⲱ⳽) V 2,[14];
7,[23]. III 71,24; 78,20.21.22; 90,19; 94,22. BG 84,10. ⲍⲓⲭⲛ̄(ⲛ̄)- V
3,13; 7,[9]. III 91,18; 99,8. See further ⲍⲣⲁⲓ̈.
ⲭⲱⲕ v. V 15,[22]. III 88,10. BG 104,18; 115,15; 121,9.11; 124,15. ⲭⲏⲕ⁺ III
85,7. ⲭⲱⲕ ⲉⲃⲟⲗ V 13,[3]; 16,15. III 85,4; 89,6; 107,20; 112,10; 113,10;
118,6. ⲭⲱⲕ ⲉⲃⲟⲗ ⲙ̄ⲙⲟ⳽ V 6,[6]. ⲭⲟⲕ⳽ ⲉⲃⲟⲗ BG 114,1. ⲭⲏⲕ⁺ ⲉⲃⲟⲗ
III 77,2; 104,8. ⲭⲏⲕ⁺ ⲉⲃⲟⲗ ⲛ̄- III 101,2. BG 94,2. ⲭⲏⲕ⁺ ⲉⲃⲟⲗ ⲍⲛ̄- III
76,18. ⲭⲱⲕ m. V 4,[2]. III 74,15; 98,14. BG 90,6. ⲭⲱⲕ ⲉⲃⲟⲗ V 14,[5].
III 86,10; 101,14. ⲭⲱⲕ ⲉⲃⲟⲗ ⲙ̄ⲙⲟ⳽ V 8,[30].
ⲭⲉⲕⲁⲁⲥ conj. III 76,11; 87,5; 97,1; 101,9; 105,6; 107,16.23. BG 87,19;
88,12; 94,11; 100,7; 104,[1].13; 105,4.17; 118,11; 119,10; 120,16;
122,7.12; 124,14.
ⲭⲓⲛ- prep. V 8,17. III 92,9; 98,13; 119,[13]. BG 80,7; 83,11.17; 87,5; 90,5;
98,6; 107,15; 124,18; 127,4. ⲭ(ⲓ)ⲛ ⲛ̄- V 1,5. III 70,4; 71,17; 74,15; 87,9;
89,16; 94,8.13; 103,21; 111,12; 113,20. BG 116,11. See further ϣⲟⲣⲡ̄.
ⲭⲱⲛϥ m. III 111,13.
ⲭⲡⲟ v. BG 88,4. ⲭⲡⲉ- III 97,6.9. BG 88,9. ⲭⲡⲟ⳽ V 8,15; 10,21. III 70,4;
78,16; 103,9. ⲭⲡⲟ ⲛⲁ⳽ V 6,22. ⲭⲡⲟ⳽ ⲉ- III 92,8. BG 80,6; 81,15. ⲭⲡⲟ
ⲉⲃⲟⲗ ⲙ̄ⲙⲟ⳽ V 10,20. ⲭⲡⲟ⳽ ⲉⲃⲟⲗ ⲍⲛ̄- III 93,20. BG 82,13. ⲭⲡⲟ m. V
2,16; 5,[22]; 10,22.[23]. III 71,20.21; 77,[2]; 94,17.18. BG 84,4.5.

ⲁⲧⲭⲡⲟ V 7,17; 10,18. BG 84,6. ⲁⲧⲭⲡⲟⲹ V 4,[23]. BG 98,6. ⲣⲉϥⲭⲡⲟ
m. V 6,6.[8]; 8,[29]; 10,10. III 96,22.23; 104,8. BG 87,16; 98,17; 103,5.
ⲣⲉϥⲭⲡⲉ- III 82,3; 106,21. BG 87,18. ⲭⲡⲟ ⲙ̅ⲡⲕⲁϩ V 1,[5]. See further
ⲉⲓⲱⲧ, ⲛⲟⲩⲧⲉ, ϣⲱⲣⲡ̅.

ⲭⲟⲉⲓⲥ m. V 11,[18]; 15,[7] twice.7.[8].[9].[10]. III 87,16.17 twice.19 twice;
94,1; 95,19; 96,15; 98,10; 100,17; 105,4; 108,17; 111,19 twice.20.21
twice; 112,21; 114,9. BG 112,<15> four times.<17> two times. ⲭⲟⲉⲓⲥ
ⲙ̅ⲡⲧⲏⲣϥ̅ III 74,20; 98,22. ⲭⲥ̅ ⲙ̅ⲡⲧⲏⲣϥ̅ BG 90,15. ⲭⲟⲉⲓⲥ ⲛ̅ⲧⲉ ⲡⲧⲏⲣϥ̅ V
4,[8]. ⲭⲟⲉⲓⲥ ⲛ̅ⲧⲉ ⲛ̅ⲭⲟⲉⲓⲥ V 7,[1]. ⲙⲛ̅ⲧⲭⲟⲉⲓⲥ V 6,17. ⲙⲛ̅ⲧⲭⲁⲉⲓⲥ
V 6,[30].

ⲭⲓⲥⲉ v.: ⲭⲟⲥⲉⲧ ⲉ- V 14,17. ⲙⲛ̅ⲧⲭⲁⲥⲓ ϩⲏⲧ III 107,9; 118,19. BG 104,4;
125,15.

ⲭⲟⲉⲓⲧ m.: (ⲧⲟⲟⲩ) ⲛ̅ⲭⲟⲉⲓⲧ III 91,20. BG 79,8.

ⲭⲱϩⲙ̅ v.: ⲭⲁϩⲙ̅ⲧ III 93,21; 108,12. BG 106,5. ⲭⲁϩⲙ̅ⲉⲧ BG 82,14.
ⲁⲧⲭⲱϩⲙ̅ BG 86,4.

ϭⲱ v. V 3,[8].

ϭⲱⲗⲡ v.: ϭⲱⲗⲡ ⲉⲣⲟⲹ BG 83,18. ϭⲱⲗⲡ ⲛⲁⲹ III 94,11. ϭⲱⲗⲡ m.: ϭⲱⲗⲡ
ⲉⲃⲟⲗ III 89,17.

ϭⲟⲙ f. V 3,13.14; 4,[29]; 5,[31]; 7,9.[13]; 8,6.[7].18; 11,21.[24]; 12,[11].15;
13,[23]; 15,[11].[19]; 17,6. III 75,12; 76,21; 78,12; 83,11; 84,4.7.21;
85,2.23; 87,20; 88,5; 90,3; 96,7.23; 99,13; 101,5; 103,1.5.12; 111,14.22;
114,5; 119,7. BG 83,10; 87,1.3.18; 91,17; 94,6; 96,19; 97,4.13; 109,7;
112,7; 113,1.14; 117,7; 121,8; 126,16. ϭⲁⲙ V 6,10; 7,29; 12,27. ⲙⲛ̅
ϣϭⲟⲙ III 88,20; 89,24. ⲙⲛ̅ ϣϭⲟⲙ ⲛ̅- V 17,[3]. III 74,8. ⲟⲩⲛ̅ ϭⲟⲙ V
17,[10]. ⲟⲩⲛ̅ ϣϭⲟⲙ ⲙ̅ⲙⲟⲹ V 2,[2]. III 71,5. ⲁⲧϭⲟⲙ BG 115,12.
ⲙⲛ̅ⲧⲁⲧϭⲟⲙ V 16,12. III 89,4; 113,9. ϣϭⲙ̅ϭⲟⲙ BG 121,7.

ϭⲓⲛⲉ v. V 4,[3]. ϭⲛ- III 94,2. ϭⲛ̅ⲧⲹ V 1,9. III 74,19; 98,18. See further
ϭⲟⲙ.

ϭⲉⲡⲏ v.: ϩⲛ̅ ⲟⲩϭⲉⲡⲏ III 113,11.

ϭⲣⲱϩ m. III 107,25.

ϭⲉⲭⲙ̅ nn. (not attested elsewhere): ⲁⲧϫⲓ ϭⲉⲭⲙ(ⲉ) ⲛ̅ⲥⲱⲹ III 72,22; 95,14;
118,[11]. Cf. ⲧⲁϭⲥⲉ, with which ϭⲉⲭⲙ̅ is parallel. ϭⲉⲭⲙ̅ may be
related to ϭⲁⲭⲙⲏ (Crum: 842b).

GREEK LOAN WORDS

ἀγαθός III 72,17; 95,10. BG 85,14. ἀγαθόν III 97,13; 114,20; 118,[13]. BG
88,14; 118,[4]. ⲙⲛ̅ⲧⲁⲅⲁⲑⲟⲥ III 97,7. BG 88,7; 125,7.

ἀγάπη V 9,6; 11,[3]. III 82,24; 97,4; 104,20; 117,23. BG 88,3; 99,14; 124,3.

ἄγγελος V 9,11.14.17.20; 11,18.19; 12,12.17; 15,13; 16,7. III 77,21;
81,[1].4.9; 84,8.17; 87,22; 88,22; 91,13; 102,9; 104,24; 105,15; 112,1;
113,4; 118,5.20. BG 78,17; 95,18; 99,19; 100,18; 107,8; 113,5; 115,5;
121,13; 124,12; 125,17.

ἄγειν. ⲁⲅⲉ III 70,18; 92,20.24. BG 81,1.

ἀγένητος BG 90,12; 91,13; 92,12.

ἀγέννητος III 71,22; 73,16; 75,9.22; 82,12; 89,16; 94,19; 96,13; 98,20; 99,9; 100,[1]; 103,20; 117,[11].

ἀθάνατος III 71,12.19; 76,23; 77,10; 78,10.23; 83,20; 85,10.18.21; 88,[3].6.15; 89,8.16; 93,23; 101,8.10.20; 106,13; 112,4.7; 113,13; 114,22; 117,[16]. BG 94,10. ἀθάνατον III 103,3.

αἰσθάνεσθαι. ⲁⲓⲥⲑⲁⲛⲉ BG 82,8. ⲉⲥⲑⲁⲛⲉ III 71,5; 93,16.

αἰών V 1,13; 5,19; 7,[31]. III 73,19; 76,9; 77,16; 81,20; 83,4.22; 84,15.18; 85,10.11.15.17.18.22; 86,11.17; 87,8; 88,2; 89,7; 90,2; 100,15; 102,4; 106,3; 108,19.22; 111,11; 112,3.22; 113,10.15; 114,3; 118,[8]. BG 93,10; 95,12; 101,18; 106,12.17; 107,6.15; 108,1.8.12.17 twice; 109,4.6; 110,3.11; 112,1; 113,9; 114,15; 115,16; 116,4; 117,5; 118,13; 119,2; 124,18. ⲉⲱⲛ V 5,[25]; 6,4.22; 7,[32]; 8,18.[25]; 9,[10]; 10,[1]; 11,[9]; 12,[4].[24].[26]; 13,4.8.15.[18].[22]; 14,[6].[12]; 15,17; 16,16.[19]; 17,[5]. III 89,10.

ἀκολουθεῖν. ⲁⲕⲟⲗⲟⲩⲑⲉⲓ III 114,[25].

ἀκόλουθον III 114,25.

ἀκρίβεια BG 82,2. ⲁⲕⲣⲓⲃⲓⲁ III 93,11.

ἀκριβῶς III 105,7. BG 100,8.

ἀλήθεια III 71,10; 74,21.

ἀμήν. ⲍⲁⲙⲏⲛ III 119,17.

ἀνάγκη III 112,23. BG 114,16.

ἀνάπαυσις III 86,14; 89,23; 114,1; 117,14; 118,[14]. BG 110,7.

ἄναρχος III 75,[2]; 99,1. BG 91,3.

ἀντωπεῖν. ⲁⲛⲧⲟⲡⲓⲧⲱ III 75,8. ⲁⲛⲧⲟⲡⲓⲧⲟⲛ III 99,8.

ἀντωπός. ⲁⲛⲧⲟⲡⲟⲥ III 75,7.13; 99,8.14. BG 91,11; 92,1.

ἀόρατος. ⲁⲍⲟⲣⲁⲧⲟⲛ III 91,12; 117,20; 118,[12]. BG 78,14.

ἄπειρος. ⲁⲡⲓⲣⲟⲛ III 76,12.

ἀπέραντος III 85,17; 96,12.19. BG 85,9. ἀπέραντον III 76,16; 93,9; 97,22; 100,23; 108,23; 118,[9]. BG 87,14; 93,19; 102,4; 106,19; 107,15; 108,15; 125,1.

ἀπολαύειν. ⲁⲡⲟⲗⲁⲩⲉ III 97,<7>. ⲣⲁⲡⲟⲗⲁⲩⲉ BG 88,6.

ἀπορεῖν. ⲁⲡⲟⲣⲓ III 91,3. BG 78,2; 79,17. ⲁⲡⲟⲣⲉⲓ III 92,2.

ἀπόρροια BG 90,7; 119,3. ⲁⲡⲟⲍⲣⲟⲓⲁ III 98,15.

ἀπόστολος III 112,19. BG 114,12.

ἄρα BG 95,5.

ἀρετή III 91,6. BG 78,6.

ἀριθμός BG 121,10.

ἅρμα III 88,18.

ἁρμόζειν. ⲍⲟⲣⲙⲁⲍⲉ (reflecting the late form ὁρμάζειν) BG 120,17.

ἀρχάγγελος V 6,[27]. III 77,20; 87,21 twice; 102,9; 111,22.23. ⲁⲣⲭⲓ-ⲁⲅⲅⲉⲗⲟⲥ V 15,11.[12]; 16,[6]. BG 95,19; 113,[2].3.

ἄρχειν. ⲁⲣⲭⲓ III 71,24; 78,20.21 twice; 94,21. ⲁⲣⲭⲉⲓ BG 84,10. ⲁⲣⲭⲉⲥ-

θαι III 77,24; 102,16; 119,14. BG 96,6. ⲡ̄ⲁⲣⲭⲓ V 6,[29]; 7,20. ⲡ̄ⲁⲣⲭⲉⲓ
    V 7,21.22. ⲡ̄ⲁⲣⲭⲉⲥⲑⲁⲓ BG 127,5.
ἀρχή V 2,10; 4,[7].11.[12]; 5,21.27.[30]; 6,[2]; 8,[2].17.[28]; 14,[4]. III
    71,15.22.23; 74,20.23; 76,13.20.22; 86,9; 87,9; 94,6.19.20; 98,24;
    101,4.6; 103,21; 111,12. BG 83,7; 84,7.8; 87,5; 91,1; 94,5.8; 98,6; 110,2;
    112,[3]. ⲁⲧⲁⲣⲭⲏ V 4,[12].
ἀρχιγενέτωρ III 82,18; 118,20. BG 119,14; 125,16.
ἄσοφον BG 82,7.
ἀσπάζεσθαι. ⲁⲥⲡⲁⲍⲉ III 81,7. BG 121,4.
ἀσπασμός V 9,19. III 81,8.
αὐτογενέτωρ III 75,7. BG 107,4.
αὐτογενής V 4,[32]. III 75,14; 97,14; 99,15; 101,19; 106,5. BG 92,1; 95,3;
    102,2; 108,16.
αὐτογέννητος III 76,<14>; 82,13.
αὐτόκτιστος III 76,17; 101,1. BG 94,1.
αὐτοπάτωρ III 75,6; 77,14; 102,1. BG 95,9.
αὐτοτέλειος. ⲁⲩⲧⲟⲧⲉⲗⲓⲟⲥ BG 98,[18].
αὐτοφυής III 76,16; 100,23. BG 94,1.
ἀφθαρσία V 3,[18].[20]; 7,11. III 74,1.4; 76,2; 78,11; 88,11; 97,11.15;
    103,4; 112,11.
ἄφθαρτος V 3,[26]. III 72,15; 73,1.19; 74,3.11; 95,9.17. ἄφθαρτον V 3,[19].
    III 97,19; 100,6; 119,[16].

βίος III 71,2; 93,13. BG 82,5.

γενεά V 5,[4]. III 75,17; 97,9; 99,18. BG 88,8; 92,6.
γενέτειρα III 77,4.
γενέτωρ III 82,15.
γένος III 73,14; 96,10; 99,18. BG 92,5.
γνῶσις V 4,8; 17,14. III 117,[9].

δεκάς V 7,[19].19.[27].
διαφορά V 3,23; 8,15. III 73,18; 74,6; 78,12; 98,9. BG 89,1.20.
διοίκησις III 70,9.12; 92,15.18. BG 80,14.18.
δυάς V 7,18. III 78,18.
δύναμις V 11,[29]. III 73,11; 78,9; 83,15.19; 87,11; 96,8.

εἰ μήτι. ⲉⲓⲙⲏⲧⲓ V 2,[12]. III 71,18; 94,2.9. BG 83,2.13.
εἶδος V 15,15.
εἱμαρμένη. ⲍ̄ⲓⲙⲁⲣⲙⲉⲛⲏ V 1,[22].
εἰρήνη. †ⲣⲏⲛⲏ III 91,21 twice. BG 79,10 twice.
ἐκ III 87,3 twice. BG 111,10.11. See further μέρος.
ἐκκλησία V 9,15; 14,[11[.16.17.[18].[23]. III 81,5; 86,16.22.23.24; 87,4;
    111,2.7. BG 110,10; 111,3.4.6.14.
ἐνθυμεῖν. ⲉⲛⲑⲩⲙⲉⲓ III 104,10. BG 99,[1].

ἐνθύμησις V 15,[23]. III 73,10; 78,7; 83,5.6; 88,9; 96,6; 102,24; 105,18; 112,9; 117,[17]. BG 86,17; 96,17; 101,4; 113,17; 123,14.

ἔννοια V 3,11; 4,[4]; 6,8; 7,[6].15.16.[25]; 8,[2]; 11,8.10.15. III 73,9; 74,16; 78,6.14.15; 83,5 twice; 87,10; 96,4; 98,16; 102,22; 103,6.7; 111,13. BG 86,18; 90,8; 96,15; 97,7.8; 112,5.

ἐξουσία V 2,11; 3,[7]; 6,25; 9,[8]; 13,[24]; 15,[19]. III 71,15; 73,5; 77,18; 85,24; 88,4.12; 91,6; 94,6; 95,24; 102,6; 104,22; 108,10; 112,6.12; 119,5. BG 78,6; 83,8; 86,12; 95,15; 99,17; 106,2; 109,8; 113,13; 114,3; 126,13.

ἐπαινεῖσθαι. επαινογ III 108,20. BG 106,15.

ἐπεί. επι 74,8; 75,8. BG 91,11; 114,16.

ἐπειδή. επιΔΗ V 4,21; 6,10.

ἑρμηνευτής III 101,12.

ἔτι III 89,1; 97,24. BG 89,8.

εὐαγγέλιον III 104,1; 119,[15]. BG 98,10; 127,8.

εὐδοκία III 117,18. BG 112,4; 123,14.

ζωή V 14,[25]. III 87,5; 111,8. BG 111,16.

ἤ V 1,8. III 70,7; 72,8; 93,7; 95,2; 96,16; 114,11 twice. BG 79,16.17; 80,11; 85,2; 117,15.17.

θέλησις III 83,9.10.

θρόνος III 88,16; 112,15. BG 114,7.

ἰδέα. ϩιΔεα III 72,6.8.9; 87,23; 94,24; 95,3; 112,2. BG 113,<7>. ειΔεα V 4,17.

ἴδιος. ϩιΔιον III 78,6; 102,21.

ἵνα V 4,14.

ἰσοδύναμις. ϩιϲοΔγΝαμιϲ III 73,12; 75,15; 99,16. ϩϊϲοΔγΝαμοϲ BG 92,3.

ἴσος. ϩιϲον III 96,8.

ἰσόχρονος. ϩιϲοχρονοϲ III 75,9.14; 99,10.16. BG 91,14; 92,2.

καθαρόν III 91,17; 117,[9]. BG 79,4.

καρπός III 97,6.10; 107,17; 117,3. BG 88,5.10; 104,14; 122,13.

κατά V 4,[9]; 7,[11].[13]; 8,17; 14,[20]. III 74,21; 78,11.12; 90,6; 103,3.4. BG 97,2.4; 122,11.

καταβολή V 1,[5]. III 70,4; 71,17; 92,9; 94,8. BG 80,7; 83,11.

καταπέτασμα III 114,21. BG 118,8; 119,1.

κόσμος V 1,6.[11]; 5,18; 8,[26]; 10,[2]; 15,[17]; 16,[19].[24]. III 70,5.10.18; 71,17; 76,10; 81,21; 88,2; 89,11.15; 92,10.16.23; 94,9; 100,15; 106,4.13.25; 107,3.8; 112,4; 113,[15].19. BG 80,8.14; 83,11; 93,11; 102,[1].13; 103,11.14; 104,3; 113,10; 116,[4].10; 120,9.

λογισμός III 73,11; 78,8; 83,8 twice; 96,7; 102,24.
λόγος III 83,10; 87,18; 111,24. BG 113,4.

μαθητεύειν. ΜΑΘΗΤΕΥΕ III 90,18. BG 77,14.
μαθητής III 90,17; 105,3; 106,9; 114,10; 119,[11].[14]. BG 77,12; 100,4;
    102,8; 117,14; 127,6.
μακάριος V 3,[1]. III 70,1; 72,19; 73,[1]; 74,10; 90,12; 95,12.16; 119,[9].
    BG 85,16; 86,3; 126,17.
μαντεία. ΜΑΝΤΗ III 91,1. BG 78,1. (reflecting an Ionic form; see LSJ, s.v.)
μέλος V 7,[10]; 8,[6]. III 78,9; 103,1. BG 96,19.
μέρος V 14,21.[22] twice.[24]. BG 119,8. ΜΕΡΟΥС BG 111,10.11. ΕΚ
    ΜΕΡΟС III 87,3 twice; 111,5.6.
μηνύειν. ΜΗΝΕΥΕ III 106,8.
μονάς V 7,18.24. III 78,17.24; 103,9. BG 97,10.
μονογενής V 5,22.
μορφή V 2,[18].[19]; 8,11.14; 15,16. III 72,4.5; 88,[1]; 91,11; 97,1;
    103,17.18; 112,2. BG 78,13; 84,14.16; 87,19; 98,2.3; 113,8.
μυστήριον III 91,8. BG 78,9.

νήφειν. ΝΗΦΕ III 101,11. BG 94,14.
νοεῖν. ΝΟΕΙ III 72,20; 73,20; 76,9.19; 90,1; 100,14; 101,4. ΝΟΕΙΕ III
    95,12.13. ΝΟΪ BG 85,18; 93,10; 94,4. ΑΤΝΟΕΙ V 3,[1]. III 72,19; 75,23.
    BG 85,17. ΑΤ̄ΝΟΪ BG 92,16. ΑΤ̄ΝΟΕΙ III 100,5.
νοῦς V 3,10; 6,6; 7,6; 8,[2]; 9,[23]. III 73,9; 77,[2]; 78,6; 96,4; 102,21; 104,8.
    BG 86,17; 96,14; 98,18.

ὀγδοάς. ΖΟΓΔΟΑС V 14,[19]. III 102,4. BG 95,13; 114,6.
οἰκονομία III 91,4.9; 92,5. BG 78,4.10; 80,2.
ὅλος. ΖΟΛΩΝ III 96,[1].
ὀνομάζειν. ΟΝΟΜΑΖΕ III 86,16; 103,23. BG 110,9.
ὀνομασία III 77,11.
οὐ V 4,15.
οὐδέ V 9,[33]. III 76,8; 81,19; 90,1; 100,14; 106,2. BG 93,9; 101,17.
οὖν V 2,[8]; 9,17; 10,13. BG 78,2.
οὐσία III 96,23. BG 87,18.
οὔτε V 2,11.12; 5,17; 8,24; 16,[12]. BG 83,8.9.10; 115,12.

πάλιν III 106,9. BG 102,7.
παμμήτωρ. ΠΑΝΜΗΤΩΡ III 82,21.
παγγενέτειρα. ΠΑΝΓΕΝΕΤΙΡΑ III 82,5.22; 106,22. ΠΑΝΓΕΝΗΤΕΙΡΑ BG
    103,7.
παγγενέτωρ III 82,17; 84,14.
πάνσοφος III 77,3; 82,20.
παντοκράτωρ III 107,3. BG 103,15; 119,9.
πάντως V 5,23.

παρθένος V 16,[9]. III 89,[1]; 113,6. BG 115,8.

πηγή V 3,15; 7,4. III 73,13; 96,9. BG 87,3.

πιστεύειν. ⲡⲓⲥⲧⲉⲩⲉ III 74,13.

πίστις V 4,[5]; 10,[12].14; 11,[4]. III 74,17; 78,4; 82,6.8; 83,[1]; 98,17; 106,24. BG 90,9; 103,9.

πλανᾶσθαι. ⲡⲗⲁⲛⲁ III 74,5.

πλάνη V 6,14. III 77,9. BG 118,17.

πλάσμα BG 119,12.18.

πλάσσειν. ⲡⲗⲁⲥⲥⲁ BG 97,17.19. ⲣ̄ⲡⲗⲁⲥⲥⲁ III 103,15.16.

πνεῦμα. ⲡⲛⲁ̄ V 1,[19]; 11,[28]; 16,10. III 86,6; 89,2; 91,12; 96,21; 97,8; 102,12; 105,2; 113,6; 117,[16].21; 118,[12]; 119,[13].[16]. BG 78,15; 81,7; 87,16; 88,8; 96,3; 100,[2]; 109,17; 115,9; 119,2.7; 122,8; 123,11.19; 125,5; 127,4.

πνευματικόν III 82,9; 83,17. ⲡⲛⲓⲕⲏ̄ V 10,16; 11,[24].

πνοή BG 121,4.

προεῖναι. ⲡⲣⲟⲟⲛⲧⲟⲥ III 75,8; 99,9.

πρόνοια V 1,[21]. III 70,20; 71,3; 91,5; 93,2.14; 108,16; 119,2. BG 78,5; 81,9; 82,6; 106,9; 122,3; 126,8.

προπάτωρ III 74,[22]; 75,2; 98,24; 99,1. BG 90,17.

πρός V 6,[22]; 9,10. III 77,17; 88,17; 102,5; 112,16. BG 95,13; 114,8.

πρωτογενέτειρα. ⲡⲣⲱⲧⲟⲅⲉⲛⲉⲧⲓⲣⲁ III 82,23; 104,17. ⲡⲣⲟⲧⲟⲅⲉⲛⲉⲧⲉⲓⲣⲁ BG 99,10.

πρωτογενέτωρ III 81,10; 82,16; 83,23; 85,13; 104,15; 105,11. ⲡⲣⲟⲧⲟⲅⲉⲛⲉⲧⲱⲣ BG 99,7.14; 100,12; 108,4.

πρωτογένητος. ⲡⲣⲟⲧ<ⲟ>ⲅⲉⲛⲏⲧⲟⲥ BG 99,<4>.

πύλη BG 121,18.

πῶς III 74,17; 95,20; 98,17; 100,18; 103,23; 106,11. BG 86,7; 90,2.9; 93,14; 98,9; 102,<9>.

σάρκινος III 108,14. BG 106,7.

σάρξ III 91,15.16. BG 79,2.4.

σιγή V 15,21. III 88,8.9; 112,8; 117,17.21.

σοφία V 6,8.9; 8,[32]; 9,4; 10,[5].[12].15; 11.[3].[4]; 15,[21]; 16,18. III 77,4; 81,23; 82,5.8.20.21.22.24 twice; 83,1; 88,6; 89,9; 90,14; 101,16; 102,13; 104,11.17; 106,16.23; 107,7.19.24; 113,13; 114,14; 119,18. BG 77,8; 95,1; 96,5; 99,[2].11; 102,17; 103,7; 104,1.17; 105,6; 109,3; 116,1; 118,[2]; 120,16; 127,11.

σπορά III 93,20. BG 82,13.

στερέωμα V 12,[28].[30]; 13,[2]; 16,16. III 84,23; 85,[1].3; 88,15; 89,7; 112,16; 113,12. BG 114,7; 115,17.

στρατία V 16,[5]. III 88,22; 113,3. BG 115,5.

συζυγία BG 95,3.

σύζυγος. ⲥⲩⲛⲍⲩⲅⲟⲥ V 8,[31]; 10,6.14. III 77,6; 81,23; 82,8; 88,7; 89,9; 101,16; 102,14; 104,11; 106,17; 113,14; 114,15. BG 102,17; 116,2.

σύμβολον III 117,19.24. BG 123,16; 124,5.

συμφωνεῖν. cΥΜΦωΝει III 70,16; 81,22; 82,7; 83,12; 92,22. cΥΜΦωΝι III
71,10; 86,4. BG 81,4; 102,16; 109,14. ϜcΥΜΦωΝι V 2,[5].
συμφώνησις. cΥΝΦωΝΗcιc III 83,2.
σχῆμα V 15,16. III 88,[1]; 112,2. BG 113,8.
σῶμα III 97,10. BG 88,9.
σωτήρ V 10,[9].13; 12,16; 13,14. III 82,2.7; 84,[2].8; 85,14; 91,7.10.24; 92,6;
94,4.14; 95,21; 96,15.18; 98,12; 100,[2].18.20; 105,9; 106,15.20; 107,22;
108,17.20; 112,21; 113,1; 114,13; 119,9. BG 78,8.12; 79,13; 80,3; 83,5;
86,9; 87,9; 90,4; 92,13; 93,16; 100,10; 102,15; 103,4; 105,3; 106,11.14;
107,17; 108,6; 114,14; 115,1; 118,1; 126,18. c̄ω̄Ϝ BG 83,19; 87,12. c̄Ϝ
V 12,9.12.

τέλειος III 72,23. τέλειον III 91,17. τεΛιοc V 7,10; 13,5. III 78,10;
95,15.20.21; 96,18; 98,12; 100,19; 105,8; 106,14; 108,19; 112,24;
114,13; 118,4. BG 79,5; 86,2.8.9; 87,12; 90,3; 93,16; 100,9; 102,14;
106,14; 107,17; 114,[18]; 117,18; 124,11. τεΛιοΝ III 103,2. BG 97,[1];
107,9.
τέρπεσθαι III 89,21. τερπε III 81,15. BG 101,2.13; 116,18. τερπΗ III
105,17.
τιμή III 97,11; 108,2. BG 105,10.
τόπος III 107,12. BG 104,8.
τότε III 103,22; 108,16; 112,19; 119,10. BG 98,7; 106,10; 114,12.
τριάς III 78,18
τριβή III 93,21; 108,11. BG 82,14; 106,4.
τύπος V 12,[3].[5].[6].[8].[10]; 12,14.19; 16,[21]. III 82,10; 83,21.23;
84,2.3.6.10; 89,13. BG 116,3.6.

ὑπηρεσία III 77,22; 81,3; 84,16; 88,23; 105,1. BG 100,[1]. ϨΗπερΗcιλ BG
107,6.
ὑπόστασις III 91,3; 92,4. BG 78,3; 80,1.
ὑποταγή III 71,16; 94,7. BG 83,9.
ὑστέρημα III 85,8.

φιλόσοφος III 70,15; 92,20. BG 81,3.
φρόνησις III 73,10; 78,8; 83,7 twice; 87,13.16; 96,5; 102,23. BG 96,17;
112,10.
φύσις V 2,[12]; 16,[4].[24]. III 71,16; 74,9; 88,20; 89,15; 94,7; 113,19. BG
83,10; 116,11.
φωστήρ V 10,[7].

χαίρειν. χαιρε V 1,3.
χάος V 13,20.27; 16,[23]. III 85,21; 86,3; 89,14.18; 113,18.20. BG 109,13;
116,10.12; 118,14; 119,10; 120,9; 121,10.
χάρις BG 88,12; 122,18.
χρηστός. Μ̄Ν̄τχρΗcτοc III 97,4. Μ̄Ν̄τχ̄c̄ BG 88,2.

χρόνος V 4,[24]; 12,[5]. III 83,22.
χωρεῖν. xωpι III 117,[10].[13]; 118,1.

ψυχή BG 120,1.3.
ψυχικός BG 121,6.

ὡς V 3,14.[19]; 16,[3]. III 73,22; 74,3; 98,7; 119,6. BG 89,11.16; 126,14.
ὥστε V 12,[29]. III 74,4; 83,14; 84,19.24.

PROPER NOUNS

ⲁⲇⲁⲙ. ⲁⲇⲁⲙ ⲡⲃⲁⲗ ⲙ̄ⲡⲟⲩⲟ(ⲉ)ⲓⲛ V 9,[23]. III 105,12. BG 100,14; 108,10. ⲁⲇⲁⲙ ⲡⲁ ⲡⲟⲩⲟⲉⲓⲛ III 81,12.

ⲃⲁⲣⲑⲟⲗⲟⲙⲁⲓⲟⲥ III 103,22. BG 98,8.

ⲅⲁⲗⲓⲗⲁⲓⲁ III 90,19; 91,20. BG 77,15; 79,9.

ⲉⲩⲅⲛⲱⲥⲧⲟⲥ V 1,[1]; 17,[18]. III 70,1; 90,12.

ⲑⲱⲙⲁⲥ III 96,14; 108,17. BG 87,8; 106,11.

ⲓ̈ⲁⲗⲇⲁⲃⲁⲱⲑ BG 119,16.
ⲓⲏⲥⲟⲩⲥ. ⲓ̄ⲏ̄ⲥ̄ III 119,18. ⲓ̄ⲏ̄ⲥ̄ ⲡⲉⲭ̄ⲣ̄ⲥ̄ III 90,14. BG 127,12. ⲓ̄ⲥ̄ ⲡⲉⲭ̄ⲥ̄ BG 77,8.

ⲙⲁⲑⲑⲁⲓⲟⲥ III 94,1; 100,17. ⲙⲁⲑⲁⲓⲟⲥ BG 82,19; 93.13.
ⲙⲁⲣⲓⲍⲁⲙⲙⲏ III 98,10; 114,9. ⲙⲁⲣⲓⲍⲁⲙ BG 90,1; 117,13.

ⲥⲟⲫⲓⲁ V 6,8.9; 8,[32]; 9,4; 10,[5]; 15,[21]; 16,18. III 81,23; 88,6; 89,9; 101,16; 102,13; 104,11; 106,16; 107,7.19.24; 113,13; 114,14. BG 95,1; 96,5; 99,[2]; 102,17; 104,1.17; 105,6; 109,3; 116,1; 118,[2]; 120,16. ⲁⲅⲁⲡⲏ ⲥⲟⲫⲓⲁ V 11,[3]. III 82,24. ⲡⲁⲛⲅⲉⲛⲉⲧⲓⲣⲁ ⲥⲟⲫⲓⲁ III 82,22; 106,22. ⲥⲟⲫⲓⲁ ⲡⲁⲛⲅⲉⲛⲉ (ⲟⲣ ⲏ)ⲧ(ⲉ)ⲓⲣⲁ III 82,5. BG 103,7. ⲡⲁⲛⲙⲏ-ⲧⲱⲣ ⲥⲟⲫⲓⲁ III 82,21. ⲡⲁⲛⲥⲟⲫⲟⲥ ⲥⲟⲫⲓⲁ III 82,20. ⲡⲁⲛⲥⲟⲫⲟⲥ ⲥⲟⲫⲓⲁ ⲛ̄ⲅⲉⲛⲉⲧⲉⲓⲣⲁ III 77,3. ⲡⲓⲥⲧⲓⲥ ⲥⲟⲫⲓⲁ V 10,[12].14; 11,[4]. III 82,8; 83,[1]. ⲡⲣⲱ(ⲟⲣ ⲟ)ⲧⲟⲅⲉⲛⲉⲧ(ⲉ)ⲓⲣⲁ ⲥⲟⲫⲓⲁ III 82,23. BG 99,10. ⲥⲟⲫⲓⲁ ⲛ̄ⲡⲣⲱⲧⲟⲅⲉⲛⲉⲧⲓⲣⲁ III 104,17.

ⲫⲓⲗⲓⲡⲡⲟⲥ III 92,4; 95,19. BG 79,18; 86,6.

ⲭⲣⲓⲥⲧⲟⲥ . ⲭ̄ⲣ̄ⲥ̄ III 104,22. ⲭ̄ⲥ̄ BG 99,9.16; 101,9; ⲭ̄ⲥ̄ where it is perhaps an error for ⲭ̄ⲥ̄ (i.e., ⲭⲟⲉⲓⲥ , q.v.): BG 83,1; 86,7; 87,9; 90,2; 100,4; 102,8; 106,11; 114,14; 117,13. (ⲭ̄ⲥ̄ in BG 112,15 four times, and 112,17 twice, is clearly an error.) See further ⲓⲏⲥⲟⲩⲥ.

PAPYRUS OXYRHYNCHUS 1081
GREEK FRAGMENT OF THE SOPHIA OF JESUS CHRIST

INTRODUCTION

P. Oxy. 1081 is closely parallel to both *SJC*–III, from 97,16 to 99,12, and *SJC*–BG, from 88,18 to 91,15. It is related, but less closely, to the parallel sections of the two *Eug* texts.

P. Oxy. 1081 was first edited and published by Hunt in 1911 (16–19), who was not aware of its connection with the as yet unpublished *SJC*–BG. Wessely republished it 13 years later; he depended on the Hunt collation, but added some restorations.[1]

In 1950 Puech identified the papyrus as a fragment of *SJC* (98, n.2; see also 1963: 245). Till included edited portions of the text in his edition of BG, but made no attempt to publish the complete text: he considered P. Oxy. 1081 too fragmentary to help with understanding the Coptic of *SJC*–BG and parr. (1955: 216) and expected Puech himself soon to publish a new edition of the papyrus (1955: 53). That edition never appeared. In 1975, Attridge published an edition based on infrared photographs, taking into account all the relevant Coptic texts with the exception of *Eug*–V, which is less useful than the other texts mentioned above.

I began working on P. Oxy. 1081 in 1970 in preparation for this volume, and at the suggestion of Alan Sparks, then Associate Director of the Institute for Antiquity and Christianity in Claremont, I wrote to Peter Parsons of Christ Church, Oxford, with the request that he examine the papyrus directly and respond to my queries. This he graciously did in May 1971 and again in November of the following year (in response to follow-up questions). More recently Attridge generously lent me the photographs he used in his edition.

The text and translation published here, then, are the result of the reworking of the fragmentary text in the light of the earlier editions (especially that of Attridge), with the aid both of the observations and suggestions of Parsons and of Attridge's photos. The numerous differences from earlier editions are discussed in the notes.

The MS consists of three large fragments of one leaf from a papyrus codex, with writing on both sides. The largest (A) measures 15.9 × 5.7 cm. The next in size (B) is 12.9 × 5.1 cm. The smallest (C) is 6.5 × 5.8 cm. "A" has the remains of the text along most of the inside margin, starting with the top lines. "B" has the remains along with outside margin for the middle half of the page. And "C" has what remains of the bottom of the page. The

---

[1] Hunt's text was reprinted by E. Klostermann, and Wesseley's, by A. De Santos Otero.

verso/recto designation given to sides one and two respectively by Hunt is misleading as these terms are used today, since, in the codex from which the leaf came, side one would have been the recto and side two the verso. The recto has the vertical fibers, while the verso has the horizontal. It is evident from a calculation of the average size of extant letters that those restored with certainty in the lacuna between the lower part of "B" and "C" require a space 3 to 4 mm. wider than that provided in the present fragment placement. The additional space (created by moving "B") would also straighten the lines that run between "A" and "B", which now would, if written out, appear slightly bowed.

In view of the above, the MS measurement given by Hunt (20.3 × 10.7 cm.) must be modified to 20.3 × 11.1 cm. The average length of the lines whose beginnings and endings are extant (16 in all) is 9 cm., according to Attridge; but this also must be changed by the addition of 4 mm. The MS is located in the Library of Cambridge University, where it has been given the acquisition number 5894. Paleographic evidence suggests that it is to be dated early in the 4th century.

Attridge holds that the text of P. Oxy. 1081 is closer to that of *SJC*–III than *SJC*–BG (8). He cites four instances where P. Oxy. 1081 agrees with *SJC*–III against *SJC*–BG: line 7 (III 97,21–22; BG 89,5–7); line 9 (III 97,23; BG 89,7); line 25 (III 98,10; BG 90,2); and line 26 (III 98,11; BG 90,2). Line 7 involves a shift of a phrase from one part of the sentence to another; line 9 involves a difference in tenses (but in fact there is no agreement among any of the texts here, and similar minor tense differences are found elsewhere also); line 25 has to do with the difference between $\overline{xc}$ and $\overline{xc}$, which might be accounted for on the basis of individual scribal error, since confusion over these terms is widespread; and line 26 involves a difference of pronominal subject, which might be the result of dittography (see BG 90,2n.). Of these, then, only the first may be significant.

As to the agreements between P. Oxy. 1081 and *SJC*–BG against *SJC*–III, Attridge cites only two: line 11 (BG 89,10–11; III 98,1–2) involving the difference of the number of the pronominal subject, which, as he says, is not significant in this instance; and line 34 (misidentified by him as line 35) (BG 90,12; III 98,19), where there is a minor addition in *SJC*–III, which is probably a scribal gloss, as Attridge says. Neither of these can be considered significant. There are two other agreements, overlooked by him, where P. Oxy. 1081 and *SJC*–BG have a phrase in common that is omitted in *SJC*–III: line 18–19 (BG 89,16–17; III 98,7); and line 38 (BG 90,17–18; III 98,24). Since the omissions in *SJC*–III in these instances could be explained as the result of homoioteleuton, one can say only that a special connection between P. Oxy. 1081 and *SJC*–BG is possible.

P. Oxy. 1081, then, is a text that is very close to the two Coptic texts of *SJC*. Its special affinities to one or the other of those texts seem too minor to permit a judgment about which one is closer to the Greek.

PAPYRUS OXYRHYNCHUS 1081
Fragment of *SJC*
(= NHC III 97,16–99,12; BG 88,18–91,15;
NHC III 73,16–75,11; NHC V 3,15–4,25)

	[	τοῖς μετὰ ταῦ]
Vertical		τα γεγονόσι[ν. εἰς δὲ]
Fibers	2	τὸ ἐμφανὲς [οὐκ ἔτι ἐ]
		ληλύθεισαν. [διαφο]
	4	ρά τε πολλὴ [μεταξὺ]
		τῶν ἀφθάρ[τ]ων. [ὁ δ' ἐφώ]
	6	νει · ὁ ἔχων ὦτα τ[ῶν ἀ]
		περάντων [ἀ]κο[ύει]ν ἀ
	8	κουέτω κα[ὶ] τοῖς ἐγρη
		γοροῦσιν [ἐγ]ὼ λαλῶ. ἔτι
	10	προ[σθεὶς ε]ἶπεν · πᾶν
		τὸ γε[ινόμε]νον ἀπὸ
	12	τῆς [φθορᾶς] ἀπογεί
		νετ[αι ὡς ἀπ]ὸ φθορᾶς
	14	γεγ[ονός · τὸ] δὲ γε[ι]νό

Line 1, Att restores [οὐ δὲ εἰς]. For restoration here of movable ν, see BDF sec. 20.

Line 2, Att restores ἐμφανὲ[ς αὐτοὶ ἡ]. For the position of the negative, relative of the verb, see BDF sec. 433. ἡ is incorrect as the augment of the pluperfect in this case.

Line 4, τε may be a mistake for δέ. Att restores [ἦν ἐντὸς]. The use of the imperfect contrasts with the Coptic of *SJC*. Regarding ἐντός, Crum cites no instance where the Coptic par., ογτε, translates ἐντός. As Att himself notes, ογτε is commonly used to translate μεταξύ.

Line 5, ν: so also Att. H brackets it. The top of the left stroke is visible. Att restored [ὁ δὲ φω]|νεῖ. However, since the Coptic calls for an imperfect tense, he has in correspondence suggested the restoration adopted here. H restored [τυγχά]νει at the suggestion of Swete.

Lines 6–8, ὁ ... ἀκουέτω: *SJC*–III has the exact par. (97,20–22) in contrast to BG.

Line 6, Both H and Att bracket the first τ. However, the photo shows the tip of the right end of the crossbar.

Line 8, Both H and Att show the second τ as certain. However all that remains is 1 mm. of the right portion of a horizontal line, which would be compatible also with π. Att is undoubtedly correct that ε should be read rather than α (H) before γρη, although the traces are not as clear-cut as he indicates.

Line 9, ουσ: Att considers all as certain. H correctly places a dot under σ. Only a trace of the bottom of the υ remains. Only a bit of the left side of the curve of the o remains, which would be compatible also with ε or σ. Of the σ only the top and bottom ends of the curve remain, which would be compatible also with ε.

Line 10, προ[σθεὶς: restored by W.

       μεν[ον ἀπὸ] ἀφ[θ]αρ

16   σίας [οὐκ ἀπο]γείν[εται]

       ἀλλ[ὰ μ]έν[ει] ἄφ[θαρ]

18   τον ὡς ἀπὸ ἀ[φ]θ[αρσί]

       [α]ς γεγονός. [ὥς]τ[ε πλῆ]

20   [θος] τῶν ἀν[θρ]ώ[πων]

       ἐπλανήθ[ησαν καὶ]

22   μὴ εἰδότ[ες τὴν δια]

       φ[ο]ρὰν τα[ύτην ἀπέ]

24   θανον. [λέγει δὲ αὐτῷ]

Horizontal   [Μαριὰμ ὅτ]ι κε πῶς οὖν

Fibers 26 [ταῦτα γιν]ώσκομεν; λέγε[ι]

       [ὁ τέλειος σ]ωτήρ· διέλθε

28   [τε ἀπὸ τῶν] ἀφανῶν κα[ὶ]

       [εἰς τ]ὸ τέ[λο]ς τῶν φαινο

Line 16, Att inadvertently omitted the bracketing of the last four letters (acknowledged in correspondence).

Line 19, Last half of line: [.] τ[ινες] (H followed by T–S); [ ] π[ληθο] (Att). τ seems more likely than π since the portion of the crossbar to the left of the vertical (all that can be seen) is longer than the crossbars of most of the π's in the MS. Both H and Att accepted the placement of the two fragments involved, relative to each other. When they are further separated by 3 or 4 mm. (see introductory discussion), then it becomes possible to make the restoration preferred by Att and incorporated above. It also makes unnecessary Att's unlikely word division.

Line 20, Initial lacuna: H (followed by T–S) restores only two letters (δέ). Att rightly finds room for three (ς δὲ).

Line 21, π: considered certain by H and Att, but all that remains is 1 mm. of the bottom of the left leg. It would be compatible also with ι, κ, ν etc.

Line 22, μ: considered certain by H and Att, but much of it has been lost to holes and flaking, and what remains is only a bit of the beginning and end and a small part of the center.

Lines 22–24, μὴ . . . [ἀπέ]θανον: Restorations made by T–S.

Line 23, φ: considered certain by H and Att, but remaining traces would be compatible also with ψ.

Line 24, An historical present is restored because of λέγει in line 26 (so too Att), but note the aorist in line 10.

Line 26, γιν]ώσκομεν: late form (see BDF: sec. 34 [4]). T–S and Att restore γιγν]ώσκομεν (Att omits the dot). All that remains of the ω is a 2 mm. vertical portion of its right side, which made it possible for H to reconstruct ι.

ε: considered certain by H and Att, but only a portion of the curve remains and there is no sign of the horizontal strokes. An ο or σ could also be read.

Line 28, ἀπό: ἐκ (Att); διά (T–S). For ἀπό rather than ἐκ, see BDF: sec. 209. Regarding διά, Crum cites no instance of the Coptic ϫιν (III 98,13; BG 90,5) being used to translate it (773a).

30 [μέ]νων καὶ αὐτὴ ἡ ἀπό[ρ]

ροια τῆ[ς ἐ]ννοίας ἀνα

32 δείξει ὑ[μῖ]ν πῶς ἡ πίστ[ις]

—τῶν [ἀ]δή[λ]ων—

εὑρ[ετ]έ[α τ]ῇ φαινομέ

34 νῃ τοῦ ἀγ[εννή]του π̅ρ̅ς̅.

ὁ ἔχων ὦτ[α ἀκού]ειν ἀ

36 κουέτω. [ὁ τῶν ὅλ]ων δε

σπότης ο[ὐ καλεῖτα]ι π̅ρ̅ ἀλ

38 λὰ προπά[τωρ· ὁ γὰ]ρ π̅ρ̅ [ἀρ]

Line 29, Att brackets the first ο, but a bit of the bottom of the letter is visible. H restores [ει]ς τọ (incorrectly reported by Att), which leaves too much unfilled space in the lacuna, as H admits. T–S suggests, as an alternative to H, εἰ]ς τέ[λο]ς (incorrectly reported by Att).

Line 30, W, T–S and Att incorrectly accent αυτη as a demonstrative. H, W, and Att do not restore ρ at the end of the line, perhaps because of concern that the letter would have been beyond the margin established by the scribe. But the vertical side shows the scribe exercising considerable freedom regarding the right margin, and there is thus no reason to think that he would not have done the same on the horizontal side when necessary. T–S restores ρ.

Line 32, Att inadvertently omitted the bracketing of the last two letters of the line (confirmed in corresondence).

Words between dashes are in the left margin of the MS. As to whether any letters preceded τῶν, H says it is not certain, "but there is a speck of ink over the ω, and the margin above is imperfect." Att claims to see more than H and on that basis reconstructs [ἡ] ἐκ. But a close examination of the photos suggests that the ink traces Att describes are mostly shadows seen through tiny holes in the papyrus—holes resulting in part from the flaking off of the vertical layer of papyrus on the opposite side of the leaf. The few genuine ink specks may have been either random drops from the scribe's pen, or the remains of a sign indicating an insertion, or the remains of the fem. article relating the phrase attributively to ἡ πίστις, or blotting from the opposite page.

Line 33, τῇ φαινομένῃ, "through that which appears": Att suggests the reference is to ἡ ἀπόρροια, "the emanation," but that would yield doubtful sense in the context. A more likely reference is ⲧⲅⲉⲛⲉⲁ ⲉⲧⲉ ⲙⲛ̄ ⲙⲛ̄ⲧ̄ⲣ̄ⲣⲟ ⲍⲓⲭⲱⲥ ⲉⲃⲟⲗ, "the Generation over Whom There Is No Kingdom" (III 99,18–20), i.e., the community of those who belong to Unbegotten Father (III 99,22–100,2).

Line 34, τ: so also Att, but H reconstructs κ. All that remains is 3 mm. of the right side of the crossbar, but it is angled up about 20 degrees, unlike any other τ found in the MS. As Att notes, the presence of the Greek loanword in both versions of *SJC* seems to resolve the uncertainty of the trace. The scribe may have been forced by an imperfection in the papyrus to make the top of his vertical stroke lower than usual, and then the crossbar was used to reestablish the former line level. T–S reconstructs ἀγ[ενή]του (omitting a dot under the τ).

Line 35, ε: so also H, but considered certain by Att. All that remains is the right tip of the horizontal stroke.

Line 36, ω: considered certain by H and Att, but all that remains is the right curve, which would be compatible also with ο.

ε: considered certain by H and Att, but only 2 mm. of the horizontal stroke remains.

χή ἐ[σ]τ̣[ιν τῶν μ]ελλόγ

40 των̣ [φαίνεσθαι. ἐ]κεῖνο[ς]
    [δὲ ὁ ἄναρχος προ]πάτω[ρ].

42 [εἰσορῶ]ν̣ α̣ὐ̣τὸ̣ν̣ [ἐ]ν̣ ἑαυτ̣[ῷ]
    [ἐσόπτ]ρῳ· ὅμ[οιος] ἑαυ

44 [τῷ φαίν]εται· α̣ὐ̣[τοῦ δὲ]
    [τὸ ὁμ]ο̣[ίω]μα ἀν[εφάνη ὡς]

46 [προπάτ]ω̣ρ θς πη[ρ] κ̣[αὶ]
    [ἀντωπὸς ἐ]πὶ ἀντ̣[ω]πῖ̣[το]

48 [τῷ προόν]τι ἀγεννήτ̣[ῳ]
    [πρι. ἰσόχρονο]ς̣ μὲν τοῦ

Line 38, Att inadvertently omitted the bracketing of the last two letters of the line.

Line 39, ν: considered certain by H and Att, but only the left stroke is visible. It would be compatible also with ι.

Lines 40–41, ν: considered certain by H and Att, but all that is visible is the top 2 mm. of the left stroke.

Att restores δὲ at the end of line 40 rather than in line 41, and omits the article in line 41. The result is that line 40 is longer in his reconstruction than one would expect, while line 41 is shorter.

Line 43, Att has εἰσόπτρῳ, but ἐσόπτρῳ is the more common form. Att restores ἑ[αυτ], but remains of both α and υ are clear in the photo.

Line 45, Att restores [ὁμοι]ώ[μα]τα ἀν[αφαίνει]. Although he makes no attempt to restore the words, H records ω after the first lacuna, and μ immediately after the second. What remains of the letter after the first lacuna is about of a circle, with the opening where one would expect if it were the right half of an ω. But the curve is rounder than with most of the ω's in the text and more resembles that of an ο. In addition, there are signs in the photo of flaking where the remainder of the circle would have been if the letter were an ο.

As to what appears after the second lacuna, Att thinks he sees not the beginning of a μ but the tail of an α (although he does not dot the α in his transcription). But α's in this text mostly have the long stroke steeply angled to the end of the tail, whereas the remnant is horizontal. It is certainly not the beginning of a μ, but is, in all likelihood, the end of one. The space between μ and α is 2 mm. and does not offer room for the τ proposed by Att. The vertical line he describes is very uncertain, and there is no sign of a crossbar, which would be expected. The reconstruction offered above agrees in number with the Coptic.

Att's reconstruction of the present active form of ἀναφαίνεν disagrees with the Coptic, which calls for an aorist and in BG, probably a middle (see BG 91,8n.). The reconstruction adopted above, although passive in form, is understood as a middle (see Smyth: sec. 814), and is compatible with the Coptic perfect without a reflexive pronoun in SJC–III.

Line 46, ω: so also H, but considered certain by Att. All that remains is about 1 mm. of the middle section of the curve on the right side. It would be compatible also with ο, θ, and φ.

Att brackets κ, overlooking the remains of the foot of the right leg, which had been seen by H. Att places ἀν, from ἀντωπὸς, at the end of the line.

Line 47, ἀντ[ω]πῖ̣[το]: Att restores ἀντ[ω]π[εῖ τῷ]. Remains of the mid-portion of ι are clear. A Greek imperfect middle is called for (see III 75,8).

Line 48, Att puts the article in the preceding line, making his reconstruction of the first

50   [ὄντος πρὸ αὐ]τ̣ο̣[ῦ φωτός]

TRANSLATION

	[to those] that came to be
Vertical	[afterward. But] they had not yet come
Fibers 2	[to] visibility.
	Now there is a great difference
4	[among]
	the imperishables." [Then he called out,]
6	"Whoever has ears [to]
	[hear] about the infinities,
8	let him hear. And I speak to those who
	are awake." Still
10	[continuing] he said: "All
	that [comes] from
12	the [perishable] passes away,
	[since] it [came] from the perishable.
14	But what comes
	[from] imperishableness
16	[does not pass away]
	but [remains] imperishable,
18	since it came from [imperishableness].
	[So, many]
20	[men]
	went astray, [and,]
22	not knowing
	[this] difference, they died."

---

lacuna here too short.

  Line 50, The second visible letter could be either ω or ο, as Att notes.

  Att reconstructs to line 52 thus: [προάρχοντος] τῷ[ν φω] | [τῶν ἀλλὰ ἀνόμοιος δυν]|[άμει].
It is not clear that ⲘⲠⲈⲦⲌⲀ ⲦⲈϥⲈⲌⲎ would have translated προάρχοντος, and ⲚⲚⲞⲨⲞⲒ̈Ⲛ is
much more likely a translation of a sing. than a pl. (see III 99,11).

24   [And Mary said to him:]

Horizontal   "Lord, how then

Fibers   26   do we know [that?" The perfect] Savior said:
              "Come

28   [from] invisible things even
       [to the end] of those that are visible,

30   and the very emanation
       of Thought will show

32   [you] how faith—in the invisibles—
       must be found through that which appears

34   of [Unbegotten] Father.
       Whoever has ears to [hear], let

36   him hear. [The] ruler [of everything]
       [is not called] 'Father' but

38   'Forefather.' For [the] Father [is the beginning]
       [of those that] are

40   [to appear; but] that one is
       [the beginningless] Forefather.

42   [Seeing] himself within himself
       [in a mirror], he [appears]

44   [like] himself, [but his likeness]
       [appeared as]

46   [Forefather], Divine Father, [and]
       [Confronter], since [he] was confronting

48   [First Existent] Unbegotten
       [Father]. [He is] indeed [of equal age] with the one

50   [before him, who is light]